PIM

21

THE SUNKEN KINGDOM

Peter James graduated in archaeology and ancient history at the University of Birmingham and pursued postgraduate research at University College, London. His other books are *Centuries of Darkness* (also available in Pimlico) and *Ancient Inventions*.

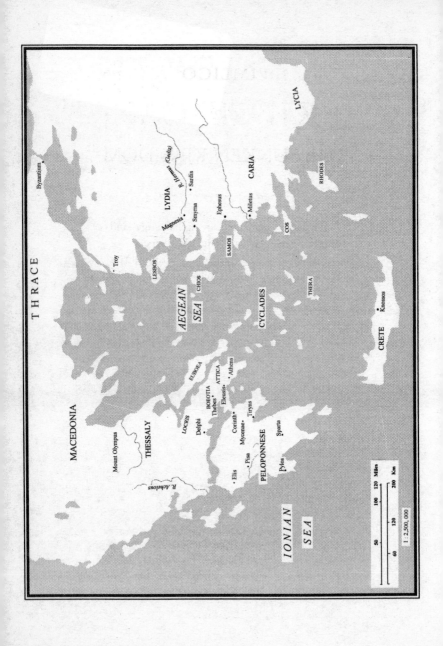

THE SUNKEN KINGDOM

The Atlantis Mystery Solved

———

PETER JAMES

PIMLICO

For Mum (Jean) and Frank
in their new life together.

PIMLICO

An imprint of Random House
20 Vauxhall Bridge Road,
London SW1V 2SA

Random House Australia (Pty) Limited
20 Alfred Street, Milsons Point, Sydney,
New South Wales 2061, Australia

Random House New Zealand Limited
18 Poland Road, Glenfield, Auckland 10, New Zealand

Random House South Africa (Pty) Limited
Box 2263, Rosebank 2121, South Africa

Random House UK Ltd Reg. No. 954009

First published by Jonathan Cape 1995
Pimlico edition 1996

1 3 5 7 9 10 8 6 4 2

Papers used by Random House UK Limited are natural,
recyclable products made from wood grown in sustainable forests.
The manufacturing processes conform to the environmental
regulations of the country of origin

Printed and bound in Great Britain by
Cox and Wyman Ltd, Reading, Berkshire

ISBN 0-7126-7499-3

Contents

The punishment of Atlas and Prometheus – from a Greek (Laconian) cup of the late 6th century BC.

Illustrations

PLATES

FIGURES

Acknowledgments

I have many people to thank for their specialist knowledge and assistance at many stages of the work. In acknowledging their help I hasten to add that they do not necessarily agree with any of the arguments expressed in this book, which are my sole responsibility.

Principal thanks are due to Dr Nikos Kokkinos (Institute of Archaeology, London) for invaluable feedback and criticism from the very inception of the project, for contributing his expertise to my trip to Lydia and for taking the photographs; to Kyriakos (Joe) Lambrianides (Institute of Archaeology, London) for his knowledge and good company on our visit to Lydia; to prehistorian Dr Nick Thorpe, Aegean archaeologist John Frankish and librarian Brian Moore for their helpful comments on early drafts. I am grateful to Alan Griffiths and Professor Bob Sharples of the Department of Greek, University College London, for providing me with many key references – and particularly to Alan, who is always encouraging despite my tendency to indulge in 'paranoid fantasies'. Geologist Dr Han Kloosterman (Utrecht) kindly gave me access to his notes on earlier geological views on Atlantis; Professor David Hawkins (School of Oriental and African Studies, London) generously answered my questions; and archaeologist Bob Porter (Institute of Archaeology) and science writer Leroy Ellenberger (St Louis) once again exhibited their amazing capacity for digging up and generously providing useful references.

My thanks also go to the British Institute of Archaeology at Ankara for providing help towards travel costs in Turkey, and especially to the academics of Izmir who made us welcome and gave so generously of their time when we visited, notably Professor Recep Mireç and Professor Ilhan Kayan. I am more than grateful to my friend Cuneyt Urşanlilar for driving us around the Manisa area. He also introduced me to the Alpinists Club of Manisa, to whom I am extremely grateful for their warm hospitality and information regarding local topography.

It goes without saying how much I appreciate the excellent work by Peter Koenig on the new line drawings, Leslie Primo's help in selecting the plates, Anthony Esposito for answering lexical queries and Francis Hitching's permission to reproduce Ken Smith's drawing (from Hitching 1978) as Fig. 2. And especial thanks to Richard Dean who saved the day by installing my new computer when the last one died on me just as I was finishing.

I should like also to thank my editors at Cape, Tony Colwell for his patience and guidance, and especially for pointing out where in the text I became long-winded, and the steadfast Pascal Cariss for weeding out some of my more excruciating metaphors and steering the text through production.

Special thanks go to my agent and guardian angel Leslie Gardner for hovering around beneficently when times were difficult, but perhaps most of all I owe an enormous debt of gratitude to classicist and editor Katherine ('the Hen') Stott, who clucked and brooded until we had hatched a better product – all for the fun of it! (When a wise publisher snaps her up it will be my loss.) And last, but not least, my thanks to Nori for being so patient when I was struggling to complete this.

Except for short passages, all translations of Plato are taken from Jowett unless otherwise indicated in the footnotes. Several new ones have been provided by Katherine Stott.

No attempt has been made throughout this book to use a consistent system for transliterating names from foreign and ancient languages. Rather I have simply chosen to use those forms which I feel are most familiar to the reader, e.g. Knossos rather than Cnossus and Cronus rather than Kronos.

Introduction

Nearly 2,400 years ago the Greek philosopher Plato posed a riddle which has baffled and infuriated scholars ever since: was his story of the lost continent of Atlantis a complete fabrication, or did some historical reality lie behind it? This question has been debated ever since Plato wrote, yet despite more than a thousand books on the subject (at a conservative estimate) there is still no agreement on what Atlantis represents and where, if at all, it was actually sited.

Most Atlantis books have been written by believers, and are attempts to identify a 'real' Atlantis behind the tale: the favourite location has always been the Atlantic Ocean (where Plato placed it), though in recent years scholars have come to believe that Atlantis was an echo of the Minoan civilisation of Crete, thought to have been destroyed by the explosion of the volcanic island of Thera. Equally firm in their opinion are the sceptics, who insist that a search for Atlantis is utterly futile, as Plato obviously made the whole thing up. Some scholars dismiss the matter out of hand, as if Atlantis was not even the brain-child of Plato, but something so unspeakably cranky that it should not be discussed. When I told an academic librarian friend that I was working on this book, he remarked that he could not approve, as the subject was 'entirely too flippant'. Why there is such hostility to the idea of Atlantis – indeed a willingness to suppress through silence a large area of Plato's work – is a thorny question which I have tried to tackle here. There is a deep-seated reluctance even to acknowledge the important message which Plato was trying to convey through writing about Atlantis, irrespective of whether it was real or not.

Attempts to vindicate Plato through archaeological or geological evidence take a leap of faith by assuming that he was not simply lying, while the sceptics, of course, take the opposite tack. Both sides can make plausible cases. Is there a way out of this dilemma? Many years ago I decided that the only strategy was to suspend any naive hope of finding a 'real' Atlantis, and to concentrate instead on the key question: did Plato have a source for his claims? He frequently illustrated his ideas with stories drawn from the rich font of Greek myth, and while he elaborated on them and freely recast them in a Platonic mould, it has never been demonstrated that he invented any of his raw material. In most cases his sources can be identified, but for Atlantis this has never been successfully achieved – hence the charge that he simply made it up. So first and foremost the Atlantis story needs to be treated in terms of literary transmission. Was Plato's account of how he came across the story likely? Where, if anywhere, should we look for the source or sources of his tale?

There was no guarantee that this approach would ever work for the simple reason that we have lost so much of the literature of the ancient world. Yet now I think it can be safely said that a source has been found and that the story behind the story can be identified. A wholly unexpected bonus from this approach is that there also seems to have been some historical reality behind the original story, and that the tale of Plato's sunken kingdom was not, after all, a purely literary device.

If I am right in my belief that the raw material for Plato's story has at last been found, then we can begin to re-examine the stratigraphy of his Atlantis writings from the bottom upwards and examine with more confidence the extra levels which Plato superimposed on the original. Plato was far from being a one-dimensional writer, and while working on this book I was constantly amazed by the number of levels on which he succeeded in writing simultaneously. Since I have concentrated on identifying the core of the story and the wider thrust of Plato's intentions, it was inevitable that some of these upper levels of meaning were neglected. For example, analysis of the detailed geometrical description which Plato gives of the Royal City of Atlantis had to remain beyond the scope of this book. An interesting case has been made by American musicologist Ernest McClain (1976) that the mathematical ratios expressed in this description reflect Plato's passionate interest in music and encode a sophisticated (Pythagorean) knowledge of music theory. Still, this is only one aspect of the story – it is not possible to explain the origin of the Atlantis story solely in terms of the extra philosophical layers which Plato added to it.

So an apology must be made for what has been omitted here. I take solace in the fact that I have tried (unlike most writers on

Atlantis) to give a passable sketch of the man and his thought – why Plato was interested in Atlantis is inseparable from the quest for Atlantis itself. Specialists may be dismayed by the lack of up-to-date reference to recent studies on the myriad facets of the master philosopher's work, but this was unavoidable. Assessing Plato's Atlantis story involves so many fields – geology, geography, mythology, history, archaeology, philosophy, astronomy and mathematics – that any attempt even to give up-to-date bibliographical references for them all would take a volume several times the size of this one. The literature on Plato himself – let alone Atlantis – is so vast that it would take a lifetime for an individual to absorb. So on this point I crave indulgence from specialists in the many disciplines touched upon. In some other respects I have been deliberately provocative – in the hope that such an approach might galvanise new thinking about Plato, who, without doubt, has been rather shabbily treated by the twentieth century.

*

In *Centuries of Darkness* I argued that the conventional dates for the Egyptian New Kingdom are wrong and that they should be lowered by up to 250 years (see James *et al.* 1991, 1991a, 1992). For example, the end of the 19th Dynasty, presently placed *c.* 1190 BC could come down to *c.* 940 BC. As the chronology of the Bronze Age in Greece, Turkey, the Levant – indeed the Eastern Mediterranean generally – is dependent on Egypt, their dates would come down accordingly. The Late Bronze Age of Greece and the Hittite Empire in Anatolia may have ended as late as 950 BC. To avoid any confusion I have adhered to the conventional dates throughout this book. The arguments put forward work on either chronology, though a lower chronology only improves them. I have accepted here that traditions from the Late Bronze Age were remembered and recorded in both Greece and Anatolia from the fifth century onwards. The possibility that such traditions could have been preserved during the long Dark Ages which intervened has often been disputed and many scholars today deny, for example, that Homer's poetry contains any real echoes of Mycenaean Greece. Removal of some 250 years from the time-scale surely makes it more credible that the legends of archaic and classical times do contain genuine memories of Bronze Age events and society.

PART ONE: ATLANTIS

CHAPTER I

The Lost Continent

In his science-fiction adventure *Twenty Thousand Leagues Under the Sea* (1869), Jules Verne relates how Pierre Arronax, a Professor of Natural History, became the guest of Captain Nemo aboard the fantastic craft *Nautilus*. Guided by his mysterious host, Arronax was treated to some spectacular underwater sightseeing. The most bizarre vista of all greeted Arronax during a walk on the bottom of the Atlantic Ocean:

> Before us lay some picturesque ruins . . . There were vast heaps of stone, amongst which might be traced the vague and shadowy forms of castles and temples . . . over which, instead of ivy, seaweed threw a thick vegetable mantle. But what was the portion of the globe which had been swallowed by cataclysms? Who had placed those rocks and stones like cromlechs of prehistoric times?
>
> There indeed under my eyes, ruined, destroyed, lay a town – its roofs open to the sky, its temples fallen, its arches dislocated, its columns lying on the ground . . . Further on, some remains of a gigantic aqueduct; here the high base of an acropolis, with the floating outline of a Parthenon; there traces of a quay . . . Further on again, long lines of sunken walls and broad, deserted streets – a perfect Pompeii escaped beneath the waters. Such was the sight that Captain Nemo brought before my eyes!
>
> Where was I? Where was I? I must know at any cost. I tried to speak, but Captain Nemo stopped me with a gesture, and picking up a piece of chalk stone, advanced to a rock of black basalt, and traced the one word:
>
> ATLANTIS
>
> Thus led by the strangest destiny, I was treading under foot the mountains of this continent, touching with my hand those

ruins a thousand generations old, and contemporary with the geological epochs. I was walking on the very spot where the contemporaries of the first man had walked.[1]

More than any other writer, Verne captured the essence of the modern vision of Atlantis: a mysterious continent, home to an advanced culture of almost unimaginable antiquity, which was lost beneath the waves millennia before the beginnings of our own civilisation. As Verne realised, the very name of Atlantis has a special, magical ring to it. Its power can evoke a wistful reaction, as James Bramwell observed:

> The name Atlantis has a sad sound. If it is pronounced ringingly, giving the first two syllables their full consonantal resonance and allowing the final sibilant to fall softly from the tongue, the effect seems to evoke an image of the surge and hiss of huge waves breaking over submerged rocks to spend themselves in white ocean foam.[2]

The nostalgic tone of Bramwell's comment, written in 1937, was not due to any implicit belief in the reality of Atlantis. He was simply infected by the romance of the subject. So many others – numbering millions – have turned their fascination with the existence of Atlantis into an article of faith. Through the medium of countless books and articles, these traditional 'Atlantologists' have given rise to a modern legend, a potent image as integral to Western civilisation as the Holy Grail or Superman. Fiction and fantasy writers – from Verne through Conan Doyle to Dennis Wheatley – have also played their part in building the image of Atlantis, working along such similar lines that it is often difficult to see who is leading whom – the fiction or the 'non-fiction' writers.

Since Verne's day, scores of pulp novels, comics and films have developed the Atlantis motif step by incredible step into a lost super-civilisation populated by high priests possessing both awesome occult powers and a precocious scientific knowledge.[3] More than 11,000 years ago the fictional Atlanteans had already developed airships, submarines, laser beams and even nuclear weapons. In many romances such deadly weaponry plays a key role in the destruction of Atlantis. The high priests somehow stumbled on elemental, 'cosmic' forces – the key to the universe itself – but the magnitude of this power turned their heads. Corrupted beyond redemption, they recklessly experimented with sinister forces which, once unleashed, escaped beyond their control and annihilated them. Nuclear explosions of extraordinary magnitude destroyed the Atlanteans' cities and the very structure of the ground beneath them.

Racked by the elements, Atlantis sank beneath the waves, never to be seen again. Never, that is, except for those authors who take the logical step of assuming that the Atlanteans were so technologically advanced that they could surely cope with a disaster as paltry as a sinking continent. Some science fiction writers have portrayed the Atlanteans as still alive today, surviving the change in their environment by constructing massive undersea domes or by genetically engineering gills.

FIG. 1   The island-continent Atlantis as conceived by the visionary scientist Athanasius Kircher. (From his *Mundus Subterraneus* 1644.) North is at the bottom of the map.

All this makes racy fiction, to be enjoyed as such. Yet, surprisingly, practically every ingredient can also be found seriously argued in innumerable non-fiction books on Atlantis. Many of these are written by psychics and occultists who use sources of knowledge very different from those familiar to historians and scientists.

A favoured method of some Atlantologists, in company with self-styled psychic archaeologists, is hypnotic regression. A subject in a hypnotic trance is taken back through numerous past lives until he or she remembers the experiences they underwent as a citizen of Egypt or Atlantis. Some say that similar results can be achieved through meditation, if the sitter is holding the right sort of crystal. The hidden power of crystals – as an aid to healing akin to aromatherapy – has long been investigated by practitioners of fringe medicine, and for some reason many of the more adventurous crystal practitioners are taken with the idea that crystal energies have a connection with Atlantis.

A few years ago I attended a London workshop on crystal energies, where only the meanest of sceptics could fail to be intrigued by the mass of anecdotal and other evidence suggesting that crystals may have unexplored and beneficial properties. So I was dismayed when the principal speaker, after orchestrating an interesting review of the evidence for crystal-power, launched into a history of crystal energies in which the existence of Atlantis as a lost super-civilisation was taken utterly for granted. We were told that crystals were used extensively in Atlantis, for healing and other purposes, but the Atlanteans had sometimes misused them. Further, crystals survive in which Atlanteans stored power or vibrations – like the recording on a compact disc – and, while the rediscovery of many of the crystals holding good energy is fostering the use of crystal-power for healing, sinister crystals exist, charged with negative Atlantean power, which are inhibiting the cause.

The literature on crystal-power – and many other 'New Age' interests – is full of such stuff. A leading crystal writer, Ra Bonewitz, even claims that it was the misuse of crystal energies which destroyed the island-continent. Now, he says, the world is at long last beginning to recover from the trauma of the Atlantean destruction – 'the reason behind the impulse being felt in so many people worldwide to study and learn more about crystals'. In similar matter-of-fact style Bonewitz informs the reader that the end of Atlantis was predicted by some uncorrupted members of the priesthood who fled to the Nile and the Himalayas to plant the seeds of knowledge. It is astounding enough to read Bonewitz's claim that the Egyptian and Tibetan civilisations were founded by Atlanteans, but his most startling revelation is still to come:

let us remind ourselves that although we have been speaking of Atlanteans as someone else, *we are* the Atlanteans. So, fellow Atlanteans, how is it going to go *this* time?[4]

If it cheers someone up on a dreary bus-ride to work to imagine that they are really a reincarnated Atlantean with limitless reserves of untapped potential, then no harm has been done. And Bonewitz, along with most of the 'New Age' thinkers on Atlantis, does write from a highly defensible moral position, chivvying his reincarnated Atlanteans to be more morally responsible *this* time with their heritage of cosmic power. If one or two of his fans were later to become nuclear scientists or genetic engineers, it would be a positive benefit to us all if they remembered the teachings they absorbed in their days of uncritical reading. As this book will show, the originator of the Atlantis story intended it partly to be a parable with an important moral.

The worst that can really be said about the psychic/occult school of Atlantis writing is that eventually it grows tedious. There is a mountain of it and any reader not actually fired with mystical zeal by the idea of Atlantean priests wielding cosmic crystal-power will rapidly become frustrated by the sheer lack of evidence and turn instead to the *bona fide* science-fiction shelf.

While the more offbeat literature on Atlantis is merely harmless fun, the very mention of it to some academics can be like waving a red rag to a bull: they laugh, sneer or even become apoplectic with rage at the idea that Atlantis may have been a reality.[5] Only subjects like UFOs and astrology seem to provoke stronger reactions. What is baffling is *why* these subjects manage to annoy academics so much. A truly dispassionate scientist should be interested in discovering why people wish to believe the incredible, and in explaining the origins, development and mechanics of such beliefs.

Atlantis is a good case in point. Through its popularity the subject has become fudged with extraneous beliefs and misconceptions which can be very off-putting to more conservative scholars. They are probably unaware that earlier this century belief in the lost continent of Atlantis was a scientifically respectable position. Indeed, the controversy over the existence of Atlantis was central to the development of modern geology (see Chapter 2). A surprising number of scientists, when insisting that Atlantis has already been explained away, show clearly that they have no idea where the story originated.

So where did it all start?

The Most Incredible Story

Most people have a vague notion that Atlantis is a Greek myth or legend, but strictly speaking it is not.[6] None of the early mythographers or poets of Greece has a word to say about it. So the story of Atlantis can hardly qualify as a 'Greek legend' like the stories of Perseus and the Gorgons, the Golden Fleece, the Trojan War, or the Labours of Heracles.

None the less, the Atlantis story does come from the Greek world. It was first recorded by the renowned Athenian philosopher Plato in the mid-fourth century BC, in two of his 'dialogues' – the *Timaeus* and the *Critias*. The vital question is: did Plato have a source for the story or did he simply make it up?

First, it is worthwhile looking at what Plato said. Plato always spoke through other people in his dialogues, and for Atlantis the mouthpiece (rightly or wrongly) was Critias, a fellow philosopher and old relative. Critias asserted that he had certain knowledge, from unimpeachable sources, about the past existence of a massive continent, 'bigger than Libya and Asia put together', at the very edge of the known world. Called Atlantis, it lay, naturally enough, in the Atlantic Ocean. Here, on a mountain near the sea, the sea-god Poseidon wedded a mortal woman called Cleito and fathered ten sons who divided the continent between them into ten kingdoms. Their leader and overall king was the eldest son, Atlas, who gave his name to the island and the surrounding sea.

The natural resources of the island continent were limitless. Almost every useful plant grew there, producing timber, vegetables, herbs, drinks, gums and materials for perfumes. Likewise, the mountains, plains, marshes, rivers and lakes were stocked with herds of animals. In particular there was 'a very large stock of elephants' – ivory was highly prized in the ancient world as a material for manufacturing luxury furniture and ornaments. Metals were also found on the island in abundance – not only those which were well known in Plato's time, but another called *oreichalkos*, which was said to be second in value only to gold.[7] Anything the island lacked was imported from the Atlantean empire overseas. In short, the kings of Atlantis 'had such an amount of wealth as was never before possessed by kings and potentates, and is not likely ever to be again' (*Critias* 114D).

On the mountain ('acropolis') where Poseidon and Cleito had mated, the kings built the capital of Atlantis, 'a marvel to behold for size and for beauty'. The land around the mountain had already been miraculously sculpted by the sea-god to protect his and Cleito's love nest. Poseidon surrounded it with concentric rings of land and sea, which were originally impenetrable boundaries since ships and sailing had yet to be invented. The central island itself Poseidon blessed with perpetual hot and cold running water in the shape of two springs (*Critias* 113).

The work of successive Atlantean kings transformed the sacred island into a glittering metropolis. They dug a channel, wide enough for a ship to pass through, to connect the rings of water and lead to the sea, where they built a harbour. The channel was then roofed over so that the sea-way was subterranean; bridges were constructed over the rings of water to connect the central acropolis with the rings of land. Defensive walls with towers were built around each ring, made from three colours of local stone: red, black and white. Some buildings were plain, but in others the Atlanteans 'put together different stones, varying the colour to please the eye'. The main defensive walls were encased in metal – the outermost with bronze, the next with tin and the innermost, protecting the sacred acropolis, with *oreichalkos*, 'which sparkled like fire' (*Critias* 115–116).

The palace complex on the Atlantean acropolis was a wonderland. In the centre, surrounded by a wall of gold, stood the temple of Cleito and Poseidon. The outside of the temple was coated with silver and the pinnacles with gold, while the roof was made of solid ivory decorated with precious metals. Inside were golden statues of the kings and queens of Atlantis, dwarfed only by a gigantic statue of Poseidon.

Nearby were the royal palace and gardens with numerous bathing pools fed by the two natural springs – some open to the air and others, with hot water for the winter, under cover. There were separate baths for the kings, private citizens, and women; and, Plato notes, even the horses had their own special baths. (The horse was the sacred animal of the god Poseidon.)

On the outer circles of land were temples to the other gods, more gardens, barracks for the royal guards, exercise grounds and, in the outermost ring, a huge circular race-course for horses.

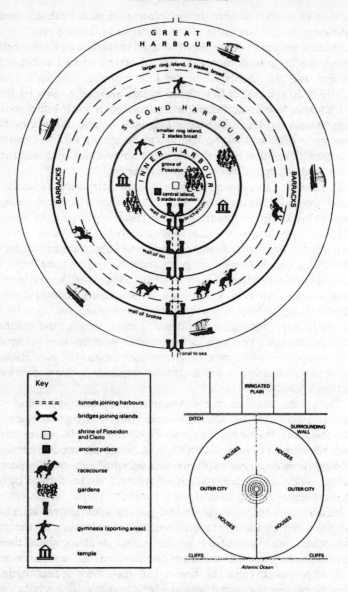

FIG. 2   Plan of the Royal Metropolis of Atlantis, following Plato's detailed description. (Bottom right) The wider setting of the city – the outskirts were surrounded by an enormous circuit wall which included houses and the harbour on the coast of the Atlantic (*after Hitching 1978*).

Beyond the city complex lay an enormous plain, criss-crossed with a network of canals used for irrigation and transport. These connected the city to the surrounding mountains, which were dotted with 'many wealthy villages of country folk', meadows, streams and lakes.

This was the Royal City and capital of Atlantis, seat of the descendants of Atlas, but there were nine other great cities, each ruled by its own king. The ten kings ruled jointly, meeting every few years to make major policy decisions, though in all matters they conceded authority to the dynasty of Atlas. His descendants were also the war-leaders, commanders of the world's largest military force. The army from the Royal City alone included 60,000 captains to organise the levies from the surrounding countryside, a fleet of 1,200 triremes and a chariot-force 10,000 strong. (For comparison, the largest known chariot-force from ancient Egypt, in the time of Ramesses II, was a mere 2,500.) Each Atlantean charioteer led a small fighting unit, comprising a rider (who jumped from horse to horse), two heavily armed foot-soldiers, two archers, two heavily armed and three lightly armed slingers, three javelin-men and four marines.

It was this powerful, well-organised army which enabled the kings of Atlantis to extend their power across the sea to our own world. Their empire reached into the Mediterranean, including north Africa as far as Egypt, and Europe as far as Tyrrhenia (Tuscany) in Italy.

Eventually, however, the fortunes of the Atlanteans began to change. In the *Critias* (120D–121) Plato describes how the Atlanteans originally shared the character of their divine ancestors: 'for they possessed true and in every way great spirits, uniting gentleness with wisdom'. Even their fantastic wealth did not corrupt them: 'They despised everything but virtue . . . thinking lightly of the possession of gold and other property, which seemed only a burden to them.' But the divine part of their nature became diluted over the generations and eventually they became corrupted by greed. Zeus, king of the gods, decided to bring about their downfall, using their greed to punish them.

The Atlanteans, already masters of half the Mediterranean, decided that Greece, Egypt and all the other free states within the region were to be enslaved. They crossed over to our world with a gigantic host of warriors, but did not meet with the instant success they had expected. The Athenians were not rich like the Atlanteans, leading a simple communal lifestyle. Already free citizens of a proud city, they led a mixed host of Greeks and 'barbarians' (non-Greeks) against the invaders and succeeded, despite being deserted at times by their allies, in repelling the Atlanteans and liberating Europe. Afterwards the Athenians raised a monument to commemorate their achievement.

What happened next is known in less detail. Plato's main work on Atlantis, the *Critias*, is unfinished, and the narrative simply breaks off. Yet a brief summary in the *Timaeus* gives the end of the story. Zeus' original intention was to reform the Atlanteans by humbling them – 'that they might be chastened and improve' (*Critias* 121C). Presumably this plan should have been completed when they were defeated in war by the relatively small state of Athens. We can only assume that the Atlanteans had not learnt their lesson, for Zeus next brought about their complete and total destruction.

'There occurred violent earthquakes and floods', and then, in one awful day and night 'the island of Atlantis . . . disappeared in the depths of the sea. For which reason the sea in those parts is impassable and impenetrable, because there is a shoal of mud in the way; and this was caused by the subsidence of the island' (*Timaeus* 25D). The Atlanteans were not the only casualties. During the same catastrophic episode, the earth opened up and swallowed the entire Athenian army. These awesome events took place, according to Plato, about 9600 BC, one thousand years before his date for the founding of Egyptian civilisation.

A 'True Story'?

There are no flying machines or high priests with occult powers in Plato's account, but the fantastic elements qualify it, on one level, as one of the world's oldest science fiction stories. It certainly reads like one, if only for the immense scale on which everything is drawn. The temple in the Royal City was three times the size of the Parthenon in Athens, while the statue of Poseidon inside, which nearly touched the roof, could have been up to 300 feet, dwarfing Nelson's Column (including plinth) at 210 feet.[8] This colossus, according to Plato, was made of solid gold.

It is this immensity, particularly in terms of the geography and time-scale, that makes the story seem so incredible. The concept of a highly advanced civilisation existing more than 11,500 years ago is breathtaking. Although some societies, notably the earliest farming communities of the Near East, were relatively advanced by 9000 BC, the example of Britain is far more typical. At that time the inhabitants of the British Isles were still in a pre-farming age: they had no pottery, and fished, gathered and hunted with tools made of flint, wood and vegetable fibres. Indeed, the Stone Age did not officially end in Britain until about 2500 BC. So what to make of the suggestion that an almost global empire – complete with majestic cities, sophisticated agriculture, complex irrigation systems, canals, bridges, ship-tunnels, temples, fleets of ships and even metal-plated buildings – existed around 9600 BC?

Of course, such reactions are based on modern conceptions. Plato's audience would not have had the benefit – or limitations, depending on one's point of view – of our archaeological and geological knowledge. Yet they, too, would have found his Atlantis tale strange. The Greeks, after all, had their own ideas about geology and history.

Although the Greeks lived in a fairly unstable environment – the Aegean basin is one of the most geologically active regions of the world – the damage they saw being wreaked by wind, wave, earthquake and volcano was all on a relatively small scale. They were used to the idea that an earthquake could cause a large stretch of coastline to collapse, destroy a city or even devastate a whole province. They also had legends (very much like that of the biblical Noah) that the whole of Greece had been submerged by deluges in the remote past. But the unheard-of Atlantic continent that Plato was describing would have been hundreds of times the size of Greece. The idea of such huge landmass being wasted at one stroke would certainly have stretched his audience's credulity.

As to the time-scale of Plato's story, the Greeks frankly admitted that their own culture was a very young one. They paid great respect to the venerable antiquity of the great civilisations of the Near East: Phoenicia, Babylonia, Assyria, and above all Egypt. For the 'ancient' Greeks, Egypt was widely regarded as the oldest civilisation in the world (with the possible exception of the kingdom of Phrygia in Turkey). They attributed to the Egyptians the invention of writing, astronomy, geometry, philosophy, most of the arts and crafts,[9] and even the first knowledge of the gods. The Greek historian Herodotus said that the names of most of the major gods came from Egypt.[10] So when Plato made his claim that a great, unknown, civilisation existed one thousand years *before* the first Egyptian kings, ears would have pricked up and wry smiles may have spread across learned faces.

This is not a hypothetical scenario. Many Greek philosophers and historians after Plato flatly refused to believe his Atlantis story. It was altogether too far-fetched. Aristotle, an ex-pupil of Plato's, was the most scathing of all. He compared Atlantis to the wall that Homer said the Achaean Greeks built when besieging Troy. One could not see it, but Homer said that it had been washed away by a wave after the city was captured. Of Atlantis Aristotle said: 'Its inventor caused it to disappear, just as the Poet [Homer] did with the wall of the Achaeans.'[11] The criticism was a trenchant one. Plato had no physical evidence with which to back up his story, and was unlikely ever to produce any. If Aristotle had been writing now he might have said that Plato had produced a hypothesis which could neither be verified nor disproved, and that to cover his embarrassment at the implausible monstrosity he had created he had swept it under the sea with a stroke of the pen.

Still, Plato saw some of the obvious objections coming. The story does seem incredible and he freely admitted it was 'passing strange' (*atopos*, more literally 'out of place'). Despite and because of this, Plato – through his mouthpieces Critias and Socrates – insisted that the account was 'wholly true', and 'not fiction but a true story' (*Timaeus* 20D, 26E) and went to some lengths to stress the respectability of the story's pedigree. His source, he claimed, was none other than Solon, a famous Athenian statesman, philosopher and businessman of the sixth century BC. Solon was one of the 'Seven Wise Men' of Greek tradition, noted for his respect for the truth as well as for his justice and wisdom. He once scolded the dramatist Thespis for including what he perceived as 'lies' in his plays. Thespis (after whom we have the word 'thespian') replied that make-believe was permissible on the stage. Striking the ground with his staff, Solon exclaimed: 'Yes, but if we allow ourselves to praise and honour make-believe like this, the next thing will be to find it creeping into our serious business.'[12] Attributing information to Solon would have been the ancient Greek equivalent of a twentieth-century American citing Abraham Lincoln as a source.

Solon, according to Plato, had meant to compose an epic poem on the subject of Atlantis. It was never finished, but some notes survived, which were handed down together with the story

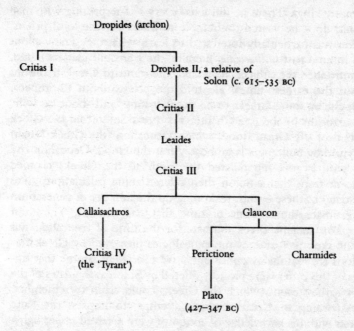

FIG. 3 Genealogy of the Critias family, as reconstructed by Davies (1971, 322–35). The date for Solon follows Miller (1969). It was Critias III (and not Critias IV as has sometimes been argued) who introduced the Atlantis account in the *Timaeus* and *Critias*.

through the Critias family, who were relatives of Solon as well as Plato. It was Critias' great-grandfather Dropides who was first told the story by Solon. Dropides related it to his son Critias, who was once asked by a friend to justify his claim that Solon had a theme which could have made him the greatest of all poets, had he turned his hand to it seriously. The elder Critias duly explained 'what Solon related and how, and who were the informants who vouched for its truth' (*Timaeus* 21D). It was this rendition that the younger Critias, who was present at the time, remembered and retold to entertain Socrates and his friends.

According to Critias, Solon came by the Atlantis story on his trip to Egypt. It was about 565 BC, early in the reign of King Amasis of the 26th Dynasty. Amasis was a great admirer of the Greeks and Solon was well received at Sais, seat of the 26th

Dynasty kings. There he did what every self-respecting wise man would do – he visited the temple to interview the local priests. Solon was particularly interested to learn what they knew about the remote past (*archaeotata*, literally 'most ancient matters'), and, to introduce the subject, he related the standard Greek traditions about the earliest times. He told the priests about Phoroneus, thought by some Greeks to be the first king, and about his wife, the arrogant Niobe (see Chapter 11). Next Solon told the Greek legend of the Great Flood, which Deucalion (the Greek Noah) survived by building a large boat. After the Flood, Deucalion and his wife Pyrrha repopulated the land: all the Greeks claimed descent from them. Solon then offered some calculations as to the dates of these events, reckoning up the number of generations to estimate the amount of time that had elapsed. The most common ancient Greek estimate for the time of Deucalion was about 1500 BC[13] and, as the genealogies preserved by Greek traditions are reasonably consistent,[14] we can safely assume that figures of this order were proudly offered by Solon as the dates of the very earliest events which the Greeks could claim to remember.

According to Critias, Solon's attempts to impress the Saite priests with his knowledge of antiquity were received rather light-heartedly. By way of response, one of the senior priests said: 'Oh Solon, Solon, you Greeks are all children, and there is not an old man among you.' The deflated Solon asked what he meant and the priest replied 'that in mind you are all young; there is no old opinion handed down among you by ancient tradition, nor any science which is hoary with age'. Having put Solon in his place, the priest went on to tell him *why* he thought the Greeks had only the poorest memory of their own past, and how the Egyptians, by contrast, had records stretching back into far earlier times (*Timaeus* 22).

The priest explained to Solon that every now and again, after enormous intervals of time, the stars change their courses in the heavens and cause the destruction of the world by fire and water. These periodic catastrophes had wiped out the oldest inhabitants of Greece, apparently along with everyone else except the Egyptians, who had survived them because of their country's special climate. The priest claimed that, as it does not rain in Egypt (though it actually does occasionally), floods from heaven did not affect them, while during universal conflagrations the River Nile would rise to give the people cooling protection. Thus, the priest said, the Egyptians had been able to preserve records of world events from the very earliest times, records which they housed in their temple archives. With regard to Greece, however, every time its inhabitants had invented writing and started making records, deluges had swept them all away, leaving only a handful of rustic survivors to start civilisation again from scratch. Only the names of a few kings were remembered.

The priest went on to make further astonishing claims. He had detailed knowledge of the race of Athenians who had existed 9,000 years before, about whom Solon and his contemporaries knew next to nothing. The priest said that these ancient Athenians had 'the fairest constitution of any of which tradition tells, under the face of heaven'. Indeed, the priest proudly added, the laws and social organisation of the original Athens closely resembled those of Egypt itself (*Timaeus* 23C, 24A).

These marvellous Proto-Athenians are an important, but all too often neglected, part of Plato's Atlantis narrative. Their very disappearance is a crucial factor in the story. As already noted, the entire Athenian army was supposed to have been swallowed by an earthquake on the same night that Atlantis sank, while their homeland was devastated by a flood. Presumably they were still on campaign against the Atlanteans, as it seems to have been a flood that devastated their homeland, Attica. This deluge was the greatest that Attica ever endured. The flooding was so severe that the shape of the Acropolis was transformed overnight (*Critias* 112A).

While it is not explicitly stated in the surviving portions of Plato's Atlantis narrative, it is clear that almost the entire race of prehistoric Athenians was supposed to have been wiped out by these disasters; the Saite priest referred to 'a small seed or remnant of them which survived' (*Timaeus* 23C). Gradually Attica was repopulated, but the new Athenians did not rediscover the art of writing for many generations. In this way, the priest explained to Solon, the Athenians had forgotten about their past and naturally they were also ignorant of their glorious achievement in defeating the power of Atlantis. The situation had been different in Egypt. The priest claimed:

> Whatever happened either in your country or in ours, or in any other region of which we are informed – if there were any actions noble or great or in any way remarkable, they have all

been written down by us of old, and are preserved in our temples [*Timaeus* 23A].

This, in Plato's understanding, was the ultimate authority for the existence of Atlantis. By his own admission, the story had travelled an extraordinarily long way: the memory of a war between two prehistoric civilisations (Athens and Atlantis) had at some point been committed to writing in Egypt, where it was preserved over several millennia. In about 565 BC Egyptian priests gave a digest of these records to Solon. The story then went from Solon to Critias the Elder, from Critias the Elder to Critias the Younger, and, at around 400 BC, from him to Plato. Plato included it in two of his last works, the *Timaeus* and *Critias*, written some time between 360 and 350 BC.[15]

The chain of transmission, long as it is, is not implausible – at least with respect to the links at the Greek end. There is no good reason to doubt that Solon visited Egypt[16] and he was, as the scenario requires, an accomplished poet. Numerous fragments of his work still survive.[17] The idea that he would have collected material on his travels for a future project is entirely in character. Likewise, the claim that the story behind Solon's projected poem could have been transmitted by means of the Critias family is eminently feasible since Solon and Plato themselves actually belonged to this well-documented Athenian family. The number of generations in the account of the transmission, stage by stage from Solon to Plato, also make it chronologically possible.

Given all these factors, the *prima facie* case for Plato having chanced upon a story brought by Solon from Egypt does not seem unreasonable. Plato went to great pains to spell out the precise circumstances of the story's transmission, particularly with respect to the role of Critias. He had heard the story from his grandfather at the tender age of ten, and would have been a fairly ancient man by the time he related it to Plato's friends. Yet, as Critias himself remarked, the old can often remember the events and stories of their youth far better than they can the recent past. Before relating the story, he spent a night rehearsing it in his mind so that he could remember it clearly (*Timaeus* 26B). And, as an *aide memoire*, he could also turn to the notes which Solon had left in the family:

Solon, who was intending to use the tale for his poem, enquired into the meaning of the names, and found that the early Egyptians had translated them into their own language, and he recovered the meaning of the several names and when copying them out again translated them into our own language. My great-grandfather, Dropides, had the original writing, which is still in my possession, and was carefully studied by me when I was a child [*Critias* 113A].

Lost Civilisations

Despite some claims to the contrary, there are no internal inconsistencies in Plato's account of the Atlantis story's transmission. Rather, the account is impressive for its harmony and for the remarkable care which Plato took in setting the background for the story. Sceptics, however, might say that there is too much circumstantial detail and that it is merely corroborative padding to give artistic verisimilitude to a ludicrously far-fetched story.[18] It is a natural enough suspicion, given what is at stake. Plato was claiming to hold nothing less than a secret key to the world's earliest history.

The question of Plato's reliability with regard to the Atlantis narrative cannot be answered in one breath. Yet, even at this early stage, the idea that he invented the whole thing, complete with a string of respectable sources to whom he was conveniently related, seems a little unreasonable. Critias the Younger was obviously alive around 420 BC, when Plato indicates he spoke to his friends Socrates, Timaeus and Hermocrates. By the time Plato wrote up his account, Critias and Socrates, at least, would have been dead – but friends of all the group would still have been alive. Would Plato have had the temerity to perjure Critias with such fantastic claims when there must have been people around to catch him out? Likewise, the idea that Plato would have implicated such a respected and famous person as Solon in an outrageous hoax seems very unlikely. Plato's family connections with both Critias and Solon would have rendered such acts totally shameful.

Even judging from the internal evidence of the *Timaeus* and *Critias*, the case for Plato having perpetrated a massive hoax seems rather forced. Beyond that there is Plato's track record – he was a pastmaster at using already available material to illustrate his philosophical arguments, and can never be shown to have relied on sheer invention.

All things considered, it seems best to assume that Plato was being sincere when he laid out the Atlantis narrative for his future readers. Of course this leaves further questions. Was he merely taken in by Critias, who for some reason – even senility? – was playing an elaborate prank? Or was Solon, despite his reputation for honesty, the inventor? The same arguments can be used for their defence as for Plato: would these eminent wise men have jeopardised their reputation and run the risk of ridicule for a mere flippancy? They may all have been sincere, of course, but simply misled by something the Egyptian priests had concocted. Or did they all play a small part, adding to the story by degrees as it came to them?

The quickest resolution to the whole matter would be for evidence for the existence of Atlantis to be found. Given the apparently impeccable credentials that lie behind Plato's story, many have thought it best to take the plunge of faith, give him the benefit of the doubt and simply look for Atlantis itself. The idea that Plato's story, shorn of its frills, holds the secret of the world's earliest civilisation is one that holds enormous appeal. Yet is it possible that Atlantis existed in anything like the way that Plato described it?

Many of the great civilisations of the ancient world have been genuinely 'lost', in the sense that memory of them had been completely – or almost completely – erased by the passage of time. For example, central and southern Anatolia (Turkey), northern Syria and parts of northern Iraq were once dominated by the mighty Hittite Empire, of which there are only the remotest echoes in biblical and classical writings. It was properly rediscovered only in 1906, when archaeologists excavated the capital city of the Hittites, complete with an imperial archive of clay tablets, near the village of Boghazköy in central Turkey. We now know that the Hittite Empire was one of the great powers of the ancient Bronze Age: it had enough military muscle to stand up to, and even defeat, its rival Egypt (see Chapter 10).

Over the last century archaeologists have uncovered even longer forgotten civilisations. In the 1970s archaeologists discovered Ebla, an enormous city in the Syrian desert, which had clearly ruled a small empire in the late third millennium BC; one wing alone of the royal library at Ebla contained so many clay tablets that it was estimated a whole generation of cuneiform scholars was needed to decipher them. The existence of such an important city-state came as an almost complete surprise to historians and archaeologists.[19]

An even greater surprise had come in 1921 when a team of British archaeologists discovered the wonderful civilisation of the Indus Valley (Pakistan). Before their work, little was known of the development of civilisation in India before the third century BC. Yet the marvels they discovered at the superbly planned prehistoric cities of Harappa and Mohenjo Daro dated as early as 3000 BC. These cities had streets of neat brick-built houses with drains connected to public sewers, and even the first western-style sitting toilets.[20] The Indus Valley script, still undeciphered, holds the promise of further surprises.

The example of the lost civilisation of the Indus Valley illustrates an inexorable trend in archaeology: the dates for the major technological advances of prehistory are constantly being pushed backwards in time. The trend is very encouraging for those who wish to take Plato's Atlantis story at its face value.[21]

A case in point is the belief among archaeologists in the 1950s that there had been a 'Neolithic Revolution' around 4000 BC in which farming and the first settled communities were developed by people still using stone tools. This picture has had to be completely revised. For example, in the 1960s British archaeologists excavated the extraordinary prehistoric town of Çatal Hüyük in southern Turkey, built in the seventh millennium BC. Covering some thirty acres, the town was a honeycomb of extremely regular brick-built houses, clustered together around small courtyards and streets. There were about 1,000 of these dwellings, which had neatly plastered interiors, some decorated with elaborate murals. The inhabitants – about 7,000 in number – grew wheat, barley and a dozen other edible plants, and raised herds of cattle. A wide range of arts and crafts were practised by the townspeople: they made pottery and simple metal tools, wove linen garments, fashioned elaborate jewellery and used mirrors of polished volcanic stone.[22] Looking at the remains from Çatal Hüyük, it is often easy to forget that they come from a time 7,500 to 8,500 years ago. In the words of Jacquetta Hawkes, the excavation of this 'precociously advanced civilisation . . . transformed our whole conception of human life and behaviour in that period'.[23]

With the dates for Çatal Hüyük we are only three millennia short of the time range indicated by Plato for Atlantis. The extraordinary prehistoric settlement at Jericho is even closer. By 7000 BC Jericho was surrounded with a defensive wall, 13 feet thick and 10 feet high, enclosing some ten acres. In the centre was a masterpiece of prehistoric construction – a solidly built stone tower more than 40 feet high, enclosing a spiral stairway. Jericho is also one of the earliest known sites for agriculture in the world: by about 8000 BC peas and lentils were being grown here and at sites in northern Syria and southern Iran.[24] At about the same time the people of the Natufian culture of Palestine had domesticated dogs, were living in permanent settlements with storage arrangements for grain and were manufacturing jewellery from stone, bone and shell. From the Aegean there is evidence of overseas trade by about 11,000 BC, when sites on mainland Greece began importing obsidian (a volcanic glass) from the island of Melos, a hundred miles away.[25]

The greatest surprise of all came from Japan in the 1960s. For a long time it was assumed that pottery must have been invented in the Near East – 'the cradle of civilisation' – by the earliest known agricultural societies. However, evidence has now come to light that some 13,000 years ago pottery was being made in Japan. By contrast, the earliest Near Eastern pottery, from Iran, dates to around 9000 BC. Not only is this later, but it is also only sun-dried rather than fired like the earlier Japanese pottery.[26]

While the idea of an Atlantic civilisation at the dawn of history may not suit current preconceptions, conventional thinking in archaeology – as in any other field – has been overthrown time and again. Does the fact that this could happen yet again allow a window of possibility, however small, for Plato's Atlantis to have been a reality?

Many of the great legends of the past have been confirmed by the archaeologist's spade. After all, didn't people refuse to believe in the existence of the great walls of Troy, described in Homer's poetry, until the eccentric German scholar Heinrich Schliemann excavated them in the 1860s? Could the golden walls of the Royal City still be waiting to be found at the bottom of the Atlantic Ocean?

CHAPTER 2

The Origin of Civilisation?

Ignatius Donnelly, the founding father of modern Atlantology, was the archetypal eccentric thinker: in every field he touched, from politics to ancient history, his views were heretical. Immensely influential and popular during his lifetime, Donnelly's role as a scourge of orthodoxy has ensured his absence from the official rolls of honour. The description of Donnelly as 'the greatest uncelebrated man in American history' is a fair one.[1]

Born in Philadelphia in 1831, into a family of Irish Catholic immigrants, Donnelly's chequered career included turns as farmer, lawyer, land speculator, businessman, editor, novelist and politician. His first major venture was as co-founder of a scheme to build a tiny midwestern town into a model community, optimistically named 'Nininger City'. The scheme flopped, and Donnelly narrowly escaped bankruptcy by converting the unsold plots of the 'city' into farmland. He moved into politics, shifting allegiance from party to party (Democrat, Republican, Populist and the quasi-socialist Mid-Road People's Party) as he defended the rights of small farmers against eastern big business, corruption and vested interests. Donnelly always remained a 'man of the people' – a committed radical, libertarian and abolitionist.

In 1859, at the age of twenty-eight, Donnelly was elected Lieutenant-Governor of Minnesota on a Populist ticket; and in 1862, as a Republican, he became its Congressman, a post he held for eight years. While in Washington, Donnelly took full advantage of the Library of Congress, reading so widely and voraciously that one contemporary rated him as 'perhaps the most learned man ever to sit in the house'. This was the other side of Donnelly's curious personality. As well as a number of novels which often expressed his political concerns – such as the abolition of slavery – Donnelly penned articles and books on a peculiar range of non-fiction topics from phrenology to the intrigues of

Elizabethan England. He was the first to develop the theory that Shakespeare's plays were riddled with cryptically coded messages revealing the identity of their true author – who was, in Donnelly's opinion, Sir Francis Bacon.

By 1870 Donnelly had been hounded out of politics by his rich opponents, and he withdrew to his house in Nininger City, by then almost a ghost town. Here, he laid aside for a while the immense labour of trying to crack Bacon's supposed ciphers, and took up another enthusiasm – Atlantis and the origin of civilisation. The work was a struggle: Donnelly was deeply in debt and, in his own words, 'there was nothing left of me but the backbone'. Still, the Donnelly backbone was a resilient one. It also needed someone with Donnelly's energy, panache and wide-ranging interests to resurrect the Atlantis question – one left essentially undeveloped since Renaissance times.

Atlantis: The Antediluvian World was published in 1882 and became an instant success: it had gone through twenty-three printings by 1890. Perhaps the most striking thing about Donnelly's book on Atlantis is its originality. No one had ever attempted to press into Atlantean service such a mass of argument and evidence. What sparked off this colossal task he never stated. One source was certainly Jules Verne's *Twenty Thousand Leagues Under the Sea*, first published in English in 1870. Donnelly's long-standing interest in Francis Bacon must also have played a part. Around 1600 Bacon wrote a romantic utopian novel called *The New Atlantis*, based on Plato's ideas. Bacon, like most other post-Renaissance scholars before Donnelly, seemed to think that Plato's Atlantis was a memory of America.[2]

The theme of Atlantis also clearly appealed to Donnelly's idealism. He skimmed over the verses of the *Timaeus* and *Critias* in which Plato describes the spiritual decadence of the Atlanteans, seeing only 'a great, rich, cultured and educated people', who had built a global empire from small beginnings. Donnelly's admiration for the pioneering god Poseidon, who spawned the Atlantean race, is undisguised: 'we see an immigrant enter the country, marry one of the native women, and settle down; in times a great nation grows around him'.[3] Where Nininger city had failed, Donnelly could make Atlantis succeed.

Donnelly's discussion of Plato's account was cursory. He saw little point in beating about the bush with literary analysis since he believed the evidence for the existence of Atlantis, exactly as

Plato had described it, was so strong. For Donnelly, Atlantis was the missing piece in the jigsaw puzzle of prehistory. Slot it into place and everything – from the distribution of flora and fauna to the rise of civilisation on both sides of the Atlantic – begins to make perfect sense.

The Lost Centre of the World

By neglecting Atlantis, Donnelly argued, academics had completely distorted history. He set out his challenge to the conventional wisdom in thirteen propositions:

1   That there once existed in the Atlantic Ocean, opposite the mouth of the Mediterranean Sea, a large island, which was the remnant of an Atlantic continent, and known to the ancient world as Atlantis.

2   That the description of this island given by Plato is not, as has long been supposed, fable, but veritable history.

3   That Atlantis was the region where man first arose from a state of barbarism to civilisation.

4   That it became, in the course of ages, a populous and mighty nation, from whose overflowings the shores of the Gulf of Mexico, the Mississippi River, the Amazon, the Pacific Coast of South America, the Mediterranean, the west coast of Europe and Africa, the Baltic, the Black Sea, and the Caspian were populated by civilised nations.

5   That it was the true Antediluvian world; the Garden of Eden; the Gardens of the Hesperides; the Elysian Fields; the Gardens of Alcinous; the Mesamphalos; the Olympos; the Asgard of the traditions of the ancient nations; representing a universal memory of a great land, where early mankind dwelt for ages in peace and happiness.

6   That the gods and goddesses of the ancient Greeks, the Phoenicians, the Hindoos, and the Scandinavians were simply the kings, queens and heroes of Atlantis; and the acts attributed to them in mythology are a confused recollection of real historical events.

7   That the mythology of Egypt and Peru represented the original religion of Atlantis, which was sun-worship.

8   That the oldest colony formed by the Atlanteans was prob-
    ably in Egypt, whose civilisation was a reproduction of that
    of the Atlantic island.

9   That the implements of the 'Bronze Age' of Europe were
    derived from Atlantis. The Atlanteans were also the first
    manufacturers of iron.

10 That the Phoenician alphabet, parent of all the European
    alphabets, was derived from an Atlantis alphabet, which was
    also conveyed from Atlantis to the Mayas of Central America.

11 That Atlantis was the original seat of the Aryan or Indo-
    European family of nations, as well as of the Semitic peoples,
    and possibly the Turanian races.

12 That Atlantis perished in a terrible convulsion of nature, in
    which the whole island sunk into the ocean, with nearly all
    its inhabitants.

13 That a few persons escaped in ships and on rafts, and carried
    to the nations east and west the tidings of the appalling
    catastrophe, which has survived to our own time in the Flood
    and Deluge legends of the different nations of the old and
    new worlds.[4]

These revolutionary proposals also give a broad overview of the
kinds of evidence Donnelly marshalled. There are several chapters
on cultural resemblances between ancient civilisations on both
sides of the Atlantic, ranging from archaeological remains to
religious rituals; other chapters present linguistic arguments drawn
from similarities in languages and scripts. By far the largest space
in Donnelly's book is devoted to the myths and traditions of the
world, on which he felt the Atlantean catastrophe had left an
indelible mark.

None of the world's ancient literature – with the exception of
the works of Plato and a few Greek writers who followed him –
actually mentions Atlantis under that name, a point which is rarely
made clear in many of the popular books on the subject. Still,
Donnelly and his successors present a dazzling array of legendary
material which, at first glance, might seem to corroborate Plato's
account.

Donnelly was the first to stress that there is a scatter of traditional place-names around the Atlantic basin which seem to

echo the name Atlantis. There is the Atlas Mountain range in north-west Africa, near which a tribe called the Atlantes lived in classical times. Apparently, Spanish conquistadores also found a town called Atlan on the coast of Venezuela when they arrived there in the fifteenth century. Most intriguing of all is the story that the Aztecs of Mexico told about their ancestral homeland. Before moving to Lake Texcoco, site of their capital, Tenochtitlan (Mexico City), they said that they had lived somewhere to the east, in a beautiful land called Aztlan. The Aztec Emperor Montezuma described it to the conquistador Hernan Cortés:

> Our fathers dwelt in that happy and prosperous place which they called Aztlan, which means whiteness . . . In this place there is a great mountain in the middle of the water which is called Culhuacan . . . which means 'crooked mountain'.[5]

The name and the mountain and water associations certainly remind one of Plato's Atlantis. Aztlan and the rash of other *atl*-places around the Atlantic formed a major plank of Donnelly's argument:

> Look at it! An 'Atlas' mountain on the shore of Africa; an 'Atlan' town on the shore of America; the 'Atlantes' living along the north and west coast of Africa; an Aztec people from Aztlan, in Central America; an ocean rolling between the two worlds called the 'Atlantic'; a mythological deity called 'Atlas' holding the world on his shoulders; and an immemorial tradition of an island of Atlantis. Can all these things be the result of accident?[6]

Add to this the claim reported by Donnelly that 'the words Atlas and Atlantic have no satisfactory etymology in any language known to Europe', whereas the Nahuatl language of Mexico contains the word *atl*, meaning 'water' which could have provided the name for the island-continent.[7] Incidentally, Donnelly's notion that the Atlantean Empire extended to the Americas as well as Africa and Europe is based on Plato's *Timaeus* (25B), which states that the Atlantean kings held sway over 'parts of the continent' which lay beyond it.

It all sounds quite persuasive until one looks at the evidence more closely. The cluster of *atl*- names around the North African coast is certainly no accident. These names all come from the Greeks, who linked them to the mythological giant Atlas. In their understanding, Atlas gave his name to the towering mountain on the coast of north-west Africa, and the mountain its name to the tribe of Atlantes (or Atarantes) who lived nearby. Either Atlas, or the mountain, gave the Ocean its name. But what about Atlantis? Do the North African names prove that it must have lain in the Atlantic, or was it located there by someone *because* of the North African names? This chicken-and-egg conundrum will be addressed later. In the meantime, one thing is clear – Atlas, the one constant element in all these names, *does* have a satisfactory European etymology – from the Greek verb *tlaô*, 'I bear', because the giant Atlas was thought to carry the skies on his shoulders. The superficially attractive Mexican *atl* is an irrelevance.

As to the mysterious Aztlan, Donnelly and his successors[8] are unfair to their readers in not giving the full context of the story told by the Tenochca Aztecs of Mexico City. Donnelly and the traditional Atlantologists are fond of citing the Aztecs' legendary version of history, in which successive world eras were destroyed by global catastrophes – even the Sun was believed to have changed during these upheavals. With these there is a genuine and striking parallel with Plato's description of a succession of catastrophes caused by changes in the heavens. If Aztlan were Atlantis one would expect the migration of the Tenochca Aztecs to be placed by their historians in one of the world's earliest 'Sun' periods, for example in the age of the 'Water Sun' which was terminated by floods and lightning, or the subsequent 'Earth Sun' age, when the world was populated by giants. Unfortunately for the traditional Atlantologists, the Aztecs made it clear that their migration from Aztlan was an extremely recent event in their version of history.[9] They dated it precisely to AD 1168, a good ten thousand years after Plato said that Atlantis sank. And although they located the 'mountain' of Aztlan in a body of water, their records show it was not the Atlantic Ocean, but a lake which must have lain in eastern Mexico.[10]

Other legends and myths collected by Donnelly to corroborate Plato's story concern much less specific matters and are harder to pin down. Many were genuine traditions concerning primeval times, such as the widespread myths of a universal Deluge. It is a curious, and as yet unexplained, fact that so many cultures of the world can tell a story about a time when the earth was submerged beneath waters, leaving a chosen few who had been warned by the gods of the impending disaster, and who then rebuilt civilisation.

Donnelly was not wrong-headed in attempting to link these myths to the story of Atlantis. The biblical tradition of Noah's Flood, for example, in which the world's earliest civilisations are wiped out by a devastating flood, is surely comparable at a general level to the tale of catastrophe told by Plato.

Donnelly's approach to the Deluge myths was a characteristically radical one. Belief in the literal truth of the Bible was still extremely strong in the late nineteenth century. Indeed, Darwin's shocking theories had made little headway in America by the time Donnelly was writing. Most people had no problem in explaining why Deluge myths were so widespread: one only had to open the Bible and read the story of Noah to realise that the world had once been punished by God with a cataclysm of waters. While still treating the Genesis account respectfully, Donnelly skirted round the most literal interpretation and argued that Noah's Flood and the stories of the Deluge were all versions of one more localised catastrophe – the sinking of Atlantis. Memories of it had then been scattered around the globe by those Atlanteans who managed to flee by boat.

Likewise Donnelly argued that the world's traditions of a Golden Age at the beginning of time were all memories of the palmy days of Atlantean civilisation. Traditions of a world centre, where the first human beings had lived in close proximity to their gods, are almost as widespread as Deluge myths. Again, Donnelly was justified in tackling them and trying to find some rationale for the common features of such legends. And again he had a convenient explanation: the Hebrew Garden of Eden, the Viking Asgard and the Indian sacred Mountain of Meru (where the gods created mankind), were all really names for Atlantis, the cradle of the human race.

Donnelly backed up his case with arguments drawn from material evidence. He could point to many similar cultural developments in the pre-Columbian civilisations on both sides of the Atlantic, such as pyramid-building, the use of hieroglyphics, and the practice of mummification and skull deformation. However, Donnelly was an uncritical scholar, and his passion for Atlantis drove him to throw everything available into the pot and rely on the cumulative effect to persuade his readers. It takes no specialist knowledge to see the weakness in arguments such as the one based on painting: 'This art was known on both sides of the

Atlantic. The paintings upon the walls of some of the temples of Central America reveal a state of the art as high as that of Egypt.'

The problem with the 'evidence' Donnelly found for Atlantis was that none of it – aside from Plato's story – was really direct, and he had nothing to clinch his case. In fact the best evidence at his disposal is usually considered the weakest – the testimony of myth and legend. Because this kind of material is susceptible to many different interpretations, in the last analysis any arguments that the world's great myths and legends reflect the existence and destruction of Atlantis are rather circular.

One cannot interpret a legend as referring to Atlantis and then use that interpretation as independent corroboration of Plato's account. The situation would be very different, of course, if Atlantis were proved to be a geological reality. The circularity of argument would be broken and there would certainly be good grounds to look at the Golden Age and Deluge traditions in a different light.

By the Light of a Volcano

What are the chances that there *is* a large land-mass submerged beneath the waters of the Atlantic Ocean? A superficial look at the character of the Atlantic sea-bed makes the prospect seem quite encouraging. Traditional Atlantologists have always been bolstered in their faith by the existence of groups of islands in the central Atlantic such as the Azores, which *look* as if they are the remains of a once much greater land-mass. The Azores are the volcanic tops of an extremely high structure known as the Mid-Atlantic Ridge that runs down the centre of the Atlantic basin, roughly from north to south.

The ridge was discovered by marine surveys carried out in the 1870s. The method used was straightforward and accurate – weights attached to cables were lowered from ships and the depths of various points on the ocean bed were noted from the amount of cable which had to be reeled out and plotted on maps. The results were introduced by Donnelly with his usual showmanship:

> Suppose we were to find in mid-Atlantic, in front of the Mediterranean, in the neighborhood of the Azores, the remains of an immense island, sunk beneath the sea – one thousand

miles in width, and two to three thousand miles long – would it not go far to confirm the statement of Plato that, 'beyonds the strait where you place the Pillars of Hercules, there was an island larger than Asia [Minor] and Libya [Africa] combined,' called Atlantis? And suppose we found that the Azores were the mountain peaks of this drowned island, and were torn and rent by volcanic convulsions . . . ?[11]

Of course he already knew the answer. The deep-sea soundings carried out by ships from the British, American and German navies had mapped out an enormous undersea ridge stretching from just west of the British Isles to the coast of South America, with a long extension running southwards between the African and South American continents. Donnelly was in good company

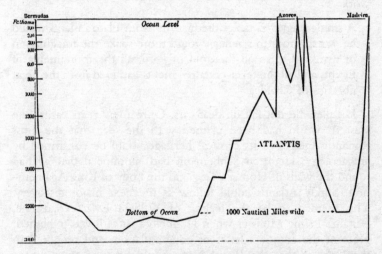

FIG. 4 The profile of the Atlantic Ridge, as revealed by the deep-sea soundings of H.M.S. *Challenger* and the U.S. ship *Dolphin* (*from Donnelly 1882*).

in his interpretation of this discovery. A member of the scientific team on the British naval vessel *Challenger* expressed the opinion that the ridge they had been exploring was the remains of 'the lost Atlantis'.[12]

The naval expeditions also confirmed that the mountainous peaks of the undersea ridge were in fact volcanoes. Donnelly was jubilant:

These facts would seem to show that the great fires which destroyed Atlantis are still smouldering in the depths of the ocean; that the vast oscillations which carried Plato's continent beneath the sea may again bring it, with all its buried treasures, to the light; and that even the wild imagination of Jules Verne, when he described Captain Nemo, in his diving-armor, looking down upon the temples and towers of the lost island, lit by the fires of submarine volcanoes, had some groundwork of possibility to build on.[13]

The only piece of evidence missing, in Donnelly's opinion, was an archaeological find from the bottom of the Atlantic. In the conclusion to *Atlantis: The Antediluvian World* Donnelly proclaimed that it was time to put the 'idle navies' of the world to work:

A single engraved tablet dredged up from Plato's island would be worth more to science, would more strike the imagination of mankind, than all the gold of Peru, all the monuments of Egypt, and all the terra-cotta fragments gathered from the great libraries of Chaldea.[14]

His plea did not fall on deaf ears. Only a few years earlier the western world had been primed with the idea that the most romantic images of its classical heritage could be confirmed by archaeology: Heinrich Schliemann had announced that he had found the walls of Homer's Troy and the body of King Agamemnon. Surely Atlantis could follow as the next major discovery. This seemed to be the feeling of William Ewart Gladstone, Britain's Prime Minister when Donnelly's *Atlantis* was published. He sent the author a letter of congratulation, and proposed to the Cabinet that the Royal Navy could be used to mount a scientific expedition to find Atlantis. The idea was, however, quashed by the Treasury.[15]

Even without the final scientific confirmation Donnelly hoped for, many believed that he already had enough geological evidence on his side to prove his point. Plato's Atlantis should be taken seriously. Donnelly followed up this success with another bestseller, entitled *Ragnarök: The Age of Fire and Gravel*, which extended his exploration of human traditions even further back in time. In *Ragnarök* Donnelly argued that the Earth had been struck by a comet about 30,000 years ago, causing many of the phenomena that scientists today attribute to the glaciers of the Ice Age. The main survivors of the catastrophe were the Atlanteans, who rebuilt civilisation on their island continent. The book concludes with a second surprise, as Donnelly presented a mass of archaeological oddities (mostly mistaken) to demonstrate that pre-glacial man was fully 'civilised', using pottery, domesticated animals, cities, metallurgy and even coins. The home of this civilisation, so old that it even gave rise to the Atlantean culture, was North America. As a reviewer in the *Pall Mall Gazette* commented: 'America, the land of big things, has, in Mr Donnelly, a son worthy of her immensity.'

Continents Adrift

Nineteenth- and early twentieth-century scholarship continued to believe in the past existence of the Mid-Atlantic Ridge as an enormous land bridge, across which flora and fauna now common to both sides of the Atlantic had once spread. While some geologists may have objected that such a land bridge had been submerged thousands – if not hundreds of thousands – of years before Plato's Atlantis, the evidence of the ridge continued to provide a highly respectable edge to Atlantological speculations for decades.

The idea of Atlantis was particularly popular among French geologists. It even made a convert of Louis de Launay, one of the most respected and powerfully placed geologists of his time. (His posts included those of Inspector General of Mines; Professor of Geology, Mineralogy and Palaeontology, École des Ponts et Chaussées; and Director of the Service de la Carte Geologique de France.) In 1905 he discussed the evidence for a northern continent joining Canada to Ireland or Spain which 'must have endured very late', but insisted that 'no attempt should be made to associate this hypothesis with the famous Atlantis of Plato, which by no means represents the memory of a geological phenomenon.'[16] By 1921, however, his view of the sinking of Atlantis had changed completely:

There is . . . for a geologist, nothing more normal and commonplace in Earth history than the disappearance of a continent under the ocean. In general such events are only of interest to geologists. But this one is more striking to the imagination because it must have occurred suddenly, and especially because it undoubtedly engulfed thousands of people.[17]

The happy co-existence of traditional Atlantology with respectable geology was eventually to be shattered by a revolutionary new theory published in 1915. A young German meteorologist and explorer called Alfred Wegener had noticed that if you cut out the continents from a map the pieces can be roughly joined together like a jigsaw puzzle. This led him to propose that all the continents of the world had once been joined together in a single landmass, which had fragmented and then slowly drifted apart. The idea had already been toyed with by a number of other scientists, but Wegener was the first to draw the global evidence together and present it in book form.[18]

The idea was particularly unwelcome to geologists who believed in Atlantis. If you fit the Americas, Europe and Africa together there is simply no room for another continent between them. Still, in 1915 Atlantologists did not consider Wegener's theory too serious a threat. Initial reaction to it from the geological community was extremely hostile and Wegener was widely treated as little better than a crank. While geologists happily accepted that landmasses can move vertically, the idea that they could slide about the planet, ploughing through the Earth's crust, seemed preposterous.

Nevertheless, Wegener's theory slowly began to pick up support. A poll taken at the annual meeting of the British Association for the Advancement of Science in 1950 showed an equal division of opinion between those in favour and those against the idea of shifting continents. Then, in the 1960s, 'continental drift' (now better known as the plate tectonics theory) became orthodoxy with almost dramatic suddenness. This complete turnaround was brought about by two other revolutions in geological thinking.

It was once thought that the Earth's crust was of more or less uniform thickness and composition, but by about 1960 it had been realised that there were substantial differences between the crust that forms the continents and that which forms the ocean bed. While the continental crust is, on average, about 35km thick, the crust beneath the oceans only reaches about 7km. Ocean floors also lack the granitic layer present under the continents. Harry Hess, Professor of Geology at Princeton University, concluded that the ocean beds are relatively young features (compared

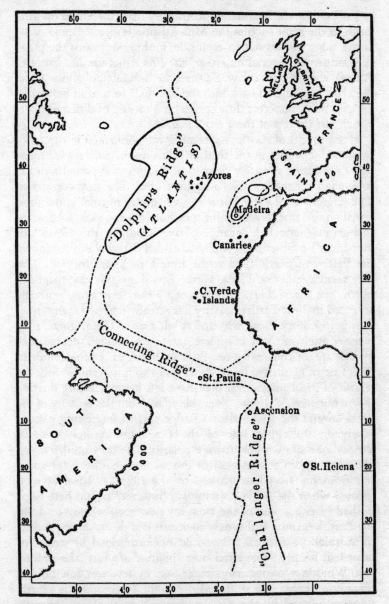

FIG. 5   The Atlantean continent, reconstructed by Donnelly from the evidence of deep-sea soundings. He implies that it was once connected to South America by a ridge of land (*after Donnelly 1882*).

to the continental landmasses) formed by magma welling up from faults in the crust such as the Mid-Atlantic Ridge. Magma rising at the ridge spreads out to each side, pushing outwards the plates of continental material on either side (the Americas and Europe/Africa); elsewhere in the world there are 'subduction' zones where the crust is ploughed back into the mantle.[19] Instead of being one lumpen mass, the crust (lithosphere) is a mosaic of different plates which rest on top of the Earth's mantle.

Hess's model of sea-floor spreading was confirmed in the 1960s by new discoveries in the field of palaeomagnetism. As sedimentary or volcanic strata are formed, the iron oxide particles in the rock align themselves with magnetic north like tiny compasses. The alignment of these particles will, under normal conditions, remain the same (even if the position of the rock relative to the geomagnetic field changes). By examining this 'fossil' (or 'remanent') magnetism, geophysicists can detect the direction of the Earth's magnetic field at the time a rock was formed. This may seem a rather odd idea, as one would imagine that magnetic north has always been to the north. But it is now generally accepted that the Earth's polarity has actually reversed many times during its history. How, why and at what speed the magnetic field reverses itself are still complete mysteries, though explanatory models are, of course, legion. For the theory of continental drift, the cause of geomagnetic reversals is not so important – only the record of fossil magnetism they have left behind. Using floating magnetometers, physicists were able to map out the polarity of the rocks around the Mid-Atlantic Ridge and an interesting pattern emerged. On either side of the ridge are parallel series of 'stripes' of rocks with alternating polarity. The only model which seems to explain this argues that the sea floor has been spreading out from the fault-line marked by the ridge. A band of rock formed when the field's polarity was 'reversed' would have been pushed to either side of the ridge by new rock welling up from the Earth's mantle. If this new rock was laid down during a time of 'normal' polarity then it would be surrounded by stripes of 'reversed' polarity. Repeated over millions of years, the process would produce two mirror-image sets of reversed and normal polarity on either side of the Mid-Atlantic Ridge. This is exactly what was found by the magnetometer surveys of the Atlantic. The palaeomagnetic stripes remain one of the best proofs of continental drift.

These developments have all been bad news for the traditional view of Atlantis. First, the idea that a large part of the Atlantic floor is formed by a submerged continent now seems to be ruled out – for one thing we would expect the crust at the bottom of the ocean to be considerably thicker than it is. Second, the reconstructed map of the Earth's continental plates (known as Pangaea) leaves no room for an Atlantic continent. Third, many similarities in fauna and flora between the two hemispheres are now explained by the continents once having been joined together, without the need for an Atlantic land-bridge. And finally, rather than being the remnants of an old, exploded continent as Donnelly saw them, the volcanoes along the Mid-Atlantic Ridge are now thought to be relatively young features. Their existence certainly conforms with the idea that the ridge is a geologically active fault-line along which new ocean crust wells up as magma.

The Balance of Evidence

To be fair to the traditional Atlantologists, the geological case against the existence of a past Atlantic continent is not completely proven, and it rests to a large extent on the primacy of theory. It is wise to bear in mind the cautionary words recently expressed by David Chester, a volcanologist who is Senior Lecturer in Geography at the University of Liverpool:

> Plate tectonics is embraced by the vast majority of earth scientists, but an occasional dissident voice is still heard. It must be stressed that plate tectonics is a model, in other words, 'an idealised representation of reality in order to demonstrate some of its properties' . . . : it is also a theory – the best available at the moment – but a theory nevertheless.

As Chester remarks, it is a sobering thought that little more than forty years ago a geologist could pronounce with supreme confidence in *Scientific American* that 'everything that is known concerning the configuration and structure of the floors of the oceans proves conclusively that Wegener's hypothesis of continental drift is wholly untenable.'[20]

There are indeed problems with the theory, not the least being the nature of the driving mechanism behind the relentless drift of the continents.[21] A number of models have been proposed:

one of the most bizarre suggests that the Earth is actually expanding (due to a change in gravity), and that the continents move further apart like pieces of cut peel on an inflatable orange.[22] And while continental drift is taught almost as an unchallengeable fact in the West, it is only now beginning to make headway in the former USSR. In the 1980s Soviet geologists still rejected the idea out of hand, deeming it to be an unnecessary piece of western scientific speculation.[23] Objections to the whole theory are also occasionally raised in the West.[24]

Such resistance to the unquestioned acceptance of continental drift has only been healthy. Many scientists, particularly during the 1970s, tended to treat the theory as the Holy Grail of geology, able to explain practically every important process seen in the record of the rocks.[25] It is manifestly not. Geologists have become increasingly aware that other processes – most notably extra-terrestrial ones – have played a crucial role in shaping the Earth's surface. The disintegration of large comets on an Earth-crossing orbit has been established by astronomers as an influential force in the events of Earth's prehistory.[26] Cometary catastrophism, once rejected by geologists as the province of the lunatic fringe, has been steadily creeping back into geological thinking over the last three decades. For example, impacts from asteroids, meteorites or comets – or a dust veil of cometary debris – almost certainly caused the demise of the dinosaurs. No other theory matches the pattern of evidence as well and only the most die-hard reactionaries in the field now refuse to contemplate such ideas.

Thus there is no single and all-encompassing theory that explains the history of the Earth's surface and the lifeforms it supports. (This might appear perfectly obvious to laypeople, but not so to many geologists, who often seem prepared to go to any lengths for the current paradigm.) All the same, we cannot ignore years of work on the part of geologists and geophysicists and wish away the evidence for continental drift. Every geological discovery of the last forty years has tended to confirm the reality of plate tectonics theory. As Chester notes, the present consensus has been reached through literally hundreds of individual pieces of empirical research and synthesis.

In stark contrast, no evidence which is acceptable by today's standards has appeared to support the idea that there was once a continent in the Mid Atlantic.[27] Those wishing to argue for its existence would also have to produce a feasible model which can explain the evidence, such as the palaeomagnetic stripes, which so strongly supports the plate tectonics theory. More than thirty years have passed since the rise of plate tectonics theory but the traditional Atlantologists have yet even to suggest such a model.

Atlantis Sinking

The past existence of a large slab of continental crust in the Atlantic does not fit the observable facts. But, supposing Plato – or his source – had exaggerated the size of his 'lost continent', is there room, geologically speaking, for something of much more limited scope to have sunk beneath the sea?

Tiny islands are known to have both appeared and disappeared from the Atlantic. The most spectacular event in recent times was the birth of Surtsey, thrown up by a undersea volcanic eruption off the south-west coast of Iceland in 1963. Surtsey still exists, but other small volcanic islands which appeared near the Azores in the eighteenth and nineteenth centuries are known to have disappeared again within a few years, or even a few days.[28] Made by the tips of undersea volcanoes, or tentacles of lava stretching to the surface, such islands are clearly of a special, temporary nature and do not provide a good model for Atlantis. They are hardly likely to have been able to support the long development needed for the kind of civilisation Plato described. At the same time, mechanisms for sinking more solid landmasses are hard to conceive. It seems the only logical way for a more sizable island to have been submerged by the Atlantic would be if the sea-level itself had risen – which indeed it did at the end of the last Ice Age (c. 9000 BC).

The region of the Azores, the highest landmass in the Mid Atlantic, is the most likely site for a theoretical mini-Atlantis. This idea was explored by the innovative British physicist Peter Warlow in 1982:

> although we must rule out the idea of there having been a large land mass in the middle of the Atlantic, there still remains the possibility of a large island. In addition, if in the region of the Azores the sea-level were to be lowered or the land to be raised by a matter of some 200 metres, then the present Azores archipelago would become the mountainous region of

a substantial island – very roughly about the size of England and Wales.[29]

As a theoretical concept, Warlow's suggestion is the best made so far in terms of the traditional location of Atlantis. The possibility of such a (non-continental) landmass cannot be denied – after all Iceland, which is roughly the size of England and Wales put together, does exist. Nor is a rise in the level of the Atlantic by 200 metres or so inconceivable. Warlow himself suggests that deformation of the Earth's crust, during the upheavals that accompanied the end of the Ice Age, could have been responsible – again, a not unreasonable idea, as the shape of the Earth is far from perfectly spherical. It should be noted, however, that Warlow does not claim to have proven the case for a 'mini-Atlantis'. He has merely opened a window, and a very narrow one at that, through which the possibility of salvaging an Atlantic Atlantis might come.

A different mechanism for a dramatic rise in the sea-level of the Atlantic comes from more orthodox geological thinking about the end of the Ice Age. The conventional explanation of the last glaciation relies on a global temperature drop. As massive amounts of water were stored in the polar caps the world's oceans would have lowered accordingly. At the end of the Ice Age the glacial sheets melted, releasing the water and raising the sea-levels again.[30] In the opinion of Professor Cesare Emiliani, a noted geochemist, these waters were released in rapid episodes with catastrophic consequences. Emiliani and his team from Miami University based their conclusions on the study of cores taken from the sediments laid down in the Gulf of Mexico. Using oxygen isotope analysis of the tiny fossils in these sediments, they discovered that there was a dramatic change in the salinity of the gulf near the end of the Ice Age. Radiocarbon dates on organic material in the sediments suggested to Emiliani and his colleagues that this change took place about 9,600 BC, contemporary with a surge in the ice sheet covering North America known as the 'Valders Readvance'. In such surges it is thought that glaciation temporarily spread (or slumped) over warmer areas, to be followed by rapid melting. Their conclusion, then, was that they had detected a massive onrush of meltwater from the decaying ice sheets of the last glaciation of northern America.

To the delight of traditional Atlantologists and the chagrin of sceptics, when Emiliani published his findings in the prestigious journal *Science* in 1975, he linked them with Plato's Atlantis:

> The concomitant, accelerated rise in sea level, of the order of decimeters per year, must have caused widespread flooding of low-lying areas, many of which were inhabited by man. We submit that this event, in spite of its great antiquity in cultural terms, could be an explanation for the deluge stories common to many Eurasian, Australasian, and American traditions. Plato set the date of the flood at 9000 years before Solon, equal to 9600 years BC or 11,600 years BP [Before Present]: this date coincides, within all limits of error, with the age of both the highest concentration of ice meltwater in the Gulf of Mexico and the Valders readvance.[31]

Emiliani did not claim to have located Atlantis, but only to have identified the background to the story. All the same, the press naturally seized on the story, while Emiliani was severely criticised by some of his professional colleagues.

Professor Herbert E. Wright of the University of Minnesota has analysed Emiliani's arguments at length and insists that the effects of the posited meltwater-flood would have been so gradual that they would barely have been noticed by coastal inhabitants. One of his arguments is sound. To arrive at the date of 11,600 BP, Emiliani and his colleagues took the rough mid-point between two radiocarbon dates from the cores: 12,220 ± 140 BP and 10,865 ± 145 BP. As Wright points out, simply selecting a mid-point of 11,600 gives a spurious effect of precision to the method.[32] The event Emiliani detected could have fallen anywhere between about 12,360 and 10,720 years ago, blurring the neat coincidence with Plato's date of 9600 BC (11,600 BP). Wright's second argument, however, is based on a logical fallacy. He assumes that the meltwaters must have arrived *across* this larger timespan, rather than at a given point within it, and then argues that this 'is certainly not a catastrophic change in cultural terms'.

Wright is clearly a gradualist, Emiliani something of a neo-catastrophist. On the evidence from the Gulf of Mexico alone, there is no way of telling which understanding is nearer the truth. However, a new sea-level curve for this period based on a series of corals from near Barbados strongly supports the abruptness of the change which Emiliani detected. About 12,500 years ago there was a sudden rise of the sea-level by 24 metres in a period of less than 1,000 years; the time-period could be considerably less, as the sea-level curve at this point swings sharply upwards, almost to the vertical.[33] Together with this there is increasing evidence that the events surrounding the end of the Ice Age were indeed catastrophic. As well as a massive shift in global climate there was widespread decimation of fauna (including the mammoths), along with dramatic fluctuations in the Earth's magnetism, including a near reversal or 'excursion' of the field by as much as 40 degrees.[34]

It is tempting to see in the massive disturbances that closed the last Ice Age a fitting context for the world's Deluge legends. Along with Warlow and Emiliani, many others have argued that the destruction of Plato's Atlantis may be linked to these events, including the Italian mathematician Emilio Spedicato, who has suggested that the Ice Age was terminated when an Apollo asteroid struck the Atlantic, causing floods of an almost global dimension.[35] All these theories, of course, take Plato's date of 9600 BC at face value, an approach which is an extremely risky proposition. If one did give Plato's date the benefit of the doubt, it is possible to blend together the best arguments of the theorists and give the traditional placement of Atlantis its 'last stand'. The net rise in sea-level between the time of the maximum advance of the ice sheets around 20,000 years ago and the 'normal conditions' of the present is calculated as being about 120 or 130 metres.[36] If we allow that the ice sheets melted in a major catastrophic episode, and if we allow for crustal deformation, perhaps aggravated by asteroid impact, maybe we should not rule out the figure of 200 metres needed by Warlow for his speculative mini-Atlantis.

This is already piling up a lot of 'ifs' in order to save Plato's face. The best, it seems, that physical science might offer is the very slim possibility of an Atlantic Atlantis on a much smaller scale than Plato described – an island no bigger than Iceland which was submerged by a dramatic change in sea-level at the end of the Ice Age. In geological terms, the area of the Azores would be the most likely location, though perhaps its traces could be sought in other corners of the Atlantic. Yet does the archaeological and historical evidence provide any justification for such a model? In other words, if it were not for Plato, would there be any need to speculate about a lost Atlantic centre at all?

Transatlantic Parallels

By far the most commonly cited evidence in favour of the existence of a real Atlantis – repeated in scores of books since Donnelly's time – concerns apparent similarities in the ancient cultures
on the two sides of the Atlantic. The argument is simple: cultural
features shared by the Americas and the Old World probably came
from a common centre and Plato's Atlantis would fill the role
nicely.

The existence of pyramids on both sides of the Atlantic is a
favourite of the traditional lobby; Donnelly claimed that 'in Atlantis, home of the gods, we find the original model of all those
pyramids which extend from India to Peru'. But do the function,
distribution and dating of the various pyramid-like structures
around the world really suggest an Atlantean origin?

Pyramid building began in Egypt about 2500 BC and continued
until Roman times. In Mesopotamia and Iran the building of
ziggurats, like truncated pyramids in shape, began about the same
time. Their function was very different. Pyramids – although
many other special functions have been claimed for them – were
basically tombs, built on a massive scale so that the pharaoh's
burial would be as eternal and impenetrable as possible. Ziggurats
were artificial mountains composed of three or four superimposed
platforms, on top of which a shrine was placed – their purpose
was to facilitate communication between the gods of heaven and
their earthly subjects.

The pyramids of Mesoamerica were flat-topped and, although
burials have occasionally been found within them, their purpose
was similar to that of the ziggurats – to raise worshippers and
their offerings nearer the heavens. Human sacrifices on top of
pyramids were an important part of Mexican life when the conquistadores arrived in 1518: Cortés, in a letter to King Charles V
of Spain, said that he counted four hundred pyramids at Cholula
alone. The structures encountered by the Spanish were, of course,
quite 'modern', the great temple at Tenochtitlan, for example,
having been completed and dedicated as recently as 1487.[37] Earlier
pyramids were built by the precursors of the Aztecs, such as the
Maya, the Olmecs and the anonymous builders of the mysterious
city of Teotihuacan in the Valley of Mexico. The Teotihuacan
people built the earliest definite Mesoamerican pyramids so far
discovered: those at Teotihuacan and nearby Cuicuilco, which

compare well in size with the Great Pyramid of Cheops at Giza, can be placed by radiocarbon dating as early as the last few centuries BC. This would mean that the age of pyramid-building in Mesoamerica overlapped with its last flourishing in Egypt and Nubia.

These dates hardly suggest a common origin in Atlantis several thousands of years BC. Even if one way to reduce considerably Plato's date for Atlantis – to, say, about 3500 BC, to meet the beginnings of the first urban civilisations – there would still be a gap of some three thousand years before the first such structures were built in Mexico. The distribution does not suggest a common origin either. If pyramid-building originated in the Mid Atlantic one would surely expect the earliest pyramid-like structures in the Old World to have been built not in Egypt and Iraq but in western Europe and north-west Africa, where there are actually none at all. In short, the pattern of evidence completely contradicts any idea that pyramid-building may have spread from a centre in the Atlantic.

The superficial resemblance between the shape and function of Mesoamerican 'pyramids' and Near Eastern ziggurats is most likely due to parallel development. The worship of deities on mountain-tops is common worldwide, and the idea of building artificial platforms to communicate with the gods could easily have been invented independently in different parts of the globe. As a pyramid shape is the most stable structure one can erect, it would be the natural choice for an imposing monument built to last.

The pyramid question is echoed in most of the other 'common' cultural features cited by Atlantologists. Aware of such problems, Lewis Spence, a Scottish mythologist and Donnelly's main successor in the early twentieth century, devised an explanatory mechanism. At some point during the Ice Age, he argued, volcanic and other disturbances split the original landmass of Atlantis into two large islands. The northern one was Plato's Atlantis, which eventually succumbed to the elements about 10,000 BC. The southern part, which Spence called Antillia, survived the catastrophe for several thousand years and eventually fragmented into the West Indies. It was from Antillia, Spence argued, that Mesoamerican civilisation received its stimulus.[38] Of all the Atlantologists, Spence was probably the most erudite and rational – his resort to such *ad hoc* explanations merely underlines the inherent weakness of their case.

There are, however, some genuine instances of cultural features shared between the civilisations of the Old and New Worlds – particularly concerning folklore and mythology. The Deluge myths of the world do, as Donnelly and the Atlantologists have repeatedly stressed, show an extraordinary pattern of resemblances.[39] Many of these common elements – such as the idea of a hero building an ark in which he rescues his family and animals – can be explained as 'logical' developments. If two peoples shared a belief that the whole world was once flooded, they might both deduce that the survivors had been saved by building an enormous boat. Much more difficult to explain are some curious similarities of small detail, such as those which exist between the Hebrew and Mexican accounts of the great Flood. The book of Genesis (9:20–21) records the following after Noah and his family disembarked: 'And Noah began to be an husbandman, and he planted a vineyard: and he drank of the wine, and was drunken . . . ' The Aztecs believed that *pulque*, their favourite alcoholic brew, was invented by Patecatl, 'the one who survived the Flood'. The Quiché Mayan classic *Popol Vuh* gives a slightly different version in which the 'four hundred sons' who survived the Flood brewed the first *pulque*, got drunk and ascended to heaven to become the Pleiades.[40] Strangely enough the Pleiades crop up again in an extra-biblical Hebrew tradition: rabbinical sources state that the Deluge was caused when God removed two stars from the constellation, leaving a hole through which the waters of the firmament rushed.[41] The recurrence of the Pleiades in these two separate traditions may have some basis in astronomical reality – for example, if widespread floods were caused by a comet or asteroid seen to have approached the Earth from the direction of the Pleiades – but no such natural explanation can be conceived to explain why the culture heroes who survived the Mayan and Hebrew Deluges were both associated with alcohol. The world's Deluge myths present a genuine problem requiring explanation, something frequently glossed over by critics of traditional Atlantology. Still, this does not mean that the Atlantologists are right. Contact between the Old and New Worlds would seem to be the only viable explanation for some of the similarities in the Deluge myths, but this contact could have taken place in many ways without needing a landbridge across the Atlantic.

There are many other pieces of evidence that suggest pre-Columbian contacts between the Old and New Worlds. For example, an extensive study of the serpent cults of the Americas and the Far East showed an impressive number of similarities in iconography and beliefs which are hard to explain in terms of independent invention.[42] Some intriguing parallels have also been drawn between some of the hieroglyphic symbols in the Maya calendar and the characters of the Phoenician alphabet.[43]

Despite dogmatic views to the contrary, the Americas were not hermetically sealed from the outside world before the time of Columbus. About AD 1000 the Vikings colonised Newfoundland, here one of their settlements has been excavated.[44] Sporadic contacts in classical times also appear likely. The Greeks seem to have been aware of the existence of America. Plato, for example, said that to the west of Atlantis lay a great continent, connected to it by a chain of smaller islands (*Timaeus* 24E-25A).[45] The Phoenicians of Carthage explored the Atlantic coasts of Europe and Africa and may have reached the Azores in the Mid Atlantic. In 1949 eight Carthaginian coins of the 4th-3rd centuries were discovered in a hoard on Corvo Island in the Azores.[46] It is easy to imagine that Phoenician and Greek ships were sometimes inadvertently carried to the West Indies. Going to America from outside the Straits of Gibraltar is actually one of the easiest sea journeys to make – one simply waits to be drawn along by the 'Canaries Currents'. In modern times there are numerous authenticated examples of craft of all shapes and sizes being carried across the ocean in this way, from canoes and sailing boats to an amphibious jeep.[47] The only difficult part about such a trip is getting back – a hypothetical Phoenician or Greek mariner would have had to follow the American coast northwards until he could catch the Gulf Stream, which would bring him back to European waters. Despite numerous claims that Phoenician inscriptions have been found in America, there is still no generally accepted evidence of Phoenician contacts.[48] Yet the possibility of some Phoenician contact cannot be ruled out. It might explain, for example, the Mayan calendar mystery. It has also been argued that transpacific contacts brought East Asian serpent cults to America between about 600 BC and AD 700.[49] And, of course, it is generally agreed that, long before these pre-Columbian contacts, the ancestors of the Amerindians migrated from north-east Asia across the land-bridge which joined Siberia and Alaska during the Ice Age. The date of the earliest arrivals is still uncertain, but probably lies between 25,000 and 12,000 years before the present.[50] Such pre-Columbian contacts provide a much simpler solution for any genuine cultural similarities between the civilisations of the Old and New Worlds than a hypothetical lost continent.

Ancient Anomalies

The occurrence of occasional scraps of 'high technology' in the ancient world is also often put forward as evidence of Atlantis, the idea being that these are merely remnants of a once-great Atlantean science, which had evolved over tens of thousands of years. The catalogue is a familiar one and usually includes such highlights of ancient ingenuity as a wooden model glider from Sakkara in northern Egypt; an ancient Greek computer for calculating positions of the stars discovered by sponge-divers near the island of Antikythera; and, perhaps most startling of all, the electric batteries found at Baghdad.

With prehistorian Nick Thorpe I have made an extensive study of the surprising feats of technology from prehistoric and ancient times. In the resulting book we examined every genuine example of 'anomalous' ancient science cited by the Atlantologists.[51] To offer them as evidence of Atlantis – or of past visitors from other worlds – can only be done by completely wrenching the articles out of context. For example, the Egyptian glider was discovered with other relics of the fourth to third centuries BC; the Antikythera computer was built during the first century BC, and the Baghdad batteries in the first century AD. To present these artefacts as remnants of a civilisation which disappeared in 9600 BC is hardly convincing.

The three finds in question actually belong to an extraordinary golden age of technological experimentation which flowered between the third century BC and the second century AD. During this time a curious number of similar technological advances were being made simultaneously in the Eastern Mediterranean and the Far East. Alexandria in Egypt was a focal point in these developments – a marvellous melting pot of Greek and Egyptian culture where science flourished under royal patronage. Inventors such as Heron of Alexandria devised contraptions ranging from syringes and executive toys to automatic opening doors and the first steam engine. Rome, of course, was another centre – the work of the Roman architect Vitruvius includes descriptions of an extraordinary range of devices such as a mechanical organ with keyboard and even a milometer! In the East, the great Chinese inventor Chang Hêng (early second century AD) made technological strides which have been described by Joseph Needham, the leading historian of Chinese science, as having 'a distinctly Alexandrian air'. Among other things he devised a milometer, an earthquake detector and a grid system for map-making similar to that being used by Greek cartographers of the time. Which way inspiration and influences went is hard to say – much may have been reciprocal. Indeed, this whole extraordinary chapter in the history of science is still a largely untold story.

Other achievements cited by the Atlantologists are more generalised than these three examples and are widely scattered through time. These include the calendars devised by the prehistoric peoples of Ice-Age Europe, the sophisticated astronomical knowledge of the Babylonians, and the extraordinary skill exhibited by many ancient peoples – from the Egyptians to the megalith builders of Europe – in shepherding enormous masses of stone into architectural wonders such as the pyramids and Stonehenge. There exists a popular misconception that the cave painters or the pyramid builders were somehow less intelligent than us, and that they must therefore have needed outside help from an Atlantean supercivilisation or even extraterrestrial visitors. The assumption is a kind of racism through time. There is actually no evidence that the human brain has 'evolved' at all over the last fifty thousand years. Modern people are merely benefiting from thousands of years of accumulated knowledge and experimentation, not from increased intellect. To underestimate the ingenuity of any ancient people is a serious mistake, and to invoke Atlanteans as an explanation of the technological wonders of the past is merely to imply that everyone else – the Egyptians, Greeks, Chinese, Indians and Olmecs included – was actually rather dim.

The Sudden Rise of Civilisation

At a period approximately 3400 years before Christ, a great change took place in Egypt, and the country passed rapidly from a state of advanced Neolithic culture with a complex tribal character to two well-organised monarchies, one comprising the Delta area and the other the Nile valley proper. At the same time the art of writing appears, monumental architecture and the arts and crafts developed to an astonishing degree, and all the evidence points to the existence of a well-organised and even luxurious civilisation. All this was achieved within a comparatively short period of time, for there appears to be little or no background to these fundamental developments in writing and architecture.[52]

These words, written in 1961 by Professor Walter Emery, an authority on the earliest Egyptian civilisation, still hold true today. The problem he raised is, of course, part of a much wider one – the apparently sudden explosion of civilisations in the Old World generally after the end of the Late Stone Age. During the fifth to fourth millennia BC, urban civilisations with cities, complex irrigation systems, temples, writing, structured hierarchies and organised bureaucracies sprang up across a broad swathe of territory reaching from Egypt, through Syria, Iraq and Iran, to the Indus Valley in Pakistan. How these developments occurred, and why they occurred when they did, has always been a moot point, something Atlantologists have used to good effect, and none more plausibly than Donnelly. Drawing his inspiration from Plato, Donnelly believed that what most archaeologists saw as the rise of Old World civilisation was the beginning of a decline – within terms of a cyclical view of history on an enormous time-scale. He argued that Egyptian civilisation was full-blown when it first appeared and that it steadily decayed thereafter. He drew attention, quite correctly, to the curious fact that ancient Egyptian medicine seems to have been been more advanced during the Old Kingdom (c. 2600–2100 BC) than it was, say, in the days of Tutankhamun or Cleopatra.[53] In Donnelly's view all ancient civilisation was an 'inheritance' – 'as "all roads lead to Rome," so all the converging lines of civilisation lead to Atlantis'.[54]

Donnelly's thinking was not out of step with that of most archaeologists of his time. In the late nineteenth and early twentieth centuries they tended to see the origins of civilisation in terms of ancient 'master races' of culture bringers. Emery, who belonged to the old school, had no doubt whatsoever that the rise of Egyptian civilisation was due to the invasion of a 'dynastic race', which settled in the Nile Valley and established kingship there. Others, such as the noted anthropologist Grafton Elliot Smith, saw Egypt not as the recipient but as the source of all civilisation. In a stream of books published between 1910 and 1940, Elliot

Smith argued that complicated techniques such as mummification could not possibly have been invented more than once. Ergo the occurrence of mummification in Peru proved beyond doubt that they were influenced by the Egyptians. Elliot Smith initiated a school of quite manic diffusionism which attributed *all* the world's ancient civilisations to a master race they called 'the Children of the Sun', who had sailed around the world spreading mummification, sun-worship and the techniques of building large stone monuments.[55]

Extreme as they were, the theories of Smith and his followers were not considered too eccentric in their day. It was widely accepted that civilisation had diffused from the Near East to Europe; the megalithic tombs of north-western Europe, for example, were thought to have derived ultimately from Egyptian models. So, just as some early twentieth-century geologists looked favourably on the idea of a lost Atlantic continent, traditional Atlantologists such as Lewis Spence also found themselves in good company with the hyper-diffusionist school of archaeology – their only disagreement concerned the location of the homeland from which all civilisation had spread. This cosy situation was to break down almost at the same time as sea-floor spreading was to spoil the Atlantologists' geological case.

After the Second World War archaeological theory went through an upheaval which was long overdue. Archaeology as a whole was going through something of an identity crisis, trying to shake off the image of being the province of dilettantes, very often old boys of the military school. The reputation was not entirely unjustified. Over the period of the two world wars much of the best archaeological work – notably in the Near East – was carried out by people with a military background. The military imbued the nascent field of archaeology with a wide range of essential skills – organisation, surveying, cartography, engineering and practical acquaintance with the topography and languages of the cultures being studied. At the same time, military men tended to see the archaeological record to a disproportionate degree in terms of military history – invasions, wars, conquests and the rise and fall of empires.

In the 1960s things began to change. Western archaeologists needed to recreate their field as a scientific discipline. The old idea of the romantic archaeologist poking around Egyptian tombs for art treasures was eschewed. Out of the same window went any idea that archaeology should serve to confirm ancient legends and traditions. In came new techniques, new technology and new methodology. The aim of archaeology was no longer to be 'the handmaiden of history'. Rather, it became a social science in its own right, its main concern being to study change within early societies by examining their material remains.[56]

An almost natural trend in the early days of the 'New Archaeology' was to reject invasions as an explanatory mechanism – such ideas had been worked to death by archaeologists of the old school and they smacked of romanticism. Diffusion became almost a dirty word – with good reason, considering the excesses of the Elliot Smith school. The new technique of radiocarbon dating brought about an enormous change in the thinking about prehistoric Europe. The earliest civilisations of Europe were now no longer dependent on vague comparisons with the Near East and could now be given their own independent chronology. Moreover, the radiocarbon dates showed that many developments thought to have been borrowed from the Near East and the Aegean actually took place earlier in Europe. In 1973 these new findings were synthesised by Colin Renfrew in his archaeological classic, *Before Civilization*, which set out to analyse the major cultural changes of prehistoric Europe – from the invention of metalworking to the development of megalithic architecture – in terms of purely local evolution. Agriculture was the only feature Renfrew allowed to have spread from the Near East (through the arrival of Neolithic farmers), though he later modified this to a model of hand-to-hand spreading of farming knowledge from Anatolia through the Balkans into central Europe.[57]

This reaction against diffusion was certainly necessary. It led, however, to a trend to reject the significance of invasions generally throughout the archaeological record. Though perhaps 'politically correct', this line of reasoning is not correct politically. If we now find the concept of master races in the past rather distasteful, it does not follow that ancient peoples had a similar understanding. Julius Caesar and Genghis Khan would laugh in the face of anyone who thought so. From a purely logical (rather than doctrinal) point of view, there is nothing wrong with the idea that there were once self-styled master races which subdued their neighbours by superior military and technological abilities – just so long as the idea does not become obsessive and lead to the interpretation of every flicker in the archaeological record as another episode of invasion and conquest.

It is hoped that we have now reached a period in the philosophy of archaeology where a more balanced view is possible of the role of invaders in the rise of civilisation. In fact, considerable evidence for foreign influence on the Gerzean culture (c. 3400–3000 BC), which preceded the First Dynasty of Egypt, has been available since the beginning of this century: a whole range of features, from the use of cylinder seals to the techniques needed to sculpt the hardest stones and build monumental structures from bricks, appear with striking rapidity.[58] They all bear the hallmark of Mesopotamian influence. During the 1960s many Egyptologists, happy with the marked trend away from diffusionism, tended to minimise this influence.[59] But now the evidence has accumulated to the point where the inevitable has to be accepted. For example, the similarities of the first brick-built buildings to those of Mesopotamia were always clear, but while such parallels remained on the general, structural level their importance could always be disputed. Recent excavations at Buto in the Delta, however, have shown that even the ornamentation of these buildings could be identical – small clay cones painted in different colours were found, just like those used in Mesopotamia to decorate walls with mosaic patterns resembling the scales on snake-skin. This 'virtually seals the argument', in the opinion of Egyptologist Donald Redford, Professor of Near Eastern Studies at Toronto University:

> Although it is perhaps premature to arrive at conclusions, the evidence for contact with Mesopotamia is more extensive and specific than can be accommodated by theory of intermittent and casual trade. It would seem that besides trade items, a *human* component of alien origin is to be sought in the Gerzean demography of Egypt. This is *not* to resuscitate the moribund 'dynastic race' theory, but we should be careful not to misread the evidence or ignore its real weight.[60]

Despite Redford's reluctance to identify the alien 'human component' with an invading aristocratic race, the influential newcomers who brought advanced techniques in sculpture and monumental architecture must surely have played an influential role in the creation of the kingdom of Lower Egypt (in the Delta). That a large influx of craftsmen could have happened without the help of an invading aristocracy is of course possible. All the same, if Redford is right about the 'human component', then it seems that archaeologists will once again have to cope with the possibility that dynastic Egypt, as we know it, originated after a foreign invasion.

I have reviewed the shifting opinions on the origins of Old World civilisation in order to be as fair as possible to the traditional Atlantologists. It is important to remember that trends are just as fundamental to thinking in geology and archaeology as they are to other fields. In purely theoretical terms, traditional Atlantologists can be encouraged by the fact that the theory of the diffusion of civilisation – possibly even by invading races – is beginning to surface again after the drubbing it took during the 1960s and 70s. However, in Egypt – the Atlantologists' favourite example of a country which was suddenly 'civilised' from outside – it is now manifestly clear that the new influences came from Mesopotamia, probably by means of the Levant.[61] Trends in thinking aside, one cannot alter the material evidence. Mesopotamian involvement was crucial in the rise of the earliest Egyptian civilisation. Atlantis, unfortunately, is no longer needed.

Atlantologists might object that this simply transfers the focus of attention from Egypt to Mesopotamia. Where did the Sumerians, the founders of the earliest great Mesopotamian civilisation, come from? Their origins too are mysterious, but a considerable amount of evidence now points to Iran as the centre where key features of Sumerian civilisation, including writing, developed.[62] Nostalgia for the mountainous terrain of Iran may have inspired the Sumerians to build the ziggurats, virtual mountains of brick, on the flat alluvial plains of southern Iraq. Nothing, by comparison, has been discovered which suggests a far-western origin for Sumerian civilisation.

There is still an infinite amount to learn about the rise and interrelationships of early civilisations, but any general pointers that there were 'lost centres' of prehistoric civilisation do not lead us in an Atlantic direction. Such centres may well be found, but they are more likely to belong on the more familiar landmasses of Asia, Africa and America.

Atlantis Rising?

The case from indirect archaeological evidence for the existence of Atlantis is extremely weak. It is fair to say that, had Plato not written about his lost continent in the Atlantic, no-one could possibly have deduced such an idea from the archaeological record of the Old and New Worlds. Atlantologists might still plead that these matters are all a matter of interpretation – which, of course, ultimately they are. What then of the direct evidence – from the Atlantic basin itself?

Over the last forty years there have been numerous claims that archaeological remains of Atlantis have already been found.[63] In 1956 marble columns were supposedly observed standing in shallow waters near the island of Bimini, which lies near the centre of the Bahama cluster off the coast of Florida. Two years later Dr William Bell claimed to have photographed one of these objects, which he described as a 'six-foot column or spire protruding from a double gearlike base embedded in the ocean floor'. In 1967 pilots Robert Brush and Trigg Adams spotted and photographed from the air a rectangular structure off the coast of Andros, largest of the Bahamas. Published photographs certainly suggest a submerged building.

Brush and Adams showed their photographs to Dmitri Rebikoff, an acknowledged expert on underwater photography. With zoologist Dr Manson Valentine, who had been searching the Bahamas for many years for evidence of lost civilisations, Rebikoff explored the Andros site in 1968 and found a building, some 100 by 75 feet, overgrown with seaweed. Valentine, who had previously been involved in archaeological work in Yucatan, compared it in plan to the Classic Mayan temple at Uxmal, and judged from its depth under water (about 6 feet) that the structure was pre-Columbian. In the same year, Valentine's attention was drawn by a local fishing guide to an unusual 'J'-shaped configuration of stones lying about 20 feet underwater off the coast of North Bimini. In the *News* of the Museum of Science in Miami (of which he is an Honorary Curator), Valentine reported:

An extensive pavement of regular and polygonal flat stones, obviously shaped and accurately aligned to form a convincingly artefactual pattern. These stones had evidently lain submerged over a long span of time, for the edges of the biggest ones had become rounded off, giving the blocks the domed appearance of large loaves of bread or pillows of stone.

Valentine's discovery, usually referred to as the 'Bimini Road', became the subject of a protracted controversy. In 1971 a professional geologist pronounced it to be naturally formed 'beach rock', fractured and eroded to give the appearance of large rounded building blocks. Undismayed, the Atlantis enthusiasts insisted that the joints between the stones were far too straight to be the result of natural cracking, and that no beach rock formations are known which are as regular or as elegant as the 'J' shape of the 'Bimini Road'. The dispute promised to run for perpetuity, until, in 1981, Eugene Shinn of the US Geological Survey published in *Nature* a summary of conclusive evidence he had collected from the stones. If the 'Road' were man-made we would not expect the grains and microstructure within the stones to be consistent from one 'block' to another. Yet they proved to be so, in every conceivable test that was applied, showing that they were laid down by natural means. Further, radiocarbon tests on shells included in the stones show that the 'Road' was formed between only about 2,500 to 3,500 years ago, far short of the 11,000 years believed by the Atlantologists. Finally, the much-vaunted hairpin curve in the 'Road' was shown to be the result of it having formed along the edge of a beach which swung around sharply – the modern beachline parallels this curve today.[64]

The 'Bimini Road' was clearly formed by natural means in the shallows of an old coastline only a couple of thousand years ago. As for the drowned 'temple' near Andros which started the whole thing, it was later shown by David Zink (English professor, diver and Atlantologist) to be a sponge storage area built in the 1930s. On a more positive note, Zink's diving team found a fragment of worked stone with tongue-and-groove jointing near the 'Road'. They also found an amorphous lump of marble that to the eye of the believer may be an eroded carving of a jaguar's head. Yet, without any other finds (such as pottery) to give them context, the objects found by Zink could well be pieces of discarded ship-ballast. Some drum-shaped stones found nearby (and claimed by Atlantologists to be pillar fragments) proved to be just that: chemical analysis shows they were made of nineteenth-century cement.[65]

Diving around the Bahamas has continued apace since the first discoveries and there has been an almost continuous stream of incredible claims. Some divers have seen – but never managed successfully to photograph – temples, pillars throbbing with energy, and even pyramids, some capped with glowing crystals. The safest explanation is that the divers involved were suffering from a severe case of the bends.

Wild claims have also been made that discoveries such as the 'Bimini Road' were predicted by the American psychic Edgar Cayce (1877–1945), hailed by some as the most successful psychic of the twentieth century. Cayce committed to paper screeds of psychic 'readings' about Atlantis, based on trances in which he claimed to have re-experienced earlier incarnations. In 1933 he predicted that a 'portion of the temples may yet be discovered under the slime of ages of sea water – near what is known as Bimini, off the coast of Florida'. The date of this discovery seemed to be predicted in another reading, made in 1940: 'Poseidia will be among the first portions of Atlantis to rise again – expect it in '68 and '69 – not so far away.'[66] Thus the discovery of the 'Bimini Road' in 1968 appeared to many to be a striking confirmation of Cayce's prophetic abilities, a claim repeated *ad nauseam* in the more uncritical literature on Atlantis.[67] In fact Cayce's prophecy was largely self-fulfilling. Brush and Adams, the pilots who spotted the Andros structure in 1967, were flying over the area because they expected to find traces of Atlantis that year. Both were members of Edgar Cayce's 'Association for Research and Enlightenment'. They then involved Rebikoff, who in turn brought in Valentine. Though Valentine says he had already been looking for prehistoric remains in the Bahamas for fifteen years before discovering the 'Bimini Road', it is clear enough that his search intensified after the initial Andros discovery. Besides, the discovery of the 'Road' – even if it had turned out to be man-made – only obliquely matched Cayce's prediction. Seen in the context of his other readings, it is clear that he prophesied the actual *rise* of a portion of Atlantis in the region of Bimini as part of a massive series of geological upheavals which would transform Europe, tip most of Japan into the sea, break up western America and produce new land in the Pacific. The process would begin in 1958, and after massive disasters in 1976, would be tied in with the Second Coming by 1998.

Were it not for Cayce's predictions, it is doubtful whether anyone would have associated the Bahama Banks findings with Atlantis in the first place. The shallow waters of the world's coastlines abound with curiosities, from geological features to sunken forests and towns. Indeed, with all the intensive diving that has been done in the Bimini region over the last thirty years it would be surprising if nothing of archaeological or geological interest had been found. Had the Bimini region been a prominent centre of Atlantis, as Cayce and his followers believe, we would surely expect something more convincing than the ambiguous scraps of evidence so far collected.

The conspicuous lack of solid archaeological evidence has daunted few hard-core Atlantologists. Investigation of the shallow waters at the edges of the Atlantic basin may have produced nothing conclusive, but Atlantologists may comfort themselves by believing that all the best evidence – the material remains of the capital of Atlantis – is of course still lurking at the bottom of the Mid Atlantic.

American expeditions, including a large-scale operation organised by the Lamont Geological Observatory, have explored much of the Mid-Atlantic sea bed, taking cores and photographs and dredging the bottom, but they have never found a single trace of (ancient) human activity. Russian scientists claim to have had more success. In 1974 the Soviet research ship *Academician Petrovsky* carried out an underwater camera survey 300 miles west of Gibraltar. In a widely publicised announcement, the chief photographer, Vladimir Marakuyev, said that two of his pictures showed a wall composed of masonry blocks about 1.5 metres high, while a third showed a short flight of steps covered with lava. The published photographs, however, must have been a great disappointment to Atlantis enthusiasts.[68] The 'walls' and 'steps' are abysmally murky shapes that could only convince the most ardent believer. Soviet science certainly tolerated, if not encouraged, Atlantis research, because it contradicted the western theory of continental drift. It also provided the Russian navy with a convenient smokescreen for espionage in the Mid Atlantic, where they were searching for places to park nuclear submarines.[69] Given the frequency of the press reports during the 1970s and 80s about Russian 'discoveries' of Atlantis, it must have been routine to take an Atlantologist on board these expeditions. No evidence was properly or convincingly published, however, and it is likely that their findings were not taken that seriously at home.

The lack of archaeological evidence from the Mid Atlantic provides the mortal wound to a literal interpretation of Plato's

Atlantis story. Whether we imagine a macro-Atlantis like Plato's lost continent, or a mini-Atlantis like that suggested by Warlow, the Azores would have been included. But when the Portuguese arrived on the islands in the fifteenth century they found them uninhabited. There is not a shred of evidence to suggest that the Azores had any prehistoric civilisation. The only possible traces of human habitation before the Portuguese are the reported Carthaginian coins of about the third century BC.

All things considered, the idea of a highly advanced civilisation having existed on a continent in the Atlantic is geologically and archaeologically implausible. Indeed, this has been the attitude of science for some decades now, except that 'impossible' is usually the preferred word. None the less, people have been searching for evidence in the Atlantic for more than a hundred years. Expedition upon expedition has been mounted, but the evidence scraped up is lilliputian compared to the immense task it is put to. We cannot rewrite world history on the basis of a few fuzzy photographs of square-shaped rocks or a single man-made object dredged from the bottom of the Atlantic. Donnelly would have been bitterly disappointed with the track record of the last century.

Is, then, the Atlantis tale just a piece of marvellous ancient science fiction, a will o' the wisp that will lead us no further than a corner of Plato's fertile imagination? There are strong reasons to doubt this. But before re-examining Plato's case, it is necessary to assess the claim, popular for several decades now, that professional geologists and archaeologists have already 'saved the day' for Plato by finding a different location for Atlantis which is scientifically respectable. Have the serious scientists really done any better than the 'cranks'?

CHAPTER 3

The Destruction of Thera

In 1900 the archaeologist Sir Arthur Evans opened up the site of Knossos on Crete, providing the first glimpse into a mysterious pre-classical world where, he believed, lay the earliest roots of European civilisation. He described his sensational discoveries as he made them in a series of articles for *The Times*, and the western world was captivated.

The palace of Knossos, as Evans found it, was built about three and half thousand years ago and was a reconstruction of an earlier complex begun around 2000 BC. It was a totally unexpected wonderland. A huge rambling structure on several floors connected by staircases, the palace included some surprisingly 'modern' features, such as lavatories with sophisticated drainage systems and the tastefully decorated royal bathroom. Exquisite frescos, perhaps unrivalled in European art for their delicacy, were scattered around the palace walls; the scenes evoked images of a highly cultured and leisured society. It was, for Evans, 'such a find as one could not hope for in a lifetime, or in many lifetimes'.[1]

Images of bulls seemed to be everywhere, from tiny carvings on seal-stones and signet rings to the dramatic frescos showing acrobats leaping over the backs of bulls. They reminded Evans of the Greek legend of the Minotaur, the creature with a bull's head and a man's body born to Pasiphaë, Queen of Crete, and confined by her husband Minos in a great labyrinth. Indeed, it was the legends of King Minos and his dynasty that led Evans to Knossos in the first place. He was hoping to find the centre where the delicately carved seal-stones of Bronze Age Crete had been manufactured. Following the legends, he had dubbed the prehistoric culture of Crete 'Minoan' (still the standard archaeological term) even before he began his excavations of the labyrinthine palace.

On 19 February 1909, an anonymously written article in *The Times* added further mystique to these discoveries. It suggested that Evans had found not only the palace of Minos, but the origin of the legend of Atlantis. The article, entitled 'The Lost Continent', is worth quoting at length – it was to spark off a controversy which has smouldered for some three quarters of a century:

> The recent excavations in Crete have made it necessary to reconsider the whole of Mediterranean history before the classical period. Although many questions are still undecided, it has been established beyond any doubt that, during the rule of the 18th Dynasty in Egypt, when Thebes was at the height of her glory, Crete was the centre of a great empire whose trade and influence extended from the North Adriatic to Tel el Amarna [in Egypt] and from Sicily to Syria. The whole seaborne trade between Europe, Asia, and Africa was in Cretan hands . . .
>
> Thus, when the Minoan power was at its greatest, its rulers must have seemed to the other nations to be mighty indeed, and their prestige must have been increased by the mystery of the lands over which they ruled (*which seemed to Syrians and Egyptians to be the far West*), and by their mastery over that element which the ancient world held in awe. Strange stories, too, must have floated round the Levant of vast bewildering palaces, of sports and dances, and above all of the bull-fight. The Minoan realm, therefore, was a vast and ancient power which was united by the same sea which divided it from other nations, so that *it seemed to be a separate continent with a genius of its own.*

The article then went on to describe the destruction of Knossos and many other Cretan cities, dated to the fifteenth century by Arthur Evans, when the Minoan empire apparently collapsed.

> As a political and commercial force, therefore, Knossos and its allied cities were swept away just when they seemed strongest and safest. It was as if the whole kingdom had sunk in the sea, as if the tale of Atlantis were true. The parallel is not fortuitous. If the account of Atlantis be compared with the history of Crete and her relationship with Greece and Egypt, it seems almost certain that here we have an echo of the Minoans.

The anonymity of *The Times* article is interesting in itself – another reminder of how cautious academics can be about discussing Atlantis. Its writer turned out to be K. T. Frost, a young scholar from Belfast, who, apparently reassured that he would not be drummed out of academia, went on to publish a fuller treatment in the *Journal of Hellenic Studies*.[2]

Atlantis Seen from Egypt?

Frost's case was elegantly argued and began with a defence of the Atlantis story against its critics, notably Professor Benjamin Jowett, then the leading translator of Plato's dialogues. Jowett had raised a number of objections to Plato's account of the story's transmission: 'How came the poem of Solon to disappear in antiquity? or why did Plato, if the whole narrative was known to him, break off almost at the beginning of it?' Jowett insisted that the story of Solon's visit to Egypt was in itself a legend, and that even if he had gone there 'he could not have conversed with the Egyptian priests or have read records in their temples'. Further, 'Whence came the tradition to Egypt?' Jowett concluded: 'Passing from external to internal evidence we may remark that the story is far more likely to have been invented by Plato than to have been brought by Solon from Egypt.'[3]

Frost found most of Jowett's objections easy enough to answer. First, there is no question of Solon's poem 'disappearing' in antiquity. Plato makes it perfectly clear that Solon never actually finished the work. It only survived as a sketch of the plot, preserved orally, and some notes on the names used in the story. On this matter Jowett was plainly wrong.

Second, Frost could certainly answer the points raised by Jowett about Solon's visit to Egypt. Casually to dismiss it as legend is to ignore the historical evidence corroborating it. Herodotus, who wrote little more than a century later (*c.* 440 BC), refers to Solon's Egyptian trip, while a verse which Solon wrote about the Nile is preserved.[4] Jowett's following point – that Solon could not have read Egyptian hieroglyphics – is an irrelevance. Plato does not say that Solon personally read the story of Atlantis in Egyptian texts but that it was related to him by the priests. Why Jowett imagined that Solon could not have conversed with the Egyptian priests is anybody's guess – he does not explain further. One assumes that Solon spoke to the priests by the same means that he spoke to anybody in Egypt or a foreign country – in Greek (if they knew it) or through an interpreter. As Frost stressed, during the 26th Dynasty Greek visitors were made most welcome in Egypt as a matter of policy: trade with Greece was encouraged, Greek maritime expertise was borrowed, and the Egyptian army was stiffened by the addition of large numbers of Greek mercenaries. Solon is said to have visited Egypt in the reign of Amasis, of whom Herodotus wrote: 'Amasis liked the Greeks and granted them a number of privileges.'[5] Chief among these was the gift to the Greeks of the Delta town of Naucratis to be their commercial centre in Egypt. The excavation of Naucratis has confirmed Herodotus' picture of a thriving Greek city in the sixth century BC. All this makes Jowett's claim that Solon had no way of communicating with Egyptian priests seem somewhat bizarre.

Finally, Frost addressed the question raised by Jowett of how the Egyptians came to know about 'Atlantis'. If Atlantis really was the Minoan civilisation, the question is easily answered because the Egyptians were certainly acquainted with Bronze Age Crete. Frost could point to imported Egyptian objects found in Crete and Minoan pottery discovered at sites of the 18th Dynasty in Egypt. Indeed, it has been found in ever increasing amounts since the time Frost wrote. Most recently Minoan frescos – showing bull-leaping and even labyrinths – have been excavated at the Hyksos centre of Tell ed-Daba in northern Egypt.[6] There was clearly an Aegean element in the foreign Hyksos dynasties that ruled Egypt for a century or so before the rise of the 18th Dynasty (c. 1550 BC).

There appear to be depictions of Minoans on Egyptian tomb paintings of the 18th Dynasty. The tombs of the viziers and other officials sometimes depict the goods brought into Egypt by ambassadors from foreign countries. The paintings provide a rich source of evidence of Egyptian contacts during this period, with men from different regions of the world, arranged in registers, bringing the characteristic produce of their countries valued by the Egyptians. There are black Nubians bearing ivory tusks, ebony, incense, gold, ostrich feathers, monkeys and other exotica; yellow-skinned Semites from Syro-Palestine bringing elaborate metal vessels, chariots, rare animals and jars with oil or wine; and, from the north, men of distinctly Minoan – or at least Aegean – appearance. They are pale-skinned, with long black hair ending in curled strands, short decorated kilts often with large codpieces, and sandals. Strikingly similar figures are depicted on the frescos from Knossos. The Cretan impression is strengthened by the goods they carry – particularly the large metal vessels with handles, decorated with bull's heads, and pouring jugs called *rhytons* in the shape of a cone or bull's head.

The 'captions' to these figures call them men from 'Keftiu' or 'the Isles in the Midst of the Sea'. Frost, along with Evans and many others, believed that Keftiu was the Egyptian word for Crete, an assumption which has been generally followed since the beginning of this century.[7] The Egyptian texts give the impression that Keftiu was a fairly remote land, lying far to the north or west of Egypt, a point skilfully used by Frost in support of his Atlantis hypothesis. If, as he assumed, the story had really been gathered by Solon in Egypt, we must try to see and interpret it from an Egyptian point of view. The Egyptians might have perceived Keftiu as a marvellous empire at the edge of the world (as they knew it), the western edge of the world if Keftiu was Crete. It is easy to see, Frost argues, how this was transformed into the story of a 'continent' of Atlantis far to the west. Frost also believed that aspects of Minoan civilisation which impressed the Egyptians may have eventually made their way into Plato's account of the mysterious island. For example, the sophisticated plumbing arrangements of the Minoans may have given rise to the Atlanteans' reputation for bathing. (Egyptian bathing facilities were fairly rudimentary.)

The Minoan bull cult, Frost argued, is reflected in the detailed account given in the *Critias* (119C-120D) of the curious rituals undertaken by the rulers of Atlantis. Every fifth year (alternating with every sixth year 'to give equal honour to both the even and the odd') the high king of Atlantis and the other nine princes came together in the temple of Poseidon, gathering at the pillar of *oreichalkos* on which the first kings had inscribed the sacred laws of the god. Here, after an elaborate ceremony involving the sacrifice of a bull, they passed judgment on any of their number who might have transgressed the laws. Bulls roamed at large within the grounds of Poseidon's temple, and the ten princes, after offering prayers, hunted them 'with staves and nooses but with no weapon of iron; and whichever bull they captured they led up to the pillar and cut its throat over the top of the pillar, raining down blood on the inscription.' The bull's limbs were burnt as a sacrificial offering, while some of the blood was mixed with wine and drunk as a sacrament by the princes as they took oaths to obey the ancient laws of Poseidon.

The point in this narrative that most struck Frost was the

hunting of the bulls: 'This cannot be anything but a description of the bull-ring at Cnossus, the very thing which struck foreigners most . . . and gave rise to the legend of the Minotaur.'[8] On a famous gold cup – of Minoan or Mycenaean manufacture[9] – found at Vapheio near Sparta, a formidable-looking bull is shown being trapped in a large net, recalling Plato's words that no metal weapons were used by the Atlantean princes to catch their sacrificial victims.

Frost suggested that elements from other, non-Cretan, cultures may have been incorporated into the Atlantis narrative by Plato; for example, 'the vast canals are derived from those of Egypt and Babylonia'.[10] But, he felt, the core of the narrative, about a lost island at the edge of the world, whose maritime power collapsed during a struggle with Athens, was essentially an Egyptian memory of Bronze Age Crete, transmitted to Greece by Solon.

Frost's model, though it had its attractions, was missing a key element. Plato talked about the demise of Atlantis in a massive catastrophe, yet it was obvious that Crete had not sunk to the bottom of the sea. The best that Frost could offer was a sudden demise of the 'Cretan Empire', caused by an invasion from mainland Greece. There is some evidence for this interpretation – from the last days of the palace of Knossos come clay tablets written in Greek in the 'Linear B' script used on the mainland. It is sometimes thought that the script was brought by Mycenaean invaders, and that the destruction of the palace, about 1450 or 1400 BC, was their handiwork.[11] This was Frost's position. He associated the Mycenaean invasion with the legend of the great Athenian hero Theseus, who thwarted the power of King Minos. Theseus penetrated the secrets of the labyrinth, slew the Minotaur (thereby relieving Athens of its deadly tribute of young men and maidens for the monster's breakfast), stove in the ships of Minos' navy to prevent them following him and even made off with his daughter, the princess Ariadne.[12] Yet the cumulative effect of these ripping yarns, even if backed with the evidence of a destruction by burning at Knossos, does not amount to anything like the dramatic end of Atlantis described by Plato.

Some years later, Evans, inspired by experience of the powerful earth tremor which shook Crete in June 1926, decided that the destruction of Knossos in the fifteenth century BC had been due not to invasion but to a devastating earthquake. Though natural catastrophe fits Plato's narrative better, an earthquake still hardly matches the drowning of Atlantis beneath the waves.

Perhaps because of this weakness, Frost's theory was ignored for many years – and almost completely forgotten. Traditional Atlantologists, meanwhile, still had the comfort of some geological respectability until the ascendancy of continental drift theory in the 1960s. To those wanting to believe in the literal truth of Atlantis, Frost's hypothesis must have seemed superfluous – an unnecessary dilution of Plato's grand story. The steady stream of books that continued to pour from the pens of traditional Atlantologists tended to veer increasingly towards the speculative and the mystical. For nearly half a century, Atlantis research remained in the doldrums.

A Bronze Age Krakatoa

In 1950 the cause was taken up again by the Greek archaeologist Spyridon Marinatos, a highly energetic and difficult character who belonged, strictly speaking, to the old romantic school of archaeology. A fierce (rather too fierce) nationalist, he was a man with a deep desire to make great discoveries about the past of his people. And, as can easily be seen from the way he spoke and wrote, he had an unquestioning faith in the truth behind the legendary past of the Greeks.

Marinatos naturally chose prime sites to work at. In the 1950s (in a joint project with the University of Cincinnati) he excavated Pylos – one of the best preserved of all Mycenaean sites and legendary seat of King Nestor, the oldest hero of the Trojan War. In the 1930s he had already excavated on the northern coast of Crete, 'in order to show if Amnisos . . . was indeed the harbour town and arsenal of Minos', as described in a tradition preserved by the Greek geographer Strabo.[13] Marinatos recovered substantial Minoan remains at Amnisos, including a palatial villa decorated with frescos of exquisitely painted lilies, which he felt confirmed the tradition.

At Amnisos, Marinatos also uncovered a building with a pit containing a large quantity of pumice. This intrigued him, for only sixty miles north of Crete lies the volcanic island of Thera, or Santorini. Eruptions have been recorded here throughout history, including one in AD 726 which threw out a mass of pumice that reached the coasts of Asia Minor, Lesbos and Macedonia. Classical sources record earlier events in AD 60, AD 46 and 198 BC. Most important, the nineteenth-century French archaeologist Fouqué had shown that there had been an eruption during Bronze Age times: houses containing Minoan vases had been excavated from the lava flows on the island.

Marinatos's mind turned towards the problem that had bothered Frost – why had the 'Cretan Empire' based at Knossos apparently fallen in the fifteenth century BC? By the time of the preliminary report on Amnisos in 1932, Marinatos had decided that nothing less than 'a great and widespread catastrophe' could have been responsible.[14] From Amnisos he could point not only to the curious finds of pumice but to the evidence of the collapsed villa walls. An unknown force had prised the massive stone blocks of the west wall out of position and bulged the wall outward, while some of the blocks from the south wall parallel to the sea were missing. Marinatos suggested that they had been removed in the backwash of an enormous tidal wave. It was a short step from here to develop the theory that Minoan civilisation had been destroyed by a huge eruption of the Thera volcano. The northern part of Crete, Marinatos suggested, had been smashed by tsunamis, tidal waves caused by the submarine earthquakes often associated with volcanoes, while earth tremors and outpourings of gas and ash had caused complete pandemonium in the Cretan cities.

A few years later Marinatos submitted a paper outlining his theory to the British archaeological journal *Antiquity*. By Marinatos's own admission, the idea was an 'audacious' one for the conservative academic world of the 1930s. Nevertheless, Marinatos was already a respected archaeologist and the paper was published in 1939, with an editorial note to the effect that 'the main thesis of this article requires additional support from excavations on selected sites. They hope that such excavations will in due course be carried out.'[15]

The war, then other work, intervened, depriving Marinatos of the opportunity to carry out the supporting excavations for three decades. In the meantime his feeling that Minoan Crete had been devastated by the eruption of Thera grew into a conviction: 'A terrible disaster struck Crete in about 1500 BC. Cities, monumental structures and two of the three palaces were destroyed for all time.'[16]

Marinatos's date for the event was deduced from an examination of the Minoan pottery found on Thera by the early French excavations, as well as that from the Cretan sites like Amnisos which were thought to have succumbed to the disaster. The effects and magnitude of the catastrophe he judged by comparison with the well-documented eruption of Krakatoa in the Dutch East Indies (now Indonesia) in 1883. After some relatively mild rumblings earlier that year, the volcano exploded with extraordinary force on 26 August, with a noise that was audible 3,500 miles away in Australia. The eruption lasted three days, belching out a cloud of ash so enormous that it remained in the atmosphere for six months, reaching as far as Europe. As a result, spectacular multi-coloured sunsets were seen almost all over the globe. The effects closer to hand were dire. The sky was completely blackened for a radius of 130 miles. Air pressure from the blast blew out lamps and smashed windows 80 miles away, and cracked walls even as much as 480 miles away. Lumps of pumice rained down over a radius of 24 miles, covering the sea with a layer up to ten feet thick. Worst of all was the massive tidal wave caused when the central cone of the volcano collapsed into the sea. Reaching a maximum height of 120 feet, it swept across the coasts of nearby Java and Sumatra, destroying 295 villages. About 36,000 people were killed.[17]

The energy released by the Krakatoa explosion is estimated to have been equivalent to 100–150 megatons, a staggering 60,000 to 90,000 times greater than the earliest nuclear bombs exploded in the Nevada desert. When the cone collapsed it left a large crater-like feature known as a caldera, some 20 square kilometres in size. The caldera left by the Bronze Age eruption at Thera was 80 square kilometres. After consulting geologist colleagues, Marinatos calculated that the Thera explosion would have been at least four times as violent as that of Krakatoa.[18]

Whatever the precise force of the explosion, the effects of the Thera eruption must have been absolutely horrendous. Marinatos could claim with some confidence that 'the inhabitants of Crete in 1500 BC lived through the same moments of terror as did the inhabitants of Java and Sumatra in 1883.'[19] The case for attributing the destruction of Cretan cities in about 1500 BC to Thera seemed reasonable and Marinatos's arguments were generally well received.

Marinatos also took up the cause of a Minoan Atlantis where Frost had left it, developing his ideas in an article published in 1950. While he appreciated Frost's general arguments he could

see the obvious difficulty with it: 'A large, prosperous and powerful island lost within the region of Egyptian awareness other than
Crete did not exist. But that they should have invented a myth
about its being submerged . . . seems difficult.' Yet Thera, Marinatos felt, could solve the problem: 'The Egyptians must undoubtedly have learnt of an island becoming submerged and this was
Thera, but being so small and insignificant they did not know of
it. They transferred this event to Crete, the island so grievously
struck and with which all contact was suddenly lost.'[20]

Storm over Thera

The Minoan-Atlantis hypothesis particularly intrigued the Greek
seismologist Professor Angelos Galanopoulos. In a series of short
articles published in the 1960s he expanded the sketch drawn by
Frost and Marinatos into a grand edifice with the explosion of
Thera as the centrepiece.

Galanopoulos argued that almost everything in Plato's Atlantis
account could be made to fit Thera and Minoan Crete. He was
even able to include the dimensions of the island-continent by
judicious reinterpretation of Plato's description and division of
some of his figures by ten. Galanopoulos augmented his case with
other traditions which he felt demonstrated Thera's impact on the
mythological record. For example, the ancient Greeks believed
that the Flood of Deucalion – which was supposed to have
swamped the whole of Greece – occurred about 1500 BC. The
date nicely coincides with that for the explosion of Thera, and
Galanopoulos argued that the myth echoed the devastation of the
Aegean coasts by massive tsunamis from the caldera's collapse.
Likewise the Exodus of the Israelites from Egypt can, according
to one reading of the biblical figures, be dated to the early fifteenth
century BC, a date preferred by the earlier Church Fathers such as
St Augustine (AD 354–430), who actually synchronised Deucalion's
Flood with the time of Moses.[21] Surely then, Galanopoulos
argued, the Plagues of Egypt which allowed the Israelites to escape
could also have been caused by Thera. The 'plague of blood' could
have been caused by the red rain that sometimes accompanies
volcanic eruptions, while the 'plague of darkness' could have been
the result of the enormous ash cloud. Galanopoulos felt that the
explosion of Thera could even explain the 'parting of the Red
Sea'. It can be reasonably argued that the 'sea' in the biblical

account was actually Lake Serbonis, a large lagoon on the north-eastern coast of Egypt. When the Thera caldera was created, the sea would have rushed in to fill the huge cavity, causing it to ebb away from the coasts of the Eastern Mediterranean. Thus, Galanopoulos proposed, the level of Lake Serbonis may have been miraculously lowered just long enough for the fleeing Israelites to 'cross on dry land'. About fifteen to thirty minutes later the tsunami would have come, rushing over the lake and drowning the Egyptian chariotry in pursuit.[22]

More than any other scholar, Galanopoulos has become identified with the Minoan-Atlantis theory, although he freely acknowledges his predecessors, including Louis Figuier, who as early as 1872 suggested that part of Thera had sunk in a volcanic explosion and given rise to the Atlantis story. Still, it was Galanopoulos, after Figuier, Frost and Marinatos, who developed the theory fully and popularised it through his articles and lectures. For Dr James Mavor, an engineer at the Woods Hole Oceanographic Institute, who first came across the idea in 1965, it was 'Galanopoulos' theory'. When he met Galanopoulos in Athens he was completely enthralled by the idea that the remains of Atlantis might lie under the Aegean waters or the lava beds at Thera.

With admirable enthusiasm Mavor immediately began plans to check the theory. He was already completing work on a deep-sea submarine, known as *Alvin*, and hit on the idea of using the vessel to probe the waters around Thera. With Galanopoulos's encouragement, Mavor pulled every string possible and, though he could not drum up the budget to get *Alvin* to the Aegean so quickly, he managed to book a week's time on the *Chain* (a Woods Hole research ship travelling the Mediterranean in 1966) to investigate Thera.

This plan was to see if the shape of Thera before the eruption conformed to Plato's description of the Royal City of Atlantis, ringed by circular canals. Mavor's first expedition did valuable scientific work in exploring the bottom of the caldera, but nothing was found to support the Atlantis theory. Nevertheless, the press released some extraordinarily misleading statements – put in Galanopoulos's mouth – about the discovery of a moat which confirmed that Thera was the Atlantean metropolis. The 'moat' was actually a natural depression at the bottom of the caldera.

Mavor developed plans for a second, land-based, expedition concentrating on survey and diving work, but also including some trial excavations. However, problems soon developed. Mavor seemed unaware that he was treading on the territory of the formidable Marinatos. Naturally enough, it had always been Marinatos's intention to take up where the French archaeologists had left off in the nineteenth century and re-excavate Thera, thereby checking his theory about the role of the eruption in the demise of Minoan civilisation. At first Marinatos was diplomatic – he needed American funds and equipment – and seemed prepared to be the Greek archaeological side of an international project. A concession to excavate on Thera was duly obtained by Marinatos from the Greek government.

When Mavor and his team arrived on Thera in 1967 they were under the illusion that they were working on a joint project. But things had recently changed. Marinatos was friendly with the fascist colonels who seized control of Greece in April 1967, and had suddenly acquired a great deal of power. Tensions between him and the Americans began to grow. One of Mavor's party, an amateur archaeologist called Edward Loring who lived on Thera, had been charged with smuggling antiquities, but, despite his acquittal, Marinatos remained hostile. Loring eventually had to leave. The others remained while Marinatos made good use of their technical skills to explore the archaeological potential of the fields near the village of Akrotiri on the southern crescent of the island. The French excavations of 1870 had already discovered Bronze Age houses here, under a shallow ash layer, and, with the help of the Americans' magnetometer and seismograph, new sites were selected for excavation.

A building was soon discovered, and Marinatos announced half-jokingly to Mavor that he no longer needed him or his friends: 'But do your tests anyway.' Under the eager spade of Marinatos house after house emerged, along with the expected Cretan pottery and even fragments of frescos. By the end of 1967 it was clear that an important and highly prosperous Bronze Age settlement had been discovered, almost perfectly preserved under a protective later of volcanic ash and tephra.

On their return to America, Mavor and his team issued a press release entitled 'A Minoan Pompeii and the Lost Atlantis'. Their version, rather than Marinatos's (which did not mention Atlantis), was snapped up by the world press. To make matters worse, the Italian press managed to muddle Galanopoulos and Marinatos, leaving the latter completely out of the story. It is hardly surprising that the unfortunate Mavor received a letter from the Council of the Athens Archaeological Society 'discontinuing entirely' his involvement in the Thera project. His licence to do underwater research at Thera was scrapped shortly afterwards.[23] Publicising scientific research with an Atlantis tag can be a double-edged sword.

1969: Year of Thera

The excavations on Thera proved to be the icing on the cake for the Minoan-Atlantis theorists. The Bronze Age town discovered at Akrotiri is nothing if not spectacular, and through continuing excavations it has now emerged as the largest prehistoric site ever excavated in Europe. The 'Minoan Pompeii' has street after street of houses, some three storeys high, with cut stone façades, their roofs cluttered with storage jars standing just as they had been left. Inside, some houses were decorated with frescos of breath-taking beauty showing bucolic life, sports, and maritime scenes with ornate ships at sail.

Most of the pottery from these houses is similar, or identical, to that used at Knossos and other Cretan sites, and it is tempting to see Thera as a Minoan 'colony'. The pottery finds, of a style known as 'Late Minoan I', clearly vindicated Marinatos by showing that the Bronze Age town on Thera was closely linked to – and contemporary with – the great palaces on Crete. They thus seemed to confirm his theory that the palaces were destroyed by the tidal waves and ash-falls from Thera's eruption.

It was a scenario dramatic enough to match Plato's Atlantis. While Crete itself had not sunk, the central caldera cone of Thera had, and its settlements had been engulfed in a mountain of ash and lava.

The new discoveries on Thera were fully exploited in 1969 by three books arguing the Minoan-Atlantis hypothesis. The first, *Atlantis: The Truth behind the Legend*, was written by Galanopoulos himself, in conjunction with Edward Bacon, former archaeological editor of the *Illustrated London News*. The second was Mavor's *Voyage to Atlantis*, largely a recasting of Galanopoulos's ideas, but including an entertaining account of the tribulations endured during his expeditions to Thera. Marinatos dismissed it in three marvellously tart sentences: 'Another book, under the self-confiding title "Voyage of Atlantis" was published during this same year, 1969. Its author is Mr J. Mavor, an expert in electrology. From the psychological point of view it may prove interesting to some scholars.'[24] The third work, *The End of Atlantis*, was written by Dr John Luce, a respected Irish classicist who later became Associate Professor of Classics at Dublin University. Luce's experience with classical texts allowed his exposition to be the most erudite and balanced; it was also prefaced with an approving foreword by no less a person than Sir Mortimer Wheeler, the grand old man of British archaeology.

All three books rehearsed much the same evidence. The mainspring of their arguments was the same as Frost's original theory – that memories of a disaster which struck Bronze Age Crete and Thera had been preserved in Egypt and eventually transmitted to Plato via Solon. By the 1970s the theory had become established as the only viable solution to the Atlantis problem. Many of its proponents, including Marinatos and Galanopoulos, were weighty academics in their own right, while the congruence of specialists in a number of fields ranging from classics to volcanology in itself seemed convincing. This was *the* experts' answer. An extremely attractive gloss was added to the case by the glamour of the Minoan and Theran cultures. As these could claim some role in the growth of European civilisation, the romantic idea of Atlantis as the mother of civilisation could still be vaunted.

As the Minoan theory ascended the throne of Atlantean studies, orthodox geologists could breathe a sigh of relief. A geologically respectable location had been found for 'the lost continent' and they were now safely off the hook.

Place and Time

An extraordinary number of academics – from geologists to classicists – still seem to imagine that the eruption of Thera has 'solved' the Atlantis mystery. The idea has now been rehashed and published so many times that it has become part of modern mythology. When Jacques Cousteau took his submarine to explore the Aegean he went not to Thera but to 'Atlantis'. On the island itself, visitors enjoy bottles of a local vintage labelled 'Atlantis Blanc de Blanc'. The whole thing, naturally, has given rise to a considerable tourist industry on the island.

With enough repetition anything has a chance of sticking in the public consciousness, but this is hardly a substitute for good evidence or arguments. The Minoan theory has always suffered from grievous problems, the most conspicuous concerning the location and date of Atlantis.

Plato himself, without any doubt, placed his lost continent in the Atlantic and not the Mediterranean. But from both the geological and archaeological standpoints the chances of an Atlantic location are infinitesimally small. So it is a reasonable step, if we wish to give Plato the benefit of the doubt, to look elsewhere for Atlantis. Given the involvement of Egypt, Italy and Athens in the story, the Mediterranean is the most likely choice after the Atlantic itself.

Yet of all Mediterranean locations, Crete seems the most unlikely candidate for the origin of the Atlantis story. The problem is that Plato himself did not recognise any resemblance between Atlantean and Cretan civilisation. Although Plato did not know 'Minoan' civilisation as we do from archaeology, the Greeks were heir to numerous traditions concerning the wonders of ancient Crete and the empire of Minos. Many things were remembered (correctly or otherwise) in Greek legend: the bull cult; the marvellous palace; the wealth of its kings; their laws, organised navy, technological expertise, overseas colonies and struggle with Athens. Plato was well aware of all these traditions, and wrote a book entitled *Minos*, featuring the legendary king as the archetypal lawgiver.[25] He was also intimately acquainted with the geography of Crete. Late in his life he selected a site there for the founding of an experimental political community (see Chapter 4). Supporters of the Minoan-Atlantis hypothesis must suppose that Plato, who made detailed studies of Cretan history, geography and culture, wrote up the Atlantis narrative without noticing the parallels which Galanopoulos, Luce and others have detected. Christopher Gill, an expert in Plato at the University College of Wales (Aberystwyth), noted the basic implausibility in the idea that the Greeks learnt about the Minoan civilisation from the Egyptians: 'For the Athenians of the Classical period had a much clearer picture of Minoan Crete (including the features most relevant to the Atlantis story) than the Egyptians seem to have done.'[26]

Further, while it is feasible that the story became relocated from the Mediterranean to the Atlantic, the Minoan school is unable to provide a convincing rationale for the transference. The major mythological figure in Plato's account is Atlas, the founder and first king of Atlantis. He is also, as will be shown later, the key to its location. A case can be made for arguing that the continent was relocated from the Mediterranean to the Atlantic because of the latter's connections with Atlas. Yet Atlas is conspicuously absent from the rich collection of myths concerning Crete. In Greek myth Atlas spawned a vast tribe of descendants but none of them has connections with Crete.

The second problem with the Minoan-Atlantis hypothesis is the date. Plato stated that the war between Athens and Atlantis took place 9,000 years before the visit of Solon to Egypt (*c.* 565 BC), which takes it back to roughly 9600 BC, long before the rise of Minoan civilisation. The Minoan Atlantologists have tried to turn this discrepancy into a virtue by the simple expedient of dividing Plato's figure by ten. The result (900 years), when added to 600 BC (a rounded-up date for Solon's visit to Egypt), gives us a date about 1500 BC, a neat match with Marinatos's date for the explosion of Thera.

Galanopoulos went on to argue that the Egyptians had mistakenly exaggerated other figures in the story by a factor of ten. For example, Plato says that the great rectangular plain that lay near the Atlantean Royal Metropolis was about 240 by 230 miles (3,000 by 2,000 Greek stades) in size (*Critias* 118A). There is no room for even a small plain on Thera, so Galanopoulos argued that it should be sought on Crete, where the central Plain of Messara is indeed roughly 240 by 230 miles. The Royal Metropolis itself, according to Plato, was 12 miles in diameter. Galanopoulos superimposed a circular city of 12 miles' diameter on a map of Santorini and found a rough match with its presumed size before the volcanic eruption. The exercise is, of course, marvellously inconsistent, as Galanopoulos reduced the size of the plain by a factor of ten, but not the metropolis. Galanopoulos was also forced to take appalling liberties with Plato's text, which makes it perfectly clear that the metropolis and plain belonged together – in fact a canal was supposed to have connected them. By using similar methods and number-juggling one could place the Atlantean metropolis and plain almost anywhere.

Undaunted by such niceties, Galanopoulos proclaimed that he had discovered the key to 'a complete and integrated solution of the Atlantis riddle':

The solution of this riddle is as simple as the mistake which created it. The Atlantis story in Plato is essentially correct in all its points except the date of the submersion of the Ancient Metropolis which was 900 and not 9,000 years before Solon, and the dimensions of the plain of the Royal City, which should be 300 × 200 stades and not 3,000 × 2,000, as given in Plato.[27]

The extra factor of ten, Galanopoulos believed, 'crept in during the transcriptions of the Egyptian records', either when Solon himself took notes from them, or when the Egyptians had made earlier copies.[28] Luce used a similar argument: 'Solon, or the priests, could have mistakenly multiplied some actual dates and linear measurements by ten.'[29]

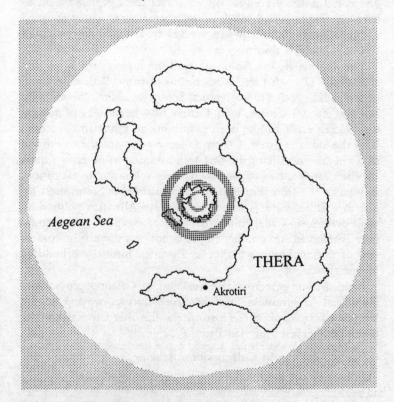

Aegean Sea

THERA

• Akrotiri

FIG. 6   The present shape of the island of Thera is due largely to the explosion in Minoan times, when the centre collapsed into the caldera. Superimposed are the outlines of Plato's Royal Metropolis, producing an apparent fit which Galanopoulos saw as significant.

Galanopoulos's factor-of-ten theory rapidly breaks down under closer examination. It may sound plausible to those using the modern decimal system, in which mathematical errors by the simple addition or omission of a zero are quite familiar. The ancient Egyptians, however, would have found Galanopoulos's argument strange. They had a decimal system, but factors were not raised by adding another digit or zero. Instead different symbols were used for 1, 10, 100, 1,000, 10,000 and so on. The symbols are extremely distinct: the hieroglyphs for 100 and 1,000 – the two which Galanopoulos would suppose became confused – are drawings of a coiled rope and a lotus flower, respectively. No-one could possibly confuse them; in fact the Egyptians seem to have carefully selected highly distinct symbols precisely to avoid such problems. That the priests would have consistently miscopied '100' as '1,000' is absurd.

The alternative, that Solon misread the hieroglyphs, is equally ridiculous. Though there is no reason to suppose that he could understand Egyptian hieroglyphics, Solon, one of the 'Seven Wise Men' of ancient Greece, would surely have been wary of making such a crass error had he been examining an Egyptian document with the aid of a priest. Common sense rules out the likelihood of a mistake occurring in oral transmission. Most early Greek travellers funded their voyages by trading. Solon was no exception, as we can see from Plutarch, who explains that Solon used his role as a ship-owner as an excuse to leave Athenian politics: he went overseas to trade, going 'first of all to Egypt'.[30] Solon would have conducted some rather hopeless business there if he had no way of distinguishing whether an Egyptian meant one hundred or one thousand!

James Mavor perceived the weakness in Galanopoulos's argument that 'the mistake' had occurred during copying of the Egyptian hieroglyphics. Unfortunately, the alternative theory he developed is even more fantastic:

> For the date to fit Galanopoulos' scheme, as he explains, the error must have been made when Solon obtained the story in Egypt . . . If the Egyptians obtained the story from a Cretan refugee who was sufficiently educated, it might have been written in the Aegean Linear A or B script. In this writing system the symbols for 100, 1,000 and 10,000 are very similar and could be easily confused.[31]

The mind boggles at the idea of a Cretan refugee struggling ashore in Egypt and sitting down to write an account of his home country: as he is about to seal the tablet in its time-capsule, he frets that future Egyptian priests might only have a shaky grasp of Linear B – will they make a dreadful mistake and think they live 9,000 years in the future rather than 900? Mavor's farcical explanation is accompanied by an illustration of the relevant numerals in the Cretan Linear script, which a child could distinguish. A more pertinent illustration would have been a coin bearing the inscription '100 BC'.

Fortunately there is no need for any of these speculations about how the Egyptians could have multiplied their figures by ten. It is difficult to say how the ancients might have exaggerated linear measurements, whether accidentally or otherwise. But with respect to dates there is considerable controlling evidence on how the ancient Egyptians themselves estimated the past. The Minoan school have all missed the point that, although the Egyptians were certainly prone to exaggerating dates, they did not do this by adding a factor of ten.

First and foremost, the figure of 9,000 years cannot possibly be due to a scribal error or misunderstanding. This becomes perfectly clear when the figure is seen in context. The *Critias* (108E) states that the war between Athens and Atlantis took place 9,000 years ago. In the *Timaeus* (23E) the Saite priest says that the Athenian civilisation was also founded 9,000 years ago. The figures are of course round ones, but it is clear that Plato meant that the Athenian civilisation that went to war with Atlantis had been founded recently. Egyptian civilisation, according to the same passage, was one thousand years younger than the Athenian.[32] This gives us the relative timescale which Plato was at great pains to describe: the priest said that Atlantis disappeared about 9600 BC and that Egypt began about 8600 BC.

As a piece of ancient chronological thinking, an age of 8,000 years for Egyptian civilisation is quite consistent with what we know from other evidence. Elsewhere Plato talks about how Egyptian art had remained static for some 10,000 years (see Chapter 7). Herodotus says that he was told by Egyptian priests that the reign of their first king Menes (i.e. the beginning of their civilisation) fell 11,340 years before the invasion of the Assyrian king Sennacherib in about 701 BC.[33]

All these figures – 8,000 (Plato), 10,000 (Plato) and 11,340

(Herodotus) – are of the same order and they surely reflect real Egyptian estimates for the founding-date of their civilisation. The antiquity of one's native culture was an important point of pride to the scholars of the ancient world. In the third century BC, after Alexander's generals had established dynasties in both Egypt and Babylonia, there even seems to have been an element of competition between the hellenistic historians of the two countries as to which country had the oldest recorded history. The Babylonian historian Berossus, for example, claimed that a dynasty lasting no less than 33,091 years ruled in his country after the time of the Flood.[34]

It is against this background that we should evaluate the statement in the *Timaeus* that Egyptian history stretches back some 8,000 years. We do not have to accept Plato's figure: the point is that it reflects the kind of estimate being bandied around in Egypt during Greek times. Herodotus even gives the calculations used by the priests, who claimed that 341 kings had reigned in Egypt before about 700 BC, each representing a generation. By allowing three generations a century, they arrived at the figure of 11,340 years.[35] The result is, of course, vastly inflated by today's archaeological understanding, which would place the beginning of the 1st Dynasty some time in the late fourth millennium BC.

It is not difficult to account for the 'mistake' made by Herodotus' informants. They very probably did have a list of 341 kings to show Herodotus – it would be quite easy to knock one together today from available sources – but the flaw in their calculation was the assumption that each king represented a separate generation. Royal dynasties rarely last longer than a few hundred years before they are toppled or replaced by fresh blood, and the idea that the kings of Egypt reigned in father-to-son succession over 341 generations is biologically improbable. At some points in Egyptian history (notably the First, Second and Third Intermediate Periods) more than one dynasty reigned in Egypt; sometimes there were as many as three or four kings ruling from separate capitals. The Egyptians chose to gloss over such untidy details, preferring like other nations to see their past in terms of a continuous, unbroken succession of rulers stretching back to the beginning of time.[36]

It is fundamental to the Minoan-Atlantis theory that Plato's story ultimately came from Egypt. It is ironic, then, that its supporters completely ignore what Plato has to say about Egypt itself. If the Minoan-Atlantis school wish to scale down the 9,000 years that the Saite priest gave for the demise of Atlantis, then to be consistent they should also scale down the 8,000 years given for the length of Egyptian civilisation in the *Timaeus*. They would then arrive at a preposterous result: that the Egyptians claimed their civilisation was founded in 1400 BC, nearly a thousand years after the building of the pyramids. The Egyptians, of course, believed no such thing.

The Minoan school would have done better to argue that the Egyptian priests had no idea of history (including their own) and had simply muddled the dates. But to take the figure of 9,000 years out of context, divide it by ten and present the sum '600 BC + 900 years = 1500 BC' as a piece of evidence in favour of the Minoan hypothesis is an exercise in number-juggling bordering on the fraudulent.

Minoan Echoes?

The Minoan theory performs miserably in fulfilling the key factors of the geographical and chronological placement of Atlantis. Faith in the Egyptian origin of the story is central to the hypothesis, but a date around 1500 BC makes nonsense of the idea that the Egyptians were involved in its transmission. Yet the supporters of the Minoan hypothesis have thrown together a mass of other evidence which seems to have made a great impression. Many people still accept their case because of the numerous parallels ostensibly drawn between Atlantean and Minoan civilisation.

A close look at these supposed 'parallels' suggests a different conclusion. Many of the points used by the Minoan school require considerable manipulation of Plato's text. To take one example, when Plato said that beyond Atlantis lay a 'true continent', which could be reached by a chain of smaller islands lying in between (*Critias* 25A), the Minoan theorists argue that the description should be seen from an Egyptian standpoint: i.e., from Crete one can cross through the islands of the Aegean to the European continent beyond. Here the Minoan theorists have completely missed the point. Whether he had genuine information or not, Plato, along with other Greek savants, was positing the existence of a transatlantic continent. To try to twist his description of the 'true continent' into a reference to Europe is simply to do him an injustice. After all, the discovery of the Americas has long since proved Plato right.

Other 'parallels' produced by the Minoan school are equally forced. For example, Plato says that the Atlanteans quarried white, red and black stone during the construction of their elaborate canal system, and that they used the stone to construct the wonderful buildings of the Royal Metropolis (*Critias* 116A-B). Galanopoulos thought he had scored a hit here by pointing out that white, red and black stone are all available on Thera. Yet they are, as geologist Dorothy Vitaliano noted, also available in other areas of the Aegean and, for that matter, many other places in the world, including the Azores, as traditional Atlantologists have stressed.[37] Further, Galanopoulos merely selected one phrase from the *Critias* without regard for the context: there are certainly no Minoan canal systems on either Thera or Crete.

Other arguments used by the Minoan school are so generalised that they are completely futile. For example, the royal palace at the capital of Atlantis was augmented and adorned by successive kings and became 'amazing to behold for the magnitude and beauty of its workmanship' (*Critias* 115D). The geologist Dorothy Vitaliano, once a supporter of the Minoan case, argued that this described 'Knossos to a "T".'[38] It also, unfortunately, describes any other palace to a 'T'.

The two arguments which the Minoan school evidently see as the strongest – since they have appeared in all the presentations since the time of Frost – concern the baths and the bull cult of Atlantis.

Plato states that in the Royal Metropolis of Atlantis there were cisterns for bathing, some in the open air, and others (with natural hot water) under cover for the winter; there were 'separate baths for the kings and for the private citizens, besides others for women, and others again for horses and all other beasts of burden' (*Critias* 117B). Vitaliano, who prepared a favourable analysis of the Minoan theory, stated that

> These details are very consistent with Minoan palace life. The palaces were equipped with baths, not only for the use of the inhabitants, but also for ritual bathing of visitors before they entered the royal presence. At Knossos at least, the queen had her own elegant bathroom.[39]

This is not the striking parallel it is made out to be. Vitaliano's ritual baths for visitors are an imaginary touch, though this is unimportant. The Minoans are not known to have built cisterns, either indoors or outdoors, for bathing. There was a lot of bathing at Knossos, but it was done in small ceramic tubs like Victorian hip baths in which the bather sat upright. These are hardly a parallel to the bathing pools of Plato, and a penchant for bathing can hardly be described as a diagnostic feature with which to 'identify' the Minoan and Atlantean civilisations. The whole point is really a red herring. In Plato's time cleanliness was considered to be civilised, so sophisticated bathing arrangements would have been a likely touch to add to the description of a high civilisation like that of the Atlanteans.

The sacrificial bull cult of Atlantis involved catching the animals without the use of metal weapons (only nooses and staves) and their slaughter on top of the sacred pillar of Poseidon. Vitaliano found Plato's detailed account of the cult one of the most persuasive points in favour of identifying Atlantean civilisation with Minoan:

> The bull is one of the most conspicuous motifs in their [the Minoans'] culture. The netting of bulls is depicted on the Minoan gold cups found at Vapheio in Sparta. Representations of bulls trussed and ready for sacrifice are also known. Bull-leaping, although more of a spectator sport, may have had religious significance at least originally. The idea of the sacred pillar lends still another Minoan parallel to this passage, one of the most suggestive of all that the Atlanteans may have been the Minoans.[40]

It all seems plausible until one remembers that bull-cults were actually extremely common in the ancient world, particularly in the Eastern Mediterranean (e.g. in Anatolia, Egypt and Palestine). There is nothing especially Cretan in the custom of bull sacrifice. As to the capture of bulls without injuring them, it was an important factor in ancient ritual that sacrificial animals should be perfect and unharmed. Regarding the supposed parallel between Atlantean practice and the scene on the Vapheio Cup, Vitaliano subsequently admitted: 'How else but with a strong net would one go about capturing a large dangerous animal alive and unhurt? This method is still used today, in taking wild animals for zoos or scientific study and release.'[41] The use of ropes and nets to capture large beasts must have been commonplace in the ancient world –

we are just lucky in having a Minoan picture of such an event – but it is of no particular significance. Nor is the occurrence of a pillar in the story very diagnostic – again, pillars were fairly common cult features in the Eastern Mediterranean, and figured prominently, for example, in the worship of the Phoenicians. The Minoans may have had sacred pillars, but there is no evidence that they actually sacrificed bulls on top of them. As it happens a precise parallel for this curious Atlantean custom can be found elsewhere in the Aegean world (see Appendix 3).

The End of Thera

In the final analysis, the much vaunted similarities between Atlantis and Minoan civilisation boil down to one factor in common: a sudden catastrophe. Yet even this is a poor match. After all, Plato said Atlantis was destroyed by earthquake and flood and not by a volcanic eruption, which is a very different matter.

Further, the Minoan-Atlantis theory has been rocked to its foundations by the recent demonstration that Thera did *not* destroy the Minoan civilisation of Crete. This possibility has been around ever since Marinatos began his excavations of Akrotiri. When the pottery finds were compared with those from the destruction levels of the Cretan palaces, they were found to be of a noticeably earlier style. The vases from Thera belonged to the Late Minoan IA phase, while those from the palaces were of the succeeding Late Minoan IB period. At first Marinatos tried to argue that the differences in pottery style were merely regional and that in effect Late Minoan IA and IB were contemporary. But continuing excavations have clarified the differences between the two styles, which are now universally accepted as successive phases that ended at least fifty years apart. The pottery problem thus posed an enormous stumbling-block for Marinatos's model. If Thera exploded before the fall of the Cretan centres, how could it possibly have destroyed them?

Still, Marinatos's theory was so attractive that faith in it was difficult to shake. Colin Renfrew noted that at the first International Conference on Thera (held on the island in 1971), 'anybody who raised his voice to say that Crete might not have been destroyed by the eruption of Thera (and I was one of those who did) was considered something of an eccentric.'[42] Debate at the second conference (1978) still seemed more concerned with deciding which model would best circumvent the notorious pottery problem than with questioning Marinatos's basic model. A number of ingenious solutions were offered. Some argued that two layers could be detected in the layer of tephra on Thera – so that the volcano could have exploded in two phases, the first destroying the town of Akrotiri, the second the palaces on Crete. Another model suggested that Akrotiri was abandoned after a severe earthquake, and that the actual eruption had occurred many years later.[43] These and other models were experimented with at the conference, but all came to naught – it was becoming crystal clear that Akrotiri was destroyed by a single volcanic eruption during the Late Minoan IA phase. Chairing the meeting, Renfrew was pleased to note that there had been a sea-change in opinion.

By the Third Conference, held in 1989, all doubts had been dispelled. Marinatos – who died on site at Thera on 1 October 1974 – would have turned in his grave. The extra excavation which *Antiquity* had called for in the 1950s to test his model had now been done, but had proved him wrong. Layers of ash and pumice from Thera have been found at other Aegean sites in contexts which undeniably date to the Late Minoan IA period. In Crete, Theran ash has now been identified at numerous sites, in levels *beneath* the destructions of Late Minoan IB. Clearly the eruption of Thera, though it may have dealt some long-term damage to the morale and economy of Minoan civilisation, could not have been directly responsible for its demise.

It now seems certain that the eruption of Thera took place anything up to 150 years earlier than the destruction of the Cretan palaces. In recent years the trend has been to push the dates for Thera back from about 1500 BC through the sixteenth century BC and even into the seventeenth. Some of the grounds for arguing this have been slender, involving leaps of faith based on the idea that the eruption of Thera was such a unique catastrophe that its effects can be traced globally. For example, the narrow tree-rings which grew in California and Northern Europe in the year 1628 have been held to reflect a severe winter caused by the Thera dust cloud, while a peak of acidity in 1645 BC found in ice-cores drilled in Greenland has been attributed to acid rain in the aftermath of the eruption. Claims that these remote-control methods provide an independent and 'scientific' means of dating the Thera eruption are extremely overblown.[44] Nevertheless, there are good arguments for arriving at a similar result in terms of *relative* rather than absolute chronology. Through detailed re-examination of the pottery finds which provide cross-dating between Crete and Egypt, it is now clear that the Late Minoan IA period must be unhinged from its traditional links with the 18th Dynasty in Egypt. Thera did not explode in the time of the great conqueror Thutmose III or his predecessor Queen Hatshepsut (early fifteenth century) as commonly supposed, but much earlier, though the LMIB Cretan palaces may have fallen about this time.[45] It seems that Thera erupted, at the latest, near the very beginning of the 18th Dynasty, possibly during the reign of its founder, Pharaoh Ahmose (conventional dates 1550–1525 BC)[46], but more probably even earlier, in the time of the Hyksos dynasties (or 'Second Intermediate Period').

Dorothy Vitaliano, as we have seen, was once a supporter of the idea that the Theran destruction of Crete gave rise to the Atlantis myth. Ironically she was the first, together with her husband, to identify Theran ash in a Late Minoan IA deposit on Crete – at Kato Zakro in 1974.[47] Disillusionment with Marinatos's hypothesis followed, and in 1978 she reassessed the Minoan case for Atlantis:

> If the natural catastrophe was not directly responsible for the demise of Minoan civilisation, does that completely rule out Crete as the prototype of Atlantis? If Plato is to be taken seriously, yes. Insistence on the reality of the Egyptian document forces us back to Frost's original suggestion, that the sudden cessation of trade just looked to the Egyptians as though Crete had sunk without trace.[48]

There would be little comfort in falling back on Frost's original theory. There was no 'sudden cessation of trade' between Egypt and the Aegean, either at the time Thera exploded, or, it seems, after the Cretan LMIB palaces fell. The Late Minoan IB period seems to have ended by the early part of the reign of Thutmose III, yet the reliefs of his viziers continue to show 'Keftiu people' bearing tribute. How or why could the Egyptians have imagined that 'Atlantis' had disappeared when its traders and ambassadors were such familiar figures on their shores during the fifteenth century BC? In short there seems to be no way, however one approaches the evidence, that Thera or Minoan Crete could have given rise to the Atlantis legend.

Given all these problems, even John Luce, one of the leading proponents of the Minoan-Atlantis theory, has noticeably cooled off. In 1978 a paper he wrote on the Atlantis problem contained this apologia:

> To interpret the Egyptian background of the narrative in this way is to keep well within the bounds of reasonable speculation. To go further (as I did in *The End of Atlantis*), and to hypothesise that Plato acquired some garbled information about *Minoan Crete* from Egyptian sources, is to venture on less firm ground . . . A reviewer of my book wrote that there is a 'sporting chance' that the Minoan hypothesis is correct. I myself have never put it higher than that.[49]

Not everyone has the intellectual honesty of John Luce. Unfortunately the same hackneyed claims about Thera are still being peddled.[50]

J. Rufus Fears is an American classics professor who has written a cogent and scathing attack on the Minoan-Atlantis hypothesis. Above all it is clear that he sees it as being unwarranted interference with the text and intentions of Plato. Fears's conclusion is worth citing if only as a measure of the passion which the subject of Atlantis can arouse:

> In order to make the equation, archaeologists and philologists have transformed every major feature of his story . . . From a no longer extant island, it miraculously reappears as Crete. Plato securely places his story 9,000 before his time. His advocates tell us that he meant 900. He measures the plain around Atlantis at 3,000 by 2,000 stadia; what he meant was 300 by 200. And so on, until, by a process of bowdlerisation, Plato's Atlantis is transmuted into a saleable product, which can exploit public interest in archaeology, ignorant fantasies about Bermuda Triangles and Shangri-Las, and contemporary morbid fascination with disasters. Commercialism has thus transformed an instructive philosophical utopia into a harbinger of *The Towering Inferno* and *Krakatoa, East of Java*. It is no tribute that classical scholarship has condoned and abetted this travesty.[51]

Fears's rather crusty remarks are unfair to Plato, in that the latter was manifestly interested in catastrophes, as well as to those who might enjoy the innocent pleasure of fantasies about Shangri-La. His point about classical scholars fuelling a modern myth about Minoan Crete is, however, well aimed.

All things considered, we must now accept that the Minoan-Atlantis hypothesis, like the island of Thera itself, has been well and truly exploded.

Which Way Atlantis?

Neither the traditional case for placing Atlantis in the Atlantic nor the more recent claim that it was Thera in the Aegean stands up to close scrutiny, but there is no shortage of other candidates in the voluminous literature on Atlantis. Over the last three centuries a positively dazzling array of places have been put forward as the 'real' site of Atlantis. North America, Ceylon, Palestine, Mongolia and Spitsbergen (together!), Carthage, Tartessos in Spain, Malta, central France, Nigeria, Brazil, Peru, the Caucasus Mountains, Morocco, the Sahara Desert, the Arctic, the Netherlands, East Prussia and the Baltic, Greenland, the South Pacific, Mexico, Iran, Iraq, the Crimea, West Indies, Sweden, and the British Isles have all, at times, had their advocates.[52]

Reviewing all these theories and dissecting them one by one would take a lifetime. Fortunately there is no real need to go through the motions. Apart from the fact that none has 'caught on' in the sense of convincing anybody, all theories about the location of Atlantis suffer from the same problem as the Thera hypothesis. The problem is one of methodology. They take as their starting point perceived resemblances between Atlantis and a given ancient civilisation or location, and then continue to heap on circumstantial evidence until a nicely rounded case appears. Such approaches generally end up trying to shoehorn every detail of Plato's narratives into the same reluctant mould.

In the late 1970s I tried to avoid these problems with a new approach. The aim was to take the least liberties possible with Plato's text, including his account of how the story was transmitted before it reached him. There is no good reason to doubt the story of Solon's visit to Egypt, so the claim that the story originated there seemed worthy of further examination. The Egyptians of the 26th Dynasty (the time of Solon's visit) did have an interest in the West. For example, there is the story reported by Herodotus that Necho II (610–595 BC), the greatest Pharaoh of this dynasty, sent a fleet of Phoenician sailors to circumnavigate Africa and return to the Mediterranean via the Pillars of Heracles.[53] On the

Atlantic coast of Europe the Celtic peoples of Britain and France told many tales of spectral lands to the west and cities sunk beneath the sea, some of which may go back to Iron Age times.[54] It is possible that Phoenician travellers collected some of these tales. As to the idea that Atlantis was a civilisation older than Egypt itself, perhaps here a distant memory of the builders of the great megalithic tombs and stone circle of north-western Europe had been incorporated. After all, the civilisation of the megalith builders did begin, as radiocarbon has shown, some time before the founding of the First Egyptian Dynasty. Megalithic chambered tombs were already being built in Portugal by 4500 BC.

In short, I wondered whether the story may have been concocted in Egypt from Phoenician travellers' tales and Celtic stories of lost lands to the west, blended with a memory of the megalith builders of the Atlantic fringe.[55] The model involved a rather awkward pastiche of elements but at least it was much closer to the spirit of Plato's text than the Minoan hypothesis. The chronological and geographical requirements of his narrative could be satisfied without any major modification. The idea of Atlantis as a western civilisation of great antiquity could be retained, and the Egyptian route for the story's transmission was followed.

Yet there were a worrying number of loose ends. First, there was the conspicuous absence of a catastrophe – the megalithic civilisation of Atlantic Europe was not wiped out by any sudden environmental disaster, either before or after the founding of Egyptian civilisation. There was no particular point in time when megalithic civilisation collapsed. For example, Stonehenge, which was started around 3000 BC in the later Neolithic was still being rebuilt in the Bronze Age, about 1500 BC, and continued to be used a cult centre until Roman times. The essential message of the *Timaeus* and *Critias* is that a great city or civilisation met its end in a watery grave. Megalithic Europe did not.

My reason for thinking of megalithic Europe in the first place was to find something that suited Plato's description of a civilisation older than Egypt itself. Yet this factor in the story clashed head-on with another element, the important role played by the Athenians in the Atlantis narrative. There were certainly no Athenians in 9600 BC and the situation is much the same even if we scale down the date to the mid-fourth millennium BC – just before the beginning of the Egyptian 1st Dynasty. The site of the future Athens had been settled but there was no city, no walled acropolis, no trace of the advanced society discussed by Plato. The idea of Neolithic Proto-Athenians marching across Europe to do battle with the megalith builders in the fourth millennium was simply absurd. Indeed, there was no city of Athens until about the fourteenth century BC. How could this be squared with the claim that the Athenian war with Atlantis took place before Egyptian civilisation began?

Finally, there was a basic implausibility in my megalithic model. Was it really possible that memories of the megalith builders were brought to Egypt and preserved there? Indeed, how could the Egyptians have known about a civilisation that was 'a thousand years' before their own?

The more one looks at it, the more suspicious becomes the Egyptian role in the transmission of the Atlantis tale. The whole question seems like a ghastly rubik cube – there seems to be no way to fit together the three main elements in the story – Atlantis, Athens and Egypt – into a reasonable historical picture, wherever Atlantis may have been. Something would clearly have to give, but what? Is it the Egyptian link? If so, why did Plato cite Egypt as his authority for the story? Or was he simply playing games with us? The story – as presented by Plato – simply could not be true, according to timescale or geography. So had Plato made mistakes? Did he really get all the story from Solon as he claimed? How much of it was his own interpretation? Indeed, what was his motive for writing about it in the first place? All this would have to be sorted out before I could get to the core of the matter.

It was time to take a long hard look at the creator of Atlantis. This led, strangely enough, not to the conclusion that Plato was a fool or a liar – only that the wrong questions about the *Timaeus* and *Critias* had consistently been asked. To discover Atlantis, ignore the opinion of the geologists, archaeologists, ancient historians and even philosophers – first ask Plato himself what he meant and why he wrote it.

PART TWO: PLATO

CHAPTER 4

Plato's World

Probing into the mind of the creator of Atlantis may seem a trifle ambitious. The scope of Plato's writing, and the depth of his thinking, is breathtaking. He has been described, quite fairly, as the inventor of philosophy as we know it, 'the first Western thinker to produce a body of writing that touches upon the wide range of topics that are still discussed by philosophers today under such headings as metaphysics, epistemology, ethics, political theory, language, art, love, mathematics, science and religion.'[1] The full range of critical literature on Plato's work runs into hundreds, if not thousands, of books, not to mention articles in learned journals.[2] Even so, there is no real consensus on even the broader aspects of Plato's philosophy, making any attempt to summarise the range of his work in a short space nearly impossible. Still, in order to understand the creation of Plato's Atlantis, we must delve a little way into his life and background.

Plato was born into a family of Athenian aristocrats – about 429 BC, during the turbulent period of the Peloponnesian War (431–404 BC) – a circumstance which was perhaps his most important formative experience.

The war began simply because Athens had become too high and mighty – a fact admitted by the eminent Athenian historian Thucydides.[3] Ten thousand Athenians, aided by a small force of Plataean allies, had succeeded in repelling the massive Persian army at Marathon in 490 BC. The Greeks won further victories at Salamis (480 BC), where the Athenians smashed the Persian fleet, and at Plataea (479 BC), where the Spartans and their allies defeated the invading land-force. The Greeks were now able to counter-attack, pursuing the invaders on to their own ground and even recapturing Byzantium. The chance of taking over the leadership of Greece was bungled by the Spartan general Pausanias when he made a bid to become the son-in-law of the Persian

Emperor, and Athens was left to lead the Greeks in the continuing offensive war. During these years Athens became a rich state: the 470s to 440s were Athens' golden age, the period when its greatest works of art and public buildings were produced.[4] Part of its wealth came from seizing the colossal amounts of bullion carried by the Persian army.[5] More came from a defensive alliance against Persia now referred to as the 'Delian League'. In practice it worked as a protection racket, with the Athenians milking money and ships from the small Aegean states which they had 'liberated'.

As far as many Greeks were concerned, the Athenians had merely replaced the Persian empire with their own. This was the assessment of Hermocrates, a prominent Sicilian statesman and the fourth character (along with Socrates, Timaeus and Critias) in Plato's Atlantis dialogues.[6] The smaller Greek states resented their loss of autonomy and their grievances were taken up by Sparta, Athens' erstwhile ally against Persia and the leading state of the Peloponnese. In 431 BC the Peloponnesians invaded Attica and a protracted struggle began which was to involve all the Greek states as far west as Sicily.

To a large degree the Peloponnesian War was a struggle between the two rival political systems of Greece. Sparta was an inland state ruled by kings, with strict social stratification and rigid social conventions. Military prowess, physical fitness and discipline were its keynotes – it is with good reason that we still speak of 'spartan' regimes. The Spartans eschewed trade and wealth, and had very little art to speak of aside from some poetry and music. Athens could not have been more different. Without kings (not counting the archons, who were elected officials holding titular kingship), it was a shaky proto-democracy run by aristocratic factions. Perched on the coast, Athens always had the potential to be more outward-looking than Sparta, and its military strength now lay in its navy. Most Athenians abhorred what they saw as the sterile existence of the Spartans and revelled in their new-found power and wealth. The Parthenon, started in 447 BC, was an artistic celebration of their triumph.

When Athens Was Atlantis

The parallels with the war between Atlantis and Athens are inescapable – except that in Plato's story the roles of Sparta and Athens have been largely reversed. In the *Timaeus* and *Critias*

Athens has become spartanised into a simple, agriculturally based state with no ostentatious wealth, defended by an army of doughty footsoldiers. There is no mention of a harbour, a navy or overseas commerce, which Plato saw as a corrupting influence (*Laws* 705A). This spartanised Athens is blended with echoes of Athens' great days *before* she built an overseas empire. The Athens of *Timaeus* (25C), either as the leader of the Greeks or alone when deserted by its allies, is able to withstand the mighty host of the Atlanteans; eventually it defeats them and celebrates its victory. One is instantly reminded of the heroic Athens of 490 BC, which almost single-handedly overcame the Persians at the (land) battle of Marathon. Plato elsewhere eulogises the achievement of the Athenians at Marathon, who 'chastised all Asia's insolent pride, and were the first to rear trophies of victory over the barbarians' (*Laws* 705A). There are, of course, echoes of the oriental despotism of Persia in the picture Plato draws of the mighty enemy faced by Proto-Athens. But most of all Atlantis resembles the 'new Persia' – the haughty, imperial and potentially decadent Athens of Plato's own time, with an unhealthy desire to dominate all its neighbours. As Vidal-Naquet put it: 'Plato's Athens meets and vanquishes Atlantis; in so doing, she really overcomes herself.'[7]

The parallels suggest that Plato's Atlantis narrative might be a parable written to contrast the relative merits of the old and new Athenian systems. To some extent it was, and the Proto-Athenian (more Spartan) way was clearly the winner in Plato's book. It has even been argued that Plato invented the struggle between Atlantis and 'Proto-Athens' to illustrate his judgments on contemporary Athens and Sparta. This is the opinion of Christopher Gill:

> I think that this view of the genesis of the Atlantis story is far and away the most convincing, explanatory of the significance of the details of the story and consistent with Plato's political position; and that, in essence, the story was intended to be a politico-philosophical myth constructed out of historical ingredients, and specifically designed as a cautionary tale . . . for an Athenian audience.[8]

Gill adds some interesting circumstantial detail to support his case. It is striking, for example, that the politician Hermocrates, who organised the Sicilian resistance to Athenian imperialism during the war, is included by Plato as one of his speakers. He could also have added another detail from the days of the

Peloponnesian War – an Athenian fortress on a small island called
Atalante (off Locris in central Greece) was wrecked by a tidal
wave in 426 BC. De Camp argued that the Atalante disaster was
one of the elements that contributed to the Atlantis legend.[9] Even
so, to argue that the *whole* Atlantis narrative was inspired by the
political struggles of the Peloponnesian War encounters some
serious problems. Gill himself admits that the theory leaves a
number of unexplained elements, such as the genuine interest the
narrative shows in prehistory.

Above all, the theory misunderstands the nature of parables:
Jesus Christ did not invent mustard seeds or prodigal sons when
he used them to illustrate moral points. We should not be deceived
by the beautiful simplicity of the Atlantis narrative into thinking
that it is a one-dimensional construction. The likelihood that
Plato included literary touches alluding to contemporary politics
does not mean we have got to the bottom of the matter and
'solved' the Atlantis mystery.

Still, the parallel with the Peloponnesian War offers a valuable
lead. No-one would imagine that a writer of Plato's skill simply
repeated the Atlantis tale verbatim as it was received from Solon.
In the colouring that makes the story reminiscent of the grand
struggle between Athens and Sparta, there is a clear instance of
Plato's own handiwork. Solon could not have included it in his
version, for the simple reason that he had been dead for two
centuries before the war broke out. Was old Critias responsible?
Unfortunately, nothing is known of Critias' thought and any
contribution he might have made to the story's development is
indistinguishable from Plato's own. Of course Critias and Plato
may have worked on the story together, but for practical purposes
it is simplest to consider the post-Solonic elements in the narrative
as an overlay added by Plato, the great architect of Atlantis.

Plato has left a hefty challenge in literary detective work. To
proceed any further requires an understanding of the mechanics
of the Atlantis narrative – its construction and its transmission.
Identifying other elements of 'Platonic overlay' is an important
step, but above all we need to answer the question – why did
Plato write it? We can only penetrate the tangle by looking further
at Plato himself.

The Failure of Politics

The Peloponnesian War had a profound effect on the intellectual climate of Plato's time. The war was, in the words of the great Greek historian Thucydides, the 'greatest disturbance' in Greek history, and after it Greece was never quite the same. The Spartans had to swallow their pride and accept Persian money in order to build a fleet and finish the war. In 405 BC, when Plato was about twenty-four, the Athenian navy was defeated at the battle of Aigospotamoi (Gallipoli peninsula in north-western Turkey). In April 404 BC in the midst of growing political upheaval at home, the Athenians capitulated. Their fields had been trampled to dust by the feet of Spartan invasions and their economy was in ruins.

The new, crestfallen, Athens was more introspective. There was no more simple faith in the god-given right of the Athenians to an empire, or in that of their aristocrats to indulge in a lavish lifestyle. Even during the war, the Athenians under Pericles were acutely aware of the moral problem posed by emptying the pockets of their Delian League allies in order to beautify Athens.[10] The leaders elected after his death in 429 BC (about the time of Plato's birth) were less conscious of such niceties. Hawkish demagogues hoping to win easy votes, they committed Athens to a policy of hopeless adventurism – the worst excess was a reckless and costly expedition in 415 BC to conquer Sicily which bordered on lunacy.

By the end of the war, many Athenians were disenchanted with democracy, and the party of the oligarchs, aiming to place control of the state in the hands of an aristocratic clique, was in the ascendant. With the collusion of the Spartan commander-in-chief, Lysander, the oligarchs established a regime known as the Council of Thirty, ostensibly to reform the Athenian constitution. They promised stability, but their initial attempts to cleanse the city of corrupt officials and troublemakers soon transformed into a massive purge of political opponents. Chief of the Thirty was Critias (IV), Plato's cousin and grandson of the Critias in the Atlantis dialogues.[11] Critias emerged as a bloody tyrant, organising a wave of arrests and executions.

Plato watched these developments with horror. Near the end of his life he described his early disillusionment with politics in a rare autobiographical piece, contained in a letter sent to his Sicilian friends about 352 BC:

As a young man, I had the same experience as many others. I expected, as soon as I came of age, to enter public life. Some events then occurred in the affairs of the city. The existing constitution – derided by many – was overthrown . . . and thirty of the leaders were given supreme power. As it happened, they included some of my relatives and acquaintances and they at once called upon me as a suitable recruit. My feelings were not surprising for a young man: I thought they were going to lead the city from an unjust to a just way of life and rule it accordingly; so I observed with deep interest. And I saw how, in a short time, these men made the old regime look like a golden age.[12]

The most heinous crime of the Thirty, in Plato's reckoning, was their persecution of his old friend and teacher Socrates, whom he described in his letter as 'the most upright man then living'. The Thirty ordered Socrates, then in public life, to arrest a citizen marked for execution. He refused, preferring to risk death himself than commit a crime. It was Socrates' firm belief that it was better to suffer wrong than to do wrong.[13]

It must have been Socrates who persuaded Plato that there was more to life than politics, enabling him to resolve his dilemma by turning to philosophy. The towering figure of Socrates overshadows the whole of Plato's writings. Indeed, it is true to say that one cannot understand Plato without Socrates. Who, then, was this extraordinary character?

Socrates

Socrates was the most elevated and yet the most down-to-earth of all the Greek philosophers. When told that the oracle at Delphi (mouthpiece of the god Apollo) had proclaimed him to be the wisest of men, Socrates remarked that the only thing he truly comprehended was his own ignorance.

Socrates was a curious man, more like a zen buddhist master than our usual idea of a Greek philosopher. Short but extremely robust, he was renowned for his ability to endure incredible hardships – many tales were told of his earlier days as a soldier. Physically unattractive (by his own admission), he made no efforts to improve his appearance, always wearing the same shabby cloak. Though a master of self-control, he loved a laugh and a drink, and had a penchant for pithy one-liners. Steadfastly unmaterialistic, Socrates watched a great mass of gold and silver being carried through the streets of Athens in ceremonial procession and passed the remark: 'How many things I can do without!'[14] On another occasion he was asked why he stayed with his wife, Xanthippe, who had the reputation of being a harridan. His answer was that if he could put up with her then he could put up with anyone![15]

Socrates held no formal classes for his teaching. He simply wandered about bantering in the market-place or at dinner parties with anyone who was interested. His teachings were communicated by avoiding confrontation. He would never clash in an argument; instead, by subtle and extended cross-examination of his opponent, he would skilfully lead them to his own position on any matter.

Socrates taught that ethics and self-knowledge were the key to wisdom. He was continuing a trend already started by the Greek sophists, who were themselves wearying of the big questions, such as the nature of the universe, which had preoccupied the great thinkers of the sixth century BC. These were the scientists of Ionia, the strip of Greek colonies on the coast of western Asia Minor (Turkey). Able to draw on the wisdom of the East (in particular the mathematical and astronomical knowledge of the Babylonians), Ionians such as the physicist Thales of Miletus (c. 625–545 BC) had made enormous strides in the understanding of planetary orbits, eclipses and even magnetism, laying the foundations for future Greek advances in geometry, geography and the natural sciences. Anaxagoras, last of the great Ionian philosophers, correctly deduced that stony matter exists in the heavens and argued that the Sun itself was a physical being rather than a spiritual one. His supposition that it was an incandescently hot stone was not too far from the truth. Science as we know it was awakening from the dream-world of ancient superstition and religion.

Along with the genuine insights of the Ionian school came droves of less valuable speculations. For example, Anaxagoras, having worked out that the Moon was a body much like the Earth, also concluded that it was inhabited. He believed, too, along with most other Ionians, that the Earth and other planets were flat. The problem with the Ionians was that they did not have the technical resources to check their cosmological speculations.[16] This led to a massive over-diversification of hypotheses.

Almost every philosopher of the Ionian school felt free to produce his own system of the universe 'with an audacity amounting to hubris'.[17]

From the standpoint of the late twentieth century – where we have to suffer perennial revisions in the understanding of sub-atomic particles, black holes and other intangibles – it is easy to sympathise with Socrates' view of the Ionian cosmologists: 'even the most conceited talkers on these problems did not agree in their theories'.[18] By the middle of the fifth century reaction began to set in. The great sceptic Zeno (whom Socrates met in his youth) produced logical paradoxes which punched holes in the Ionian understanding of space, time and motion, and philosophers turned from the question 'How was the world made?' to 'How is knowledge of the world possible?'

This was Socrates' attitude. Why bother with unverifiable hypotheses about the cosmos when there were far more pressing concerns at home? Athens was already approaching a moral crisis. The Greek general Xenophon, in his youth an admirer and friend of Socrates, summarised the master's main concerns:

> His own conversation was always about human things. The problems he discussed were, What is godly, what is ungodly; what is beautiful, what is ugly; what is just, what is unjust; what is prudence, what is madness; what is courage, what is cowardice; what is a state, what is a statesman; what is government, and what is a governor?[19]

Indeed, Socrates generally avoided going beyond matters of which he had personal experience. The dictum 'know thyself', supposed to be a divine truth uttered by the god Apollo himself, lay at the heart of his teachings and was his starting point for understanding the nature of man and god alike.

Socrates imbued the Athens of the late fifth century BC with a new spirit of enquiry. Young men from all walks of life and political persuasions were attracted by the freshness of his thinking. But when Socrates touched on the question of the gods he came into conflict with the state – this time the democratic government which had been restored in 403 BC. Though he had never uttered a single blasphemous sentence, the powers-that-be were concerned that Socrates' analysis of the state religion might eventually challenge their own authority and they brought him to trial.

This tragic turn of events is sometimes spoken of as something of a mystery, but it should be remembered that blasphemy trials were quite common in fifth-century Athens.[20] Anaxagoras, who spent the end of his life there, was only one of a number of other philosophers brought to trial. The conservative Athenian public were genuinely shocked, for example, by Anaxagoras' claim that the Sun and Moon were not divine beings.

In Socrates' case there was another charge besides irreligion. His circle had included men who became political undesirables, notably Plato's cousin Critias, leader of the notorious Thirty, and the dashing young general Alcibiades, who led Athens into a series of spectacular military disasters during the Peloponnesian War, including the ill-fated Sicilian expedition. It was implied that Socrates' influence on these men in their youth had been a bad one – and that Athens could do without such an unconventional educator. (As it happens, Socrates had done his best to restrain Critias and Alcibiades in their excesses.)

After a hearing at which he was accused of atheism and corrupting the youth of the city, Socrates was condemned to death. Sent to prison, he committed suicide by swallowing hemlock. It was the example of Socrates' life – and death – that fired Plato's conviction that only philosophers, rather than politicians, were worthy to shape and rule society.

Disillusioned, Plato left Athens for Sicily where he continued to record Socrates' teachings. He presented them in dramatised form, as dialogues among Socrates and his circle of friends. (Plato himself does not appear – at least not under his own name.) The occasion was very often a drinking party, in Greek *symposion*, the most famous being the subject of the *Symposium*, one of the two dialogues thought to have been written up in Socrates' lifetime. These had been happier days for Plato.

Of Plato's personal life little is known. Though apparently in good company in Socrates' circle, where gay relationships were the norm, Plato's attitude towards homosexuality was confused.[21] 'Platonic love', in Plato's own understanding, was an elevated concept of the love between two men. (Women were not included.) Contrary to the modern understanding of the term, sex could play a part in 'platonic' relationships. The misunderstanding came in simply because Plato stresses the spiritual side of these relationships – for example in the anecdote about how Socrates shared a bed with the beautiful young Alcibiades, whom everyone fancied, and left him untouched. There is no good evidence that Plato himself had any close relationships; he seems to have remained a bachelor although it was considered usual for Athenians of his time to marry, whether homosexually inclined or not.

Plato sometimes gives the impression of a rather lonely man, who spent his time committing to paper conversations, real or imaginary, with his old mentor. He must have missed Socrates deeply. After some twelve years of wanderings he returned to live in Athens, where he founded his philosophical Academy, but his relationship with his home city continued to be one of love mixed with hate. In Plato's last works, there is a brooding, pessimistic mood, contrasting with the 'sunny, mischievous intellectual adventures in the early Socratic dialogues'.[22] The mood of individual dialogues can almost be used to measure how much the real Socrates and his ideas shine through Plato's writing. This, of course, is a moot point, as Plato is our main source for Socrates, who left no writings himself.[23]

The game of distinguishing the dialogues with real Socratic content from those which are purely Plato has long been a favourite one of literary critics. Though no-one can be certain, it seems fairly clear Socrates himself speaks most strongly in Plato's earliest dialogues – as might be expected when memories of him were most fresh. In the middle and later ones, including the connected series The Republic, Timaeus and Critias, Socrates has become more of a 'talking head', with Plato providing the script.[24]

So Plato was both the transmitter and interpreter of Socrates' teaching, and, in his later writings, he was responsible for transforming it. The relationship of the two men has been compared to that between Christ and St Paul, although in the case of Socrates and Plato the two men knew each other personally. Others might argue that Judas Iscariot would be a closer match for Plato: long after Socrates' death, Plato effected a complete, though unwitting, intellectual betrayal of his master.

The Ideal State

With Socrates as his example, Plato became primarily a social and political philosopher. Certainly his best – in the sense of most coherent – work was on these matters. His highspot was The Republic, which exhibits a level of political analysis of extraordinary sophistication for the fourth century BC.

Disillusioned by every political system around him, Plato attempted to draw a blueprint for an entirely new kind of state. The order of *The Republic*'s contents is rather baffling for the modern reader. Plato's analysis of the various political systems already on offer, which one might have expected at the beginning, occurs instead at the end, just before some final essays on the theory of art and the immortality of the soul. Though he wrote in prose, Plato was as much a poet as a philosopher, and the construction of his work always has its own inspired flow.

When he gets round to it, Plato's analysis of the kinds of political system available in his time is brilliant. He groups them under four headings: timarchy, oligarchy, democracy and tyranny. Timarchy, a word which Plato coined himself, described the society of the Spartans and Cretans (both tribes of the Dorian branch of the Greek family) in which kings, limited in their power by respect for tradition, shared control of the state with the aristocratic military class: its defining features were 'respect for authority, abstinence of the soldier-class from agriculture, industry or business, the maintenance of common messes [for the military class] and attention paid to physical and military training' (*The Republic* 547). Oligarchy, in Plato's time, meant straightforward rule by the rich, while tyranny did not necessarily have the negative connotations it has today.

Plato arranged his description of the four types of society into a pseudo-historical evolution, or rather descent, from timarchy, which he considered to be the most original and ideal of the four kinds of state. Each type of system carries within it the seeds of its own destruction. In a timarchy there will be greed for money, an excess of which will topple it and convert it into an oligarchy; the oligarchs' obsession with money leads them to neglect their own education, and when the common man sees that his masters are no better than himself the oligarchy topples and is replaced by democracy; and a democracy will fall when its desire for freedom turns into licence, lawlessness and chaos, providing the right circumstances for the takeover of a strong man who will impose tyranny.

As a historical phenomenon such an evolution is, of course, quite unreal, and it was intended as an abstract framework for a psychological study of the available political systems.[25] Recent history would have provided Plato with many examples of changes in government (including those at Athens) which did not fit such a pattern. Still, Plato certainly believed that, of all available constitutions, timarchy was the nearest to the ideal. He also believed, if things were left to themselves, in an inexorable law of decline from perfection.[26] The purpose of *The Republic* was to provide an improved version of the timarchy in which change, and the inevitable slide through oligarchy and democracy into tyranny, would be arrested. Plato had invented social engineering.

The new state was to be ruled by a group known as the Guardians, subdivided into two classes: the Rulers, who would be the government and the generals, and the Auxiliaries, who would 'assist the Rulers in the execution of their decisions', i.e., act as army, police force and civil service. The third class was to be everybody else – from shop-keepers to farmers – and very little is said about them except that the Guardians, like good shepherds, would have their interests at heart.

Plato's aim was to maintain stability in the Guardian class. To prevent quarrels, greed and the growth of capitalism they were forbidden all private property, except the barest essentials. In fact their lifestyle was to be communist. There would be no private dwellings; instead the Guardians would live together like soldiers in camp and eat from common messes, their food provided by the third class in return for the protection which the Guardians afforded them.

There was to be complete equality between the sexes: men and women were to share a common education and have the same opportunities and duties, including army service. As men and women were to live the same lives, the family was to be abolished. Breeding would now be done in a different way. The population would be strictly regulated by allowing selected male and female Guardians – only those of the best stock – to meet at mating festivals, where, to prevent any arguments, they would choose their partners by drawing lots. The children of these unions would be raised in state nurseries and groomed for their role as future Guardians.

Education was paramount in Plato's brave new world. Sports and military practice were considered healthy pursuits, but art, literature and music were to be strictly controlled and censored to purge them of unedifying elements. Even Homer's poetry was deemed unsuitable for the Guardians – the greedy squabbling deities of the *Iliad* provided bad role models. Poetry and music must be of a sober nature, with no extravagance or wild rhythms.

'There was to be no jazz in the Republic', as historian of science George Sarton wrily noted.[27]

The aim of this rigid educational system was to groom the Guardians in a system of ethics based on philosophical principles. But who was to be the ultimate arbiter on points of dispute? Plato decided that the Rulers themselves needed a ruler, and set above them a leader who was a Philosopher King, a mixture of saint, monarch and general. He, and his hereditary heirs, were to be obeyed without question. This was an absolute prerequisite for the existence of the ideal state.

We can see at this point how far Plato had strayed from the spirit of Socrates' teachings. It is a bitter irony that the character of the Philosopher King was based on Socrates himself, who, if offered the job, would have rejected it out of hand. Socrates did not believe in imposing his ideas by authority. He felt that if he posed the correct questions, his audience would convince themselves about right and wrong. After all, learning is only remembering and we all contain the seeds of wisdom. This recalls the zen buddhist adage that we are already enlightened, but have simply forgotten it. And Socrates, like a zen master, might have been tempted to whack Plato around the head for his stupidity. Unfortunately, he was not around when Plato strayed from the path. Not everyone had the wisdom of Socrates, or the inherent faith in human nature that he miraculously preserved even until the time of his death. Plato had lost some of his idealism, and his passion for stability had led him to the stage where he was prepared to crush freedom.

When trying to digest the unpleasantly totalitarian side of Plato's 'ideal state', it should be borne in mind that democracy in any shape or form was still a relatively new idea to the Greeks, and one that was utterly alien to their neighbours. Democracy as a concept was invented by the Athenians, but it was not something that they believed should be automatically extended to every inhabitant of a given country. It was discovered as a way of sharing power among the ruling class, at best with an extension to the middle class, which included industrialists, shop-keepers, artisans and farmers. Seen in its context – against a background of other societies in the Mediterranean and Near East where kings ruled with almost unlimited powers – the Greek experiment with democracy was a striking departure from the norm. Yet it was limited by the fact that the economy of ancient Greece was ultimately based on the manual work of a massive number of slaves or serfs. Any notion of freeing them from their work or giving them rights in state decisions was simply inconceivable. It would be rather like a modern Westerner giving away his washing machine, computer and car, as well as his means of income. Freeing the working class would have meant such unimaginable dislocation that there would be no state or society left to discuss. The Spartans, great rivals of the Athenians, had few slaves as such but held down a massive population of serfs, known as the *helots*, whose labours provided the economic backbone of the state.

So the social ideas expounded in Plato's work, repugnant as they might seem to us today, were far from peculiar in his own day. Plato was a philosopher's philosopher, and the unfortunate totalitarian tinge to his social schemes sprang from his undying conviction that only trained philosophers were really capable of steering the ship of state. Slaves and manual workers could not be expected to know anything about philosophy – they simply did not have the necessary education.

Indeed, for Plato, wisdom was a divine gift in itself, something of which only a few select mortals could surely partake. *The Republic* is peppered with references to truths which Plato honestly believed he had drawn from another world, a perfect dimension which lies beyond this one.

The World of Ideas

Plato's world view was not a simple one. It was a highly complex metaphysical position, with its roots firmly based in the colourful world of pagan Greek religion, where all of nature was inhabited and controlled by gods.

Ancient Greek religion itself was a complex system. On one level it resembles the polytheism of modern Hindu worship, which has changed little for thousands of years. The gods were like packets of energy encapsulating many apparently diverse aspects of the world. One god, Apollo, was the Sun, but he was also the god of medicine, music and the arts generally. The patronage of another god, Hermes, was so varied that it included diplomacy, banking, travel, divination, writing, phallic urges, stealth, theft, scientific knowledge and invention. He was also thought to be the guide of souls to the Underworld and the god of the planet Mercury.[28]

How and why such diverse elements were thrown together under one aegis by the Greeks is an open question that may never be fully answered, but the relationships do make sense. One can start at almost any point in the circle formed by Hermes' attributes and proceed along a quasi-logical path. To begin, at random, with his planetary identification, Mercury is an inner planet, occupying a position between the Earth and the Sun, which was often considered by the ancients to be a 'central fire' of the universe. The idea that Hermes was the messenger of the gods thus seems apposite, as does his association with speed. Mercury is the fastest moving of all the planets. Speed and his role as herald then lead to Hermes' connection with communication and related aspects. Even the phallic associations can be linked up, through the rapidity and mercurial nature of the male erection. But to discover where the god Hermes originated by this means is rather harder: it is possible to start almost anywhere in the circle, say with the phallic aspect, and travel through all the associations again.

Today the expression 'life's rich tapestry' is employed to describe the way that things strangely interweave in our own tiny lives. The tapestry metaphor is a good one for the polytheistic view of the universe. Visible, everyday life lies on one side (the front) of an elaborate tapestry. The threads forming the patterns might appear to be connected in a hidden way which can only be revealed by seeing the other side of the tapestry. In philosophical terms the gods were like the knots on the reverse side of the tapestry, providing the unseen connections between different and otherwise apparently unrelated aspects of the world. Such a view is fundamental to all occult philosophies (essentially polytheistic and pagan in origin) in that they see everything in the universe as interrelated, from the heavens to the plants in one's back garden.

Plato took the old polytheistic beliefs and refined them into a philosophy in which the divine essences behind the universe were a first principle. It was something like the knots behind the tapestry that Plato was trying to get at when he developed his concept of the World of Ideas in *The Republic*: behind this material and imperfect world lies another, composed of Ideas or Forms which are eternal and perfect.

The concept of intangible realities could be arrived at in more than one way. Absolute beauty and absolute wisdom, for example, are aspects of a truth to which philosophers aspire. Unless, of course, they are wasting their time, something which Plato naturally found repugnant, then these verities must exist, quite independent of human effort. Mathematics provides another route – it was already sufficiently advanced by Plato's time for sages to realise that maths could demonstrate the reality of things that apparently do not exist. For example, mathematicians happily play with the concept of the square root of minus one, something which has no place in this world but happily exists in pure logic.

Plato's World of Ideas was not a bizarre form of escapism. It might appear strange to us, but to the educated pagan mind of his own time the concept would have seemed elegant. People had always believed that the world was populated by invisible entities, and Plato had merely offered an explanation that seemed to encompass both science and religion. Gods and spirits (or daemons) were included in his philosophy as a kind of interface between the perfect World of Forms and the material universe.[29] Qualities such as truth, virtue and justice already exist before they enter our world, and we only experience them as the dimmest reflections. The idea is illustrated in *The Republic* (514–519) with an extended metaphor about some wretched prisoners, tied up since birth in such a way that they can only see the back wall of the cave that is their 'world'. They can only interpret our world in terms of the shadows cast by passers-by just outside the cave. It was his fascination with the World of Ideas and its corollary of pre-existence that kindled Plato's interest in history and was eventually to lead him to his grand narrative of the struggle between Athens and Atlantis.

Plato and History

If one had to summarise the core of Plato's philosophy in very few words, the statement 'knowledge is memory' would be about the closest one could get. In an early dialogue, the *Meno*, Socrates demonstrates the principle by helping a slave solve a geometric problem. He gives him no clues, but simply prompts him to think by asking questions; and so the slave arrives at the correct solution to the problem. (It is rather unconvincing, but that is another matter.) All this, Socrates said, is explained by the immortality of the soul:

> The soul, as it is immortal and has been born many times, has seen everything both here and in the other world, and has

knowledge of them all. So we should not be surprised if it
remembers the knowledge, or virtue, or anything else it once
possessed. All nature is akin, and the soul has learned all things,
and so when a man has recalled a single piece of knowledge –
or as we say, learned it – there is no difficulty in finding out
the rest, if he keeps his spirits up and does not tire of the
search; for enquiry and learning are only recollection.[30]

This was the doctrine on a spiritual level, and it is easy to see
how Plato progressed from this to a belief that knowledge could
be recovered on a historical level. It was natural to assume that
nearer the Creation souls were in closer touch with the world of
perfection; in Plato's words, they 'still remembered, so far as
possible, the teachings of the Creator and Father' (*Statesman*
273B). The idea was expressed by Professor G. R. Morrow, one
of the few classicists to appreciate fully the importance of Plato's
historical research in another, broader, sense: 'the Nous whose
ordering principle the philosopher follows as his guide is already
embodied, for the eye of the philosopher, in the materials of
human history.'[31]

Morrow's view is based on a meticulous study of the historical
content of Plato's last and longest work – the *Laws*. Here Plato
completed his scheme for an ideal state, set out as the plan for
an experimental settlement called Magnesia on the island of
Crete. This utopian colony was to realise the ideals he had already
set out, with the difference that full stress was now given to the
value of a legal code, something which received scant attention
in *The Republic*, where the imaginary philosopher king ruled like
an emperor with absolute authority. 'The reader of the *Republic*
who picks up the *Laws*', remarked its translator Trevor Saunders,
'is likely to have difficulty in believing that the same person wrote
both.' Still, as Saunders continued, the apparent change of mind
on Plato's part is best understood in terms of the different character
of the two works. *The Republic* is really setting out a goal which
is so idealised that it remains entirely theoretical and utterly unat-
tainable; the *Laws* is *The Republic* 'modified and realized', tempered
by the practical considerations of the physical world.[32]

As raw material for the projected city-state of Magnesia, Plato
used the laws, customs and educational systems of the Dorian
states of Sparta and Crete. It is here that Plato's character as an

arch-traditionalist is fully revealed. This was Morrow's conclusion from his study of the *Laws*:

> Again and again we have seen Plato take in hand some familiar historical institution – for example, the popular courts, the music and gymnastics of Athenian education, the worship of the Olympians – or some deeply rooted tradition – such as respect for the rule of law, or the devotion of citizens to their polis – and, in the light of the larger end which it is adapted to serve, make it over into a form fitted for his model city. Outright invention plays almost no part at all in his work . . . Plato is more like a gardener than carpenter in the tenderness with which he treats his political material, and in the care with which he prunes and shapes it for more luxuriant growth.[33]

In short, as Morrow notes, Plato's vision of the never-to-be-built Magnesia was not 'an irrelevant creation of philosophical imagination, but an ideal rooted in the soil of Greek history'. For history also read prehistory. The *Laws* not only offer a brilliant analysis of the Persian monarchy and the political systems of contemporary Greece but also Plato's vision of the remote past: going backwards in time through the founding of the Dorian states and the political systems at the time of the Trojan War to the development of society after the destruction of civilisation by the Flood in the time of Deucalion (*c.* 1500 BC). (In modern archaeological terms it is a journey back in time through the Iron Age to the Bronze Age.) Later in the *Laws* (713) Plato goes back even further, to the very earliest human society that memory could recall: in the Golden Age ruled by the god Cronus:

> Still earlier, ages before the cities whose settlement we have discussed, a greatly blessed government and settlement is said to have existed in the time of Cronus, an example that has been the blueprint for living in the best of today's cities.[34]

The Golden Age

Plato's understanding that there was a perfect society at the beginning of time was, like all his others, a refinement and outgrowth of traditional Greek beliefs. The idea is implicit in Greek myth. The poets told that when the world was young, gods and mortals mingled and feasted together; then, due to the sins of mankind, the relationship was broken. One of the oldest Greek myths on record traces mankind's gradual descent from bliss into his present state of turmoil.

The myth is found in the works of the Greek farmer and poet Hesiod, a close contemporary, possibly even predecessor, of Homer (eighth century BC). Hesiod's *Theogony* contains the best-known version of the birth and succession of the gods. The ancient Greeks had no concept of a creation as such, but believed that everything had been born from a primeval state called Chaos. From Chaos, said Hesiod, arose the goddess Gaea (Earth). She gave birth to her own spouse, Uranus (Sky), and their children were the mighty Titans. Led by the youngest, the wily Cronus, the Titans rebelled against their father Uranus and castrated him. The rain of blood fertilised Earth, who brought forth the Giants, the Furies (Erinyes) and Ash Nymphs (Meliae); Uranus' genitals fell into the sea, where the goddess Aphrodite sprang from the foam that gathered around them. Fearing that he would be treated in a similar way by his own offspring, Cronus swallowed his children as they were born. Only the child Zeus was saved by his mother, who tricked Cronus into swallowing a stone in his place. With the collusion of Gaea, Zeus forced Cronus to vomit up his siblings (Poseidon, Hades, Hera, Demeter and Hestia) and a long war began between the two generations of gods. Eventually Zeus and his party triumphed and Cronus and the Titans were cast into the Underworld. Zeus and his siblings (with the exception of Hades, or Pluto, who became ruler of the Underworld) established their seat on Mount Olympus; the remainder of the Twelve Olympians were made up by a fourth generation of gods, the select offspring of Zeus.

In his other major poem, *Works and Days*, Hesiod traced the human counterpart to this divine succession – the generations of mortals who had inhabited the earth. Each 'generation' was an age, named after a metal, beginning with gold and descending through the baser metals to iron. The people of the Golden Age lived in the time when Cronus was still king. They lived a carefree existence, perpetually feasting. There was no need to till the earth, which provided food in abundance. People never grew old, and 'when they died, it was as though they were overcome with sleep'. Why the Golden Age ended Hesiod does not state, but it is implied that it was connected with the fall of Cronus.[35] The people of the Golden Age still dwell on earth as kind spirits, the guardians of mortal men.

The people of the Silver Age which followed were of much poorer quality; 'it was like the golden age neither in body nor in spirit'. Children were a hundred years growing up, then spent a short and valueless life: 'they could not keep from sinning and wronging one another, nor would they serve the immortals . . . Zeus was angry and put them away' and they became spirits of the Underworld.

The Brazen Age came next, when a third generation of men, sprung from ash trees, populated the world. Their armour, tools and even houses were made of bronze. 'Terrible and strong' they were hard-hearted and violent; their addiction to warfare eventually wiped them out.[36]

Next came the Age of Heroes, a respite from the constant degeneration of mankind because the gods had intermingled with men to produce a race of demigods.[37] These were the familiar heroes of Greek myth, many of whom were said to have fought and died in the wars of Thebes and Troy. Some of them were granted immortality by Zeus, and were removed to the Isles of the Blest far away in the ocean stream at the edge of the world. (Cronus was liberated by Zeus from the Underworld to be their ruler.)

Finally, after the last Heroes had gone, came our own generation, the Age of Iron, in which 'men never rest from labour and sorrow by day, and from perishing by night'. Hesiod ends his story with a gloomy prediction about how things in this age will degenerate to a point when children will be born with grey hairs. When that time comes Zeus will destroy us.

This succession of ages was the basic scheme of the Greek view of prehistory and it was also to provide the framework for Plato's investigations. In the same way that he treated Greek religion, Plato accepted and refined it, then nudged it towards rationalisation. The form of government during the Golden Age became one of his favourite themes. The wise god Cronus who ruled during the Golden Age 'was of course aware that human nature . . . is never able to take complete control of all human affairs without being filled with arrogance and injustice'. In the same way 'that we don't put cattle in charge of cattle or goats in charge of goats, but control them ourselves', Cronus placed us under the guidance of a superior species, appointing spirit regents to act as guardians (*phulakes*), or shepherds, of the human race and 'the result of their attentions was peace, respect for others, good laws, and a state of happiness and harmony among the races of the world' (*Laws* 713).

Plato's treatment of the Hesiodic Golden Age shows the skill he employed in treating the old legends. He made up nothing, but simply gave the existing elements a 'Platonic twist', turning the good spirits of the dead men of Hesiod's Golden Age into its rulers. The Golden Age myth then became the keystone and authority of his political philosophy. Thus the ideal and original form of government was that by the gods. Only by struggling back to reach the divine part of human nature can we devise a perfect state:

> We should do all we can to emulate the way men lived in the time of Cronus and, following what spark of immortality there is in us, we should run our private and public lives, our homes and our cities, accordingly, by law based on reason.[38]

So the further one went back in time, the nearer one found the perfect archetypes and models for human life and behaviour. Though Plato first treats the Golden Age myth in the *Statesman* – a short work which forms a bridge between the *Laws* and *The Republic* – it can be seen from his choice of the word Guardians (*phulakes*) that when he wrote *The Republic* he was already thinking in terms of the traditional account given by Hesiod, who uses exactly the same word for the spiritual regents of Cronus.

Plato accepted the myth as a useful one: 'The story has a moral for us even today, and there is a lot of truth in it. Where the ruler of a state is not a god but a mortal, people have no respite from toil and misfortune.' There was no way to turn back the clock and restore direct divine rule to the world, so Plato studiously worked through the strategies by which we can attempt to mirror the conditions of the Golden Age. In *The Republic* the guardianship of spirits was to be replaced by philosophers, whose intense training would enable them to recover the 'spark of immortality'. By the time he wrote the *Laws*, Plato seems to have accepted that the rule of the 'Philosopher King' was rather too hopeful, and instead outlined a legal code which he felt was consonant with divine wishes. Neither approach worked, but the crucial point is that Plato, along with all the ancient Greeks, believed that the human

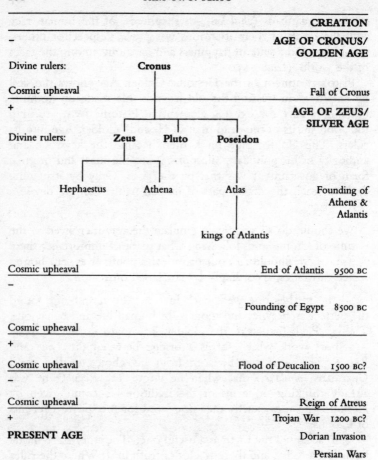

CREATION

AGE OF CRONUS/
GOLDEN AGE

Divine rulers: **Cronus**

Cosmic upheaval   Fall of Cronus

+   **AGE OF ZEUS/
                                               SILVER AGE**

Divine rulers: **Zeus   Pluto   Poseidon**

Hephaestus   Athena   Atlas   Founding of
                                                   Athens &
                                                   Atlantis

kings of Atlantis

Cosmic upheaval   End of Atlantis   9500 BC

–

Founding of Egypt   8500 BC

Cosmic upheaval

+

Cosmic upheaval   Flood of Deucalion   1500 BC?

–

Cosmic upheaval   Reign of Atreus

+   Trojan War   1200 BC?

PRESENT AGE   Dorian Invasion

Persian Wars

FIG. 7 Tentative reconstruction of Plato's scheme of prehistory, based on clues in the *Timaeus, Critias, The Republic* and *The Statesman*. Each world age ended with a cosmic upheaval and destruction of the world by flood or fire. Whereas Hesiod had a scheme of five world ages (Golden, Silver, Brazen, Heroic, Iron = Present), Plato evidently extended the series, as he placed the Atlantis deluge two catastrophes before the Flood of Deucalion. In the *Statesman* he argued that during the Golden Age time and the universe ran in the opposite direction to the way they do now. People sprang from the Earth fully grown and ended their life as infants. In the next age (when Atlantis flourished) time ran as it does now. Since then he claimed there have been two more complete reversals of time and the universe. The present order came about in the reign of Atreus (two generations before the Trojan War), when Greek tradition claimed that the Sun and Stars reversed their direction. Periods of 'normal' (our) time are indicatd by a + sign, reversed (Golden Age) time by a – sign.

condition had undergone an irreversible change. The end of the Golden Age fulfils the same mythological role as the biblical story of our expulsion from the Garden of Eden.

The Silver Age of Atlantis

What then happened after the Golden Age, when direct divine guidance was removed from the world? Plato was not one to do things by halves, leaving us dangling by a thread on such an important philosophical question. This is where the story of Atlantis comes in. Though it is not often appreciated, the discussion of the history of the human condition begun in the *Statesman* and *Laws* is directly continued in the *Timaeus* and *Critias*.

Plato never explicitly states it – and his audience probably did not need to be informed – but the saga of Atlantis clearly fits into the mythical Silver Age.[39] This is evident from a number of indications. Atlantis must have belonged to a time after the Golden Age, as the state of Atlantis had kings, laws and all the other political paraphernalia that were unnecessary during the time that divine regents of Cronus ruled the world. Yet Atlantis clearly belongs to the highest antiquity possible. The catastrophe which destroyed it is described as the 'third' before the great Flood in the time of Deucalion. The Greeks counted inclusively, so in our reckoning this would be the 'second' catastrophe before Deucalion's – there is no room to place Atlantis anywhere but during the Silver Age (see Fig. 7). Plato's narrative begins with the dividing up of the world into spheres of interest by the new generation of gods that followed Cronus – Poseidon, notably, claimed Atlantis as his own. This again places it immediately after the Golden Age and the fall of Cronus. Finally, in Hesiod's account the people of the Silver Age sealed their own fate by their hubris, or 'mad immoderation', which led Zeus to 'put them away'.[40] As Plato makes clear, it was the hubris of the Atlanteans which led to their destruction.

Change had been impossible during the Golden Age, but in the Silver Age our relationship with the eternal was fundamentally different. We were now on the road of inexorable decline, something that affected even the semi-divine Atlanteans:

> While their divine nature remained in them . . . and remained well-disposed towards god . . . they retained their true and

wholly great minds, and treated both their ever-changing fortunes and each other with gentleness and wisdom. They scor-
ned all but virtue, and thought little of their existing prosperity,
bearing easily the burden of gold and other possessions. Their
wealth did not make them drunk with pride or cause them to
lose control and go to ruin . . .

But when the divine part in them grew faint through fre-
quent mixing with a large mortal part, and their human nature
prevailed, then they could no longer bear their prosperity and
they became unseemly. To one truly able to see, they looked
ugly, but to those unable to see what makes a genuinely happy
life, they seemed all that is fine and blessed, filled as they were
with unbridled ambition and power.[41]

Throughout his later works Plato developed this theme of
mankind's decline from grace. As each new world age began,
civilisation would rise again, only to become corrupted as its
'divine spark' became weak. It would then be destroyed – by
its own efforts or by the action of the gods. Belief that any society,
without special guidance, would decline to the worst state possible
was the driving force behind much of *The Republic*, where mechanisms were outlined which would prevent such change; the *Laws*
which followed was another attempt at upholding and preserving
a 'perfect' society by legislation.

Always the traditionalist, Plato followed the cyclical view of
mankind's history given by Greek myth in which we had fallen
step by step from the state of grace enjoyed during the Golden
Age. As a philosopher, however, Plato needed to explain these
changes: why was the human race always fighting against decline?
The view he held is almost diametrically opposed to the naive
version of modern social Darwinism, in which 'progress' is seen
as an inevitable consequence of evolution.

Today's prehistorians study change in past societies by developing models that help to explain their internal workings. At the
same time they must take on board all relevant information about
anthropology and environment, as well as working within an
accepted framework of human evolution. Plato explores very
similar areas in his later works, though of course his framework
of the past was very different from our own. He had become, to
all intents and purposes, an ancient Greek prehistorian. The title
of the world's first prehistorian has never been accorded to Plato

but it would be well justified.[42] From the time when he began to explore ancient societies in *The Republic*, in the middle part of his writing career, his works become increasingly preoccupied with prehistory and related matters. The most important works of his last period of writing – the *Statesman*, *Timaeus*, *Critias* and *Laws* – are all concerned with prehistory. It was this 'evidence of a genuine interest in historic and prehistoric investigation' in the *Timaeus* and *Critias* that gave Gill pause for thought when he developed his theory that the Atlantis story was merely a 'philosophical myth' about contemporary Athens.

It is now clear how much of Plato's life led up to the writing of the Atlantis narrative – his education with Socrates, his disillusionment with Athens and its politics, his ambition to construct a blueprint for an ideal state, and his belief that earlier societies had once been much nearer that ideal. He had also developed a burning desire to explore (through theoretical means and by examining traditions) how the earliest societies had responded to the challenges they faced and to discover the reasons why they had failed. Far from being simply a moral comment on contemporary Athens, the Atlantis story was an integral part of Plato's description of our relationship with the universe.

CHAPTER 5

A Platonic Affair

In *The Republic* Plato had succeeded, to his own satisfaction at least, in drawing up the plans for an ideal society. He now wanted to test the theory by exploring it further. At the beginning of the *Timaeus*, which is represented as a continuation of the dialogue in *The Republic*, Socrates requests a story in which the ideal state can be seen in action – a kind of philosophical pantomime.

Critias then says he actually knows a true story which will fit the bill eminently, and he describes the struggle between prehistoric Athens and Atlantis. The model state in the story is not Atlantis, but ancient Athens, idealised along the lines of Sparta and the society described in *The Republic*. Atlantis is its antithesis. The Proto-Athens of his tale is flawless – not a single criticism of its constitution or behaviour is offered, only praise for the honour and bravery it exhibited in standing up to, and repelling, the unprovoked attack by the aggressive Atlanteans. This 'very great exploit, worthy indeed to be accounted the most notable of all exploits' was the story that Critias introduced to his audience.

Then, after a brief summary of the Atlantis story, the dialogue veers off into a long discussion of cosmology. Though he begins the *Timaeus* as philosophical ring-master, Socrates remains silent throughout the rest of the work as he listens to the speech given by a Sicilian astronomer called Timaeus.

How much of what follows is Plato's own work is a moot point. In classical times Plato was accused of plagiarism: in Sicily he had supposedly purchased a copy of a work by the Pythagorean scientist Philolaus of Croton and transcribed the *Timaeus* from it.[1] Philolaus made some radical departures from earlier astronomical thinking, and may have been the first to depart from a 'fixed earth' model by attributing motion to the Earth.[2] So the charge of plagiarism presumably applies to the astronomical portion of the *Timaeus* rather than the Atlantis narrative. Still, the idea that

Plato simply copied Philolaus' work wholesale is unconvincing. That he collected and used earlier writings on astronomy is no surprise, and while there is certainly much Pythagorean thinking in the *Timaeus*, doubtless derived from Philolaus and others, there is also much influence from other schools of thought. The result is Plato's own synthesis.[3] It is, however, another radical departure from the pure teachings of Socrates, who despised cosmological speculations.

Exactly how Timaeus' speech relates to the Atlantis narrative is a question of vital importance – generally glossed over in works on Atlantis – which will be addressed shortly. First we need to examine its contents, which purport to bring us from the origin of the universe down to the origin of man. (Critias and Hermocrates are scheduled to talk about Atlantis and later history on subsequent days.)

What Was the *Timaeus*?

The *Timaeus* begins by establishing that there must have been a creation. There are, Timaeus argues, two kinds of existence: that which *always* exists and never 'becomes' and that which is always 'becoming' yet never really exists. If 'becoming' is interpreted as 'changes state', the distinction is easier to comprehend. Things that never change are eternal – they are therefore perfect and belong to the World of Ideas. The world we exist in is clearly not of this type. It changes constantly, always 'becoming' but never actually arriving at a finalised state. In these terms then, it does not exist, at least in the same way that the eternal, unchangeable World of Ideas does.

For those unfamiliar with Plato's thinking, this may take some swallowing, but as first principles of philosophy go, it is hard to see where since Plato's time they have been improved upon. (Descartes' 'I think therefore I am' has hardly got us very far.) Following Timaeus' logic further, if the universe we live in is always in a state of 'becoming', it is not eternal, so must have had a starting point. Ergo, there was a beginning.

After making suitable apologies that the very nature of his subject means his presentation will fall short of the truth, Timaeus takes us step by step through the creation. As he could only have had good intentions, the 'God of gods' would naturally have used the best of models for his handiwork – Himself. He therefore created the universe as a single, living entity. The Cosmos is therefore a god in itself, a mirror image of the Eternal. As it has a material form it is spherical, the most perfect of shapes. The Creator set Soul at the centre and began its history with the motion most suitable to a sphere by setting it spinning (*Timaeus* 33B–34B).

So Timaeus presents us with a pretty story of God trying to do his best to replicate his own perfection. But this is undercut by expressions such as 'as far as possible', which run through the account. The point is that if the Creator had made a *totally* perfect creation, then he would have simply cloned himself and we would have ended up with two Gods. This, clearly, was not what happened. The conclusion, tacitly accepted throughout the *Timaeus*, is that God was using imperfect materials which were *already* in existence before he began his task. Thus, in his first response to Socrates, Timaeus states:

> God desired that, so far as possible, all things should be good and nothing evil; wherefore, when He took over all that was visible, seeing that it was not in a state of rest but in a state of discordant and disorderly motion, He brought it into order out of disorder.[4]

The idea of a Creator who does not create his own raw materials might seem strange, but it was commonplace in ancient thinking. In fact most Greeks before Plato's time did not think in terms of a single creation at all. The 'creation' described by Plato was actually an act of organisation and the 'creator' really an Artificer. In the *Timaeus* he is called a 'demiurge' (*dêmiourgos*), the ancient Greek word for a craftsman or workman.

The rest of the *Timaeus* takes us through the creation of the gods (including the Olympians), the planets and their orbits, the human body, sensations, and the arrangement of the elements, with God constantly struggling to impose order on the irrational materials at his disposal. Plato had a similar job trying to reconcile the perfect intentions of the Creator with visible, mundane realities. Plato's apparent fondness for perfectly circular motion created particular difficulties when it came to explaining the movements of the stars and planets. Interpretation of the astronomical sections is also muddled by his belief that soul pervades the universe, and that, for example, for every human soul there is a star which is linked to it. While many see the idea as one of sublime, poetic beauty, the materialist critic will see things differently. George Sarton, one of the greatest historians of ancient science, positively ranted: 'the astrologic nonsense that has done so much harm in the Western world and is still poisoning weak-minded people today was derived from the *Timaios*.'[5] It is all, of course, a matter of taste.

Yet it has to be granted that interpretation of the *Timaeus* is a minefield. Astronomy, mathematics, philosophy and biology become blended together into what seems like a bizarre dream-world, haunted by geometrical spectres from Plato's World of Ideas. The patient reader can see the intention behind it all, and it is quite a magnificent one. Plato had already discovered that abstract geometrical forms (e.g., mathematically conceived circles as opposed to those drawn on paper) are the only thing that is completely perfect. God's perfect thoughts – the World of Ideas – may therefore be approachable in mathematical terms. The idea has electrified scientists and sages through the centuries since the *Timaeus* was written. Naturally, Plato fell short of the mark – but it is no criticism of him to state that he did not succeed in providing a total game-plan for the universe. The achievement of the *Timaeus* is quite breathtaking considering it was written in the fourth century BC, something apparently forgotten by those modern critics who become strangely impatient with its curious mixture of myth and mathematics. Like any ancient text on cosmology, only a sympathetic eye can appreciate and understand it. Read the wrong way, it can seem like the most ghastly intellectual gibberish.

It has even been suggested that it is the unintelligibility of the *Timaeus* that has ensured its continued fascination over the centuries: as no-one could quite understand its cosmological ramblings, it was assumed to hold extraordinary insights which the reader was too embarrassed to admit he could not grasp. This was Sarton's brutal assessment:

The success of Plato's astronomy, like that of his mathematics, was due to a series of misunderstandings: the philosophers believed that he had obtained his results by the aid of his mathematical genius; the mathematicians did not like to discuss the same results because they ascribed them to his metaphysical genius. He was speaking in riddles, and nobody dared to admit that he did not understand him for fear of being considered a

poor mathematician or a poor metaphysician. Almost everybody was deceived, either by his own ignorance and conceit
or by his subservience to fatuous authorities. The Platonic
tradition is very largely a chain of prevarications.[6]

And then, of course, it is just possible that Plato's work has not
yet been fully understood . . .

Was Plato a Bad Astronomer?

It would be more than a tragedy to leave the last word to Sarton,
who was notoriously crabby about everything Plato wrote. In
different circumstances his reactions might have been amusing,
but Sarton was a senior academic whose comments were part of
a serious campaign to discredit Plato during the 1940s and 50s.
The campaign – actually the culmination of centuries of hostility
towards Plato's philosophy – has had a profoundly negative effect
on the study of much of his work, specifically the *Timaeus*.
Naturally, this has hardly encouraged serious study of the Atlantis
story in its context. In fact, the meaning of Atlantis is intimately
linked to Plato's vision of the cosmos.

With Plato's mathematics Sarton is not too unfair, admitting
that Plato may have had some hand in the discoveries usually
attributed to him – geometric analysis, problematic analysis and
the realisation that there are only five regular solids.[7] But when it
comes to what Sarton calls 'the astronomic fancies of Plato', he
is loath to give him credit for anything, even when testified by
impeccable sources:

> According to Aristotle, Plato believed that the Earth rotates
> around its axis; according to Theophrastos, 'in his old age Plato
> repented of having given Earth the central place in the universe,
> to which it had no right'. These two sayings have caused
> polemics, but we are justified in rejecting them, because they
> contradict Plato's own writings.[8]

In this respect it is surely safer to believe the ancient witnesses
than to follow Sarton. Aristotle was a firm believer in a fixed
Earth and he intended his statement about Plato's beliefs as a
criticism. As Plato's pupil, he should have been well acquainted
with his teachings, published and unpublished. Theophrastus studied with both Plato and Aristotle and succeeded the latter as head

of the Lyceum at Athens. On any other matter Sarton would simply have accepted their testimony.

As it happens, Sarton is wrong on all counts. There is nothing strange in the idea that Plato could have known that the Earth rotated, or that it did not stand at the centre of the universe. These very ideas characterised the theories of Philolaus, who, as has been shown, was one of Plato's sources. As for Sarton's statement that Aristotle's and Theophrastus' claims 'contradict Plato's own writings', one has to look no further than the *Timaeus* to find the concept of the Earth's rotation – although this is masked by most translations. Here there is a circular problem of some magnitude. Unfortunately, it has been assumed for the best part of this century that Plato was a bad astronomer.[9] Accepting this to be the case, translators have merely reinforced the belief by refusing to admit that Plato could have had any advanced knowledge about the solar system. The translation for the Loeb Classical Library by Bury renders the controversial passage from the *Timaeus* as follows:

> And Earth, our nurse, which is globed around the pole that stretches through all, He framed to be the wardress and fashioner of night and day . . . (*Timaeus* 40B–C)

The 'pole that stretches through all' is the axis of the universe. As to the meaning of the extraordinarily vague word 'globed', Bury explains it in a note: 'The word (*eillesthai*) (or *illesthai*) is taken by some to imply "oscillation" or "rotation" . . . ; but it seems best to suppose that Plato is here regarding the Earth as stationary.' Seems best? Why, one might ask?[10] Any dictionary of ancient Greek (such as Liddell and Scott's) will include one of the primary meanings of the verb *eilô* as 'to turn or whirl round, revolve, like *eilisso*, *gê eillomenê* (or *illomenê*) the earth turning on its axis'. No dictionary gives 'globed' as a translation. Jowett also avoided the obvious, translating the word as 'clinging', though in a footnote he allowed the alternative 'circling'. Lee's widely read Penguin translation gives 'winding', adding that 'the meaning of these words, and in particular the word here translated "winding" . . . have been much disputed'[11] – a mild way to describe a controversy which has actually continued since Roman times.[12] Lee passes responsibility for the translation 'winding' to Cornford, who devoted no less than fourteen pages to the problem in his commentary on *Timaeus* (1937). Cornford agreed that the word implies motion, and that rotation was probably intended, but, on the grounds that this is difficult to square with the other motions in the universe described by Plato, he concluded that 'whatever motion *illomenên* might mean, Plato was wrong'.[13] One marvels at the kind of logic that can arrive at such a solution – even if Plato knew the Earth turned on its axis, he was *still* 'wrong'!

The translation 'rotates' is the only one out of all those offered that makes sense of the context – and this is how Aristotle, whose knowledge of the scientific vocabulary of ancient Greece was surely better than any modern translator, clearly understood it, citing this very passage from the *Timaeus*.[14] How else, one might ask, could the Earth be described as 'wardress and fashioner of night and day'? The only other feasible explanation offered to date – that by virtue of remaining static the Earth controls the succession of day and night (as the Sun circles the Earth) – is hardly as convincing.

I have elaborated this point to show the depth of the problem involved with the study of Plato's astronomy and cosmology. How can astronomers or physicists be expected to assess Plato's work when they have to judge from such unsympathetic translations? Can the rest of Plato's astronomy have been interpreted correctly when translators, commentators and astronomers all believe that he was ignorant of the Earth's rotation?

Plato may not have been an innovative astronomer, or even a practical one, but this does not make him a 'bad' one. In fact his work reveals a brilliant synthesis of the best results of the Ionian and Pythagorean astronomers. It includes many other surprises apart from possible knowledge of the Earth's rotation. Plato knew the correct order of the planets, in terms of distance from the Earth. He was right in insisting that, despite their apparent behaviour, the planets move in circular orbits.[15] He also knew that the Earth is a sphere which stands unsuspended in space ('heaven'), and that it has existed for millions of years; that the planets move through their own volition (and not because they are attached to invisible spheres); that the planets and stars rotate on their axes; that the Moon receives its light from the Sun; and that the heavenly bodies 'are not actually those small things that they appear to be, but each of them is immense in its bulk' – for example, the 'Sun is larger than the whole of the Earth, and all the planets are of amazing size'.[16] Altogether, not a bad checklist for someone writing more than 2,300 years ago.

What is more remarkable is that Plato was able to synthesise and popularise such knowledge at a time when the very discussion of astronomy – at least in Athens – was still considered to be a rather dangerous, anti-social, pursuit. Looking back from the more enlightened era of the second century AD, Plutarch explained the attitude to astronomy that prevailed shortly before Plato. He was discussing the terror which a lunar eclipse inflicted on the Athenian army besieging Syracuse in August, 413 BC:

> This they saw as a supernatural phenomenon, a sign sent by god to announce some fearful calamity. Anaxagoras, through his understanding and courage, was the first man to attempt an explanation of the illumination and eclipse of the moon; but his was a recent theory, not well reputed. In fact his book, circulated secretly, was read by few and cautiously received. In those days there was no tolerance for natural philosophers or visionaries, as they were known; they were accused of explaining away the gods and substituting for them blind forces swayed by necessity. For this reason Protagoras was exiled [411 BC], and Anaxagoras was sent to jail [432 BC] until Pericles, with great difficulty, managed to get him released, while Socrates, though he had nothing to do with these matters, was put to death for his connection with philosophy.
>
> It was only later that the brilliance of Plato's fame removed the stigma from the study of astronomy and opened up the subject for all to study. This was due to his own example and because he made natural forces subject to divine principles.[17]

Plutarch went on to explain how Dion of Syracuse, whom Plato had educated in astronomy, was completely unperturbed by a lunar eclipse that occurred in 357 BC. Such was the influence of the *Timaeus*, characterised by Sarton as the fount of astrological superstition![18] Plutarch, by putting Plato's efforts into context, proves himself on this point to be a far better historian of science than Sarton. Plutarch also reminds us of the extraordinary nature of Plato's achievement – he managed to reconcile the earliest results of scientific astronomy with theology, in a model where God himself was subject to the restraints of necessity.

Enter Aristotle

What, then, brought about the extraordinary reversal in thinking from Plutarch's belief that Plato's work on astronomy freed man from superstitious fear of the heavens to the diametrically opposed view of Sarton, who claimed that 'the influence of *Timaios* upon later times was enormous and essentially evil'? Needless to say, Sarton was equally disparaging about the subject of Atlantis, which he saw only as inspiring 'speculation of a peculiarly irrational kind'.[19]

I have said that interpretation of the *Timaeus* is a 'minefield'. A more apt metaphor would be a battlefield. This single book of Plato's has been the main subject of a protracted war that has been raging between two scientific and philosophical giants since the fourth century BC: Plato and his student Aristotle. It is a war of which very little is heard today, although it is one which is still quietly raging away in modern science.

The differences between Plato and Aristotle need a brief introduction. To summarise them all would simply be to repeat the entire works of both, since Aristotle took evident delight in disagreeing with his old teacher at every possible opportunity. Plato himself was reported to have said about his erstwhile star pupil: 'Aristotle spurns me as colts kick out the mother who bore them.'[20] In the centuries that followed, the meaning of both Aristotle and Plato to their audiences has changed immensely, with different emphases being placed on the various aspects of their work. The war between the two philosophers is something like an endless struggle between two titanic jellyfish.

Some of the more lucid attempts at defining the battlelines may help. In the nineteenth century, Platonist Thomas Taylor summed up the quintessential difference between the two philosophers: Aristotle, even when considering theology, did so in physical terms; Plato, on the other hand, considered even physics theologically.[21] In the twentieth century, the perceptive science writer Arthur Koestler described the differences between Plato and Aristotle as follows:

> They were truly twin-stars, born to complement each other; Plato the mystic, Aristotle the logician; Plato the belittler of natural science, Aristotle the observer of dolphins and whales; Plato, the spinner of allegorical yarns, Aristotle the dialectician

and casuist; Plato, vague and ambiguous, Aristotle precise and pedantic.[22]

Koestler's last comment is perhaps the most important. Aristotle was basically a classifier. Developing an approach to the natural world that was based on observation and classification, he practically invented the sciences of biology and zoology. But classification is not all of science: if classification is faulty it will obviously give disastrous results. Yet Aristotle's preciseness has often given his work a scientific air even when his results were ludicrous.[23] Plato, on the other hand, seemed to appreciate that it was better to be roughly right than precisely wrong.

Cosmos and Change

A fundamental thread running through the many differences between Plato and Aristotle was their attitude to change. The nature of change is a bugbear for most systems of philosophy and was almost a preoccupation of the philosophers of Plato's time. By deciding that the material universe had not been created from perfect matter, Plato neatly solved the problem. The Eternal did not change; but this universe, which was an imperfect replica of the 'real thing', *could* – everything was actually in a state of perpetual decline as it slid further away from its perfect original. With regard to the regularity of the cosmos, Plato was capable of reconciling two viewpoints – the ideal and the mundane (what we might call 'real') – between which he clearly distinguished.[24] In the *Timaeus* the accent is more on the ideal, hence his *apparent* stress on the circularity of planetary orbits which has caused so much confusion. In *The Republic* (529) he wrote:

> The stars in the sky, though we rightly regard them as the finest and most perfect of visible things, are far inferior, just because they are visible, to the true realities; that is, to the movements and bodies in movement whose true relative speeds are to be found in terms of pure numbers and perfect figures, and which are perceptible to reason and thought but not visible to the eye.

Plato was, of course, absolutely right. The behaviour of the stars and planets cannot be described with perfect precision, any more than one can plot exactly the movement of grains in a hot rice pudding. Where does one grain end? Which part of Mars are we measuring from, and to where? No mathematical formula exists, for example, to describe the exact perigrinations of the Moon, which is still (we are told) wobbling after its capture by the Earth, as well as vibrating from its last encounter with a large meteorite. As Plato said, everything – even the stars – falls short of the perfection offered by mathematics.

In the past Plato has been severely criticised for this train of thought, especially as it concludes with the idea that for the real study of astronomy we should 'ignore the visible heavens'. In Plato's defence it might be said that some astrophysicists seem to have been dutifully following his advice for some time now, cashing in nicely with such purely mathematical concepts as 'black holes', 'missing masses' and unintelligible 'histories of time' which have absolutely nothing to do with observable phenomena. (One over-prolific physicist has said that the Sun must have stopped working – because it does not fit the mathematical predictions of how it 'should' behave![25]) Plato hardly meant to encourage this kind of stuff: elsewhere in his writings he gave far more stress to observational astronomy and it was his insistence on the mathematical nature of the problem that led, through the Academy, to the rapid progress of astronomy in the centuries following his death.[26] Most commentators gloss over the middle part of Plato's discussion, where he states quite clearly that there are irregularities in the solar system which are likely to befuddle astronomers' calculations:

> He [the genuine astronomer] will think that the heavens and all they contain were made by their creator in the best possible way. On the other hand, in the relation of day to night, their relation to the month and that of the month to the year, or the stars' relation to these and to each other, he will think it strange to imagine that these things – visible and material objects – are constant and never-changing.[27]

Complementing this, Plato believed that there had been periodic and massive changes in the universe which decimated the Earth with flood and fire. This is how he explained the myths of the Deluge and Phaethon, who scorched the Earth when he tried to drive the chariot of the Sun-god: 'the truth of it lies in the occurrence of a shifting of the bodies in the heavens which move round the Earth, and a destruction of the things on the Earth by fierce fire, which recurs at long intervals' (*Timaeus* 22D). These shifts also caused watery catastrophes, including the one which destroyed Atlantis and its rival Athens. It is not only the *Timaeus* that talks of these cosmic upheavals, but the *Statesman* as well. In this short work, a pendant to *The Republic*, Plato states that the universe must suffer from such periodic upheavals, because complete constancy is a quality which belongs only to the Eternal himself. Because the universe is made of imperfect matter, it must undergo changes. In the *Statesman* Plato discusses at length the idea that the universe periodically reverses its motion and actually runs in the opposite direction – 'of all the changes of the heavenly motions, the greatest and most complete'.[28]

Aristotle would have none of this. Rejecting Plato's view of a separate World of Ideas, he argued that Ideas and physical forms were inseparable aspects of existence – not an unreasonable view except for the conclusions to which it led Aristotle. Where Plato argued that there was divine essence in the stars, Aristotle felt that the stars actually were divine. As they were divine they were immortal and perfect, and thus fundamentally different from the Earth, which was imperfect and made of gross matter. The heavens, he argued, were made of a lighter, purer substance, known as 'ether' (*aithêr*).

In this way Aristotle drew a sharp division between the heavenly spheres and those below them. It had to be accepted that the Moon was imperfect – Greek astronomers at this period had appreciated that lunar eclipses were due to the Earth casting its shadow over the Moon. So Aristotle, dividing the universe into nine spheres (the outermost two for the 'prime mover' and the fixed stars, the rest for the planets), decided that the lowest or lunary sphere was imperfect like the Earth but that all the heavenly spheres beyond the Moon were made of super-refined, flawless ether.

As the heavenly spheres were perfect they could not be subject to change. Heaven, Aristotle declared, 'is eternal, suffers neither growth nor diminution, but is ageless, unalterable and impassive',[29] a belief which he claimed was borne out by human observation. He also insisted that no changes in the heavens were reported by the ancients. (Here he is guilty of the sin of omission. As well as the Phaethon story, Plato cited in the *Statesman* the well-known legend of Atreus and Thyestes, which describes how the Sun once

FIG. 8 Aristotle's conception of the universe, which has often been compared
to the skins of an onion. The Earth, composed of the four elements (in
ascending order earth, water, air and fire), is surrounded by the concentric spheres
of the planets. (From Petrus Apianus' *Cosmographia per Gemma Phyrsius restituta*
published in Antwerp in 1539.)

reversed its motion.) Supremely confident in the perfection of the
heavens, Aristotle rejected the beliefs of the Ionian scientists, who
used terrestrial analogies for celestial changes: 'It is absurd', he
wrote, 'to make the universe to be in process of change because
of small and trifling changes on earth, when the bulk and size of
the earth are surely as nothing in comparison with the whole
universe.'[30] His argument may have sounded very plausible to an
audience which was unaware that the rest of the universe *is* made
of exactly the same stuff as the Earth.

Aristotle was just as wary about terrestrial change. Unlike Plato,
he discarded the testimony of legends recounting the periodic
devastation of the world by fire and flood. It is clear that he

rejected the Phaethon story, which tells how the Earth was incinerated by a massive disturbance in the heavens. Aristotle refers to the view of some Pythagoreans who regarded the Milky Way as a trace of this catastrophe – it was the trail left by a star that had been dislodged from its place by Phaethon's careering chariot. It was a weak argument, but Aristotle countered it with an even weaker one – he argued that the Milky Way was an atmospheric rather than an astronomical phenomenon.[31] As for the universal Deluge, which the Greeks thought had occurred at the time of Deucalion, Aristotle argued that it was merely a local event, caused by the River Achelous flooding a small area around Dodona in northern Greece.[32]

It is clear, then, why Aristotle dismissed as a fabrication Plato's story of the sinking of Atlantis. He did so because he rejected the entire historical view of Plato, in which the Earth was periodically destroyed by cosmic catastrophes. Where Plato's world was an unstable, dangerous place, Aristotle's was almost the complete opposite – fundamentally different viewpoints which coloured all their teachings on astronomy and cosmology.

The Decline of Neoplatonism

Aristotle's prestige was enhanced by becoming personal tutor to Alexander the Great, and when his pupil took the Macedonian throne, Aristotle returned to Athens to found his own institution, the Lyceum (335 BC). This was to be the cradle of the 'peripatetic' philosophers, supposedly named after their habit of strolling about as they meditated. Despite these successes, Plato's authority continued to outshine Aristotle's for many centuries to come. Plato was immensely popular throughout the hellenised world, and the Academy he founded at Athens to continue his work lasted a staggering nine centuries.

The *Timaeus* went on to become one of the most widely read books of the classical world and it would be impossible to overestimate its importance for the thought of all later periods. Its description of a single Creator god held great appeal for many early Jewish and Christian writers. The subject is too vast to touch on here, except to note that many – notably the Jewish writers Josephus and Philo (first century AD) and the famous Church Father St Clement of Alexandria (second century AD) – assumed that Plato had drawn his inspiration from the writings of

Moses. This made the *Timaeus*, for many centuries, a respectable subject for Christian discussion. Even the Atlantis story was reinterpreted in terms of Christian demonology. The Christian writer and teacher Origen (third century AD), who studied Platonism in Alexandria, saw it as an allegory, with the war of Athens and Atlantis symbolising the struggle between the spirits that animate the universe.[33]

Pagans, of course, claimed the *Timaeus* for themselves and eventually it became their shield against the rising power of Christianity. Offering a refined and mystical system of philosophy, it provided a counterweight to the growth of the new religion which was especially useful as Christians themselves respected it. Julian, last pagan Emperor of Rome (AD 360–363), relied on it heavily in his polemical writings against Christianity, contrasting the creation account of Plato with that in Genesis, believed to have been written by Moses. Which, Julian asked, was more sublime?[34] The argument cut little ice with the Christians who believed that Plato had copied Moses. Following this belief, St Augustine (AD 354–430) was able to express openly his admiration for Plato, and particularly for his account of the Creation.[35] Augustine also noted that Aristotelian teachings had to all intents and purposes been subsumed into Platonism by his time: the most notable philosophers of the Peripatetic school, like the Academics (from Plato's Academy), were now calling themselves Platonists.[36]

By the sixth century official Christianity had begun to harden its attitudes. There had been many bitter struggles between the Church and paganism, and when a re-energised 'Neoplatonism' began to flourish in Athens, the Roman Empire, now the strong right arm of Christianity, had to react. In 529 the Emperor Justinian shut down the Academy and passed a decree banning philosophical teaching in Athens.[37] Many of the scholars who had collected around Damascius, last Director of the Academy, pressed on to Mesopotamia, and then to Persia. They carried with them the seeds of Greek science, which was, a few centuries later, to flourish in the Muslim world while Europe rotted in an intellectual dark age.

The study of Plato was effectively suppressed in the eastern (or Byzantine) half of the Roman Empire. In the west it still flourished. The *Timaeus*, one of the few of his works to be translated into Latin, became synonymous with Plato – and almost with

Greek philosophy. For many western Europeans it was one of the few important pagan writings from the ancient world of which they were aware, and it continued to be studied and copied until well into the twelfth century. Then came the change. Texts of Aristotle, Archimedes, Euclid, Ptolemy and others had recently been rediscovered through the medium of Arab translations, and for a short while there was the promise of an early renaissance. What happened was almost the opposite.

Aristotle rapidly became adopted by the Church as *the* scientific textbook, and all else became neglected. He was less of a mystic than Plato, whose teachings of personal spiritual quest were perceived as a potential threat to papal and ecclesiastical authority. Plato's writings were rather too stimulating for the medieval Church. He encouraged people to think for themselves too much. A war that had been long forgotten started anew and the persecution of Plato began afresh, Neoplatonic teachings only being preserved in western Europe among fringe groups. For the rest of the Middle Ages Aristotle reigned supreme, while the association of Plato with the unorthodox was steadily reinforced.

Aristotle and Astronomy

The marriage of Aristotle to the established Church must surely be the grimmest development in European intellectual history since Christianity wedded Rome. Aristotle himself encouraged enquiry and investigation but, as Arthur Koestler noted, medieval schoolmen studying his work 'made the mistake of taking in what it actually said – and insofar as the physical sciences are concerned, what it said was pure rubbish. Yet for the next three hundred years this rubbish came to be regarded as gospel truth.'[38]

Another reason for the zeal with which the medieval Church took Aristotle to its bosom was the comfortably stable picture which he drew of the universe. On theological grounds it really should have opted for Plato's view of a world periodically ravaged by fire and flood – it was far more compatible with the Old Testament, which is brimming with natural catastrophes, from Noah's Flood and the destruction of Sodom and Gomorrah to the apocalyptic visions of the prophets. Indeed, the early Christian thinker Cosmas Indikopleustes (sixth century AD) argued that the story of the deluge that destroyed Atlantis was simply stolen from the Babylonian version of Noah's Flood.[39] As it happened, the Church – in an extraordinary exercise in doublethink – opted instead for Aristotle's view that the heavens are somehow not connected to the Earth. Koestler explained the attraction of Aristotle's model for the medieval Church:

> This splitting-up of the universe into two regions, the one lowly, the other exalted, the one subject to change, the other not, was to become another basic doctrine of medieval philosophy and cosmology. It brought a serene, cosmic reassurance to a frightened world by asserting its essential stability and permanence, but without going so far as to pretend that all change was mere illusion, without denying the reality of growth and decline, generation and destruction. It was not a reconciliation of the temporal and the eternal, merely a confrontation of the two; but to be able to take in both at one glance, as it were, was something of a comfort.[40]

The effects of Aristotle's teachings on science were hideous. Not only was progress retarded; the clock was effectively turned back on scientific knowledge by some two thousand years. The statement made by A. N. Whitehead in his classic *Science and the Modern World* is as staggering as it is true: 'In the year 1500 Europe knew less than Archimedes who died in the year 212 BC.' Actually, it is an understatement – the Ionian and Pythagorean philosophers of the 6th–5th centuries, not forgetting Plato of course, had a better understanding of astronomy and many other fields than the scholars of the later Middle Ages.

The expression 'the dead hand of Aristotle' has been used to describe the stifling effects which his mistaken ideas were to have on science over the next two thousand years. The stranglehold of the 'dead hand' was always most lethal in the field of astronomy. Sunspots, for example, were observed in medieval times, but their existence was rigorously denied as there was no mention of them in Aristotle's encyclopedic works. Likewise, Tycho Brahe had difficulty convincing people that he had observed the birth of a new star in the constellation Cassiopeia in November 1572. The heavens, according to Aristotle, simply could not exhibit blemish or change.

Aristotle effectively banned other fundamentally important phenomena from astronomy (and earth history) by misclassifying them. He argued that comets were 'exhalations' of vapour from the lower atmosphere ignited by fire in the upper air, completely reversing the (correct) opinion of the Pythagoreans, who had taught that comets should be considered like planets – as bodies distinct from the Earth with their own orbits and periods of revolution.[41] Likewise Aristotle classified meteors ('shooting stars') as an atmospheric phenomenon along with rainbows, aurorae and haloes. This is correct in that meteors are caused by small particles of matter burning up as they enter the Earth's atmosphere but it led scientists to ignore their real origin. Meteorites are extraterrestrial bodies large enough to survive the friction of the Earth's atmosphere and land. Despite the view of the Ionian philosophers that stony matter exists in space, Aristotle's insistence that the heavens were made of pure ether led to the understanding that meteorites as such did not exist. Their existence was officially denied until the nineteenth century. When a shower of meteorites fell in France on 24 July 1790, three hundred witnesses sent written statements to the French Academy, together with samples of the stones – the Academicians merely ridiculed them for their ignorance in believing a 'physically impossible phenomenon'.[42]

The worst of Aristotle's astronomical crimes, of course, was his insistence that the Earth stood fixed and unmoving at the centre of the universe. Plato probably allowed that the Earth rotated on its axis, and late in life, if Theophrastus is correct, he subscribed to the Pythagorean view that the Earth is not the centre of the universe. On these points, as usual, Aristotle took issue with his teacher, and the effects were disastrous. Koestler summarised the tragedy of this development in suitably dramatic terms:

> The Ionians had prised the world-oyster open, the Pythagoreans had set the earth-ball adrift in it, the Atomists dissolved its boundaries in the infinite. Aristotle closed the lid again with a bang, shoved the earth back into the world's centre, and deprived it of motion.[43]

The Church elevated Aristotle's teachings to the status of absolute dogma, and it was this that led Giordano Bruno to the stake in 1600 and forced the ageing Galileo to undergo his humiliating trial and imprisonment thirty-three years later.

Renaissance

The vicissitudes of the *Timaeus* are inextricably bound up with the history of astronomy, major trends in which have usually gone hand in hand with those in cosmology, philosophy and sometimes even theology. Astronomy, 'queen of the sciences', often calls the tune and the great scientific discoveries of the Renaissance – made by Copernicus, Kepler, Brahe and Galileo – were all in this field. It is no coincidence that Aristotle's teachings about the cosmos were worthless and that the Middle Ages were so benighted generally.

As has long been recognised, the Renaissance happened when the iron grip of Aristotle was forcibly thrown off. Dissatisfied with the Church, radical scholars began to turn from the Aristotelian teachings of Thomas Aquinas to those of the Florentine Platonist Marsilio Ficino, who published new Latin editions of Plato's works in the 1480s. By 1536 Peter Ramus was able to receive a standing ovation at the Sorbonne for his lecture on the theme 'Whatever is in Aristotle is False'.[44]

Science now turned again to Plato. Geographers were intrigued by the description given in the *Timaeus* and *Critias* of another continent which lay to the west of the site of Atlantis, and was once reached from there by a chain of islands. Directly or indirectly, it was one of the inspirations for Columbus, who inadvertently proved Plato right on this point when he discovered the Americas. But the most important Platonic revival was in astronomy. Johannes Kepler (1571–1630), for example, drew much of his inspiration directly from the *Timaeus*. Kepler's belief that 'geometry provided the Creator with a model for the decoration of the whole world' is pure Platonism. Fascinated by Plato's observation that mathematics only allows five perfect solids, Kepler developed a model whereby the distances between the planets follow the same ratio as those between the five perfect solids if they were arranged nesting one within the other. (Imagine a cube enclosing a sphere, with a pyramid inside the sphere and so on.) The idea may sound strange to modern science, but it was typical of the way in which Renaissance scholars worked. Moreover, Kepler's model worked, accurately describing the distances of the planets to within a few per cent.[45] From his Platonic model of the solar system Kepler derived his three laws of planetary motion, which laid the foundations for Newton's work and indeed all future studies in astrophysics.

When he defended himself against his critics, Galileo Galilei (1564–1642) appealed to the authority of the ancients, notably the Pythagoreans and the Platonists. The idea that the Earth moved, he noted, was believed by 'Pythagoras and all his followers, by Herakleides of Pontus (who was one of them), by Philolaus the teacher of Plato, and by Plato himself according to Aristotle.'[46] In Britain the Renaissance saw the growth of a Platonist movement at Cambridge, led by Henry More and Ralph Cudworth. The Cambridge Platonists, who were neither poor astronomers nor poor Greek scholars, were firm in their belief that Plato described the motion of the Earth in the *Timaeus*.[47]

Ironically enough, the efforts of the Renaissance scientists who were inspired by Plato were eventually to do him out of a job. His faith that mathematics held the key to nature's secrets was adopted by Kepler and Newton, who believed that they were piling up evidence that the universe had a geometrical design, and hence a Creator. Science, however, did not follow this route. As post-Newtonian science came to regard itself as a substitute for – and then the legitimate successor of – religion, mathematics came to dominate the cosmological picture so much that God himself was ousted from it, a process completed during the Darwinian revolution of the late nineteenth century.

Science now adopted a completely mechanistic and materialist view of the universe and the debt which the Renaissance owed to mystics like Plato was eventually to become an embarrassment. In particular orthodox science came to treat anything that smacked of astrology as complete anathema. Neoplatonism, like most ancient mystical philosophies, was steeped in astrology and, as a scientific phenomenon, was consigned to the offical junkbox of history. The orthodox version of the history of science has even recast the great heroes of the Renaissance – most of whom actually dabbled in Platonism, astrology and alchemy – in the mould of the modern scientist. It then churlishly derides them when their behaviour does not always conform to the idealised model – Kepler has been denounced as a 'theological crank', Galileo as a 'cheat' and Newton as a periodic 'lunatic'. It was, it seems, only a matter of time until Plato was subjected to similar treatment.

Plato's Final Downfall

Plato did continue in favour in western European intellectual circles until well into the middle of this century. Then came the crash – Platonism as a fashionable philosophical stance barely survived the disaster.

The reaction began largely with distaste for Plato's supposed decadence. In a study of Plato's morals published in 1931, John Jay Chapman homed in on the *Symposium* and condemned it as a piece of propaganda in favour of 'pederasty'. (Chapman meant to say homosexuality.) He rounded this off with a critique of Plato as a logician and literary artist. Three years later *The Platonic Legend* by Warner Fite, Professor of Philosophy at Princeton, continued the criticisms of Plato's ethics and documented what the author felt was an important 'discovery' – the society recommended by Plato in *The Republic* was basically undemocratic. There have always been – and always will be – criticisms of Plato's ideas, but the timing of these particular studies, which might otherwise have left little mark, meant that the anti-Platonic sentiments they expressed rapidly snowballed. In the 1930s the political ideas expressed in *The Republic* were being taken up and abused by totalitarian groups in central and eastern Europe. Nazism in particular claimed authority from *The Republic* for its ideas on social engineering.[48]

The Atlantis theme itself was adopted and remoulded by Nazi theorists. Plato's belief that the world was periodically destroyed suited the apocalyptic visions of the Nazi party, which revelled in the belief that the destruction of the world by fire would cleanse it and augur a new age. Between the two world wars a crank Austrian inventor called Hans Hörbiger developed a theory that the earth had been home to a series of super civilisations, destroyed by successive cosmic upheavals. The last had occurred during the capture of the Earth's Moon, and caused the destruction of Atlantis. Of great appeal to the Nazis, and to Hitler personally, was Hörbiger's cyclical view of history: the catastrophes would occur again and the races of demi-gods which ruled Atlantis and even earlier civilisations would return.[49] This mystical side to National Socialism was discussed with the Führer on many occasions by Hermann Rauschning, the Governor of Danzig. One of Rauschning's observations, made in 1939, reveals the way in which Atlantis had unfortunately been elevated into an icon of esoteric history:

> At bottom every German has one foot in Atlantis, where he seeks a better Fatherland and a better patrimony. This double nature of the Germans, this faculty they have of splitting their personality which enables them to live in the real world and at the same time to project themselves into an imaginary world, is especially noticeable in Hitler and provides the key to his magic socialism.[50]

Of course the super-Atlantis of Nazi occultism has nothing at all to do with the *Timaeus*. Nor is there any fascism as such in Plato's work. But these were grave days for democracy, and intellectuals in Britain and the United States were keen to dissociate themselves from a thinker who had become the unwitting ally of totalitarianism. As a result, during the Second World War an amazing campaign of vilification developed in the West against the author of *The Republic* and *Timaeus*.

Plato Today, written by Richard Crossman, a leading philosopher of the British Labour Party, took Plato on an imaginary journey through the modern world of 1939 and had him nodding with approval at the expediency of the 'noble lies' of Goebbels and Stalin. The attack on Plato came to a climax in 1945 with *The Open Society and Its Enemies* by the Austrian liberal and philosopher Karl Popper, which unreservedly characterises Plato as a black-hearted, dangerous totalitarian. Popper, who became Professor of Logic and Scientific Method at London University in 1949, is one of the undoubted heroes of modern scientific thinking. Unfortunately, in *The Open Society* he gets carried away to an appalling degree. Extraordinary liberties are taken with the basic sources (Plato's writings) and all sense of historical perspective is jettisoned.

In 1953 Ronald Levinson, Professor of Philosophy at the University of Maine, was prompted to write a lengthy volume *In Defense of Plato*. His chapter headings, including 'Was Plato an Abnormal Personality?' and 'Was Plato a Totalitarian?', reveal the charges that were now constantly being laid at Plato's door. Levinson confessed to being left rather breathless by the 'variety and virulence' of the accusations:

> Who would have thought the old man had such bad blood in

him? Defamer of his native Athens, betrayer of his master Socrates, racist, statist, propagandist unabashed, equivocating, man-hating, boy-loving, frustrated aristocratical snob – one was prepared for an imputation that the marble statue had feet of clay; we hear, instead, that it is composed entirely of mud.[51]

By the time things began to calm down in the mid-1950s, the damage had been done. As has been shown, Western science had had a long, but never very comfortable, relationship with Plato. He may have been one of the many inspirations for the Renaissance, but he was always – and still is – someone to be held at arm's length, with the distaste that authority always holds for the unorthodox. There was an almost audible sigh of relief when it was 'discovered' in the 1940s that Plato was merely a fascistic pervert – he could now be safely dumped from the scientific rolls of honour. When Sarton published his *History of Science* in 1952 he simply had to quote chunks of Popper's anti-Platonic tirade to justify his lop-sided treatment of Plato's political writings and then his philosophy generally.

Sarton could now confidently state that the *Timaeus*, 'considered for thousands of years as the climax of Platonic wisdom, modern men of science can only regard as a monument of unwisdom and recklessness.' As justification Sarton skilfully played the astrology card, in the tirade against the 'astrologic nonsense' spawned by the *Timaeus* cited earlier. Actually there is no mundane astrology in the *Timaeus* at all, and even Sarton admits that it does not 'degenerate into petty fortunetelling'.[52]

So it came about that a large part of Plato's work, on astronomy, cosmology, physics, geology and prehistory – his interests in later life, was quietly omitted from the curriculum of what is worth further serious study. The bulk of subsequent scholarship on Plato has been concerned with his efforts as a pure philosopher and 'sociologist' – the logic, dialectics, ethics, jurisprudence, etc. – in short the basically Socratic elements of his work – as well as with *The Republic*, which is still a favourite subject for analysis and criticism. As for the rest, they have been largely dropped. Studies of Plato's scientific work are rare, and sympathetic ones even rarer.[53] They have been actively discouraged by the statements of scholars such as Sarton and Benjamin Farrington, Professor of Classics at University College Swansea and a leading historian of classical philosophy and science. In the various editions of his work *Greek Science: Its Meaning for Us* (published between 1944 and 1969), Farrington admits the importance of Plato in philosophical history, but explains that

> We are not here concerned, except incidentally, with philosophy . . . We merely wish to caution against the mistake of regarding Plato as being equally important for the history of science. *From the scientific point of view, the* Timaeus *is an aberration.*[54]

In the same work Farrington throws out the extraordinarily bald statement that 'Plato has contributed nothing to science'. At the same time he takes a barefaced Aristotelian stance, arguing that even when Aristotle reversed the *correct* opinions of his predecessors he was justified as he was somehow acting 'scientifically'![55]

Nothing of the *Timaeus* can properly be understood without this background, although the above is only the briefest of sketches – necessarily, as the whole matter is still largely uncharted territory. Even the broad sweep of events, let alone the subtleties, has yet to be properly chronicled. A huge obstacle faces anyone attempting to interpret the vicissitudes of the Neoplatonist tradition – the desperate lack of information. In 1994 it could still be pointed out that the persecution of Neoplatonist paganism 'in all its physical, artistic, social, political, intellectual and psychological dimensions, has not as yet formed the object of scholarly research.'[56] Even the basic textual material for understanding the beliefs of Plato's successors is in short supply. In 1976 Robert Temple complained of the obstacles which stand in the way of an assessment of the Neoplatonist role in the history of science. Proclus (AD 410–485) was *the* leading Neoplatonist in the sense of being the most prolific and influential pagan philosophical writer of his day. Yet, as Temple notes, little of Proclus' work is actually available in English translation, except for those prepared by Thomas Taylor at the end of the eighteenth and beginning of the nineteenth centuries. Although Proclus wrote a lengthy *Commentary on the* Timaeus *of Plato*, which includes discussion of the Neoplatonist interpretations of Atlantis, this is only accessible to the English reader through a translation published by Taylor in 1820. As Temple rightly notes: 'The non-specialist reader will never have heard of Proclus, one of the greatest intellects of history.'[57] Such is the power of the 'dead hand of Aristotle'. And little has changed since Temple wrote.

Why Atlantis?

We can now return to Atlantis, the starting point used by Plato
for his contentious cosmological work. Whatever has been made
of it in the past, and whatever we make of it now, the *Timaeus*
must have represented to Plato a highspot in his work. Its aim,
after all, was to provide nothing less than a complete explanation
of 'Life, The Universe and Everything'. It ends with these words:

> We can now claim that our account of the universe is complete.
> For our world has now received its full complement of living
> creatures, mortal and immortal; it is a visible living creature, it
> contains all creatures that are visible and is in itself an image of
> the intelligible; and it has thus become a visible god, supreme
> in greatness and excellence, beauty and perfection, a single,
> uniquely created heaven.[58]

What, then, was the story of Atlantis doing in Plato's grand
philosophical account of cosmos and nature? Or, conversely, why
was Plato's account of Atlantis, with which the *Timaeus* opens,
interrupted by an astonishing digression on the creation of the
universe? At first glance the two elements seem to make strange
bedfellows.

The question has attracted little serious attention. To take one
example, the 550-page *Cambridge Companion to Plato* published in
1992 has no discussion of Atlantis at all! And while discussion of
the *Timaeus* continued *ad nauseam* before the 1940s, in the *Cambridge Companion* it is referred to only occasionally and tangentially
– for example as evidence that Plato still held his belief in the
World of Ideas late in life. The *Critias*, which is exclusively
concerned with the drama of Atlantis *vs.* Athens, is only referred
to in discussions of the chronological order of Plato's works, and
is given no entry in the bibliographical guide to studies of single
works.[59] Other recent bibliographies follow the same pattern[60] –
the *Critias* is given no individual entry for the simple reason that
barely any studies have been written.

Where discussion of the *Timaeus* has continued, Atlantis is
usually hived off as an intrusive, irrelevant element. In Cornford's
standard commentary on the *Timaeus*, translation and discussion
of the Atlantis section occupies a mere eleven pages out of nearly
four hundred; no attempt is made to link the story to Plato's
cosmology or political views. 'I find it extraordinary', Vidal-

Naquet remarked, 'that these problems are scarcely even mentioned in the great commentaries on the *Timaeus*.'[61] The other side of the coin is that most books on Atlantis simply skim over Plato's views as if he developed the concept in a vacuum. If both occur they are strangely separated. Sir Desmond Lee was commissioned by Penguin Books – clearly with an eye to the Atlantis market – to translate the *Timaeus* and *Critias* together. He discusses the cosmological side of the *Timaeus* in the Introduction; for Atlantis he refers the reader to the Appendix, which is largely concerned with a discussion of the pros and cons of the Minoan hypothesis. The reluctance to deal with Atlantis as an integral part of Plato's thinking is almost pathological.

This is a very odd state of affairs, given the importance of the *Timaeus* in the development of Western philosophy, theology and science and the role of Atlantis as the historical centrepiece of this influential dialogue. One of the few recent studies of the Atlantis problem from a classical perspective, by Daniel Dombrowksi, remarks on this puzzle: 'there has been a poverty of *philosophical* interest regarding Atlantis, which is a strange condition since it was the *philosopher* Plato who was the originator of the myth of Atlantis.'[62]

One almost feels that Plato is being deprived of his say in the matter. The answer lies in the historical developments that I have just reviewed – including the rejection of the scientific worth of Plato's work after the 1930s, from which scholarship is only beginning to recover. There was also a further development of even more ugly dimensions – a dramatic shift back to an Aristotelian stance in astronomy during the same decades which was to dampen even further serious study of the message in the *Timaeus*. Koestler hit the nail on the head when he referred to Plato and Aristotle as the twin stars of Western philosophy and science, though a better metaphor is the two little weather-figures on an old-fashioned barometer – when one (wet) pops out the other (dry) goes in, and vice versa. With a horrible inevitability, when Plato goes out of favour Aristotle's influence simultaneously creeps back in.

Fortunately, through the work of more adventurous classicists in recent years, the place of Atlantis in Plato's thinking is beginning to re-emerge. Ironically enough, the key to the meaning of Atlantis in Plato's cosmic scheme lies in the purely terrestrial question of ancient Athens.

CHAPTER 6

Athens of the Heroes

Pierre Vidal-Naquet, one of the few classicists to appreciate that the Atlantis narrative has never been properly studied in context, offered the following highly perceptive guidelines for the would-be Atlantis investigator:

> There are three rules for the historian who wishes to understand the myth of Atlantis. He must not sunder the two cities that Plato has linked so closely together. He must constantly refer himself to the physics of the *Timaeus*. And consequently, he must relate the historical myth whose structure he is trying to explain to Plato's 'idealism'. The success of a properly historical interpretation depends entirely upon the extent to which this preliminary task is performed.[1]

Plato's idealism and the physics of the *Timaeus* have now been examined. It remains to put the third element into place – Atlantis' rival state Athens.

The war between the two powers is clearly an important appendage to Plato's vision of cosmogony. It briefly introduces the *Timaeus*, which then gives a history of the universe from the building of the cosmos to the creation of mankind. In the *Critias* Plato returns to the Atlantis theme, treating it in detail as an important episode in prehistory where the conflict between two different kinds of early society is analysed. The idea that he simply 'made up' the whole story of the war between Athens and Atlantis seems improbable. Put simply, would Plato have jeopardised the credibility of the *Timaeus*, containing his most important discoveries about the nature of the universe, by sandwiching it between slices of complete fiction?

It is also relatively easy to test Plato's probity on one half of the Atlantis-Athens story. The early history of Athens was hardly an unknown quantity. The official version of Athens' prehistory was still in a formative stage at the time Plato wrote, but at least one history of Attica from the earliest times had already been written (by Hellanicus, c. 400 BC); Thucydides' history of the Peloponnesian War also contains a digest of Athenian prehistory; and the plays of the great fifth-century dramatists (Aeschylus, Sophocles and Euripides), as well as the speeches of orators (such as Plato's older contemporary Isocrates) are full of allusions to Athens' legendary past.[2] So there is enough material available from the fifth and fourth centuries to answer the question – was Plato's vision of Athens' past the product of his own imagination? And beyond that, how does that vision square with archaeological reality?

One thing is clear from the outset – the idealised prehistoric Athens in the *Timaeus* and *Critias* was not something that Plato created specially for the Atlantis narrative. The same image occurs elsewhere in Plato's writings, notably in a dialogue known as the *Menexenus*, in which Socrates parodies the extravagant praise which Athenian orators customarily heaped on the city. A brief analysis of the Proto-Athens described in the *Timaeus*, *Critias* and *Menexenus* shows that almost all the elements involved were the stock-in-trade of Athenian legend and pseudo-history.

The origin of Plato's prehistoric Athenians is their most important characteristic. He calls them autochthonous, i.e., native to their land (*Critias* 109D), echoing the Greek belief that some people actually sprang from the soil like plants. Of all Greek peoples the Athenians were particularly proud to claim earth-born status.[3] The most famous sons of the Attic soil were the earliest Athenian kings. Homer describes the primeval ruler Erechtheus as 'a child of the fruitful Earth' and the fifth-century tragedians and later mythographers call his predecessors 'sons of the soil'.[4] One of their number, Erichthonius, was said to have been born when Hephaestus, god of fire and craftsmanship, became inflamed with passion for Athena and came on her leg. The disgusted goddess wiped off his semen and threw it on the ground, accidentally impregnating the Earth goddess (*Gê*). Thus King Erichthonius was born.[5] Plato was probably referring to this ribald tale when he said that the Athenians were the offspring of 'Earth and Hephaestus' (*Timaeus* 23D-E). His audience would have recognised the allusion.

The point of such stories was to contrast the pure – native – blood of the Athenians with that of Greek peoples with more remote origins. Racism, of course, was not unknown to the ancient Athenians. In the *Menexenus* (245D) Socrates contrasts those with Anatolian, Phoenician and Egyptian blood, who are 'naturally barbarians though nominally Greeks', with the 'pure' Athenians: 'whence it comes that our city is imbued with whole-hearted hatred of alien races.' This supposed purity set the Athenians apart from the Spartans, who claimed descent from the hero Heracles. He was thought to be descended from the family of Danaus, which arrived in Greece from Egypt or Syria.

FIG. 9   The Earth Goddess Ge (Gaea) gives the child Erichthonius to Athena, as depicted on a 4th-century Athenian vase. In attendance are (left) Hephaestus and (right) the snake-legged Cecrops, king of Athens (*from Cook 1940*).

The advantage of being 'earth-born' was that the Athenians were in total harmony with their land, which cared for them literally as a mother does her children. The Earth-goddess provided her Athenian offspring with wheat, barley and the miracle of the olive and made Athena and Hephaestus 'their governors and tutors', to teach them the arts of agriculture and manufacture (*Menexenus* 237E–238A; cf., *Timaeus* 23D, 24C–D; *Critias* 109C).

The idea of the Athenians' special status was not peculiar to Plato. It is echoed, for example, in the speeches of Isocrates, who tells us the Athenians were 'neither of mixed origin nor invaders of a foreign territory but . . . sprung from the soil itself, possessing in this land the nurse of their very existence and cherishing it as fondly as the best of children cherish their fathers and mothers.'[6]

The *Timaeus* and *Critias* heap further praise on the Proto-Athenians for their almost single-handed defence of Greece, indeed Europe, against the Atlanteans. This certainly reflects the battle of Marathon, but it seems that, like Plato, the Athenians believed they had *always* been the bulwark of Greece.

The *Menexenus* (239B) summarises some of their legendary achievements. The Athenians defended the sons of Heracles against the King of Tiryns, and the Thebans against the Argives, and repulsed the invasions of Eumolpus from Thrace and the Amazons from Asia. These events were all themes of Athenian legend long before Plato wrote.[7] The *Menexenus* refers to 'still earlier invaders' of Greece, which suggests that Plato may already have had the Atlanteans in mind. It was only for these invaders that Plato claimed to have special knowledge, as provided by his relative Solon. Overall, the image of the Athenians as the historic defenders of Greece – against Thracians, Amazons and come what may – was not Plato's invention. It is implicit in Athenian tradition and echoed in the writings of the earliest Greek historians, who record that the Athenians were the only major people of their country never to have been dislodged from their native lands.[8]

Although the *Timaeus* (23C) heralds the original Athenians as having 'the noblest constitution of any nation under earth of which we have heard tell', Plato is sparing in his details about its exact nature, giving only the general impression that it was ruled by an aristocracy akin to the Guardians of his *Republic*. The Egyptian priests told Solon the names of prominent Athenians from the time of the Atlantis conflict (*Critias* 110A). They are familiar as the names of primeval Athenian kings (including Cecrops, Erichthonius and Erechtheus) from the standard traditions, but Plato refers to them not as kings but as heroes. The assumption that he saw these rulers as limited or constitutional monarchs is borne out by the *Menexenus* (238C-D), where Socrates says that Athens had always had a mixed constitution, approved by free-born citizens. Some, Socrates explained, call it a democracy, others something else, but 'it is, in truth an aristocracy backed by popular acclaim; for we always have kings, who are sometimes hereditary and sometimes chosen.'

Again, the belief that Athens had a special constitution as far back as the Heroic Age was not Plato's invention. For example, the fifth-century tragedians describe Athens in the time of the hero-king Theseus as a haven of free-speech, where the rule of law and justice prevailed.[9] During the 6th-5th centuries the idea was developed that Theseus had not only united the Athenian people but also granted them supreme rule. His method was explained in various ways.[10] The most contrived was that of Isocrates, who sidestepped the anomaly of Theseus as sole ruler in a democracy as follows:

> He made the people masters of the government, and they on their part thought it best that he should rule alone – believing that his sole rule was to be trusted more and would be more equitable than their own democracy.[11]

In the same speech Isocrates implies that the earlier kings of Athens, as far back as Erichthonius, had ruled in a similar manner: their style of kingship was utterly superior to that at the great centres of Mycenae and Thebes, where incest and murder were rife and stability was never achieved. The proof, Isocrates claimed, was that the descendants of Erichthonius ostensibly held the Athenian throne in father-to-son succession for numerous generations. Thus the kingdom inherited by Theseus was 'the securest and greatest of all kingdoms'.[12] These words could have come straight out of the *Timaeus* and *Critias*. Plato was not alone in his belief that the constitution of prehistoric Athens was unique.

In the *Timaeus* (24A) the Egyptian priest told Solon that if he wanted a glimpse of life in prehistoric Athens he only had to look at contemporary Egypt – since both societies had been founded by the same goddess, Athena. The caste system in Egypt was similar to that once operative in Athens, with a strict division of the populace into different classes: priests, warriors, craftsmen (subdivided into particular skills), shepherds, hunters and farmers. The military class was kept apart from all the rest and was bound by law to devote itself exclusively to the art of war.

All of this smacks of Platonic invention, particularly as he was accused by his contemporaries of copying Egyptian institutions for his ideal Republic.[13] Yet there *were* Athenian traditions concerning priestly clans believed to have held office since the Heroic Age.[14] Plutarch, too, has related that King Theseus divided the Athenian population into three classes: the aristocracy or *Eupatrides* (literally 'those who should do well from their fatherland'), the *Geôrgoi* ('farmers') and the *Dêmiourgoi* ('craftsmen').[15] Plutarch (second century AD) was a meticulous recorder of legends who relied heavily on the (now lost) works of early mythographers such as the Athenian Pherecydes (fifth century BC). The difference between the three-fold class-division reported by Plutarch and Plato's claim that there were six groupings in Proto-Athenian society suggests that Plutarch's statements about Theseus' reforms are free of Platonic influence. Once again, it seems that Plato was working within the traditions about prehistoric Athens current in classical times.

One thing not attested by any tradition is the communist life-style of Athens' prehistoric rulers. According to the *Critias* (110C-D; 112C), the warrior caste of Proto-Athens dwelt apart from the rest of the population in communal quarters. They owned no private property and were provided with their subsistence needs by the ordinary population. They led a simple lifestyle and pos-sessed no gold or silver. This concept, which seems to come straight out of *The Republic*, is almost certainly Plato's wishful thinking.

Prehistoric Athens: Legend and Reality

All that Plato added, then, was a political twist to traditional material. He himself stresses that he is writing about the Athens of familiar Greek legend, saying in the *Timaeus* (110B) that the priests narrating the Athenian-Atlantean war 'mentioned most of those names which are recorded prior to the time of Theseus, such as Cecrops, and Erechtheus, and Erichthonius, and Erysich-thon, and the names of the women in like manner.'

Plato is a little vague – deliberately so, it seems, as to which Athenian king was ruling when Atlantis sank, though we are at liberty to make a guess. Tradition held that during the reign of Cranaus, the successor of Cecrops, Greece was devastated by the Flood of Deucalion. According to one tradition, when Deuca-lion's ark landed he fled for safety to King Cranaus at Athens.[16] Plato was probably aware of this tradition, but he did not link the two events because he was following an unorthodox time-scale which placed his story right outside the traditional parameters. Plato actually states that the flood in question was the 'third before' that in the time of Deucalion. (As ancient counting of this kind was inclusive, in our terms this means the second.) As has been shown, Plato placed the struggle between Atlantis and Athens in the Silver Age of Greek tradition – most other Greeks would have placed the earliest age of Athens in the mythical Brazen or Heroic Ages. Why Plato chose to break with the traditional time-scale and place the Atlantis-Athens war in such an early age is a key question which will be addressed later.

Otherwise, Plato's story is much closer to the mainstream of Greek myth than is often assumed. Without a word from Plato, the Greeks already believed that prehistoric Athens was home to a well-organised society of earth-born men, brave defenders of Greece as well as their own land, patronised by the deities Athena and Hephaestus and ruled over by heroic kings at a time when there was a universal deluge. The recasting of the lifestyle of the prehistoric Athenians – into a model for the communist Guardians of the *Republic* – and the backdating of the time-scale are the only two elements peculiar to Plato. It was with some confidence that Plato could put into the mouth of Critias the claim that the tale he had to tell was absolutely true – with respect to the Athenian side of the story, at least.

The real surprises come with the comparison of Plato's Proto-Athens and the archaeological record. A number of details in his account concern tangible matters which can be checked against excavated evidence. Plato's prehistoric Athens was the capital of a united Attica; its citizens were literate and its society was well organised with a high degree of specialisation in skills. It was completely surrounded by a single-circuit wall, with the military aristocracy living in dwellings on the northern side of the Acropolis, and one spring supplying their settlement with water. The city's downfall was brought about by natural catastrophes. The scene was an Attica once greater in size and with much richer soil.

Does Plato's description match the archaeological record? There is no point looking for any Athenian archaeology from 9000 BC. The earliest settlement at Athens goes back to the fourth millennium, and there was no city as such until Mycenaean times. So, setting aside for the moment Plato's own rather exotic time-scale, and following the more traditional assumptions, it is Mycenaean Athens of the Late Bronze Age that needs examination. Its remains produce an amazing series of correspondences with Plato's description: –

Federalised Attica

As Plato uses 'Athens' as a name for the whole country of Attica, he must have seen it as the capital of an already united country. (The plural name for Athens, *Athenai*, reflects the union of different states into one.) He also defines its boundaries as stretching eastward to the Isthmus of Corinth and northwards to the Asopus river.

Is it credible that Mycenaean Attica was already a united state? This is what Athenian traditions held – it was thought that under King Erechtheus the last independent state within Attica, Eleusis, was absorbed into the kingdom, after the war with Eumolpus. Then, under Theseus, the country was federalised, with the government of the whole of Attica being centralised in Athens. In some versions all the citizens of the country were resettled in the capital. While historians used to assume that the tradition of Theseus' federalisation was concocted during the sixth century BC, when the tyrant Peisistratus actually united the country, archaeological finds may have radically changed the picture. Excavation of Brauron, one of the twelve cities of Attica believed to have been united with Athens by Theseus, has shown that its Mycenaean settlement was abandoned at the end of the Late Helladic IIIA period (conventionally dated to *c.* 1300 BC) – there was no trace of burning or other destruction. In the words of John Papadimitriou, excavator of Brauron:

> It has now been shown, by the limited excavations of the Acropolis of Brauron, that the unification of Attica did not occur in the historic epoch, a little before Peisistratus, as one had believed until the present, but in prehistoric times . . . The tradition which attributes this political reunion to Theseus is true.[17]

Not all archaeologists would agree with Papadimitriou's assessment. Even so, the idea that Attica may already have been united during the Heroic Age, just as Plato and his contemporaries believed, is no longer rejected out of hand.

Literacy

The disasters that struck down Athens and Atlantis left only 'unlettered survivors', thereby breaking continuity in history (*Timaeus* 23B; *Critias* 109D–E). It follows that Plato saw the Proto-Athenians as a literate people. The Mycenaeans, as is well known, kept their palace accounts on tablets using a non-alphabetic (syllabic) script now known as 'Linear B'. Linear B tablets have been found at several Mycenaean sites, including Knossos, Pylos, Mycenae, Tiryns and Thebes, and it seems reasonable to assume that all the main palace centres employed a bureaucracy versed in this script. No examples have been found as yet at Athens, but this does not mean that the script was not used there in Mycenaean times. No Mycenaean palace has been excavated at Athens; if one had been situated on the Acropolis – the most likely place – its remains would have been obliterated by later building activity on the rock. However, an amphora inscribed with Linear B has been excavated at Eleusis, the second major centre of Mycenaean Attica, where the legendary King Eumolpus ruled.[18]

Plato's claim that only the unlettered survived the catastrophe that destroyed Proto-Athens is close to reality. If literacy did not completely die out at the end of the Mycenaean Age (conventionally *c.* 1200 BC), it certainly suffered: Linear B went out of use, to be replaced eventually by the Greek alphabet.[19]

Social Organisation

The swashbuckling society described in Homer's *Iliad* and *Odyssey* bears very little resemblance to the regimented world revealed by the Linear B tablets. As the classicist James Hooker has pointed out:

> Whatever the Greeks of the Dark Ages and the poets of the Homeric tradition preserved of the Mycenaean culture, they know nothing of the complex economic system, and little of the political structure, which obtained in a Mycenaean state. It has been truly said that in such matters there is a wide gulf between the actual world of the Mycenaeans, with its complex orders of functionaries and highly differentiated economy, and the simple and largely unstructured society depicted by Homer.[20]

Strangely enough, there is no such gulf between the society of Plato's Proto-Athens and that revealed by the tablets. In fact the highly stratified, specialised society described by Plato sounds remarkably like the real Mycenaean world. Within Plato's larger social divisions (priests, soldiers, craftsmen, shepherds, hunters, farmers) there were more specific distinctions. The craftsmen, for example, were subdivided into different kinds, 'of which each sort works by itself without mixing with any other' (*Timaeus* 24A-B). The same high degree of specialisation can be seen in the Linear B world, where 'manual occupations of great diversity were followed by well-defined and specialised groups',[21] such as several different kinds of smith.

The Pylos and Knossos tablets reveal identical economic systems, so it is generally assumed that Mycenaean society was run on similar lines throughout all the great city states. The Athenians during the Heroic Age would have been divided into highly specialised professions just as Plato described. Was this simply a lucky, though educated, guess on his part, or did he have access to traditions about earlier society which were passed over by Homer?

Circuit Wall

In the *Critias* (112B) Plato states that the military class of prehistoric Athens dwelt on the top of the Acropolis 'round the temple of Athena and Hephaestus, surrounded by single wall like the garden of single house'. Immediately recognisable in this description is the circuit-wall of 'cyclopean' masonry built by the Mycenaeans around the summit of the Acropolis during the thirteenth century BC (see Fig. 10). Parts of the Mycenaean circuit wall can still be seen (see Plate 2) and would surely have been visible in Plato's day. To his credit, Plato correctly included the wall in his description of Mycenaean Athens.

Warriors' Houses

The warrior caste of Proto-Athens built their houses on the north side of the Acropolis, though they used the southern side during the summer months (*Critias* 112B-C). Archaeological work has shown that Mycenaean settlement on the Acropolis tended to concentrate in one area on the northern side,[22] providing striking confirmation of Plato's description. Where Plato derived his information from is anybody's guess, but the settlement on the northern side of the Acropolis seems to have been unknown to earlier historians such as Thucydides, who stated that before the time of Theseus the city 'consisted of the present Acropolis and the part below it facing southwards'.[23]

The Spring

In the *Critias* (112D), Plato describes the spring of prehistoric Athens:

> There was a single spring in the area of the present Acropolis, which was subsequently choked by the earthquakes [at the time of the Atlantis disaster] and survives only in a few small trickles in the vicinity; in those days there was an ample supply of good water both in winter and summer.

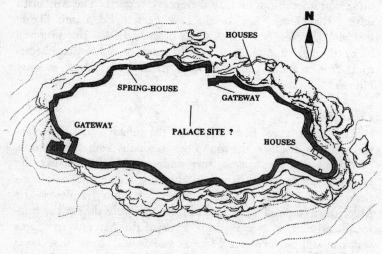

FIG. 10 Plan of the fortifications which surrounded the top of the Athenian Acropolis in Mycenaean times (*after Broneer 1956*).

Plato's account was dramatically confirmed during the American excavations of 1936–8, when the artificial spring built in Mycenaean times on the northern slopes of the Acropolis was rediscovered. The spring was one of the greatest engineering feats of the Mycenaean world, far superior to similar operations carried out at Mycenae and Tiryns where the inhabitants only managed to reach unprotected water sources outside the fortified areas. At Athens the Bronze Age inhabitants succeeded in sinking a shaft through a natural cleft *within* the citadel, reaching a spring 120 feet underground; an elaborately constructed stairway descended to a depth of about 112 feet beneath the Acropolis, at which point the water could be reached with jars on ropes.

Plato also seems to have been right about why the well fell out of use. The American excavators surmised that an earthquake was responsible. The wooden underpinning of the stone steps had given way, the stairway had crashed down and the shaft had filled with debris. To judge from the broken pottery lost in the water and around the stairs, the earthquake took place near the end of the thirteenth century BC. The well was never used again. Oscar Broneer, who directed the excavations, suggested that the memory of the catastrophe which destroyed the well – 'especially if accompanied by loss of human life' – may have become the subject of local legend.[24] It seems that during classical times only 'small trickles' from the spring were still visible. Somehow Plato succeeded in correctly deducing that the spring belonged to the same age as the circuit wall.

It is clear that Plato's account contains more genuine memories of Mycenaean Athens than is generally acknowledged. There remain two questions concerning the physical history of Proto-Athens. Was Mycenaean Athens brought to an end by natural disasters? And had Attica undergone serious environmental change since the days of the first Athenians?

A Mycenaean Catastrophe?

The *Timaeus* and *Critias* describe in no uncertain terms how Proto-Athens – the noblest civilisation of the prehistoric world and the only state in Europe that could withstand the tyrannical might of Atlantis – came to its end. While on campaign against the Atlanteans, its army was swallowed up by the same earthquakes that sank the lost continent; massive floods scoured their homeland in Attica of its once-rich soil and reduced the great rock of the Acropolis to a fraction of its former size. Was Plato right in thinking that the Mycenaean world came to an end through such natural disasters?

The problem is inextricably related to the broader question of why the Bronze Age civilisations of the Near East and Eastern Mediterranean suffered three periods of major disruption. The ends of Early, Middle and Late Bronze Ages are marked by widespread destruction and abandonment of sites. The close of the

Early Bronze Age (*c.* 2300 BC) saw particularly momentous events. The urban civilisations of Greece, Turkey and the Levant were destroyed; in Anatolia alone over 300 archaeological sites have been identified (including Troy) which were burnt or deserted at this time. In Mesopotamia the great Akkadian empire, which had united the small city-states of the Euphrates and Tigris, disappeared.[25] In Egypt the Old Kingdom, the age of the great pyramid-builders, came to a close and the country slipped into anarchy.

A cause for these upheavals was first suggested by Professor Claude Schaeffer, the doyen of French Near Eastern archaeology. The three massive breaks that punctuated Bronze Age civilisation were acutely clear at the key site of Ugarit (Ras Shamra), which Schaeffer had been excavating since 1929. During the war years he immersed himself in library research at Oxford and discovered that practically every known site in the Near East had been destroyed at the same times that Ugarit suffered. Each band of destructions could be closely synchronised. What immense forces, he asked himself, could have caused such devastation? Schaeffer concluded that the Early and Middle Bronze civilisations had been literally shaken to the ground by earthquakes, in episodes of unusual seismic upheaval of unknown cause. For the Late Bronze Age he adhered, at that time, to the traditional explanation that the destructions throughout the Eastern Mediterranean were caused by migrating invaders, such as the 'Sea Peoples'.[26]

Schaeffer's theory was largely ignored by archaeologists and the whole subject became dormant. Then, in 1966, a series of lectures given at Cambridge University by the American classicist Rhys Carpenter suddenly transformed the collapse of Mycenaean civilisation into one of the most hotly disputed issues in archaeology. Carpenter's theory was that a drastic change in climate had brought about the collapse of Bronze Age civilisation. In Carpenter's model, the prevailing climate of much of Greece became significantly warmer – and hence drier – around 1200 BC. The resulting drought caused widespread famine, and eventually the peasantry sacked and burnt down the palaces of their betters who of course held the lion's share of the remaining foodstocks. He envisaged similar famine-spawned revolutions in the heartland of the Hittite Empire (central Anatolia) and elsewhere in the Eastern Mediterranean. Egyptian texts of this period suggest that both the Libyans and Hittites were suffering from food shortages; the

Egyptians had to send the latter grain supplies.[27]

When his slim but highly controversial volume of lectures was published as *Discontinuity in Greek Civilization*, Carpenter chose as the Foreword the passage from the *Timaeus* in which the Egyptian priest described to Solon the periodic destructions of civilisation by fire and water. Carpenter interpreted them as episodes of drought and flood.[28]

The debate which grew up around Carpenter's work has never been fully resolved. It is not an easy matter to determine ancient climatic patterns. Various attempts have been made to corroborate Carpenter's model by utilising written evidence from Mesopotamia, comparisons with better-established environmental records from central European archaeology and the tree-ring record from central Turkey.[29] The problem is that in most of these cases nobody is sure what is being compared to what. Very different dating methods are used for each of the strands of evidence (historical, radiocarbon and dendrochronology, respectively) and no-one, least of all those of us who feel that the archaeological dating of the ancient Near East is askew by some two hundred years, was entirely convinced that Carpenter's model could be verified by bringing together material from such disparate fields.

Carpenter's theory concentrated exclusively on widespread famine caused by drought, and he tended to ignore the effect of earthquakes, still the worst environmental hazard in countries like Greece and Turkey. The excavators of a number of key Greek sites, including Mycenae itself, suggested that earthquakes had indeed been responsible for destructions at the end of the Late Bronze Age.[30] At Ugarit in Syria, another twenty seasons of work had convinced Schaeffer that he was wrong in his original assessment that the city had been destroyed by invaders. Instead he had found evidence of earthquake *and* drought: its collapsed walls were covered with a layer of pale dusty soil, contrasting starkly with the rich red earth of the Late Bronze levels.[31]

Neither the climatic nor the earthquake model for the destruction of Late Bronze Age society won its case and during the 1980s and 90s a number of scholars began investigating more subtle models for the collapse of Late Bronze Age society. These 'systems collapse' theories concentrated on internal weaknesses in the societies affected, largely the social and economic problems inherent in such highly structured societies. The role of mass migrations and invasion in the destructions was increasingly underplayed – with good reason as the evidence is weak – and factors such as peasant revolt given more stress, coming some way to meeting Carpenter's model. The theorists did, however, tend to gloss over the actual causes of site destruction as being rather incidental, leaving out explanations of how an oppressed peasantry could suddenly rise up and throw off their highly organised masters. The evidence, as it stands, shows that most of the palace economies of the Late Bronze Age world were thriving until the point of their actual demise.

In 1991, with the help of several colleagues, I tried to assess the patchy record of evidence and draw some picture of why the Bronze Age in the Eastern Mediterranean came to a close. The real historical circumstances, we agreed, were certainly very complex. A combination of causes was most likely involved. For example, an episode of severe earthquakes or climatic disaster could have sounded the death knell for a Late Bronze Age economic system already weakened by other factors. A change in climate and a peak in earthquake activity could have come together, with a single, as yet unidentified, cause. In Greece, where tremors are still the main environmental hazard, severe earthquake seems the most likely trigger for such a collapse.[32] Knock-on effects would have been crucial, as the palace-based economies of the Late Bronze Eastern Mediterranean and Near East were highly interdependent. If a trading partner relied upon for essential supplies (such as grain, olive oil or metals) went down, then the difficulties of coping with any local problems caused by famine, flood or earthquake would be immensely magnified. One straw can break a camel's back.

At about the time we wrote, the case for a catastrophic end to the Bronze Age was being meticulously re-examined by the American classicist Robert Drews.[33] Drews treats the main sites under discussion in turn and argues that in almost every case the evidence for natural disaster is equivocal. In one sense he is right. When an archaeologist discovers a collapsed stone wall it is sometimes extremely difficult to determine whether the causes were natural or due to the action of man. Did it fall or was it pushed? As for fire damage, it is hard enough in modern cases to detect whether a building was destroyed by arson or accidental causes (from a dropped cigarette to an electrical fault), even with immediate inspection by experts. Imagine the problems when dealing with a palace or farmhouse burnt down three or four thousand years ago. Deliberate firing by raiders or invaders is the explanation that most frequently springs to mind. On the other hand, it is a fair statistical guess that a number of sites thought to have been burnt by enemy action must have met their end through a variety of other causes – an oil-lamp upset by an earthquake, a blast of lightning, or a child playing with a domestic fire. The description of a site's destruction given in the official publication is very much a question of judgment on the part of the excavators. An unequivocal answer is generally elusive: there are not many sites like Thera.

Drews questioned, for example, Schaeffer's understanding that the end of Ugarit came about through earthquake and drought. The destruction of its walls Drews attributes to raiders – and he can point to the evidence of numerous arrowheads found in the destruction which *may* have belonged to aggressors. He argued that the layer of powdery yellow material covering Late Bronze Age Ugarit was from the burning of its brick and stone structures. Drews's strongest argument was that no single piece of unequivocal evidence could clinch the idea that earthquakes or climatic upheaval had seriously affected the city-states of the Late Bronze Age Mediterranean – even in Greece, where one would suspect that earthquakes must have played a crucial role. This might once have been the position but some dramatic new discoveries – not published when Drews wrote – have now completely changed the picture.

The Flood at Tiryns

The Bronze Age palace at Tiryns, south of Mycenae on the Argolid plain, was first discovered by Heinrich Schliemann in the 1870s and the site as a whole is now being excavated by the German Archaeological Institute. Klaus Kilian directed the excavations until his death in 1992. He searched the ruins of the city burnt about 1200 BC (at the end of the Late Helladic IIIB period), but could find no trace of the foreign invaders often supposed to have been responsible. There was complete cultural continuity with the succeeding Late Helladic IIIC (LHIIIC) settlement, except that the focus of the settlement outside the upper town on the citadel shifted. To explain these developments Kilian suggested that the town had been hit by an earthquake which triggered a raging fire. With similar developments in evidence at

Mycenae, Kilian argued that the earthquake had struck all the cities of the Argolid Plain.[34]

Drews was highly critical of Kilian's model and argued that Tiryns (and all the cities of the Eastern Mediterranean destroyed at the end of the Bronze Age) fell to raiders, a possibility which Kilian discussed only fleetingly – and with good reason, for the excavations revealed no sign of military activity in the destruction level. Indeed, his earthquake hunch has now been corroborated in spectacular fashion.

In 1987 the German Archaeological Institute sponsored geo-archaeologist Bernhard Zangger to examine the ancient environment of the Argolid Plain. By drilling cores through the soil around Tiryns, Zangger discovered that part of the lower town had been buried under a mass of mud near the end of the Late Helladic IIIB period (c. 1200 BC). Lack of stratification in the mud showed that it had been laid down in one single event, like the flash floods occasionally caused by streams, except that flash-flood deposits are usually measured in centimetres. Parts of the eastern town of Tiryns were covered by up to five metres of sediment. Catastrophes of this magnitude are not caused by a heavy downpour. Only a river could have carried the enormous slurry of mud that suddenly engulfed the town.

In Zangger's reconstruction, Tiryns was hit by an earthquake which dammed the river running south of the city and drove it from its previous course. It then raced towards Tiryns bringing a mud landslide with it. This would explain the enormous engineering efforts made by the Tirynthians shortly after the disaster. Several kilometres inland they built an enormous barrier across the river, and dug a channel to divert its waters into an old streambed nearby. The dam was a success and still determines the course of the stream today.[35]

The discovery is an exciting one; Zangger himself wonders whether his first test drilling 'may one day be considered the most important auger core in Mediterranean archaeology'.[36] Perhaps not quite; but few cores from this region can have produced such dramatic results. Plato, for one, would have been delighted. Zangger's work scotches once and for all the arguments of those who refuse to accept that natural disasters played a part in the downfall of Mycenaean civilisation. Zangger himself was once of this mind: 'As a scientist I was (and still am) strongly opposed to explaining the demises of civilisations by natural catastrophes.'[37]

With the Mycenaeans, Zangger's own discoveries forced him to make an exception. Tiryns would not have been alone in feeling the effects of the earthquake. It was of such magnitude that it would have also devastated the cities of Mycenae and Argos, which lie only a short distance away on the same plain, and would probably have hit most other centres in southern Greece.

Although the Mycenaean world continued after the disasters at the end of the Late Helladic IIIB period, it changed markedly. Trade with the Levant broke down almost completely, and the archaeological record shows continuing turbulence and destruction. The best interpretation of these events, especially after the Tiryns discoveries, is that the Mycenaeans were hit by a series of disastrous earthquakes, possibly accompanied by climatic change, which exacerbated the severe economic and political difficulties besetting the Eastern Mediterranean at the time. While some cities continued to flourish, the major centres such as Mycenae, Tiryns, Pylos and Gla never recovered their former grandeur and, in little more than a century, possibly even less, the Mycenaean Age had closed for ever. Athens, as it happened, was one Mycenaean centre to survive the catastrophe, although life there was seriously disrupted. The carefully constructed water supply for the citadel was destroyed by earthquake and the houses (which Plato mentions) on the northern slopes of the Acropolis were abandoned. The city would have also suffered economically from the collapse of its neighbouring cities, and it is usually believed that Attica became a centre for refugees from the Argolid and Peloponnese. Though there was continuity between the Athens of the Bronze and Iron Ages, Mycenaean Athens – along with the rest of the Mycenaean world – was finished. Plato's claim that Proto-Athens came to an end during a time of natural catastrophe is vindicated.

Plato the Geologist

Plato rounded out his picture of prehistoric Athens with a series of acute observations on geology. According to the *Critias*, the noble race that fought the Atlanteans lived in a much more fertile Attica than that known to Plato and his contemporaries. In classical times the Acropolis of Athens was, as it is now, a bare rock. Not so in the age of the Heroes, according to Critias. Nine thousand years ago, he stated, the Acropolis was a far more prominent feature of the landscape, flat on top and covered with soil. At the same time that Atlantis was destroyed the Acropolis was eroded to a fraction of its former size. All the soil on it was removed by 'the action of a single night of extraordinary rain' (*Critias* 112A). It was not just the capital which suffered. Most of Attica's once-rich topsoil was washed away during the Atlantis catastrophe and the other floods which followed. What remained was 'something rather like the skeleton of a body wasted by disease; the rich soft soil has all run away leaving the land nothing but skin and bone' (*Critias* 111A).

Plato not only described the process, he also explained it. Originally, he said, Attica had a deep, rich, loamy soil which absorbed the rains and drew them into hollows, forming springs and streams. (Plato pointed to shrines which still survived from the Heroic Age as evidence that these springs once existed.) The problem was that the sea around Attica, a long thin peninsula of land jutting out into the Aegean, is extremely deep. When floods came, the soil was simply 'carried out and lost in the deeps'. In other countries, where the surrounding waters are more shallow, silt washed down from the highlands collects and forms an alluvial deposit, which acts as a barrier to further erosion of the soil.

The classical scholar Arthur Platt noted that 'this statement of denudation by Plato is, I believe, the first ever made, certainly the first upon so grand a scale . . . Plato therefore must have the credit of the first distinct enunciation of a most important geological doctrine.' Yet, as he also observed, Plato had never been given his due: 'Sir Charles Lyell, in his history of the progress of geology, has entirely omitted the name of Plato as an original geologist, and I am not aware that this omission has ever been corrected. Yet it is in reality a serious one.'[38]

Platt's words, written in 1889, fell largely on deaf ears. Anyone searching through the mountain of literature on Plato for a discussion of his contribution to geology will be disappointed – though there are a few exceptions. Though highly sceptical of the historicity of Atlantis, the Czech scientist Zdenek Kukal was deeply impressed by Plato's account of Attic geology. Regarding Plato's discussion of how deep soils absorb moisture, forming springs and streams, Kukal remarked that 'even a professional hydrologist would not be ashamed of such a description'.[39] Zanger has also taken up the defence of Plato as a pioneering geologist and noted the profundity of his observations; 'no modern geologist, for example, has equalled the unerringness of Plato's comparison between soil erosion and the skeleton of a sick man.'[40]

On a theoretical level Plato's description of the geological processes which have produced the present, rather barren, landscape of Attica is actually flawless. The only problem is the time-scale involved. Plato's broad observations do not link so well with the civilisation he described. Zangger thinks that the upheavals at the end of the Bronze Age could have produced an episode of unprecedented soil erosion. Even so, there is no evidence that the Acropolis was covered in rich soil during Mycenaean times. As Zangger notes, the Eden-like conditions described by Plato may have prevailed shortly after the last Ice Age (during the Mesolithic or Middle Stone Age period), but not seven or eight millennia later. Ironically enough, Plato's date of 9500 BC for Proto-Athens, while archaeologically impossible, would suit modern dating of the geological evidence.

It would be arrogant, with the benefit of hindsight and modern techniques of geological and radiometric dating, to scoff at Plato for mismatching the relative dates of the archaeological and geological material. Given his conviction that Athens of the Heroes had been destroyed by natural disasters, it was a brilliantly intuitive leap to link this with observations about Attica's past geological condition.

Earth and Water

Years of further research will be needed to establish a detailed model of the role played by natural upheavals in the end of the Bronze Age. In the meantime, the new evidence from Tiryns has reinstated the role of natural disaster in the collapse of the Bronze Age in the Eastern Mediterranean and Near East. Plato's belief that 'Athens' of the Heroic Age was destroyed by earthquake and flood is far from being an eccentric view. If we read 'the Mycenaean world' for Proto-Athens, then it is fair to accept that the most promising model of twentieth-century scientific research has now reached a position already argued by Plato in the fourth century BC.

Putting the Athenian part of the Atlantis narrative in context allows a much firmer grasp on the meaning of the story as a whole. Even before addressing the central problem of whether Plato had genuine source material for the Atlantis side of the story, it is possible to tackle the question raised at the end of the last chapter – what does the story have to say in terms of Plato's philosophy and what is it doing in the *Timaeus*?

Vidal-Naquet rightly insisted that any understanding of the Atlantis-Athens story must 'constantly . . . refer to the physics of the *Timaeus*', and he attempted the task himself in 1964.[41] Analysing Plato's vision of prehistoric Athens, Vidal-Naquet identified three essential elements. First, it was conspicuously land-based: even though surrounded by sea, Proto-Athens had no harbours. Second was the city's 'oneness'. This can be seen in its political unity as one state (unlike Atlantis with its ten kings) and even in local details such as the single fountain on the Acropolis. Third, Proto-Athens was changeless, its constitution fixed with the aim of keeping the warrior class at a steady number (about 20,000, *Critias* 112D). Even the style of housebuilding remained constant (*Critias* 112C). Vidal-Naquet used these points to argue that Proto-Athens was the political expression of the 'Same', Plato's term for the divine essence within the universe which is eternally unchangeable (see Chapter 5). The birth of the Athenians from the Earth would support this idea. Of the four elements, earth, air, fire and water, Plato specified earth as the one that cannot be transformed: although it can undergo change and combination with other elements, it will always revert back to earth (*Timaeus* 56D).

Then what of Atlantis? As Vidal-Naquet admits, he cannot exactly contrast the 'Same' quality of Athens with an 'Other' quality for Atlantis. The 'Other', as Plato saw it, was the factor of changeability in the Universe, which of course does not exist by itself. Yet change was certainly characteristic of Atlantis. While the nature of Plato's Athens seems fixed for ever, Atlantis appears to be in a state of continuous creation. Its capital city begins as a settlement on an island-mountain formed by Poseidon and is steadily added to by each successive ruler. The Atlantean kingdom then expands to include, by degrees, the whole Atlantic continent, the chain of islands and parts of the unknown continent lying to the west, and finally the Afro-European landmass as far as Italy and Egypt. Vidal-Naquet also notes that the combination of two elements – earth and water – is fundamental to the Atlantean way of life. The Atlantean kings are descended from the sea-god Poseidon and the earth-born nymph Cleito, and the capital city is composed of concentric rings of land and water. Thus the dual nature of the Atlanteans – susceptible to the influences of both earth and water – appears to contrast strongly with the monotonous earthiness of the Athenians.

It all sounds plausible, though a little more abstruse than even Plato might have intended. On closer examination, however, Vidal-Naquet's erudite analysis begins to break down. The difference between the land-based character of Athenian power and the water-based character of Atlantean is indeed explicit in the text. Yet it is hard to press the point much further, as Vidal-Naquet attempts, into the area of Plato's physics. Vidal-Naquet's argument essentially hinges on the idea that, while Athens was unified, the image Plato painted of Atlantis was composed of dualisms. Vidal-Naquet is a structuralist and, like all structuralists, aims to analyse things by breaking them down into pairs of contrasts and opposites. Having satisfied himself that Atlantis had a dual nature, Vidal-Naquet neglected to apply the same scrutiny to Athens.

Plato's Proto-Athens was also full of dualities: its weapons were the shield and the spear; its rulers lived on top of the Acropolis, but its craftsmen below; while the aristocracy had their main quarters on the north side of the Acropolis, they spent summer on the southern side; the city had two patron deities, Hephaestus and Athena; and, perhaps fatal for Vidal-Naquet's theory, Plato did not present the Athenians as being the offspring of Earth alone, but of Earth *and* Fire combined. So the idea that there is an enormous contrast between the duality of Atlantis and a monolithic 'unity' of Athens begins to seem rather forced.

The real trouble with Vidal-Naquet's idea that Proto-Athens was the embodiment of changelessness is that it *did* change – it fell with a bang at the same time as Atlantis sank. Vidal-Naquet's explanation of the story thus falls short of the mark. The superiority of land-based to land and water-based civilisations is something that comes into play in Plato's tale, but it is unrealistic to imagine that his highly complex narrative was written solely to illustrate this point.

Fragile Environment

In 1981 Daniel Dombrowski, a classical scholar from St Joseph's University in Philadelphia, published a study which got to the heart of the matter far more directly than Vidal-Naquet's structuralist approach. Dombrowski's paper makes its point so clearly that one wonders why the obvious had not been realised long ago and become a matter of common knowledge. As so often in Platonic studies, the literal meaning intended by the author is strangely overlooked. Dombrowski notes:

> Most explanations of the story of Atlantis fail to answer the most important question of all: if *Athens* was such a noble and well-governed city, why did *she* ever deteriorate? Unlike the moral deterioration of the state in Book Eight of the *Republic*, this ideal state was destroyed through violent earthquakes and floods ... Most important, however, is the fact that it is here that the connection between the story of Atlantis and the main part of the *Timaeus* is established. Ancient Athens is *not* destroyed through bad leaders, but through what seems to be an irrational chaotic part of nature.[42]

Here Dombrowski hits the nail firmly on the head. It is implicit throughout the *Timaeus* that there is an irrational element in the universe. As we have seen, it is an essential tenet of Plato's thinking that only God himself can be perfect. We have also traced his logic in arriving at the conclusion that God must have used as the building blocks of creation raw materials that were already pre-existent. These materials, unlike the Creator, contained the seeds of imperfection. The *Timaeus* is largely the story of the Creator's struggle to impose rationality on these forces. The irrationality inherent in the raw materials of creation was expressed through periodic cataclysms in the universe – some so extreme that the solar system reversed its motion and time itself ran backwards. Though God may watch over us, the universe has always been, from our point of view, an unstable place.

The key to all of this, as Dombrowksi realised, is the concept of environment – from the cosmic to the mundane. In this sense Vidal-Naquet was right in stressing the earthbound character of the Athenians and the mixed (terrestrial and maritime) background of the Atlanteans. But if the *Timaeus* and *Critias* are re-read with the word 'environment' (rather than Vidal-Naquet's 'elements') in mind, the whole matter becomes crystal clear.

The *Timaeus* begins with a description of the periodic catastrophes that have afflicted the world. When fire destroys the Earth, 'those who live upon the mountains and in dry and lofty places are more liable to destruction than those who dwell by rivers or on the seashore.' When the cataclysm is caused by a deluge, the Egyptian priest told Solon that 'the survivors in your country are herdsmen and shepherds who dwell on the mountains, but those, who like you, live in cities are carried by rivers into the sea' (*Timaeus* 22D–E). The stability and longevity of his own civilisation, the priest stressed, was due entirely to the Nile, 'our never-failing saviour', which preserves the Egyptians from both kinds of disaster.

The *Timaeus* then goes on to explain in metaphysical terms why our widest environment – the universe as a whole – is inherently unstable by taking us back to the Creation. As a historical pendant to the origin of life, the tale of two early civilisations is told. Their contrasting characters are formed by their very different environments, a point which Plato stresses by the lavish amount of detail which he gives in the *Critias* concerning the geography of the two countries. Plato's descriptions of the flora and fauna, layout, mountains and irrigation system of Atlantis, or the soil conditions of Proto-Athens, are not elaborate window-dressing, as has often been assumed, but the very meat of the story. In the end, of course, both civilisations succumb to natural disasters.

The understanding that environment is a key factor in the shaping of societies is a commonplace today. Not so in Plato's time. As Dombrowski remarks, 'the connection between geography and history may be so common-sensical to a modern reader as to blind him to the important insight Plato is making here, an insight whose origin was rather recent . . . '[43] The only writer to touch on the theme before Plato was Herodotus, who was also intrigued by the special environmental conditions of Egypt.

The role of the environment in the rise and fall of civilisation became an important feature of Plato's philosophy, which he continued to explore after writing the *Timaeus* and *Critias*. These two dialogues were originally planned as the first parts of a trilogy covering a grand history of universe and man. After Timaeus and Critias a third guest, the Sicilian statesman Hermocrates, was also to make a speech (*Critias* 108A). His contribution, in the projected dialogue *Hermocrates*, would presumably have taken Plato's interpretation of history up to the present. It seems that it was never written – at least as a separate work – though most commentators believe that the material planned for Hermocrates' speech was recycled in Plato's *Laws*.

Here, in a lengthy historical excursion, the last few millennia of history before Plato's time are described. A man named Cleinias and an anonymous Athenian discuss the fact that 'thousands upon thousands of states have come into being, and at least as many, in equally vast numbers, have been destroyed'. In trying to pin down why such changes have taken place, the Athenian asks Cleinias: 'Do you believe there is any truth in the ancient stories?' 'Which stories do you mean?' asks Cleinias. 'Those', replies the Athenian 'that say that people have been repeatedly annihilated by deluges, pestilences and many other causes, so that only a tiny fraction of the human race survived.' Cleinias agrees that 'that sort of thing strikes everyone as entirely credible', and the two go on to analyse together the way in which civilisation could have risen again after the last flood (i.e., Deucalion's). Themes familiar from the *Timaeus* recur – of how cities built on plains and near the sea would have been destroyed 'root and branch', while the best part of the survivors would have been illiterate hill shepherds. New communities would gradually establish themselves on the high ground and for a long time would co-exist in peace. There was no shortage of land and, with the art of mining lost, the shortage of metals also meant a shortage of weapons. Only at a later stage, and through growth of numbers, would mankind spread down again to the plains and coasts and set up the full machinery of civilisation – with all the inherent corruption and need for increasingly complex political systems that this implied. These developments after the last flood were merely repeating a cycle which had continued for thousands, or even millions of years as successive civilisations were gradually established, then cut down in their prime.[44]

The moral expressed in the *Laws* is the same as that identified by Dombrowski in the *Timaeus* and *Critias*. It is simple but profound: absolute good and absolute evil do not exist (in this world), and although an ethical orientation is doubtless the best one for a given society or political state to take, that alone will not guarantee its survival. Forces beyond its control, ultimately natural ones, will eventually destroy it. It is a message that the twentieth-century Western world might well heed, since it now has the godlike power to aggravate or ameliorate its natural environment.

1 Roman portrait, copied from a Greek original, representing the philosopher Plato. (Replica in Cambridge.)

2 The Parthenon of Athens. In the foreground is a surviving part of the Mycenaean wall which once completely surrounded the Acropolis. Plato attributed the wall to a marvellous civilisation of prehistoric Athenians, rivals of the Atlanteans.

3   The royal Lydian cemetery of Bin Tepe ('Thousand Hills').

4   The burial mound of King Alyattes (d. 560 BC), father of Croesus.

5 Kara Göl, a small, mysterious lake near the top of Yamanlar Dagh once favoured as the site of the sunken city of Tantalis.

6 The Hittite god at Kara Bel.

7 'Cybele' (Tash Suret), the Bronze Age carving some three hundred feet up on the north face of Mount Sipylus. Thirty feet high, it depicts a seated goddess. According to Pausanias it was the first statue of the Mother of the Gods and was carved by a son of Tantalus.

8, 9, 10 The rock of Niobe, daughter of Tantalus, on the northern slopes of Mount Sipylus, near Manisa. Seen as one approaches from the mountain road, Niobe appears to be an ordinary outcrop of rock. From the side, details of the rock head are clearly seen.

11, 12, 13   The 'tomb of St Charalambos' (Pausanias' 'tomb of Tantalus') –
front, interior and side views.

14, 15, 16   Above the ravine of Yarikkaya, on the north side of Mount Sipylus, is a steep-sided crag of rock, on the top of which are a series of curious rock-cuttings, including the 'throne of Pelops' described by Pausanias. Below, the ravine is a narrow, sinuous passage running deep into the mountainside.

17 'Cybele', the Mother Goddess, as seen from the fields below.

18 The plain towards the Gediz (Hermus) Valley as seen from beneath the carving of Cybele. Until the middle of this century a lake covered the fields shown in the foreground.

Plato and Catastrophism

Earlier chapters have touched on the controversies between the uniformitarian and catastrophist views of earth history. The gradualist (uniformitarian) position – established as a tenet by the geologist Charles Lyell in the mid-nineteenth century – holds that the Earth's past can only be interpreted in terms of processes that are visible today. This means that all the events apparent in the geological column have to be explained in terms of very gradual developments. Even mass extinctions, including the death of the dinosaurs, must be seen as a result of processes such as the slow drifting apart of the continents. Uniformitarianism also extended its influence to the interpretation of the human past. It is still generally believed by most geologists and archaeologists that there have been no major upheavals in climate or environment since the last Ice Age, and that even the Ice Ages themselves began and ended gradually. Catastrophists, while accepting the role played by uniformitarian processes, also believe in the importance of sudden, destructive episodes involving earthquake, volcanic activity and floods, often on an almost global scale. Causes invoked range from inherent instabilities in the Earth's crust to extra-terrestrial causes, such as supernovae, meteorite and asteroid impacts or brushes with the dust contained in cometary tails. Some catastrophists consider that such events continued into the historical period and that their memory is preserved in the mythological record.

It is quite clear on which side of the fence Plato sat. Put simply, he was a catastrophist. While Dombrowski stressed the crucial role of geography in Plato's view of the past, he did so with insufficient force. He omitted any mention of catastrophism, essential to understanding Plato's view of how environment has shaped history.

Once the catastrophist perspective is recognised, the meaning of the *Timaeus* and its curious mixture of cosmology and human history ceases to be a mystery – it is all about the unstable nature of the universe in which we live. So why have modern philosophers studying Plato shied away from stating the obvious? Clear statements, like the following made by Levinson, Plato's defender in the 1950s, are exceedingly rare:

> Plato is operating with a theory of 'cultural catastrophism': through the vast, perhaps infinite reaches of time past, civilized

communities have arisen by slow steps from rude beginnings
to various degrees of cultural maturity (he formulated no periodic law requiring perfection at any point), and then, through
the agency of catastrophic floods, plagues, and the like, have
been thrown back to their primitive conditions.[45]

There are scores, possibly hundreds of books on the philosophy of
Plato that don't contain even a passing reference to his catastrophist
views.[46] Why? The only answer can be that for most of this
century catastrophism has been a very dirty word in scientific
circles. The catastrophist ingredient in Plato's work, though plainly
present, has simply been ignored. Its omission from descriptions
of Plato's world view was easily managed in an intellectual climate
which assumed that his scientific speculations were, in any case,
completely valueless: why bother with refutations of something
that has become irrelevant to the history of science? It amounts
to an appalling conspiracy of silence in which Plato's views, no
matter whether they were right or wrong, have been effectively
and systematically suppressed.

A simple psychological mechanism explains, on one level, why
scientists generally abhor the idea of past catastrophes: to accept
that they happened in history implies they may happen again.
Nobody likes the idea of rocks falling on their heads or their
house being shaken to the ground by an earthquake. This innate
fear seems to have engendered attempts to describe our wider
environment in ways that exclude such possibilities. Astronomers
have long preferred the illusion of a neat, tidy and predictable
universe – an illusion that goes back to Aristotle, who taught that
the universe was unchangeable and that the heavens were perfect.
In the eighteenth and nineteenth centuries there was a steady
erosion of Aristotelian astronomy in matters of detail: through the
sheer weight of evidence it had to be accepted that sunspots,
comets and meteorites were genuine astronomical phenomena.
But during the same centuries that these discoveries came to be
accepted, the very essence of Aristotelian thinking was creeping
in by the back door and re-entrenching itself at the heart of
science – largely through the work of Isaac Newton.

The real Isaac Newton was a very different person from the
popular image often drawn of him. He was a deeply religious
man whose aim was to demonstrate, by use of mathematics, the
brilliance of God's handiwork. In this he followed Plato's inspir-

ation, but in other respects the deity he worshipped was very different from Plato's. Newton's God was not subject to necessity and had no problems struggling to impose his will on an imperfect creation: He is all-powerful and, through choice, protects the world from large-scale catastrophe. Divine Providence was actually a far more important law in Newton's world than gravity, which he also conceived in spiritual terms.[47] Though Newton once entertained the idea that comets could collide with the Earth (a theme which preoccupied his contemporaries), his religious convictions led him increasingly to the view that Providence would not allow such a thing to happen – although he never completely ruled out the idea that Noah's Flood may have been caused by such a catastrophe. Near the end of his life Newton even argued that comets play a beneficial role in God's regulation of the solar system, by recharging the Sun with their energy. As to the evidence of past catastrophes, Newton's advice, as relayed by his disciple Colin MacLaurin, was simply to turn a blind eye. MacLaurin noted that 'ingenious men' had argued from the evidence of rocks and fossils that 'great revolutions have happened in former times on the surface of the earth', and that 'some philosophers' (a clear reference to Newton's former colleagues Edmund Halley and William Whiston) 'explain these changes by the revolutions of comets, or by other natural means'. But, MacLaurin explained, 'it does not appear to be a very important question to enquire whether these changes are produced by the intervention of instruments [e.g., comets] or by the same immediate influences which first gave things their form.'[48] In other words, God may have stepped in personally, now and then, to adjust or clear up his own creation.

By dint of the brilliance of his laws of motion, Newton managed subtly to impose a neo-Aristotelian world view on Western science. The whole package was swallowed at once. It is widely thought that Newton – and following him the great French astronomer Pierre Laplace – proved through mathematics that the solar system (even the universe) is stable, when they did no such thing.[49] Newton merely *believed* that Providence kept the world safe from disaster, while Laplace, as it happens, actually accepted that we were in a fairly vulnerable position. Nevertheless, this steady view of the cosmos, thought to be mathematically proven, came to dominate all other fields of learning. Astronomy, as has already been stated, tends to act as the 'queen of the sciences'.

The perfectly stable, trouble-free universe of Newton and Laplace was the background against which Sir Charles Lyell developed his uniformitarian understanding of geology and palaeontology.[50] (Lyell, as Platt noted, omitted any mention of Plato in his survey of geological pioneers.) And Lyell stood behind Darwin, whose model of biological evolution required millions upon millions of years of uninterrupted, catastrophe-free prehistory.

The teachings of Newton, Lyell and Darwin still form the core of modern astronomy, earth history and natural sciences. The contribution of this trio has of course been enormous. The only regret is that the imposition of their teachings, by the Newtonians, uniformitarians, and neo-Darwinists, has usually been at the expense of all other viewpoints – notably that of the catastrophists. Lyell's teachings did not immediately win favour, especially outside Britain. In the early twentieth century, many French geologists were still prepared to countenance such ideas as the sudden disappearance of an Atlantic Atlantis, but by the middle of the century catastrophist speculation of any kind had reached a nadir.

The last chapter referred to the barefaced Aristotelian stance taken by many scientists from the 1930s to the 1950s. In a world of increasing political instability, the belief that Earth, left to itself, was after all basically a safe place became increasingly popular in the West. Extreme catastrophist interpretations of the past among Nazi philosophers and historians would only have contributed to the repugnance catastrophism evoked among Western scientists in the immediate post-war period. Plato's writings repeatedly discussed the idea of global cataclysms beyond the control of mankind and this was yet another reason they were discarded in the 1940s.

So it was that the Aristotelian world view became supreme again. It may be difficult to believe that a Greek philosopher who passed away more than two thousand years before could have such a subtle and pervading influence. Yet some of the bizarre developments in astronomy around the middle of the century certainly suggest this.

First there was a complete hardening against the idea of global catastrophes in the recent past. It was very bad timing that during this very period Immanuel Velikovsky (a psychoanalyst and Russian émigré living in New Jersey) produced one of the most extreme catastrophist models of all time. Velikovsky argued that near-collisions with other planets had caused many of the catas-

trophes described in the Bible (and by Plato), and produced a
new model of the solar system which was a picture of instability:
the planet Venus, for example, he believed to have been a comet
as late as the second millennium BC.[51] If Velikovsky had produced
his speculations at any other time the reactions would not have
been so virulent. As it was, the scientific establishment of America
closed ranks and conducted a vicious campaign to discredit and
even suppress his work – to the point of engineering the sacking
of some individuals partial to Velikovsky's theories.[52] Much of
what took place in this shameful episode of scientific history was
orchestrated by a prominent and extremely powerful astronomer
named Harlow Shapley, who on more than one occasion expressed
his firm conviction in the benign nature of the universe.[53]

It seems no coincidence that over the same period astronomers
were busy remodelling their view of comets to make them harmless. Before the middle of this century theories regarding the
composition of comets always allowed them to contain fairly
substantial – and therefore dangerous – chunks of material. In
1890, for example, the British astronomer Sir Norman Lockyer
had proposed that the nucleus of a comet was composed of a
swarm of hundreds of millions of meteorites (each of which could
average 100 pounds mass). By the 1940s, however, any relationship
between comets and meteorites was increasingly denied, despite
the protests of H. H. Nininger, then the leading expert on meteor-
itics.[54] Instead, Fred Whipple's 'dirty snowball' model came into
favour. This proposed that comet nucleii are largely a mixture of
frozen gases and dust. (Whipple, incidentally, was Shapley's chief
assistant, and then successor as Director of Harvard College
Observatory.) While it was originally allowed that the dust
included rocky fragments the size of meteorites, the new model
gradually came to transform comets into a kind of cosmic candy-
floss.

Whipple's 'snowball' model was widely popularised as scientific
fact. The British public, who have learnt most of their basic
astronomy from Patrick Moore, have been fed repeated statements
to the effect that 'a comet is a flimsy body, made up of small
particles – mainly ices – together with extremely thin gas. It has
even been said that a comet "is the nearest approach to nothing
that can still be anything".' That Moore agreed with this assessment as recently as the 1980s is clear from another passage: 'Are
there any scientific grounds for the dread of comets . . . ? Brilliant

though they sometimes become, comets are flimsy, ethereal things.'[55] Ether (*aithêr*) is of course the very word used by Aristotle to describe the intangible, harmless material of which the stars were made. Moore was naturally flabbergasted when, in July 1994, hefty fragments of the disintegrating comet Shoemaker-Levy ripped enormous holes in the atmosphere of the planet Jupiter.[56]

Apart from the diehards, it is now increasingly accepted that the 'dirty snowball' went much too far in minimising the solid nature of comets and hence the dangers they present. Analysis of the core of Halley's comet has proved it to be quite substantial, and the 'dirty snowball' model has now quietly been dropped, even by Whipple. During the 1980s and 90s the link between comets and meteorites – which do undeniably hit the Earth – has begun to be accepted again.

In the post-war years instability and catastrophe were gradually allowed back into the picture by astronomers and geologists. Such totally un-Aristotelian phenomena as the explosion of stars (supernovae) and the decimation of the dinosaurs by asteroid or cometary impact have now become standard features of the cosmic repertoire – though it should be noted that such disasters are still only generally allowed at respectably safe, literally astronomical distances of place and time. Events that took place 65 million light years away or 65 million years ago will not unduly distress anyone. There is still a long way to go before Aristotle's influence is fully shaken off. Only a very small number of this more avant-garde astronomers – together with scientists in other fields – have been pushing the idea, based on very solid evidence, that large-scale catastrophes continued into much more recent times.

It is now much more than ten years since two British astronomers, Victor Clube and Bill Napier, demonstrated the existence of at least one very large comet on an earth-crossing orbit during Bronze Age times. It seems reasonably well established that sizeable pieces of debris from this disintegrating cometary body, impacting with the Earth as meteorites, would have once been a regular menace. Immediate effects would have included earthquakes and flooding (due to tidal waves), while changes in climate would have been brought about by dust clouds.[57] Meteorites need not have landed directly on ancient civilisations, or even in inhabited areas, but their impact, in sufficient size or numbers, would actually produce the effects seen at the close of the great Bronze Age periods – simultaneous earthquakes and climatic upheaval. Perhaps

Plato was right after all when he said that the catastrophes which punctuated civilisation's jerky progress came from the heavens.

While catastrophism and catastrophe theories are slowly re-entering the natural and mathematical sciences, classical archaeologists, historians and philosophers have been dragging their feet rather stubbornly – in fact they often seem to be unaware of the relevant developments in the physical sciences. Plato, who should really receive credit for having developed the first integrated model of scientific catastrophism (taking in evidence from history, philosophy, mythology, astronomy, geology and even archaeology), has still to be recognised for his extraordinary achievement. Whether he was right or wrong is not the point. It now behoves classical philosophers to set the record straight and begin to teach what it was that Plato repeatedly tried to communicate in the *Statesman*, *Timaeus*, *Critias* and *Laws*. The very least that could be said is that Plato's catastrophist picture of our environmental history is a point of view which twentieth-century science seems to be rapidly coming to appreciate.

A Tale of Two Cities

It is now clear why the story of the creation and the Athens/Atlantis tale belong together in the *Timaeus*. A modern equivalent might describe the violent history of the universe from the big bang to the death of the dinosaurs, through the events of the Last Ice Age to the contemporary threat of meteorite and comet impact.

Clear too is the purpose of the Atlantis narrative in the *Timaeus* and *Critias*: to illustrate Plato's view that environment is the key factor shaping not only the character of societies but also, ultimately, their fate. Many good societies had crumbled in the past – not through their own fault but simply because of the way the universe is constructed. Plato's view that the rise and fall of civilisations is part of a natural process beyond human control seems justified. It is becoming increasingly appreciated that the fall of the great civilisations of the Early, Middle and Late Bronze Age Mediterranean were triggered by major environmental upheavals.

On a more specific level, the background for Plato's story of a marvellous Proto-Athens was the real world of Mycenaean Greece, about which he made some remarkably accurate statements. He combined extant traditions with his own observations and interpretations – but he did not invent Proto-Athens. If one half of the Athens *vs* Atlantis story is based on a genuine tradition which has some historical basis, what about the other half?

CHAPTER 7

The Egyptian Connection

Looking at Plato's score-sheet so far, the result is a mixed one. For his description of prehistoric Athens he earns an admirable nine out of ten: none of the raw materials was invented and the skill with which he blended traditional claims with his own observations and political prejudices is admirable. In so doing he produced a remarkably accurate sketch of Mycenaean Athens, especially striking when one considers that nothing similar was attempted by any other writer in classical times, either earlier or later.

The same investigation, however, throws a very different light on Plato's claim that the Atlantis story originated in Egypt. The details given about the glories of prehistoric Athens are not the gleanings of Egyptian priests. Can we really believe that a priest of Sais relayed the information regarding the Mycenaean wall at Athens, the well to the north of the Acropolis or the eroded landscape of Attica? These are the observations of a someone intimately acquainted with the local history and geology of Attica – in other words, Plato himself. Solon and the Critias family may also have made a contribution, but it matters little whether the account of Athens was entirely Plato's work. The story of Proto-Athens, from its 'perfect' political constitution to the image of a once-fruitful Attic soil, is a manifestly Athenian construct. Egyptian priests simply don't come into it.

In the past, neglect of the Athenian part of the Atlantis tale has led to a lopsided attitude towards the claimed Egyptian origin of the story. The absurdity of the Athenian material having come via Egypt is actually an important and often overlooked clue. Here is an important watershed: is it possible that the story as a whole did not spring from an Egyptian source after all?

It is worth remembering at this stage that Plato is really the sole ancient source for the Atlantis story. There are a few other classical references to Atlantis but these are clearly derivative and do not claim to have gone back to the story's supposed source. Only one classical author has been thought to provide independent testimony of the story and its Egyptian origin – Crantor (c. 340–275 BC), a student of Plato who wrote some of the first commentaries on his work.

It has been stated by many writers on Atlantis that Crantor verified the claim that there were Egyptian records of the story. Luce, a leading proponent of the Minoan theory, was impressed that Crantor apparently 'went to the length of sending a special enquiry to Egypt to verify the sources of the story, and the priests replied that the records of it were still extant on "pillars".'[1] The German Atlantologist Otto Muck gave further details in a version where Crantor visited Egypt in person:

> Crantor came to Sais and saw there in the temple of Neith the column, completely covered with hieroglyphs, on which the history of Atlantis was recorded. Scholars translated it for him, and testified that their account fully agreed with Plato's account of Atlantis . . . Perhaps this priceless document is still hidden in the silt of the Nile.[2]

The combined testimony of the inscribed Egyptian pillar and the witness of Crantor, coming so soon after Plato, sounds impressive. The problem is that the whole scenario is imaginary. None of Crantor's original writings have survived, and the story of his detective work in Egypt turns out to come from a simple misreading of the commentary on the *Timaeus* written by the Neoplatonist scholar Proclus in the fifth century AD (see Chapter 6). Since Crantor has so often been invoked as a star witness, it is worth quoting the passage from Proclus, following the translation prepared by Taylor in 1820:

> With respect to the whole of the narration about the Atlanteans, some say that it is mere history, which was the opinion of Krantor, the first interpreter of Plato, who says that Plato was derided by those of his time for not being the inventor of the *Republic*, but transcribing what the Egyptians had written on this subject; and that he so far regards what is said by these deriders as to refer to the Egyptians this history about the Athenians and Atlanteans, and to believe that the Athenians lived conformably to this polity. Krantor adds that this is testified

to by the prophets of the Egyptians, who assert that the particulars are written on pillars which are still preserved.[3]

This last, rather bald, sentence is Crantor's sole contribution to the case. It hardly suggests the dramatic confirmation that modern writers have seen and there is nothing to indicate whether Crantor saw such 'priceless documents' at first hand or learnt about them from travellers. At is happens, there is no reason to believe that Crantor is referred to at all in this part of the passage. Taylor's translation, as Alan Cameron pointed out in 1983, is not as literal as it should be. In the original Greek of Proclus the subject of the last sentence is not 'Crantor' but 'he'. As Cameron showed, 'the run of the passage points more naturally to Plato'.[4] Crantor was thus simply repeating the claim made by Plato in the *Timaeus* and *Critias*. Thanks to Cameron's study, one of the great myths of Atlantology has at last been laid to rest.

Plato in Egypt

The removal of Crantor from the picture leaves Plato as the only witness that the story came from Egypt. At this juncture it is necessary to throw in the intriguing but somewhat neglected tradition that Plato himself visited Egypt.

The trip is mentioned by several classical writers. According to Plutarch, Plato paid for the voyage by selling oil.[5] The trip is not directly mentioned in Plato's extant works, but then he gives away very little autobiographical information. Yet the twenty or so references to Egypt in Plato's writings suggest he was familiar with the country on a first-hand basis. Most references are brief allusions, but those with more detail provide valuable insights as to how ancient Egypt was seen by the early Greek visitors; they are also remarkable for the accuracy of the statements they make about Egyptian civilisation.

The dialogue *Phaedrus* (274–275) puts into the mouth of Socrates a charming tale about the Egyptian god Thoth. It tells how Thoth invented mathematics, geometry and astronomy, and games such as draughts and dice. Oddly, his most important invention, writing, got a cool reception when Thoth presented it to Thamus (or Ammon), king of the gods. Thoth believed that writing would improve the wisdom and memory of the Egyptians, but Thamus said that the discovery was 'a receipt for recollection, not memory'. Thamus feared that writing would make the Egyptians lazy as they would no longer have to exercise their memories. The story was used by Socrates to illustrate his belief in the importance of memory.

There is nothing like this tale in surviving Egyptian literature. On the other hand, the circumstantial details provided by Plato are perfectly accurate. Thoth was indeed the Egyptian god of wisdom and, as Plato noted, the ibis was his sacred bird. The Egyptians knew him as the 'scribe of the gods' and the divine inventor of writing as well as the other arts and sciences. None of this is mentioned in Herodotus or other earlier writers – Plato was the first Greek to describe Thoth. He also correctly portrayed Ammon as king of the Egyptian gods (Amun), whose seat was at Thebes.

The most telling of all Plato's comments – with particular relevance to the Atlantis story – are those made in the *Laws* (656–657) about Egyptian art. Long ago, he says, the Egyptians realised that the forms of dance taught to children should be 'virtuous ones'. So they compiled a pictorial list of respectable dancing styles and exhibited them in their temples:

> No painter or artist is allowed to innovate upon them, or to leave the traditional forms and invent new ones. To this day, no alteration is allowed either in these arts, or in music at all. And you will find that their works of art are painted or moulded in the same forms which they had ten thousand years ago – this is literally true and no exaggeration. Their ancient paintings and sculptures are not a whit better or worse than the work of today, but are made with just the same skill.

Plato's observations on Egyptian art are impressive. Although the art of the Egyptians did change through time, they generally tried to avoid this. To the Egyptians the idea of progress would have seemed a strange one. Rather, they believed that truth (*ma'at*) and all other universal values were established by the gods at the beginning of time, and all history was a process of either lapsing from or returning to those standards. It was the pharaoh's duty to defend these values. During the Saite 26th Dynasty (665–525 BC), when the Greeks first began their intimate acquaintance with Egypt, there was a particular return to the arts and styles of the Old Kingdom (third millennium BC), and some Saite products really are indistinguishable from those made two thousand years earlier. The only problem with Plato's observation is his time-scale for Egyptian history, which in fact stretches back no more than three thousand years before his time. Yet in the *Laws* Plato talks of ten thousand years, equivalent to the nine thousand years of Egyptian civilisation referred to in the *Timaeus*.

As Luce remarked, Plato's observations on Egyptian life, religion, art, music and philosophy have a cumulative effect: they are so fresh and accurate that they are unlikely to be based on anything other than first-hand impressions.[6] Although some of his remarks, such as those about art, could have been made by viewing imported antiquities, it seems more likely that Plato did go to Egypt.[7]

This likelihood has suggested to some a different route for the Atlantis story. Luce, for example, argued that it was Plato himself that brought the story back.[8] The theory carries the natural rider that Plato invented a role for Solon as the story's transmitter. There are several problems with this idea. First, there is the evidence that Solon *did* visit Egypt.[9] If both Solon and Plato visited Egypt, on what grounds can Plato be preferred as the transmitter of the Atlantis story? Second, the theory accuses Plato of fabrication, and of implicating his great-grandfather Critias in the fraud. Finally, if Plato did hear the story himself in Egypt, why did he not simply state that he could corroborate its origins? The simplest answer is that, if he went to Egypt, he did not encounter the Atlantis motif there. Thus Luce's theory suffers from a number of faults and sheds no new light on the problem.

Does Plato's apparent inability to find the Atlantis story in Egypt blow his claims for an Egyptian origin? To be fair, the answer must be 'not entirely'. It is not hard to think of reasons why he failed to confirm the story for himself. Notably, Plato did not have Solon's rank as an Athenian head of state and may simply not have been able to obtain the same kind of interview with the Saite priests. However, this only reinforces the impression that the story was not widely known in Egypt. No-one else, for example Herodotus, mentions it, and the claimed independent witness, Crantor, is the result of misunderstanding of a difficult text.

Herodotus

Was the Atlantis story really known in Egypt at all? The material about Proto-Athens clearly was not. Then what of the details in the *Timaeus* and *Critias* concerning Egypt itself? There are actually serious grounds for believing that these are largely a pastiche drawn from the writings of Herodotus, rounded out with Plato's own observations on Egyptian culture. Many passages in Plato's writings show that he was well acquainted with Herodotus,[10] and n particular his description of Egypt. For example, the *Timaeus* (24B-C) describes the great emphasis that the Egyptians placed on traditional wisdom, 'deriving from the divine principles of cosmology everything they need for human life down to divination and medicine.' This clearly echoes Herodotus, who, after explaining that the Egyptians were the first to learn the art of divination from the gods, immediately turned to the subject of medicine.[11]

When the extraordinary claims about Egyptian history made by the Saite priests in the *Timaeus* are examined, the suspicion that Plato was borrowing from Herodotus shades into certainty. The story of the periodic and catastrophic changes in the heavens, which Plato says was told to Solon, reads extraordinarily like another passage from Herodotus. Egyptian priests, Herodotus says, told him that 11,340 years had elapsed since the time of the first pharaoh, during which time the world had undergone several enormous upheavals:

> During this period, they said, the sun changed its characteristic position four times, rising twice where it now sets and setting twice where it now rises. The people of Egypt were unaffected by this – nothing was different about the produce from the land or the river, nor was there any change in illnesses or deaths amongst them.[12]

This brief version in Herodotus contains the same three conspicuous elements as Plato's account – the great age of the Egyptian civilisation, the periodic changes in the heavens, and the survival of the Egyptians through these upheavals. The role of the Nile as saviour of the Egyptians is also stressed in both versions. The ostensibly great age of Egyptian civilisation is the background to all these claims: Herodotus' figure (11,340 years) is of the same order as those given by Plato (10,000 and 8,000 years). The condescending response supposedly given to Solon by the Egyptian priests, that 'all Greeks are children', is also paralleled in Herodotus, who relates that the earlier Greek visitor Hecataeus was derided when he told the priests of Thebes that he could trace his ancestry back sixteen generations.

The accounts in Herodotus' *History* and Plato's *Timaeus* are clearly two versions of the same story. In fact they are so close in all essential elements that it seems pointless to invoke the alternative – that somehow Solon was told exactly the same things in Egypt as were related to Herodotus a hundred years later. There is simply no need to involve Solon as the transmitter of any of the Egyptian material. It is far more likely that Plato simply modified the account he had read in Herodotus, confirmed and augmented by his own impressions of Egyptian culture.

Literary analysis can now account for two of the players in Plato's drama about Egypt, Athens and Atlantis: neither the Egyptian nor the Athenian material in the story came from Egypt via Solon. Where does this leave the all-important third figure of Atlantis?

The problems that arise from the idea that the Atlantis story came from Egypt have already been noted. If we accept the claim in the *Timaeus* that Atlantis was an older civilisation than Egypt, an impossible situation is reached. How could the Egyptians have had knowledge about a civilisation that preceded their own? Even supposing that they had preserved memory of it through the period when they were experimenting with hieroglyphic writing, why should they then have written it down? If it was a culture unconnected with their own, what would have been their motive?

Ancient Egyptian interest in foreign countries was fairly limited. Tales were told of foreign lands, but they always concerned Egyptian contact, such as the story of Sinuhe, which tells of an Egyptian official of the 12th Dynasty who, in about 1900 BC, went into voluntary exile in Palestine and Syria; he returned to relate his adventures in these strange foreign lands.[13] Yet such Egyptian descriptions of foreign countries are exceedingly cursory – restricted to brief descriptions of the local terrain, customs and resources which would be of interest to future travellers or conquerors. The idea of writing about the past of a foreign land – unless it concerned, for example, past diplomatic relations – is characteristically un-Egyptian. Even under the 26th Dynasty, when Egypt was beginning to look much further afield, nothing even touching on the history of other lands was written. Strictly speaking, this kind of history writing was only begun by the Greeks in the fifth century BC.

Yet Plato's account claims that Egyptian priests held detailed records of a war between Atlantis and Athens which had taken place thousands of years earlier – and that the same records provided detailed descriptions of the two lands and the societies they sustained. Even if it is allowed that the events took place within the span of Egyptian history, rather than before it, the whole mechanism of its transmission is utterly incredible.

The conclusion is rough – particularly for the traditional Atlantologists and the Minoan theorists, who share the same belief in the claim that the Atlantis narrative came from Egypt. It would be easy, as well, to conclude further that Plato's testimony is, after all, fraudulent and that as Egypt had nothing to do with the story's transmission, then neither did Solon. It would be a conclusion that would please sceptics and Plato's detractors. Before condemning Plato, however, there is another route that should be examined – one that has never actually been explored.

Let us suppose that Solon *was* the originator of the story as Plato claimed. Could the belief that he collected the tale in Egypt simply be based on a misunderstanding? As is known, Solon travelled elsewhere in the Mediterranean, including Cyprus and the kingdom of Lydia (in western Turkey), though the trip to Egypt was perhaps his most famous. It is possible that Solon picked up the story somewhere else on his travels, but that exactly where was forgotten by its guardians in the Critias family. If this were the case, it might have been assumed that the story came from Egypt. Respected for its antiquity by the Greeks, this would seem, in the absence of better information, to be the most likely source of a tale about remote prehistory. If Plato followed this assumption he might simply have added – from his own knowledge and reading of Herodotus – the required historical background to the story that Solon supposedly heard in Egypt. In this case Plato would be guilty of innocent over-restoration of his patchy source material, rather than outright fraud. While the possibility that Solon found the Atlantis story outside Egypt seems a long shot, it is worth asking where else he might have heard it. The search produces some surprising results.

'Glittering Scheria'

A source for the Atlantis motif much closer to home than Egypt was first suggested some three hundred years ago by the Swedish scholar Olof von Rudbeck (1630–1702).[14] The source is none other than Homer's epic, the *Odyssey*.

Homer relates how, near the end of his travels, Odysseus was shipwrecked on a magical island called Scheria, home to a happy and prosperous race known as the Phaeacians. Befriended by the princess Nausicaa, Odysseus spent a long time at the Phaeacian court, where he rewarded her father, King Alcinous, for his hospitality by relating his famous adventures. Another three books – there are twenty-four in all – are concerned with describing Odysseus' adventures among the Phaeacians themselves. Homer took obvious delight in detailing their customs – from their feasting to their games – and his account of their idyllic lifestyle rates as the world's earliest description of a utopian society.[15]

Homer's glittering island of Scheria comes second only to Atlantis for the range of geographical identifications suggested for it. While some ancient Greeks favoured Corfu, modern writers have located the Phaeacians in Crete, Tartessus (Spain), Heligoland (in the North Sea), Lanzarote (Canary Islands) and, most recently, Troy.[16] Where Homer really imagined it lay is a problem that has never been solved, and probably never can be. Homer's geography – outside of the Aegean – is notoriously vague. With the guidance of later Greek writers it is fairly safe to locate some of Odysseus' adventures – such as those with the Cyclops and the narrow scrape between Scylla and Charybdis – in the waters of the Central Mediterranean around Italy and Sicily. Beyond that, Homeric geography clearly belongs to the world of fantasy. Nothing adds up, particularly concerning the Phaeacians – all attempts, both ancient and modern, to pinpoint them have proved futile. Homer states that the Phaeacians were the remotest of all human beings, living at the very edge of the world. Yet at another point he says that a return trip from Scheria to Euboea, the largest island off the eastern coast of Greece, was made by Phaeacian sailors in a single day. When Homer adds that the Phaeacian sailors regarded Euboea as 'the world's end',[17] it immediately becomes clear that this is purely mythical geography. Eratosthenes, the Greek geographer of the third century BC, hit the right note when he said: 'Whoever would find the places Odysseus visited must first find the cobbler who made the leather bag where Aeolus kept the wind.'[18] (Aeolus, god of the winds, was encountered by Odysseus earlier in his adventures.)

All the same, the depiction of the Phaeacians as a utopian society living at the fringes of the world has naturally invited comparison with Atlantis. Since von Rudbeck's time many classical scholars have taken it as read that Homer's Phaeacians was an inspiration for Plato's Atlantis – possibly *the* major source of the story.[19]

There are indeed many comparisons to be made between Plato's lost kingdom and Homer's Scheria. Both were islands situated at the edge of the world. Both were blessed with luxuriant vegetation and a temperate climate. The royal gardens of both were watered by dual springs. The Phaeacians, like the Atlanteans, were a nation of sailors. The kings of Atlantis and Scheria alike claimed descent from the sea-god Poseidon, the only god named in the two accounts as having a temple in the capital. Bulls were sacrificed to this god by both Atlanteans and Phaeacians. And the Phaeacians, like the Atlanteans, were fabled for their wealth. This is how Homer described the royal palace of Alcinous:

> The brilliance within the high-ceilinged rooms of noble Alcinous was like the sheen of the sun or moon: for the inner walls were copper-plated in sections, from the entering in to the furthest recesses of the house; and the cornice which ran around them was glazed in blue. Gates of gold closed the great house: the door posts which stood up from the brazen threshold were of silver, and silver, too, was the lintel overhead: while the handle of the door was gold.[20]

The Atlantean use of precious metals as a building material certainly finds a parallel here. Is Plato's Atlantis, then, merely the glittering Scheria of Homer writ large?

Plato certainly borrowed much of the epic colour for his Atlantis creation from Homer's Scheria. This is only natural, but the comparisons cannot be pushed too far. If two writers from a similar culture want to describe a utopian civilisation they will certainly end up with many similarities. From the perspective of both Homer and Plato it was essential that a utopian society would be blessed with luxuriant vegetation, palaces of gold, everflowing fountains and the like. Most of what Plato apparently took from Homer's Scheria may even have been unconscious borrowing – most literate Greeks of his time would have had the words of the Poet impressed on their memories from the earliest age. None of the similarities between Scheria and Atlantis are so specific or peculiar that they could not have been gleaned from elsewhere (including Plato's own imagination) – although the cumulative effect may suggest Homer's influence.

The vast differences between Scheria and Atlantis must also be remembered. The most important elements in the Atlantis story are missing from Homer's account – the demi-god Atlas who is father to its dynasty of kings, the spiritual decline of the Atlanteans, the destruction of the island by earthquake and its sinking beneath the waves. Homer's Phaeacians remain close to the gods – and they did not, as far as we know, meet a catastrophic end. In the *Odyssey* the Phaeacians are punished by Poseidon for helping Odysseus go home: on its return, the ship they sent him in is turned to stone and rooted to the sea-bottom in view of the Phaeacian harbour. It is not stated whether Poseidon carried out his further threat of surrounding their city with a ring of mountains; the *Odyssey* leaves Scheria as Alcinous is conducting a sacrifice of twelve bulls to Poseidon to avert his wrath.[21] Even if we are to imagine that Poseidon did carry out the second part of his punishment, its intention was clearly to quarantine the Phaeacians from the rest of humanity so that they would cease being indiscriminately helpful to strangers – but *not* to destroy them. There is no parallel here to the disappearance of Atlantis beneath the waves.

Nor is Scheria anything like the aggressive empire of Atlantis. Homer's utopia is a place which barely has any contact with the rest of humanity, let alone armed warfare. Where are the enormous domains of Atlantis and its hordes of well-organised chariotry and infantry? (Homer says that the Phaeacians did not even possess bows and arrows.[22]) And where is the life-and-death struggle with a Greek nation that forms the introduction to the *Timaeus* and the centrepiece of the *Critias*?

As Vidal-Naquet rightly concluded, 'the parallelism does not explain everything – even if it ought certainly to figure in any discussion of Plato's relation to Homer.'[23] All that glitters is not gold, and glittering Scheria, while undoubtedly one of Plato's sources (conscious or otherwise) for some details employed in the Atlantis story, was not the source for its core elements.

Return of the Deluge

To pair the tale of the disastrous end met by prehistoric Athens, Plato would surely have used a story about a similar catastrophe. A folklorist appraising the Atlantis story would recognise in it a fairly common motif – the story of a kingdom submerged beneath the waves because of the sin or negligence of its inhabitants.[24] The Celts of Europe told – indeed still tell – a variety of stories woven around this theme, such as the famous tale of the lost land of Lyonesse off the coast of Cornwall.

There was no need for Plato – or his putative source Solon – to go as far as the Atlantic seaboard to discover a story with this motif. The Near East had its own flourishing tradition of deluge stories. In the familiar biblical version, the Flood was brought about by the sins of mankind. In the closely related tales from Mesopotamia, the motive behind the gods' sending of the flood-waters was somewhat different. One Babylonian version states that the gods were fed up with the racket that the human race was making: 'The land became wide, the people became numerous, the land bellowed like wild oxen . . . '[25] Disturbed by the din, the gods decided on the simple expedient of exterminating the human race. The Babylonian Deluge story dates back to at least the early second millennium BC and is a later version of a Sumerian tale already current in the third millennium BC.

The early Christian writer Cosmas Indikopleustes claimed that Plato's story of the ten Atlantean princes was merely a garbled version of the ten kings of Babylonian legend who ruled before the Flood (see Chapter 5). His comparison was wide of the mark: Plato wrote of ten kings ruling simultaneously, whereas the Babylonian rulers (like the ten generations from Adam to Noah) were a succession. Yet, despite the apparent crassness of Cosmas's theory, there may be some truth in his claim that the *Timaeus* was influenced by Babylonian thinking about the Deluge.

Plato's theory of historical catastrophism was based firmly on the testimony of tradition. His own people had long told tales of great cataclysms, from the clashes of the gods and Titans to the floods of Deucalion and Ogyges and the universal conflagration caused by Phaethon. By the fourth century BC, when Plato wrote, Greek philosophers had also been exposed to the rich traditions of the Near East, largely through the medium of the Persian Empire. It would seem unlikely that Plato had never come across the Babylonian Flood story – it is much more reasonable to suppose that he did, and that knowledge of Near Eastern traditions reinforced, or even inspired, his ideas that history had been interrupted by repeated catastrophes.

About 280 BC a Babylonian priest called Berossus wrote a history of his people in Greek, to reach the wider audience now provided by Alexander's unification of the Greek and Persian worlds. It was not a simple political history, but comprised, in Berossus' own words, 'the histories of heaven (and of earth) and sea and the first birth of the kings and their deeds'. In other words, it began with creation and cosmogony and included, according to the Roman writer Seneca, the following astrological theory of terrestrial catastrophes:

> Some suppose that in the final catastrophe the earth, too, will be shaken and through clefts in the ground will uncover sources of fresh rivers which will flow forth from their full source in larger volume. Berossus ... affirms that the whole issue is brought about by the course of the planets. So positive is he on the point that he assigns a definite date both for the conflagration and the deluge. All that the earth inherits will, he assures us, be consigned to flame when the planets, which now move in different orbits, all assemble in Cancer, so arranged in one row that a straight line may pass through their spheres. When the same gathering takes place in Capricorn, then we are in danger of the deluge.[26]

This passage in Berossus has been the subject of heated controversy. The way 'the deluge' and 'the conflagration' are referred to as both past and future (almost timeless) events clearly suggests a cyclical theory of star-spawned catastrophes, very close to that taught by Plato and the Stoic philosophers that followed him. They set great store by the concept of the 'Great Year', when all the cycles of the Sun, Moon and stars are completed and the heavenly bodies return to their original positions.

So did Babylonian science affect Plato, or did Greek philosophy influence Berossus on this point? The fact that Berossus was supposed to have settled, later in life, on the Aegean island of Cos has reinforced the suspicion that he was drawing on Greek ideas. Further, some scholars have argued that the astrological material attributed to Berossus (including the above passage) was actually written by a later, even more hellenised writer, who is referred to as 'pseudo-Berossus'.[27] This extreme view ignores the fact that the ancient Mesopotamians were obsessively interested in the effect of the stars on our history, as thousands of cuneiform tablets recording the configuration of the heavens attest. Babylonian astrologers believed that similar events would occur under the same planetary influences. Naturally they were interested in planetary cycles and by early Persian times they had already determined with reasonable accuracy the cycles of all the planets except Mercury.[28] Surely Babylonian astrologers would have been tempted to experiment with the predictive powers of longer-term cycles. While Berossus' theory of the recurrence of catastrophes after a given astronomical cycle (or 'Great Year') is not explicitly stated in cuneiform texts, it has all the hallmarks of Babylonian speculation. As Drews put it: 'There is to date no evidence that the Great Year originated in Greek philosophy, and so no reason why it should be denied to the scholars of Babylon.'[29]

Disappearing Islands

Plato cast his net widely. When he developed his theory of periodic catastrophes he clearly drew on the Egyptian story reported by Herodotus that the Sun had changed its course in the heavens several times, sometimes rising in the east and sometimes in the west. He also seems to have drawn on the Babylonian idea that the world suffered catastrophes when there was a particular configuration of the stars. Given this, could Babylonian ideas have provided anything closer to the Atlantis motif than the general idea of a universal deluge?

A Babylonian story that has some of the right ingredients is the legend of Dilmun.[30] This was an island paradise in the Persian Gulf especially loved by Enki (or Ea), god of the sweet waters. On Dilmun, Enki mated with the goddess Ninhursag – just as Poseidon did with Cleito on the primeval island of Atlantis – and they spawned a number of minor gods. There, however, the similarity to Plato's story ends. Far from being destroyed by the gods, Dilmun remained divinely blessed. It eventually drifted into history as a key point on the trade route between Mesopotamia and India, and is now known as Bahrain. Far from being destroyed in the universal deluge, Dilmun actually became the home of Utnapishtim, the Babylonian Noah, after he was granted immortality by the gods.

For an island paradise which did disappear, the Egyptians can do slightly better. An ancient Egyptian novelette, now known as *The Tale of the Shipwrecked Sailor*, comes very close in terms of genre to the yarns told about Sindbad the Sailor in *The Arabian Nights*. The hero of the story is an Egyptian courtier sent by the pharaoh to inspect his mining interests overseas. When his ship was wrecked by a storm, the courtier was the sole survivor, thrown up by the waves on a mysterious island blessed with fish, birds and 'all sorts of excellent vegetables'. The courtier survived there quite happily for some days until, 'with a noise like thunder', a giant snake appeared, announcing itself as king of the island, called Punt. He guaranteed the courtier safe passage home, then uttered a strange prophecy: 'It will happen that when you depart from this place, this island will never be seen again, for it will become water.'[31] The shipwrecked sailor returned home safely to tell his tale.

The usual assumption is that the island paradise ruled by the serpent-king disappeared beneath the waves after the Egyptian traveller left, suggesting to some that the Egyptians did, after all, tell stories of lost lands like Atlantis.[32] This possibility is a mixed blessing for the Minoan theorists. It is crucial to their theory that the story was learnt by Solon in Egypt, but they cannot use the *Shipwrecked Sailor* to support their arguments as it was written during the Twelfth Dynasty (*c.* 1930–1750 BC), long before the explosion of Thera on any dating.

What nobody seems to have analysed is whether the *Shipwrecked Sailor* does in fact describe the submergence of an island. The story does not say that the island sank, only that the serpent-king predicted that it would 'never be seen again, for it will become water'. What did he mean? Knowledge of ancient Egyptian is not so precise that we can be absolutely sure of the meaning of such a vague expression. The serpent-king may have meant that the island would vanish into thin air, as things can do in fairy stories, or that it would simply drift away – leaving only water. As a folk-tale concept, the idea of the 'floating island' was not unknown to the Egyptians.[33] The name of the serpent-king's island is also significant. He called it Punt, which is the name of a spice-rich area on the eastern coast of Africa well known in Egyptian texts from the Old Kingdom (third millennium BC) to the Saite period (seventh century BC).[34]

The point is that no Egyptian could have believed that Punt

had disappeared hundreds of years ago. So the idea that a Greek visitor such as Solon might have been told the *Tale of the Shipwrecked Sailor* with an ending in which the 'island' of Punt sank beneath the waves can be safely ruled out. It was not the source of the Atlantis story.

The upshot is that nothing has been found from Greece, the Near East or Egypt that compares to the Atlantis story. Tales with similar motifs are known, but none provides the right combination. It might be argued that a combination of motifs from a number of stories would provide practically all the ingredients of Plato's Atlantis: a pastiche of Herodotus' Egyptian history with a dash of Babylonian astrology and flood legends, blended with images from Near Eastern tales of island paradises and Homer's wonderful Phaeacians, garnished with political overtones of the Persian and Peloponnesian Wars and a soupçon of Greek myth. It is an interesting melange. All these ingredients may well have been employed by Plato. Yet it would be much more satisfying if we could find something with *all* the important elements in one tale, to which we could confidently point and say, *this* must have been Plato's source.

If Plato had such a source, the only way to trace it is to follow something far more diagnostic and far more particular to his story than generalised motifs such as flood stories and paradisical islands – common material for storytellers in the ancient world. The rich literature and folklore of Egypt certainly cannot provide an answer to the 'missing' source of Plato, if indeed there was one. The key to the whole problem has been staring mythologists in the face since the story was written, but has been strangely overlooked. Strangely, because it concerns a well-known figure of Greek myth – Atlas, the eponym and first king of Atlantis.

PART THREE: TANTALIS

CHAPTER 8

In Search of Atlas

When Gerard Mercator, in the late sixteenth century, decided to use Atlas holding the globe as the frontispiece for a collection of maps, he turned him into one of the most enduring images of the classical world. Ever since, cartography books have been called atlases. Yet despite his familiarity as an icon, Atlas remains a little-studied and enigmatic figure.[1] Who was he?

Plato calls him the first king of Atlantis and the son of Poseidon. Greek myth reckoned the sea-god to be the father of a host of wayward giants (including the Cyclops killed by Odysseus),[2] so Poseidon would not make an unlikely parent for the colossal Atlas. Yet the poets reckoned Atlas to be one of the Titans, the race which ruled the world before the Olympians were even born. Atlas was usually ranked with the second generation of Titans, as the son of Cronus' brother Iapetus (see Fig. 11).

In the sons of Iapetus we encounter the most colourful branch of the Titan race. Whereas some of the earlier Titans were faceless abstractions – such as Themis ('Justice') and Metis ('Thought') – each of Iapetus' sons has his own story. Atlas' most famous brother was Prometheus, whose name means 'Forethought'. Having fore-seen the downfall of the Titan race, Prometheus became, for a while, an ally of Zeus and the Olympians. He is best known, however, as the friend and patron of the human race, and later Greek writers even said that Prometheus created men from clay. Eventually Prometheus took the part of his protégés against the jealous Olympians. He stole fire from heaven and gave it to mankind. For this crime, Zeus punished Prometheus by staking him out on the Caucasus mountains (at the eastern end of the Greek world). Here his liver was pecked out by an eagle, but because Prometheus was immortal it grew back each night and was pecked out again, leaving him in agony for thousands of years until Heracles slew the eagle and released him.

To punish mankind for their part in the theft of fire, Zeus created the first woman, Pandora. He presented her to Prometheus' brother, the muddle-headed Epimetheus ('Afterthought'), who ignored his brother's warning not to take gifts from Zeus. Pandora arrived at Epimetheus' house with a jar – her famous 'box' – filled by Zeus with every conceivable evil. When she opened it, she unleashed all the ills of the world. In so doing Pandora was the Greek equivalent of the biblical Eve, similarly portrayed by the (presumably male) creators of Hebrew tradition as the woman responsible for the wretchedness of the human condition.[3]

Surprisingly, Prometheus – the saviour of mankind – was never worshipped in temples of his own, perhaps because the Greeks feared they would once again incur the wrath of Zeus. Yet the Greeks claimed descent from him. They believed they were all descendants of Prometheus' son Deucalion, who had survived the Flood thanks to his father's warning.

The counterparts of Prometheus and Epimetheus, awkward allies of the Olympians, were Iapetus' other two sons, Atlas and Menoetius. They were outright rebels against the new order and were punished accordingly. Menoetius was struck down in battle by Zeus' thunderbolt,[4] while Atlas, war-leader of the Titans,[5] was singled out for a more special punishment. He was

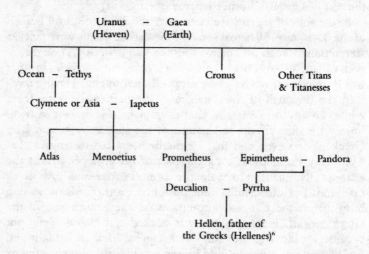

FIG. 11   The family of Iapetus.

banished to the ends of the earth and condemned to hold up the sky for all eternity.

There were conflicting views on the location of Atlas' punishment. Some placed him in the extreme north, in the land of the people known as the Hyperboreans ('Beyond-the-north-winders').[7] Hesiod said he stood in the deepest part of the underworld (Tartarus), but also located him at the 'borders of the earth':[8] perhaps he pictured him as being so colossal that while his feet rested in the underworld he also loomed the very edge of the Earth's disc. The most common, and it seems the oldest, location for Atlas' punishment was at the remote western edge of the world. Our earliest sources, Pindar and Herodotus, are from the fifth century BC,[9] but the idea may have been current as early as Homer. During his wanderings Odysseus was stranded for seven years on Ogygia, the island of Calypso, which, in the broad outlines of the *Odyssey*'s sketchy geography, might have lain in the Atlantic: 'This wave-beset, wooded island is the domain of a God-begotten creature [Calypso], the daughter of baleful Atlas whose are the pillars that prop the lofty sky: whose too are the deepest soundings of the sea.'[10] The Atlantic would be a good place for Homer's wizard-like Atlas who 'knows the sea in all its depths.'

The western location for Atlas eventually became the standard view. Here, near the Atlantic coast of western Morocco, lay the majestic mountain (or rather range of mountains) known by the Greeks as Mount Atlas. According to one tradition Atlas was transformed into the mountain when Perseus showed him the deadly Gorgon's head.[11] Pomponius Mela, a Roman geographer from Tingentera (near Gibraltar), gives a beautiful account of this mountain region, showing why it was thought such a fitting place for the pillar of heaven:

> In the midst of the sandy region is Mount Atlas, rearing its enormous mass, steep and inaccessible by reason of the sharp-pointed rocks that surround it on all sides: the higher it gets, the more it diminishes in size; its summit is higher than the eye can reach: it loses itself in the clouds; also it is fabled not only to touch with its top the sky and the stars, but even to support them.[12]

Though it was natural enough for the Greeks to place the sky-supporting Atlas at such an imposing site, there remains a conundrum of fundamental importance to the Atlantis question. Was the Titan named after the mountain or the mountain after the Titan? It has been argued that the Atlas Mountains took their name not from the Greek, but from the word *adrar*, which in the language of the native Berbers of North Africa means 'mountain'. That a local word was the origin of 'Atlas' seems to be supported by Herodotus, who says that a Libyan tribe called the 'Atarantes', or 'Atlantes', lived around a mountain which they called 'the Pillar of the Sky'.[13]

At first glance it might seem reasonable that the names of the tribe, the mountain, and even Atlas himself, were derived from the Berber *adrar*. The problem is that there is a respectable etymology for Atlas in the Greek root *tlaô*, meaning 'to bear, to endure' or 'to dare'. And, as Martin Bernal pointed out in 1991, the Berber people actually called Mount Atlas not *adrar* (a word attested only since the nineteenth century) but Deren or Durin. (Strabo and Pliny call the mountain Duris.)[14] The Berber word *adrar* could even be borrowed from the Greek Atlas, rather than the other way around; it may have been adopted, for example, during Roman times, when the area was part of the province of Mauretania.

At the very most, when the Greeks first arrived in Morocco they found the locals using a word for mountain (*adrar*) with a similar ring to Atlas, which inspired them to christen it after their mythical giant.[15] Rather than the Titan being named after a local Berber word, it seems that the Greeks named the mountain, the tribe and, of course, the Atlantic Ocean, after they had decided to locate the legendary Atlas in this region – sometime after the seventh century BC when they became familiar with north-western Africa on a first-hand basis. This is an important point for Atlantis research. If Plato had a genuine source at his disposal connecting Atlas with a lost kingdom, it does not automatically point us in an Atlantic direction. Where, then, was Atlas located before he was removed to north-west Africa?

Atlas' role as the world pillar – in north-western Africa or elsewhere – was of course only at the end of his career, when he had been expelled to the fringes of the world by the Olympians. Before this, as one of the Titans, he must have held sway over part of the known world. (Cronus, for example, was particularly associated with Italy and the central Mediterranean.[16]) Myth, confusing as it can be in the way it freely transposes elements in time and space, can still have its own internal logic. If Atlas was banished to the west he must have been expelled from somewhere. Indeed, the Sicilian poet Pindar (early fifth century BC) explicitly states this. Referring to Atlas' punishment in the west, he wrote that 'the famous Atlas indeed is still bearing up against heaven's weight, *banished from his ancestral lands and possessions*'.[17]

The Isles of the Blest

A number of sources help to reconstruct Atlas' mythical career before he was banished. At Tanagra in Boeotia (central Greece) he was said to have sat at a place called 'the Pole' (*Polos*), where he contemplated the heavens and the underworld.[18] He was also especially associated with Arcadia, the mountainous wooded country in the centre of the Peloponnese. Here, his wife Pleione bore him seven daughters, the Pleiades (who later became a constellation).[19] According to one account, Atlas once ruled as King of Arcadia, where his grandson Dardanus succeeded him. Dardanus ruled there for a while with his sons, until they were separated by a flood; he then went to Anatolia where he founded a new dynasty at Troy, descendants of the Pleiad Electra.[20] Atlas' other daughters married into, or gave rise to, a number of important mythological dynasties – at Thebes, Olympia (or Lesbos), Sparta and Corinth (see Appendix 1).

The romantic alliances and descendants of the Pleiades were the subject of a book by the historian Hellanicus, who was born on Lesbos in about 500 BC. The name used by Hellanicus for the project is rather surprising: *Atlantis*. The title does not mean what it might seem at first glance. 'Atlantis' can mean simply 'daughter of Atlas', and this was clearly the intention of Hellanicus who wrote similar genealogical guides for the descendants of other famous mythological daughters. However, the interest of the *Atlantis* does not end there. Hellanicus wrote before Plato and his work could have provided some information – not only for its title but for one of its themes. A fragment of the *Atlantis*, discovered among the papyri from Oxyrhynchus in Egypt, gives part of a list of Atlantid descendants and includes this line: 'Poseidon mated with Celaeno [daughter of Atlas], and their son Lycus was settled by his father in the Isles of the Blest and made immortal.'[21]

These lines inevitably evoke Plato's account of the founding of

Atlantis – where Poseidon mates with Cleito and their son Atlas (together with his brothers) becomes ruler of a marvellous island. The Isles of the Blest, where Lycus settled, was an otherworldly place where select heroes were taken by the gods to live as immortals. They were usually thought to lie beyond the western edge of the world,[22] which might be seen as a parallel to Plato's location of Atlantis. Things are not always that straightforward in Greek myth, however, and there were other candidates for the location of the Isles of the Blest much closer to the centre of the Greek world. The mythical ruler of the Isles of the Blest was Rhadamanthus, who in his mortal lifetime was a Cretan ruler with an empire including many of the coasts and islands of Asia Minor (Turkey).[23] Strangely enough, Isles of the Blest occur twice in the area of his earthly domains. One of the names for Crete was the 'Blessed Isle',[24] while Diodorus says that 'Isles of the Blest' (*macarôn nêsoi*) was used for the string of islands along the Aegean coast of Turkey, including Lesbos, Chios, Samos and Rhodes. They took their name either from King Macareus ('Blessed') of Lesbos, or from the mildness of their climate and richness of their soil.[25] Interestingly enough, Diodorus connects these eastern 'Isles of the Blest' with deluge stories: he states that seven generations after Deucalion's Flood another flood devastated the region, particularly the mainland of Asia Minor opposite. The islands recovered more quickly, and, being envied by their neighbours, acquired the name of 'Blest'.

Diodorus must have been using traditions collected from the 'East Greeks' of the islands and coasts of Asia Minor. Was Hellanicus, when he wrote of Lycus, son of Poseidon, drawing on the same material? After all he came from the island of Lesbos himself. His character Lycus reappears in Diodorus as one of a group of wizards from another island, Rhodes, where they were believed to have acted as tutors of the young god Poseidon. When the Flood came, Lycus fled the island and moved to the mainland to found the kingdom of Lycia.[26]

These traditions provide a perfect illustration of the kaleidoscope effect in Greek myth, with the same elements and names (Poseidon, Lycus, Isles of the Blest and the Flood) reshuffled into a number of different configurations. The geographical locations show we are dealing with a little-known complex of East Greek stories and suggest that the 'Isles of the Blest' where Lycus, grandson of Atlas settled were the Aegean islands off Turkey rather than in the far west. A second connection with these islands comes from another grandson of Atlas – Oenomaus, according to some, the king of Lesbos.[27] When we remember that a third grandson, Dardanus, was the founder of Troy, the impression grows that there was a special interest in Atlas among the Greeks of the coast and islands of Asia Minor. Indeed, the family of Atlas seem to have been especially connected with this region.

His father Iapetus somehow crept into the Bible in the guise of one of Noah's sons, Japheth, who was the father of the Ionian Greeks and a number of other, mainly Anatolian, peoples.[28] Iapetus was remembered as an ancestor in Cilicia in south-eastern Anatolia, where Atlas' sister Anchiale was said to have founded two cities.[29] Iapetus' wife, Atlas' mother, was even called 'Asia'.[30] Asia was originally a geographical term for the kingdom of Lydia on the Aegean coast of Turkey. It was later applied by the Romans to Anatolia as a whole, and it was from here, 'Asia Minor', that the whole continent eventually took its name. These explicit connections strongly suggest that the 'ancestral lands' of Atlas mentioned by Pindar were thought to be in Anatolia (Asia Minor).

The search for Atlas as a king has brought us to the east rather than the west, which was merely his place of banishment. What do the myths mean? Are they simply trying to say that the Greeks learnt the curious idea of a giant who supports the skies from Anatolia? As it happens, the mythology of the Hittites of ancient Turkey provides explicit parallels to the Greek concept of Atlas. This should really be no surprise. It has long been known that much of Greek myth and religion, if it was not directly borrowed from the ancient peoples of Anatolia, certainly shared a common ancestry.

A Hittite Theogony

The awesome struggles of the Titans and Olympians for control of the universe described in Hesiod's *Theogony* are so closely paralleled in Hittite texts that they are undeniably the same stories, seen through different cultural filters. The discovery of these texts, first published in the 1940s, meant that Greek myth could no longer be discussed in a vacuum. In the words of a leading mythologist, Joseph Fontenrose, it was no longer possible 'to deny ... any genetic relation between Greek and Asiatic mythologies'.[31]

Like Hesiod's, the Hittite version is concerned with the succession of divine rulers over the universe.[32] First Alalus was king in heaven, but he was deposed by his cupbearer Anus and 'went down to the dark earth'. Anus took the throne of heaven, but after nine years his servant, the crafty Kumarbis, rebelled and Anus was driven before him 'like a bird'. Kumarbis seized his feet and dragged him from the sky, biting off his genitals and swallowing them. Anus hid himself in heaven and Kumarbis became king, but the awesome mouthful he had swallowed was to be his downfall. He was now pregnant with three 'terrible' gods: the Storm-god Teshub, the River Aranzakh (Tigris) and Teshub's minion, Tasmisus.

What happened next is unclear from the broken text. Kumarbis spat out something and a god sprang from the ground. Meanwhile the Storm-god inside him was being coached by Anus to rebel against Kumarbis. In an effort to subdue the new forces growing around him, Kumarbis tries to devour one of his sons – presumably the god he spat out. The story ends when the Storm-god escapes from Kumarbis' body. With the help of his brothers he defeats Kumarbis and seizes power.

The structure and even the characters can be recognised in Greek myth. Alalus is matched by the Greek figure Chaos. The Sky-god Anus plays the same role as the similarly named Greek god Uranus ('Heaven'), who was also emasculated by his successor (Cronus). In both accounts, new gods appear when the earth or sea is fertilised by the semen of the sky god. Kumarbis and Cronus are conspicuously similar gods, associated with agriculture and renowned for their wisdom, and they were both deposed by new deities that grew inside them. In both cases the three new gods were led by the Storm-god – the Hittite Teshub or the Greek lord of thunder Zeus – who becomes the present ruler of the universe.[33]

The Hittite texts were written in the thirteenth century BC, on the generally accepted dating system, and certainly no later than the tenth century BC on a revised scheme. In any case, they predate Hesiod's *Theogony* by at least two centuries. This in itself does not show Greek borrowing from the Hittites, for it is a mistake to assume that the earliest recorded version of a myth is necessarily the oldest, and therefore the 'original'; both versions could have been drawn from a common source, namely a shared Indo-European tradition. This is not the case with the 'Hittite

Theogony', where the names of the gods are not Indo-European. They were actually names taken from the eastern neighbours of the Hittites, an enigmatic but highly influential people called the Hurrians, who occupied a broad swathe of territory through northern Mesopotamia, eastern Anatolia and northern Syria. The Hurrian origin of the story explains the inclusion of the River Tigris (not in Hittite territory) and, more important, the character Anus, oldest god of heaven. He is immediately recognisable as the Mesopotamian Sky-god Anu, known already in the earliest Sumerian texts from around 3000 BC. The Hurrians became acquainted with Anu in northern Mesopotamia and then he was borrowed by the Hittites. During the second millennium BC a whole panoply of Hurrian religious elements – myths, the names of gods, their iconography – was officially adopted by the Hittite Empire.

All this scuppers the idea that Hesiod and the Hittites borrowed from a common Indo-European source, strongly suggesting that the Greeks leant heavily on Anatolian inspiration for their myth of the divine succession. This is generally agreed: what is debated is where, when and exactly how much.[34] Given that even the Greek name for Heaven, Ouranos (latinised Uranus), seems to have been derived from the Sumerian Anu (via Hurrian Anus), one can only accept that the mythological debt of the Greeks to the ancient peoples of Anatolia was enormous. And the more the Hurrian myths are investigated, the more similarities appear.

The Hittite Atlas

In a sequel to the Hittite story of the divine succession there is a perfect analogy to the classical Atlas. There were many struggles between the Storm-god and the party of Kumarbis, as there were between Zeus and the Titans and Giants. One attempt made by Kumarbis to overthrow the new gods involved the creation of a superbeing called Ullikummis. Made of diorite (a hard stone), Ullikummis grew at an alarming rate – a cubit a day and an acre every month – and at his birth Kumarbis placed him on the shoulder of Ubelleris, a primeval figure who holds up both the sky and the earth. Ubelleris is so colossal that he is oblivious to most of the world's events. These are Ubelleris' words, from a dialogue between him and the god Ea:

When they built heaven and earth upon me I did not know anything. When they came and severed the heaven from the earth with a cleaver, I did not know that either. Now my right shoulder is a little sore. But I do not know who that god is.[35]

Here, unmistakably, is the Hurrian/Hittite Atlas. Like Ubelleris, Atlas belonged to a race that preceded the present rulers of the universe. Atlas was sometimes said, like Ubelleris, to hold not just the sky, but the entire world – as he is still pictured today.[36] And, just as Hesiod's Atlas stands at the House of Night in Tartarus, so Ubelleris' feet rest on the 'dark earth', the Hittite underworld. The two are even characterised in a similar way. Ubelleris' unawareness of events happening around him, even those on a cosmic scale, suggests a slow-wittedness paralleled in the Greek tale of Heracles and the apples of the Hesperides. Heracles tricked Atlas into collecting the apples by offering to take over the burden of supporting the sky. Atlas fetched the apples and was about to take them off to Mycenae himself when Heracles asked him to take over the sky again for a moment while he padded his head with a cushion. Atlas was taken in and Heracles made off with the apples.[37]

The Rebel Mountains

The literary evidence for Ubelleris is unfortunately restricted to this one story, but there is more to learn from the rich iconography of Hittite art. Ubelleris seems to have been conceived as a cosmic mountain, upon whose shoulders the universe rested. As it happens, such an Atlas-like figure was one of the most popular motifs of Hittite art during the Late Bronze Age (15th–13th centuries BC).

In the same way that Atlas became a favourite motif in Greek and Roman art – as a support for anything from a roof to a candle – there are scores of Hittite depictions of similar 'supporting' deities, or *atlantes*. They fall into two groups. One kind is the bull-man, a semi-human figure with a bull's head and cloven hoofs instead of hands and feet. The second kind is the mountain god, depicted with a lumpy skirt representing stony slopes, and crowned with a helmet with multiple horns (a sign of divinity in the ancient Near East).[38]

The bull-men are almost always depicted with their arms raised, supporting an enormous burden. The clearest example of their function comes from the extraordinary rock sanctuary at Yazilikaya (near Boghazköy), completed by the Hittites in the thirteenth century BC. Here, on the inner faces of a natural rock gallery, the Hittites carved images of the entire Hittite/Hurrian pantheon – the frieze probably shows the gods, young and old, friend and enemy alike, gathered to celebrate New Year's day with the Storm-god.[39] The figures include the two bull-men whose job was to keep heaven and earth apart: above their heads they hold the Hittite hieroglyph for 'heaven', while their feet rest on the hieroglyph for 'earth'.[40] Further along the line a group of six mountain-gods appear, hands raised in pugilistic fashion. On this occasion they are shown as free agents. More often they appear in Hittite art with arms raised to support the sky, or in the attitude shown at the very centre of the main Yazilikaya frieze: here, facing his queen, the goddess Hepat, stands the Storm-god Teshub, his feet planted on the bowed backs of two subservient mountain gods.

FIG. 12 Hittite rock drawing from Imamkülü in eastern Turkey (*after Frankfort 1969*).

Hittite artists were often not content with one set of *atlantes*. On a rock carving at Imamkülü in eastern Turkey, a row of three men carry on their raised arms three mountain gods, who in turn support on their bowed shoulders the Storm-god and his bull-drawn chariot.[41] On a rare Hittite ivory found at Megiddo in Palestine, all the degrees of heaven are depicted in a heap of *atlantes* arranged like an RAF motorcyclists' display (see Fig. 13).[42]

These pieces show the Hittite use of *atlantes* on a small scale. At Eflatun Pinar in central Turkey they can be seen on a monumental scale (see Fig. 14). Here a number of large stone blocks were placed together near a spring as the plinth for two enormous

statues of gods. The façade shows two layers of bull-men supporting winged sun discs over smaller images of the gods. Above and
around them another double layer of bull-men support another
sun-disc canopy. (The Turkish name for the site means, curiously
enough, the Spring of Plato! The reason is unknown.)

Suffice it to say that the Atlas-figure was a common feature of
Hittite art, from monumental sculpture to the fine, miniature
work on seal-stones. Both kinds, bull and human, ultimately
represent mountains,[43] but it is the human-shaped mountain-gods

FIG. 13   Hittite ivory plaque discovered at Megiddo in Palestine. At the top two
figures of the Sun-god stand in heaven, with winged canopies held over their heads
by demons. They are supported by three rows of *atlantes*, including bull-men,
mountain-gods and sphinxes, who stand in turn on a row of bulls. At the very
bottom is the earth (*after Loud 1939*).

who are of most mythological interest here. Of these the holy
mountain called Tudhaliyas was of particular importance. He gave
his name to a succession of Hittite Emperors (Tudhaliyas I to IV),

who incorporated the signs for 'mountain' and 'god' in their royal insignia (*aedicula*). One seal of Tudhaliyas IV (late thirteenth century BC) gives a more elaborate version of the king's name, in which these signs are replaced by a detailed image of the mountain-god Tudhaliyas, wearing the triple-horned crown and scaly skirt and brandishing a mace. As Maurits van Loon notes, this seal depicts Tudhaliyas as 'privileged among mountain gods in being armed and free to move his feet.'[44] Textual confirmation comes from a Hittite ritual for the building of a new palace, in which the king repeatedly invokes him (together with four other named mountains) not to come and interfere in the ceremonies: 'Mount Tudhaliyas, stay in thy place!'[45]

FIG. 14   The Hittite monument at Eflatun Pinar. It now stands in water from a nearby spring, which probably formed a focal point of a local religious cult (*from Perrot & Chipiez 1890b*).

The overall picture given of these Hittite mountain-gods is of an order of older deities, subdued by the new gods but always hovering in the background as potential trouble-makers. Van Loon suggests this is why the mountain-gods in Hittite iconography are frequently depicted with raised fists like a boxer. He interprets these figures as 'vanquished champions of the older generation of gods, their former aggressiveness (or perhaps their present submission?) indicated by the raised fists, and their defeat and punishment by their bent caps.'[46] We are inescapably reminded of the Greek Titans and their relatives the Giants, last representatives of the pre-Olympian regime, whom the myths often represent as being changed into or held in place by mountains.[47] Even though he had been transformed into a mountain, the rebellious warrior Atlas was still capable of walking about (at least when Heracles temporarily released him).

It may seem strange to ask where the Greeks got the idea of Atlas from. Atlas as we know him is a peculiar product of the classical world. Whatever sources we found for this concept (or any other), they do not downgrade the contribution of the Greeks (and Romans) who, through their art and literature, transformed Atlas into an immortal icon. But everything starts somewhere, and the Greeks themselves were keen to acknowledge the debt they owed, particularly in religious matters, to their Eastern Mediterranean neighbours. Many cultures, of course, may have independently arrived at the concept of the skies being supported by an anthropoid figure. For example, a rock painting from Scandinavia, from around 1000 BC, shows an Atlas-type figure carrying a sun disc above his head.[48] The Egyptians also believed in a god called Shu, the air personified, who bodily separated his parents Nut (the Sky) and Geb (the Earth).[49] In the case of the Hittite *atlantes*, the sheer weight of the detailed similarities – both literary and iconographical – demonstrate an organic relationship with the Greek concept of Atlas. It only remains to note that the Anatolian icon of a figure supporting the sky or sun-disc has antecedents in Hurrian art of the early second millennium – notably from the seals of the Hurrian kingdom of Mitanni of northern Mesopotamia.[50] The iconography, like the stories of 'Kingship in Heaven' and Ubelleris, seems to have travelled from east to west. In the absence of contrary evidence, we have to see the Greeks, at least in this respect, as being on the receiving end of the line.

The Trojan Connection

Nothing conclusive has ever been offered to link either Atlantis or Atlas with Egypt. Instead, there is a mass of evidence which points a mythological finger away from Egypt and towards Anatolia as the home of the Atlas concept. There is literary evidence (the giant Ubelleris), an amazingly rich seam of iconographic material, and statements by Greek mythographers which specifically link Atlas's family with Anatolia. If the idea of Atlas himself came from Anatolia, maybe the story of his sunken kingdom also came from that region . . . ?

At this point in my research a book appeared which did require an Anatolian background for the Atlantis tale – though ironically the author stuck to Plato's understanding that the story came from Egypt. This is Bernhard Zangger's *The Flood from Heaven*, published in 1993. Zangger is the geoarchaeologist who discovered the dramatic evidence at Tiryns showing that a large-scale catastrophe struck the Mycenaean world. Recognising that this upheaval was reflected in Plato's story of Proto-Athens, Zangger was prompted to go further. Plato said that Proto-Athens was destroyed by earthquake and flood at a time when it was at war with Atlantis. Surely then, Zangger reasoned, Atlantis must be the same as the great enemy of Mycenaean Greece – Troy. The Trojan War, if it was indeed a real event, must have taken place near the end of the LHIIIB period – about the time of Zangger's Tirynthian flood and some of the other Mycenaean disasters.[51]

Zangger believes that news of the Trojan War and the catastrophes that followed in Greece could have reached Egypt as they were happening. He also suggests that some Greeks, in the period of wanderings as they returned home from the war, actually settled in Sais.[52] Memories of the Mycenaean and Trojan civilisations were then blended into a narrative account by the priests of Sais, who preserved it down to the time of Solon. In short, the story of Atlantis was an Egyptian version of the tale of the Trojan War.

Zangger's hypothesis is an interesting mish-mash of good points and bad. Of the good points none, however, is conclusive. Troy in its heyday was certainly a magnificent and wealthy city, famous for its mighty fortifications – fitting the more general requirements for the Royal City of Atlantis. While it cannot be credited with an overseas empire as such, Troy may have held sway over a larger area than the immediate vicinity of the 'Troad' and would certainly have controlled sea traffic and trade between the Aegean and the Black Sea. Near Troy were two springs, described by Homer: 'In one of these the water came up hot; steam rises from it and hangs about like smoke above a blazing fire, but the other, even in summer, gushes up as cold as hail or freezing snow or water that has turned to ice.'[53] These are reminiscent of the hot and cold springs of Atlantis mentioned by Plato, except that the Atlantean ones were inside the Royal Metropolis, whereas Homer's springs were the 'sources of Scamander's eddying stream', a point some way outside the city. The general landscape of Troy also bears some resemblance to the Atlantean Royal City, located by Plato fifty stades from the coast on a 'mountain that was low on all sides' amidst a fertile plain. The mound of Troy lies in a plain and is situated fifty stades (or nine kilometres) from the nearest natural harbour on the coast.

Such parallels make a plausible case but are far too generalised. Many ancient cities were founded on hills for defence purposes. There were also obvious advantages to locating one's city near the sea (but not too close because of pirate raids), on a fertile plain and with access to secure water supplies such as springs. Together such points merely confirm that Troy, as ancient cities went, was extremely well situated – the reason why it thrived for some three thousand years. Of course Plato's Atlantean Metropolis shares features with many successful ancient cities. Plato studied these matters for the perfect society he was planning in the *Laws*, and fully understood the importance of a city's geographical setting. He also knew his Homer, and Zangger would be hard-pressed to prove that superficial resemblances between Troy and the Royal City of Atlantis did not come directly from the *Iliad* and the *Odyssey*, rather than having taken an immensely roundabout route via Egypt and Solon.

Among Zangger's stronger arguments, one of the best is that the mythical genealogies counted the royal house of Troy as descendants of Atlas (see Appendix 1). On the other hand, as has been noted, several other dynasties claimed descent from him – both on the Greek mainland and on the islands. Zangger was correct in recognising Atlas as a key pointer to the origin of the Atlantis story, though, as we shall see, another royal house linked with him emerges as a far better candidate for the Atlantids of Plato.

Another good argument – but again not conclusive – is the one Zangger offers concerning the location of Atlantis. Plato places his island-continent 'beyond the Pillars of Heracles', a geographical clue which may be more ambivalent than it first appears. It seems that as well as the more familiar Pillars at the western end of the Greek world, there was thought to be another pair at the eastern end. According to the late Roman commentary on Virgil's *Aeneid*: 'We pass through the Pillars of Hercules in the Black Sea as well as in Spain.'[54] It is easy to see how the ancients would have perceived the narrow Straits of the Dardanelles as a doublet to those of Gibraltar – situated at opposite ends of the Mediterranean and leading through to adjoining seas. The Pillars of Heracles at each extreme were conceptual markers signifying the limits of the known world of familiar Mediterranean waters. Troy lies next to the Dardanelles, not exactly 'beyond the [eastern] Pillars of Heracles', but, allowing for further corruption in the transmission of the story, Zangger can reasonably argue that this is how the location of Atlantis might have been moved from the Troad to the far west.

So much for Zangger's good arguments. Beyond this, unfortunately, he takes the narrative far too literally and, like the supporters of the Minoan hypothesis, succumbs to the temptation of trying to make everything that Plato said fit the Trojan model. Much of this effort is unnecessary. Having satisfied himself that there was confusion about which Pillars of Heracles were involved, he should have left matters there and assumed that other geographical details were added by Plato to the core of the story once it had been transferred to an Atlantic location.

For example, Zangger has great difficulty with Plato's statement that the ocean beyond the Pillars of Heracles used to be navigable in the days of Atlantis. Zangger's interpretation is that methods of navigating the Dardanelles known to the Mycenaeans were lost by the Greeks during the Dark Ages which followed the Bronze Age. The argument would be a difficult one to explain to Iron Age fishermen – Zangger forgets that information about tides and currents was not the exclusive province of the Mycenaean palaces. He also glosses over what Plato really meant: a few lines on, the *Timaeus* (25D) explains that 'the sea in those parts is impenetrable, because there is a shoal of mud in the way; and this was caused by the subsidence of the island.' Plato's intention is clear. That an earth scientist should gloss over the obvious meaning of such a passage is rather worrying. By the time of Plato – and Solon for that matter – the Black Sea was thronged with Greek colonists. The Atlantic, on the other hand, was still a mysterious quantity. For Zangger to argue that Solon or the Egyptian priests of Sais imagined that the Black Sea was clogged with mud underestimates their intelligence.

Coming down to the micro-geography of Atlantis, Zangger

takes great pains to superimpose its canal system on the topography of the Trojan Plain, claiming that traces of massive hydraulic works linking the city to the sea can still be seen on the surface and on old maps. The problem is that the features from which Zangger works may well be of far more recent date. He frankly admits that his 'reconstruction of the Trojan coastal plain, inspired by the Atlantis legend and derived from surface observation only, contradicts the most recent geoarchaeological reconstruction of this area.'[55] It does indeed. Intensive geological surveys of the Troad have been carried out in recent years in conjunction with the new excavations at Troy. Most notably, Professor Ilhan Kayan of the Ege University (Izmir) has made a detailed study of the Trojan coastline in Bronze Age times.[56] If there were ancient canal beds running down to the sea, his work would surely have discovered them. Not a trace has been found.[57]

Zangger would been wiser to leave out such arguments altogether since they only weaken his case. To judge the Trojan theory as fairly as possible, it is better to overlook the extra frills which Zangger has added and concentrate on the core of his case. What remains is slender – Troy was an ancient, well-situated and powerful Bronze Age city, ruled by kings claiming descent from Atlas; and it was at war with Greece about the time the Mycenaeans suffered a series of natural catastrophes. But is this enough to provide a convincing prototype for Atlantis? Surely something important is missing . . .

The most conspicuous fault in Zangger's case, as I stressed in a brief review,[58] is that Troy, unlike Atlantis, was not annihilated by a natural catastrophe. Troy, of course, was supposed to have been sacked and burnt by the invading Achaeans, an event usually matched in the archaeological record with the destruction of Troy level VI or VII. Troy VII, which used to be the favoured candidate for Homer's Troy, was burnt, almost certainly by enemy action. In recent years the slightly earlier level of Troy VI has attracted more support. The original understanding that its walls were wrecked by earthquake has been challenged, leaving room for Homer's Achaeans as the cause. It has also been argued that a combination of earthquake and enemy attack was responsible.[59] Whatever the case, neither destruction – Troy VI or VIIa – was fatal. In each instance the city was immediately rebuilt by the inhabitants and there was no break in occupation.

The sinking of Atlantis beneath the waves in a single day and night is the central motif of Plato's story. If Atlantis (say, like Egypt) had survived, then Plato would never have been able to begin his extended cycle developing its lost history. The point is never properly addressed by Zangger, who fudges matters and even tries to imply that it was the destruction of Proto-Athens by earthquake and flood which was the main theme of the story, Atlantis being added in as something of an afterthought. More words are indeed devoted to the demise of the Athenian army in the *Timaeus*, but in the *Critias* it is the end of Atlantis which is prominently placed at the beginning of the narrative:

> Atlantis . . . which was an island greater in extent than Libya and Asia [together], and when afterwards sunk by an earthquake, became an impassable barrier of mud to voyagers sailing from hence [the Mediterranean] to any part of the ocean.

The *Critias*, of course, ends with the gods plotting the punishment of the Atlanteans, who had lost their nobility of character.

In a book entitled *The Flood from Heaven* (a complete misnomer), it is strange that Zangger glosses over the whole matter of the destruction of Atlantis, which is left dangling like a loose thread. This says little for the Trojan case. An Atlantis that did not sink beneath the waves is no Atlantis at all.

Perhaps with good reason, Zangger is reassuringly undogmatic about his Trojan theory. While obviously fond of it, he also makes an honest attempt to point out some of the difficulties it raises, and in the last analysis he stresses that, above all, he hoped the book would start new discussion. This is also the view of Anthony Snodgrass, Professor of Classical Archaeology at Cambridge, who wrote the foreword for the book. While admitting that it is not difficult to take issue with some points in Zangger's case, he felt that 'a better response would be to pursue the many new ideas advanced here, possibly in different directions from that followed by the author.'

In this respect I offer Zangger thanks for helping to channel my own Atlantis research in a new direction which uncovered a far more promising line of investigation.

The Missing Flood

To give Zangger's theory a last chance, it seemed worthwhile checking the rich mythology of Troy to see if he had missed something – such as a tradition linking Troy with a flood. Zangger had produced no geological or mythological evidence, or even attempted to argue, that a disastrous flood (like the one detected at Tiryns) had hit the Trojan Plain.

There was a tradition which associated Dardanus, the founder of Troy, with a flood. Dardanus, son of Zeus and the Atlantid Electra, originally ruled over Arcadia; when a flood came, Dardanus escaped from Arcadia, using a makeshift boat to reach the Aegean island of Samothrace. From here he migrated to the Troad where he established a new dynasty.[60] Still, Dardanus' flood would not help Zangger's case. The myth localises it in Arcadia. Even if it were the same as the universal deluge in the time of Deucalion, which some sources maintain, there would have been no Troy for it to destroy. Dardanus was yet to found it.

Though it did not seem worth pursuing the case for a Trojan origin for Atlantis any further, it led me to check through traditional material on Anatolian floods. Some of the most intriguing tidbits of Greek legend are not to be found in the familiar versions of the myths in Homer and Hesiod but in the local legends preserved in the writings of ancient scientists and 'information collectors'. The wealth of local data collected by the Greek geographer Strabo (first century AD) includes this gem quoted from a writer of the fourth century BC:

> Democles . . . records certain great earthquakes, some of which long ago took place about Lydia and Ionia as far north as the Troad, and by their action not only were villages swallowed up, but Mt Sipylus was shattered – in the reign of Tantalus. And lakes arose from swamps, and a tidal wave submerged the Troad.[61]

Here is a tradition Zangger could well have taken into account, but again the time-frame means that it would not support his Troy-Atlantis model. Zangger identifies the struggle of the 'Athenians' against Atlantis with the Trojan War. In terms of the mythological sequence of events, this was much later than the time of the legendary King Tantalus, reckoned to be an early contemporary of Ilus of Troy,[62] whose grandson Paris abducted Helen and initiated the war. The genealogies place Tantalus at least three generations before his descendant Agamemnon, who led the Greeks against Troy (see Appendix 1). Greek historians and chronographers commonly dated events in their prehistory by placing them in relation to the Trojan War. If Democles said that the tradition placed the flooding of Troy in the time of Tantalus, then his audience would have immediately understood that he meant several generations before the Trojan War.

So Tantalus' flood is not the missing link in Zangger's Troy-Atlantis argument. Troy was a dead-end as far as Atlantis research was concerned. Still, I had come up with something far more interesting, a tradition concerning a widespread episode of earth-quake and flooding some generations before the Trojan War. Tantalus, whose name even had a similar ring to that of Atlantis, now began to intrigue.

The Great Sinner

Who was Tantalus? One of the more bizarre figures of Greek myth, he has bequeathed two words to the English language – one for the 'tantalus', a case holding a pair of decanters for whisky and water which only allows those with a key to help themselves; the other is the verb 'tantalise'.

Both words were inspired by the everlasting torment to which Tantalus was condemned in Hades for sins committed during his lifetime, made famous by a passage in Homer. The words are those of Odysseus, who was permitted a brief glimpse of the Underworld:

There too was Tantalus in sorry plight, put to stand chin-deep in a pool. He gaped with thirst: but could not reach the water to drink it. As often as the old man bent towards it in his frenzy, so the water disappeared, swallowed into the ground which showed blackly below his feet. A god made it dry. Over the pool high-foliaged trees hung down their fruit, down to his head. Pears there were, and pomegranates, rosy apples, sweet figs and leafy olives. Yet every time the old man eagerly stretched out his hand to grasp, the wind would toss them cloud-high away.[63]

What had Tantalus done to deserve this horrendous punish-ment? Different versions of his legend give weight to different crimes, though there is more agreement on his status before his fall from grace. He was a king of divine ancestry, almost a demi-god, his father being the mountain-god Tmolus or even Zeus himself. Though there were later attempts to locate his activities in Greece (at Argos or Thebes), the majority of our sources make his kingdom Lydia in Asia Minor. Lydia was a gold-rich country, and just as Croesus, one of its rulers in historical times, became a byword for wealth, so did his predecessor Tantalus. The poets played with the resemblance of his name to the word talent – the heaviest Greek weight for gold.[64] Tantalus was not only rich – he socialised with the gods and became an intimate of Zeus himself.

It was from this elevated position that Tantalus fell. He conspired with one Pandareus to steal the golden mastiff which had guarded Zeus in his infancy,[65] though this was a relatively minor misdemeanour. His most heinous crimes were actually committed at the dinner table of the gods. When Tantalus was invited by the Olympians to share their banquet of nectar and ambrosia, he was rash enough to steal some of the divine food to share with his mortal friends.[66] Others say his fault was simply that he could not control his tongue[67] and that he revealed the secrets of the gods: 'being admitted to the common table of the gods and to all their intimate talk as well, he made known to men happenings among the immortals which were not to be divulged.'[68]

Another story has it that he invited the gods to dinner on Mount Sipylus, where, either to test Zeus' omniscience, or in the naive belief that the sacrifice would please the gods, Tantalus killed his own son Pelops and made him into a stew. The gods were understandably disgusted and Zeus struck Tantalus down with a thunderbolt. They restored Pelops to life, replacing with porpoise ivory the shoulder accidentally eaten by the goddess Demeter.[69]

The mythical consensus, if it can be described as such, was that Tantalus was a rich and powerful king who overreached himself by desiring too much. The Greek writer Athenaeus, citing an older (probably sixth century BC) work about the return of the heroes after the Trojan War, expressed the essence of his crime in a different way:

> The writer of the *Return of the Atreidae* says that Tantalus came and lived with the gods, and was permitted to ask for whatever he desired. But the man was so immoderately given to pleasures that he asked for these and for a life like the life of the gods. At this Zeus was annoyed, but fulfilled his prayer because of

his own promise; but to prevent him enjoying any of the pleasures provided, and to keep him continually harassed, he hung a stone over his head which prevents him from ever reaching any of the pleasant things near by.[70]

Here was a promising line of enquiry for Atlantis research. The fabled riches of Tantalus recall those of the Atlantean kings: 'the wealth they possessed was so immense that the like had never been seen before in any royal house' (*Critias* 114D). Tantalus was an intimate of the gods, a station matching the majesty of the Atlanteans, whom Plato describes as close to the gods in spirit. Then comes the sin of over-presumption and greed, common to both king and kingdom, and finally the downfall due to the wrath of the gods.

Between Heaven and Earth

There are other curious links between Tantalus and Atlas, beginning with an array of genealogical connections. Tantalus' mother, the nymph Pluto (whose name means simply 'wealth') belonged to the Titan family, and was daughter of Cronus or Oceanus – in either case she would have been a cousin of Atlas. Tantalus himself, according to a late tradition, married one of the seven daughters of Atlas, the Pleiad Dione.[71] However, most traditions did not count Dione as a Pleiad but as one of the original six Titanesses, daughters of Uranus and Gaea.[72] If it was this Dione who married Tantalus it would place him in the senior generation of Titans and make him an uncle rather than son-in-law of Atlas. The details of these mythological variants are less important than the general relationships they establish. As Carl Kerenyi noted, through Dione 'the genealogists connected Atlas, an old god of the race of the Titans, with the king of Lydia [Tantalus].'[73] The Roman poet Ovid represents Tantalus' arrogant daughter Niobe as being particularly proud of her Atlantid blood:

> I am the daughter of Tantalus, who was the only mortal ever allowed to participate in the banquets of the gods: my mother is a sister of the Pleiades, and Atlas, the mighty god who carries the vault of heaven on his shoulders, is my grandfather.[74]

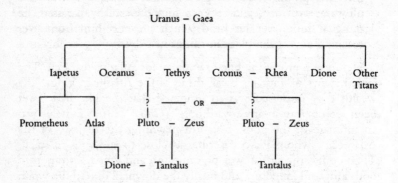

FIG. 15   Tantalus' links with the Titans.

Marriages with Atlantids continue through almost every generation of Tantalus' descendants. Tantalus is credited with only four
children, one of whom, Broteas, died childless. Little is known
of his son Dascylus, except that his son Lycus, ruler of the Marian-
dynian tribe of the Black Sea coast,[75] shared his name with two
Atlantid cousins (see Appendix 1). Tantalus' two other children,
Pelops and Niobe, both married descendants of Atlas. Niobe's
children died young, but three of Pelops' descendants married
Atlantids (see Appendix 1).

The Atlantids and Tantalids, are so closely intertwined that
mythologist Bernard Sergent argued they were originally the same
family.[76] This implies that at some point a direct identification
was made between Atlas and Tantalus. Are they in fact merely
two names for variants of the same character?

Re-examining the mythological fate of Tantalus reveals an
important parallel with Atlas. Homer's description of the torments
suffered by Tantalus in the Underworld has become the most
famous: it was his graphic picture of eternal thirst and hunger
which gave rise to the word 'tantalise'. Yet Homer's version was
a minority one. The idea that Tantalus was punished by 'having a
stone impending over him'[77] was far more common. The tradition
of a punishment involving a stone is not a late variant. Pindar
(early fifth century) knew of it – he talks of 'an overpowering
curse, which the Father hung over him in the semblance of a
monstrous stone, which he is ever eager to thrust away from his
head'.[78]

The post-Homeric *Return of the Atreidae* cited above, was written by the sixth century at the latest, and provides a version that combines the hunger-and-thirst motif from Homer with the threat of the 'stone over his head'. In fact the story probably goes back to the time of Homer or even earlier, as it had already become proverbial for a menacing danger by the days of Archilochus, an elegiac poet of the mid-seventh century. A fragment of his work says: 'Let Tantalus' rock not hang above this island.'[79]

More detail of the awesome stone is given elsewhere. According to the Scholiast on Homer's *Odyssey*, Tantalus was tied to the rock by his hands, just as Atlas' brother Prometheus had been.[80] While one might imagine that the stone was in Hades, in the version given by Euripides (mid-fifth century), it is specifically placed in the sky. In his play *Orestes*, Tantalus' descendant Electra describes how 'Tantalus hovers in mid-air in dread of a rock that looms above his head.' Later she exclaims:

> I wish I could go to that rock strung in suspense between sky and earth by golden chains, the whirlwind borne *bolos* that came from Olympus, to cry in lamentation to old father Tantalus . . .[81]

The stone of Tantalus, at least in Euripides' opinion, was no ordinary chunk of rock. In his commentary on *Orestes*, Martin West explains that since a *bolos* is a detachable lump of earth, the gods must have made it by breaking a piece off Olympus. 'The idea is probably not just that the rock is blown about by the winds but that it flies round in a circular orbit with Olympus at the centre, like a celestial body. Tantalus is also airborne, somewhere close to the rock, presumably attached to another chain.'[82]

What this curious stone orbiting Olympus on golden chains may have been is suggested by a reference in another of Euripides' plays, the *Phaethon*, where the Sun itself is referred to as a golden *bolos*.[83] Ancient commentators on Euripides and other texts corroborate this: 'Some understand the stone to represent the sun, and Tantalus, a physicist, to be paying the penalty for having proved that the sun is a mass of white-hot metal.'[84] The allusion to Euripides' earlier contemporary Anaxagoras, tried for blasphemy for teaching that the Sun was an incandescent rock, is clear.

Many ancient writers clearly conceived Tantalus' rock to be a celestial one and Kerenyi argues this is the original version of the tale.[85] A similar view had already been advanced by Cook, who suggested that 'the change from the world above to the world below probably hangs together with the conception of Tantalus as a Giant or Titan.'[86] The Titans were said to have been consigned to the Underworld after their defeat.

So the almost certainly older view of Tantalus is of a primordial giant or Titan, whose punishment for rebelling against the gods was to be chained – or to support – a celestial rock, perhaps the Sun. The image is extraordinarily close to that of the Titan Atlas, and according to the ancient Scholiast on Euripides the idea was current that the 'rock' held up by Tantalus was actually the sky[87] – a view which completes the circle and makes the punishments of these two great sinners identical.

With this growing weight of evidence it was becoming difficult to avoid the conclusion that Tantalus was actually a variant of the familiar Atlas figure. Having reached it through examining the primary sources alone, I was then pleased to find that the basic identity of Atlas and Tantalus had been recognised for well over a century; in fact it was first suggested in 1836 by the German scholar F. Creuzer.[88] As Sergent remarked in 1987:

> it was long ago observed that Tantalus is none other than a doublet of Atlas, as is shown by their names (derived from the same root, the verb *tlaô*, to carry), their homologous relationships (of titanic type) with the gods, and the myth that assigns to both the function of holding up the earth or a mountain or a rock.[89]

There is a further parallel, involving a curious link with music. Atlas had a reputation as a master lyre-player,[90] an attribute which is rather baffling until we remember his maternal link with Lydia (Asia), one of the great musical centres of the ancient world. One of his descendants was Amphion, king of Thebes, the husband of Tantalus' daughter Niobe. Amphion improved on the four-stringed lyre used in Greece by adding an extra three strings. His playing was so skilful that he was said to have been able to make trees and rocks move. The massive stones of Thebes' walls simply leapt into place as he played. One source specifically attributes Amphion's skills to his kinship with Lydian Tantalus[91] – though of course Atlas would have done just as well.

The stories of Atlas and Tantalus could have cross-fertilised at times when their underlying identity was appreciated. This may be the case with Atlas' lyre-playing, though of course it is difficult to detect whether reciprocal influence was involved or whether the myths were simply travelling along convergent paths. In Hellenistic times attempts were made to 'rationalise' both the Tantalus and Atlas myths, following a trend known as 'euhemerising', after the writer Euhemerus (*c.* 300 BC) who claimed that the gods were simply great historical personalities of the remote past, whose exploits had been exaggerated. (The wonders achieved by Alexander the Great provided the inspiration for his model.) According to Diogenes Laertius, who wrote up the lives of the famous philosophers for a Roman audience, Tantalus was a scientific forerunner of Anaxagoras; like him Tantalus discovered too much about the real nature of the heavens and was punished for revealing that the sun was merely an incandescent stone.[92] A similar 'explanation' of the cosmic aspect of Atlas was reported by Diodorus Siculus, who relied heavily on Euhemerus:

> They also say that he [Atlas] perfected the science of astrology and was the first to publish to mankind the doctrine of the sphere; and that it was for this reason that the idea was held that the entire heavens were supported on the shoulders of Atlas, the myth darkly hinting in this way the discovery and description of the sphere . . .[93]

Thus were both Atlas and Tantalus reinterpreted as pioneers of astronomy. Similar myths, it seems, have similar momentum.

If Tantalus was basically a Lydian version of Atlas,[94] how and when did they acquire their underlying similarities? One possibility is that Tantalus, like Atlas, began his mythological career as the god of a mountain, a 'world-pillar' that supported the skies.[95] Certainly Tantalus was very strongly associated with the Lydian Mount Sipylus. According to Antoninus Liberalis, Zeus punished him in the same way that he did many of the Giants – he struck him down with a thunderbolt and then finished him off by dropping the mountain on his head.[96] There was also a mountain named after Tantalus – not in Lydia but on the island of Lesbos which lies opposite.[97] Atlas, of course, lends himself very nicely to the idea that he began as a mountain-god.

It is reasonable to conclude that the figures of Atlas and Tantalus were both *largely* developed from beliefs about rebellious mountain-gods, condemned to being cosmic pillars by the new generation of deities. As Anatolia is so rich in traditions about such rebellious mountain gods, it seems likely that they both evolved here. Indeed, they may once have been the same figure, and perhaps the question should be how this character divided into two. Since Atlas became more at home in Greece, it would be best to see him as a Greek version of Tantalus, rather than *vice versa*. To go any further in penetrating the mutual origins of Atlas and Tantalus is beyond the scope of this book and must await new breakthroughs in mythological studies.

Here it is enough to note that Atlas and Tantalus were mythological equivalents and that this may not have gone unnoticed in ancient times. Thus the Lydian Tantalus may easily have been 'translated' by a Greek into the more familiar Atlas for convenience of understanding. I am thinking, of course, of Plato's source – presumed to be Solon. There is already enough evidence to suggest that the Tantalus saga was connected with the source for the Atlantis story – his fabulous wealth, his closeness to the gods, his fall from grace through hubris and his association with a catastrophe of earthquake and floods all find parallels in the story of Atlas' descendants as set out in the *Timaeus* and *Critias*.

However, it is possible to go much further. As already stressed, the complex figure of Tantalus may only be partly based on a mountain-god. There is too much about him as a king – with a capital city, empire, a tomb and a dynasty of descendants whose influence stretched as far as Greece – to assume that this is the whole picture. Somewhere along the way, traditions about a local king – fictional or real – must have been blended with that of a mountain-god.[98] If Atlas was the equivalent of Tantalus, then the origin of Atlantis may be found in the kingdom of Tantalus. What was supposed to have happened there during the great catastrophe which Democles reported?

The Lost City

The most detailed account of the disaster which occurred in the reign of Tantalus comes from Pausanias, author of the first guide book to Greece. Pausanias lived under the Emperor Hadrian (117–138 AD) and seems to have been brought up in Magnesia (modern Manisa), a Greek city which lay at the northern edge of Mount Sipylus. Though his guidebook only really covers the Greek mainland, Pausanias gives occasional glimpses of the sights 'back home'.

In his book on Achaea (the northern province of the Peloponnese), Pausanias includes an interesting digression on the nature of the extraordinary disaster that struck the Helike one winter's night in 373 BC. The city was utterly destroyed by a series of momentous earth shocks, and Pausanias analysed the disaster in graphic detail, noting that 'the character of the shock itself is not always the same. The original observers and persons instructed by them have been able to distinguish different classes of earthquakes . . .'

In the 'gentlest' kind of earthquake, Pausanias reported that buildings may be violently shaken by tremors, but often snap back roughly into position afterwards; 'a reverse tremor throws back what has already toppled.' The second kind of earthquake 'destroys everything that is the least unsteady: whatever it strikes it instantly overthrows, as with the blow of a battering-ram.' But third on the Pausanias Richter scale was the following:

> The deadliest kind of earthquake is illustrated by the following comparison. In an unintermitting fever a man's breathing is quick and laboured, as is shown by symptoms at various points of the body, but especially at the wrists; and they say that in the same way the earthquake dives under buildings and upheaves their foundations, just as molehills are pushed up from the bowels of the earth. It is this kind of shock that leaves not a trace of human habitation behind.
>
> They say that the earthquake at Helice was of this last kind, the kind that levels with the ground; and that, besides the earthquake, another disaster befell the doomed city that winter. The sea advanced far over the land and submerged the whole of Helice, and in the grove of Poseidon the water was so deep that only the tops of the trees were visible. So that between the suddenness of the earthquake and the simultaneous rush of the sea, the billows sucked down Helice and every soul in the place.

Earthquakes of this magnitude must have been rare, even in classical times. Pausanias, however, knew of an analogy from his homeland:

> A like fate befell a city on Mount Sipylus: it disappeared into a chasm, and from the fissure in the mountain water gushed forth, and the chasm became named Lake Saloe. The ruins of the city could still be seen in the lake until the water of the torrent covered them up.[99]

The name of the unfortunate city Pausanias omits to tell us, but it is supplied by the Roman encyclopaedist Pliny (writing about 75 AD), in a passage discussing settlements in the interior of Asia Minor that 'no longer exist'.[100] Pausanias' 'Lake Saloe' at Sipylus appears in Pliny's work as 'the marsh of Sale' in the district of Magnesia. Underneath the marsh, he says, lies the ancient capital of Maeonia (the old name for Lydia), which had been devoured by an earthquake. According to Pliny it was known as Sipylus, and before that 'the very celebrated city in the same place that used to be called Tantalis' – in other words the city of Tantalus. The parallels amassed between Atlas and Tantalus can now be completed by a pair of cities with strikingly similar names – Atlantis and Tantalis – and strikingly similar histories of destruction, by earthquake and flood.

It already seemed at this stage that the story of Tantalis could be the missing source behind Plato's Atlantis. But this only raised more questions. How did Plato come by the story? Why did he place it in the Atlantic and what made him think that it related to events nine thousand years before his time? And, to start at the beginning, if Tantalis lay behind the legend of Atlantis, what lay behind the legend of Tantalis?

FIG. 16   Tantalus' punishment in the underworld, from a wall painting by Polygnotus, c. 450 BC.

CHAPTER 9

In the Kingdom of Tantalus

It was with some trepidation that I first went to Lydia in May 1994 to see if I could locate the lost city of Tantalis. After all, I was looking for a legendary site that might never have existed. A number of friends had asked what I expected to find and my answer was a cautious 'nothing'. No one likes egg on their face and I had no idea whether even Lake Saloe, at whose bottom Tantalis was said to lie, could be located. Pliny described it as a marsh (*stagnum*) – if this was already the case by the first century AD, there might be no visible sign of a lake, let alone a city, after the passage of nearly two thousand years. The task in hand was to discover where it was *supposed* to have been. Anything more would be a bonus.

Candidates for the lake, the lost city of Tantalus and other remains of his dynasty had been suggested by writers as long ago as the mid-nineteenth century. George Bean, a modern archaeologist well acquainted with the area, gave a perfunctory summary of their attempts: 'Since the exploration of the country began in modern times, great efforts and many words have been expended in the attempt to identify there various features on the ground. For the city and the lake of Tantalus no satisfactory results have been achieved.'[1] I had tried to weigh up the different cases, but no amount of library research, poring over antiquarian reports and inadequate maps, could resolve the matter. Only going to Mount Sipylus and coming to grips with its topography at first hand held any promise of answering the dozens of questions which had arisen – not only regarding the location of the legendary city of Tantalis, but also from the surprising possibility that the Atlantis legend originated in a tale of disaster from the Aegean coastal region of Turkey.

As companion and photographer on the reconnaissance trip I was fortunate to have my good friend the polymathic Nikos

Kokkinos. While his formal qualifications concern the archaeology of Roman Palestine, Nikos is equally at ease discussing the
archaeology of Mycenaean Greece and Iron Age Cyprus, classical
Asia Minor and the Hellenistic world as a whole. Having another
generalist as companion was invaluable.

We were extraordinarily lucky in having, for the first week of
our trip, the company of another old friend, Kyriakos Lambrianides. By sheer coincidence, the doctoral thesis Kyriakos was completing concerned the archaeology of the island of Lesbos and the
Anatolian coast opposite. Study of the settlement and exchange
patterns between Lesbos and the mainland during the Early
Bronze Age had led him southwards along the coast to the area
of the Gediz Valley, the heartland of the later kingdom of Lydia.
At this early period (c. 3000–2000 BC), the 200-mile-long Gediz
River was already a vital artery of cultural exchange, involving
connections as far as Lesbos. Mount Sipylus, where the city of
Tantalus was supposed to have been, lies right next to the Gediz
Valley, about thirty miles inland from where the river joins the
Aegean Sea.

Before we went to Lydia, Kyriakos was able to give me a
general profile of the archaeology of the Gediz Valley, from the
Bronze to Iron Ages. Throughout this period, ancient settlers
were drawn to the river and its tributaries, not only for the
obvious advantages of the waterway and the broad fertile plain it
flowed through, but for the exceptional mineral resources to be
found in the surrounding mountains. It is difficult to determine
when these mineral resources were first exploited. Legend said
that Tantalus drew his wealth from the metal mines in Lydia and
neighbouring Phrygia. Lambrianides drew my attention to the
Early Bronze Age burials at Ahlateli Tepecik by the side of Lake
Marmara, one of the largest inland stretches of water in western
Turkey, only a few hours' walk to the north of the Gediz. Here,
the grave-goods of a relatively simple fishing community were
surprisingly rich in their variety of metal objects: finds included
copper-bronze daggers and pins, a lead bar, gold earplugs and
silver decorative items. The gold, at least, appears to have been
of local origin.[2] It was gold, panned from the river Pactolus, a
tributary of the Hermus (Gediz), which was later to make Lydia
one of the richest countries of the Eastern Mediterranean.

Legend has it that King Midas, ruler of the neighbouring
kingdom of Phrygia, got rid of the 'golden touch' by bathing in

FIG. 17 Map of Anatolia (Turkey) showing principal sites mentioned.

the Pactolus, whose sands for ever after gleamed with gold.[3] When we visited the Lydian capital of Sardis we saw the Pactolus, now reduced to a small stream. There is still a little gold in it today, though not enough to make panning economically viable.[4] But Sardis' wealthy past is clearly visible from the grandeur of its archaeological remains.[5] The site is enormous, and although the ravages of time and invasion – Sardis was burnt to the ground by the Ionian Greeks in 499 BC – mean that there is little to see of the original Lydian city, the magnificent buildings of later times, such as the Greek temple of Artemis, the luxurious Roman gymnasium and the beautiful synagogue built by the city's Jewish community, all stand as reminders of how Sardis was once one of the most economically successful cities in the world. The gold dust of the Pactolus made the Lydians into a regional super-power and its kings into near-legends.

The expression 'as rich as Croesus' still survives. Croesus was a real king, the last ruler of an independent Lydia. He controlled

all of western Anatolia – including the Greek cities on the coast
– and posed the only serious threat to the growing might of the
Persians. He gambled on war with Persia and lost. Sardis was
conquered by Cyrus the Great in 547 BC and turned into the seat
of a Persian satrap. It is to the Lydians that we owe the invention of our monetary system. They learnt how to separate the
gold from silver in the natural alloy (*electrum*) in the river ore, and
issued standard coinage in both metals, stamped with royal insignia.[6] The Persians copied the idea and set up a royal mint at
Sardis. Though the Greeks had also learnt coinage from the
Lydians by about 600 BC, it was the Persian Empire that established
the system almost globally, imposing one monetary standard
from the Aegean to the Indus Valley and from Egypt to southern
Russia.

About an hour's drive to the north of Sardis, on the other side
of the Gediz, lie the enormous earthen burial mounds of the
Lydian kings. The limestone ridge on which they are situated is
now known as Bin Tepe ('Thousand Hills'), a strange landscape
where the unnatural shape of the 'hills' dotted across it, sometimes
as far as the eye can see, creates an unreal effect. At the eastern
end of Bin Tepe is one of the very largest mounds, apparently the
tomb of King Alyattes, father of Croesus (see Plate 4). Herodotus
says the enormous amount of work taken to construct it was paid
for by the citizens of Sardis, with stone pillars erected on the
mound to record the contributions made by each group. (He
added in his usual dry fashion that 'calculations reveal that the
prostitutes' share was the largest.'[7] Which burial belonged to which
king is uncertain: even the mound usually thought to be the
burial place of the great seventh-century warrior Gyges may
belong to a later Lydian prince.[8] The problem is that the largest
mounds have never been properly excavated – due to the obvious
engineering difficulties posed by burrowing into the base of a
huge mountain of soil. Between 1964 and 1966 the excavators of
Sardis drove a tunnel right through the centre of the 'Gyges'
mound but still did not find a tomb chamber. They eventually
gave up. The director of Sardis, George Hanfmann put it nicely:
'in the battle of man against mound, the mound won.'[9] Thus,
strange though it may seem, the tombs of some of the ancient
world's richest kings remain relatively untouched.

Tantalus, reputedly as rich as Croesus, was thought to have
ruled Lydia long before the kings buried in these mounds. Croesus

belonged to the dynasty of the Mermnadae, which was founded by Gyges, a king attested in Assyrian records about 650 BC. According to Herodotus, Gyges took the throne from King Candaules (a.k.a. Myrsilus), the last in a long line of rulers who traced their ancestry back to the Greek hero Heracles. The Heraclid dynasty began shortly after the time of the Trojan War (traditionally dated *c.* 1200 BC),[10] and before them Herodotus tells us that the kingdom was ruled by the family of Lydus, who gave his name to the Lydian people. Before him the kingdom was known as Maeonia.[11] It is at this remote, Maeonian, period that the traditions place King Tantalus. How best to approach such a legendary character? With all such matters, it is best to proceed from the 'known' to the 'unknown' – and Sardis itself provided a good vantage point from which to work backwards in time into the murkier past of prehistory and legend.

Lydians and Achaeans

The tradition of the Heraclid kings of Sardis takes us back to the beginning of the Iron Age (conventionally *c.* 1200 BC). It is difficult to assess the belief that this dynasty descended from the lion-skinned, roguish demi-god Heracles of Greek myth. The more exotic tales relate how, after offending the gods, he was sent to Lydia to become the slave of Queen Omphale. Her husband Tmolus, who gave his name to the mountain behind Sardis (and according to some was the father of Tantalus), had died, and Omphale kept Heracles as plaything and lover at her court. Greek poets were supposedly scandalised by the way she made him wear drag, a reflection of the Greek view of Lydia as a mainspring of dangerous oriental 'softness' and decadence. A descendant from this strange liaison later took the throne of Lydia, founding the Heraclid dynasty.[12]

All this is a fairy-tale and it is hardly likely that a real Mycenaean Greek hero called Heracles actually visited Lydia and founded a dynasty in this way. I was surprised, then, to find a more sympathetic approach to the historicity of the Heraclid tradition in the publication of Sardis by its current American excavators. For them, the story of the Heraclids 'may indicate the arrival of Mycenaean warriors who seized the rule of Sardis and were then assimilated.'[13] Evidence for Mycenaean activity at Sardis comes in the form of large numbers of painted sherds (LHIIIB-C) dating to the 13th–11th centuries.

The background to the Sardis case is the weight of the evidence which has now accumulated for Mycenaean involvement far up the Gediz valley. It is perhaps not so surprising that Mycenaean pottery (from as early as about 1400 BC) has been found on coastal sites such as Miletus and Ephesus. At Ephesus a Mycenaean tomb (of the fourteenth century BC) was discovered underneath a car park.[14] The Mycenaean material at Sardis comes from much further inland, a good fifty miles from the coast. Mycenaean pottery (on sherds from as early as the fourteenth century) has now been found as far east as Alasehir (classical Philadelphia), another thirty miles beyond Sardis.[15]

Of course the presence of Mycenaean pottery does not prove that Mycenaeans personally delivered it – it may have been acquired by trade. But this possibility has to be balanced against historical evidence that the Mycenaeans *were* active in the region, possibly as early as the fifteenth century BC. In 1924 the Swiss scholar Émile Forrer announced that he had identified Homer's Achaeans in archives of the Hittites from Boghazköy. These refer to a western country called Ahhiyawa, whose king was of great enough status to address the Hittite Emperor in writing as 'My Brother'. The name Ahhiyawa, Forrer reasoned, was simply Achaea, the land of the Achaeans, and only mainland Greece itself was capable of supporting a kingdom of this rank. At first his ideas received some acceptance, then doubts set and alternative identifications for Ahhiyawa were experimented with – including Troy, Thrace and Rhodes. Now, however, after decades of doubt and controversy, it has been generally agreed to accept the inevitable – Ahhiyawa was, after all, Mycenaean Greece, and its kings resided at Mycenae.[16]

It is now clear that Hittite texts from the late fifteenth to thirteenth centuries describe almost constant interference by Mycenaean kings in the affairs of the Aegean coastal states. This discovery is momentous, although the academic world as a whole has been rather slow to reveal what a sea-change has happened. The political and military struggles of Ahhiyawa to establish its power on the Aegean coast of Anatolia provide a perfect historical background to the story of how the kings of Greece combined under the leadership of Agamemnon to crush the power of Troy and its Anatolian allies. In short, we may be only a spit away from finding contemporary, documentary proof of the Trojan War. (Indeed, that evidence may already be lurking, unrecognised, in a cuneiform tablet from Boghazköy.)

The combination of historical and archaeological evidence now puts a completely different complexion on the legends about early Greek connections with Lydia – including those of the Heraclids and Tantalus. Despite some of the wilder imaginative frills, the traditions about early Lydia are reasonably consistent internally, and what they relate fits the archaeological evidence quite comfortably.

The reign of the Heraclids at Sardis traditionally began around 1200 BC. Going backwards in time, the next we hear of the Lydian region is from Homer. In the second book of the *Iliad*, Homer gives a catalogue of the allies of Troy that came to defend it in its long war with the Greeks. The Lydians are included, under their earlier name of Maeonians. Homer evidently saw them as a rich people: his Maeonians fought in chariots, drawn by horses with ivory cheek-pieces, and their military help was obtained by the Trojans at great expense. Their lands included 'snowy Tmolus' (the mountain just to the south of Sardis) and 'the swirling streams of Hermus and Hyllus where the fishes breed'. The Gygaean Lake (Marmara) is described as their 'mother'.[17] These clues place them in the area stretching north of Sardis, with a shift of focus to the other side of the Hermus (Gediz) Valley, towards Lake Marmara (the Gygaean Lake) and the classical river Hyllus (modern Kum Chai).

Archaeological research has tended to confirm Homer's claim that the lands north of Sardis were settled at the time of the Trojan War (Late Bronze Age). It has been a long-range goal of the excavators of Sardis to identify and study the pre-Lydian cultures of the area, and large-scale excavation at Ahlatli Tepecik, on the shore of the Gygaean Lake, began in 1967. While early work suggested that there was a break in occupation after the Early Bronze Age, a Late Bronze Age burial has now been discovered. Middle or Late Bronze Age storage jars have been found nearby.[18] Ahlatli Tepecik is the first prehistoric settlement site on the lake to be extensively excavated and there must be many other prehistoric sites around this lake which are still awaiting detection. Further to the north, pioneering survey work had already been carried out in 1959–1960 by David French of the British Institute of Archaeology at Ankara.[19] He identified numerous mounds north-west of the Gygaean Lake, some near the River Hyllus of Homer's poetry and many more further west towards Mount Sipylus, which contained the grey pottery characteristic of Troy cities VI and VII – the two candidates for the city sacked by Homer's Achaeans (see Chapter 8).

Current research by Turkish archaeologists, notably Recep Meriç at the Dokuz Eylul University in Izmir, has been steadily filling in the 'blank' area between the old British survey north of the Gediz, and the American work around Sardis to the south. He has already identified a string of small fortified positions, of Late Bronze Age date, running along the Gediz Valley, which he feels were built by the locals as a defence system against the Hittites.[20] Where then was the heartland they were defending?

Between Myth and Reality

Hittite texts show that the Aegean coastal region during the Late Bronze Age was structured into a pattern of small kingdoms known as the Arzawa Lands. Which state was top dog tended to change, but it is known from the texts that around 1300 BC the overall King of Arzawa had his seat at Ephesus (Apasas), near the coast.[21] Where the centre of Arzawa was before that date is not known. Arzawan archaeology is still in its infancy.

Here the traditions bring in Tantalus and his kingdom on Mount Sipylus, the focus of our reconnaissance trip. The more overtly mythological sources talk of Sipylus in rather fantastic terms, recalling, for example, the banquets held on the mountain by Tantalus where even the gods were invited. Other sources concern more down-to-earth matters. The Greek geographer Strabo speaks of Tantalus as a king who exploited the mines 'round Phrygia and Sipylus', and infers that Sipylus was the name of a city or kingdom as well as a mountain.[22] This is indeed what the Roman writers Pliny and Solinus thought: they both named Sipylus as the past capital of Maeonia, also giving its alternative name of Tantalis.[23]

There seems to have been some doubt in classical times that the city of Sipylus really disappeared, as legend had it, during a devastating earthquake. Strabo wrote in defence of the tradition:

The story of Mt Sipylus and its ruin should not be put down as mythical, for in our own times Magnesia, which lies at the foot of it, was laid low by earthquakes, at the time when not only Sardis, but also the most famous of the other cities, were in many places seriously damaged. But the emperor restored them by contributing money . . .[24]

Strabo was referring to the massive earthquake of AD 18, which destroyed twelve cities of Lydia and required an empire-wide relief scheme by the Romans to repair the damage.[25]

The story of the devastation of Sipylus in prehistoric times was not something cooked up by Roman writers to make their geography books more interesting. There is the tradition recorded by the hellenistic writer Democles about the earthquakes which shook the whole coast as far as Troy in the reign of King Tantalus and 'shattered' Mount Sipylus. There are also two impeccable sources from the fourth century BC: ironically, Plato and Aristotle. Plato wrote in the *Cratylus* (395D-E) of the terrible misfortunes which befell Tantalus when he lost the favour of the gods: 'in his life the last was the utter overthrow of his country, and in Hades, after his death, the balancing of the stone above his head.' Aristotle described a rare kind of earthshock of extraordinary violence, in which 'large quantities of stone come to the surface, like the chaff in a winnowing sieve. This kind of earthquake it was that devastated the country round Sipylus.'[26]

Earlier still, the mid-fifth century mythographer Pherecydes told how Tantalus' kingdom on Sipylus was engulfed by an earthquake. About the same time, both Sophocles and Aeschylus wrote plays about the related tragedy of Tantalus' daughter Niobe, which are now unfortunately only known through fragments. In one preserved fragment, Aeschylus presented Tantalus mourning the downfall of their homeland in the company of his daughter Niobe.[27] The woes of the house of Tantalus became a favourite theme of the dramatists. Although his descendants eventually became kings of Mycenae and the conquerors of Troy, the fatal wrath of the gods incurred by old Tantalus never dissipated. Aeschylus' *Agamemnon* referred to the 'spirit of hate, whose strong curse weighs hard upon the house and heirs of Tantalus'.[28] For the rest of their time the descendants of Tantalus slaughtered each other in a roller-coaster ride of madness, infanticide, matricide and fratricide that makes Hamlet's family seem happy. Agamemnon, for example, was murdered in his bath by his wife immediately on his return from the Trojan War. The last scions of

Tantalus' family were driven from Mycenae and eventually returned to their ancestral land of Asia as leaders of Greek colonies.[29] As Aeschylus said in his lost tragedy about Niobe, 'God implants guilt in man when he wishes to destroy a house utterly.'[30]

The tradition of Sipylus' devastation was an early and persistent one, though this is not the impression obtained from the standard handbooks of Greek myth. These tend to concentrate on Tantalus' famous punishment in Hades and neglect to draw together the sources that describe the downfall of his kingdom. Yet it was an integral part of the Tantalus legend, repeatedly acknowledged by the poets.

Other traditions survive about the importance of the lost kingdom of Tantalus. The Lydian historian Xanthus (a contemporary of Herodotus) says that armies of his countrymen got as far as southern Palestine in the time of Tantalus; here Tantalus' brother Ascalus was supposed to have founded the city of Ashkelon.[31] The Greeks, for their part, believed that the ancestor of Mycenaean kings had come from Sipylus. Pelops, son of Tantalus, was supposed to have left his father's kingdom and taken over Pisa, near Olympia in southern Greece. According to the most famous version of the legend, Oenomaus, king of Pisa (and a grandson of Atlas), offered the hand of his daughter to anyone who could beat him in a chariot race. Those who lost would be killed. With the connivance of Oenomaus' charioteer Myrtilus, Pelops won. Oenomaus was dragged to his death during the race, and Pelops took his daughter and his throne.[32] By degrees Pelops and his sons extended their power, until Atreus was accorded the throne of Mycenae by its people.[33] Pelops' family became so powerful that his name was eventually given to the Peloponnese ('Island of Pelops').

Is the legend of Pelops carving out a kingdom in Greece a mere fairy tale? The scholars of antiquity took it in all seriousness, and believed that cultural traces of the Lydians whom Pelops brought with him from Sipylus could still be detected in Greece.[34] Strangely enough, the legend has yet to be seriously analysed in the light of modern knowledge about the Bronze Age political scene.

The idea of a prince from one country taking over the throne in a relatively distant one is not at all strange. The monarchies of the Bronze Age Mediterranean, like those of modern Europe, preserved their mystique by taking spouses of equal status from their 'brother' monarchies overseas. This mutually supporting system included Egypt, Babylonia, Hatti (the Hittite Empire), Mitanni (the Hurrian kingdom in northern Mesopotamia) and, for a while, Arzawa in western Anatolia. In the mid-fourteenth century King Tarkhundaradu of Arzawa wrote to Pharaoh Amenhotep III to discuss a marriage alliance. Shortly afterwards a son of the Hittite Emperor Suppiluliuma nearly succeeded Tutankhamun in Egypt but was murdered on his way to marry the boy pharaoh's widow.[35] If such dynastic interchanges were possible between Anatolia and Egypt, there is no reason to suppose that they did not take place between Anatolia and Greece. Indeed, a letter from a Hittite emperor describes how one Tawagalawas, brother of the king of Ahhiyawa, came to him to ask for a kingdom.[36]

Even the idea that Pelops won his throne through a chariot race seems less bizarre when it is remembered how important chariot-handling was to the elite of the Late Bronze Age. The story of the charioteer Myrtilus changing allegiance from the Greek king Oenomaus to the Anatolian prince Pelops is strangely echoed in the letter from the Hittite emperor about the Achaean Tawagalawas. The emperor refers to a charioteer who 'used to step on the chariot with me and with your brother Tawagalawas'. The letter reveals a surprising amount of intimacy between the two royal groups, who apparently shared a charioteer at some point. As the Sardis excavation report notes: 'We now know that it would have been quite possible for a Lydian prince to teach chariotry to Mycenaean princes in the fourteenth and thirteenth centuries BC.'[37]

Finally, the existence of a Mycenaean kingdom at Pisa (at first glance a rather unlikely idea) now seems to have been confirmed by its identification in an Egyptian list of Aegean kingdoms drawn up in the fourteenth century BC.[38]

While it was once easy to dismiss the story of Pelops as fanciful legend,[39] today it has to be accepted that all its important elements are comfortably at home in the world of the Aegean Bronze Age. If the legend of Pelops contains a kernel of truth, then the search for the lost kingdom of Sipylus is also the search for the ancestral seat of the Mycenaean kings.

A Hittite Kingdom?

The idea that the Lydian kingdom of Tantalus played a special role in early Greek history was familiar enough in the nineteenth century, when archaeologists were less edgy about taking leads from myth and tradition. The existence of such a kingdom on Mount Sipylus was cheerfully accepted and many nineteenth-century explorers searched the mountain for remains of the lost city of Tantalis. These gentlemen-explorers often had far more time and resources than any modern researcher could afford. Their work, in terms of drawings, plans and descriptions, was often meticulous. It was also vital, as we were to discover, given that some monuments and features of the landscape have now completely disappeared. Having their work to hand was an enormous advantage. We could add to this the extra accumulated knowledge of a further century's archaeological, geological and historical research.

Our first port of call, literally, was the modern city of Izmir. Izmir, or Smyrna as it is known to the Greeks, was hailed in Roman times as the jewel of the Mediterranean world. Today it is a busy industrial and commercial centre, the third largest city in Turkey, best known to Western travellers for its airport, where people stream into coaches and head for the Aegean beach resorts and the famous classical sites on the coast. If you are travelling in the other direction looking for archaeology many locals may look rather quizzical – surely all the best remains, Sardis aside, are near the coast, at Ephesus, Pergamum. . . . Maybe so, maybe not. Beautifully preserved classical towns all have their place in the scheme of things, but there is more to be discovered in the still relatively unexplored territory immediately inland.

Sir William Ramsay, the first great British explorer and archaeologist of Anatolia, wrote in 1880 that 'no part of the Greek world is richer in tradition and in the memories of a prehistoric past than the district that lies within the limit of a day's excursion from Smyrna.'[40] Ramsay was talking about the hinterland of Smyrna, behind which lie two mountains, or rather a small mountain range divided into two halves (Fig. 19). Smyrna itself lies on the coast just below the western foothills of the mountain of Yamanlar Dagh. Separated from Yamanlar by a lower ridge to the east lies the second mountain, Manisa Dagh. Scattered around the mountains are so many enigmatic remains, including rock

FIG. 18 The Hittite god at Kara Bel.

carvings, tombs and walls, that it has taken a whole century of exploration and study to identify and date them correctly. Most are quite late (classical, hellenistic and Roman), but two monuments have always stood out as being undeniably pre-Greek.

On the northern side of Manisa Dagh, carved three hundred feet up in the side of the mountain, is a colossal sculpture of a seated Mother Goddess (Plates 7 and 17). Called Tash Suret ('stone image' in Turkish), it is now best known simply as 'Cybele', the name of the Great Mother Goddess of the Phrygians, whose cult later spread to Greece and Rome. Thirty feet high, it is carved in a deep recess, where, to the right of the figure's head, is a short inscription in Hittite hieroglyphics. This is too worn to give much useful information,[41] but its existence, together with the general style of the carving, shows that the sculpture should be classed generically as Late Bronze Age Hittite. Some consider it early Hittite in style, which could place it anywhere between the fifteenth and thirteenth centuries BC.

The second monument is to the south of Yamanlar, in a pass called Kara Bel ('Black Pass'). Carved on a cliff face on the eastern side of the road, and facing southwards, is an image of a Hittite god, set in a shallow niche about eight feet high and six feet wide (Plate 6). The figure, which is more than life-size, holds a bow on his shoulder and a staff in front of him and wears typical costume – a conical crown, short kilt and sword with a crescent-shaped pommel. The iconography is so close to that of the Hittite rock sanctuary of Yazilikaya that it must be of about the same date, the thirteenth century BC. The Kara Bel figure was originally made famous by Herodotus, who described a pair of figures flanking a road near the way between Smyrna and Sardis.[42] Realising that they were not the product of any Greek artist, and unaware of the Hittites, Herodotus believed that the figures had been carved by the great Egyptian conqueror Sesostris:

> There are two images of this man carved on the rocks in Ionia . . . on either side is carved a man nearly seven feet high, holding a spear in his right hand and a bow in his left, and the rest of his equipment being part Egyptian, part Ethiopian. Across his chest, from shoulder to shoulder, runs an inscription cut in hieroglyphs, saying 'By the strength of my shoulders I won this country.'[43]

Herodotus' description is a little garbled, but clear enough to see that he was describing the Kara Bel relief. The hieroglyphs do not run across the chest but are clustered to the side of the figure, and of course they are in the Hittite sacred script, not the Egyptian. The second figure mentioned by Herodotus was a mystery until 1875, when it was found some yards away, hidden by undergrowth. Carved on a loose slab of rock and badly damaged, it was similar to the first figure.

Whether the reliefs were an official product of the Hittite Empire or were carved by a local (vassal?) monarch, aping the imperial style, has never been agreed. That they are basically

Hittite is in no doubt, while their function is fairly self-explanatory. The armed figures, positioned on either side of a mountain pass, must be some kind of territorial markers. They faced south, so were designed to greet travellers (or invaders) going north along the pass and remind them they were now entering a different land. They may have been left to mark the limits of a royal Hittite campaign, or carved simply as markers showing the border of a particular district or kingdom. In any case, the land being protected lay to the north, in other words the region of Sipylus.

What is most remarkable about the Hittite reliefs of Sipylus and Kara Bel is their very occurrence this far west. A glance at a distribution map of Hittite rock reliefs shows Sipylus and Kara Bel as isolated blobs some 150 miles further west than the nearest other example, and well over 300 miles from the Hittite capital at Boghazköy. Their existence led most scholars earlier this century to accept that the Sipylus region had been the seat of a local Hittite or client Hittite kingdom. David Hogarth, writing in the first edition of the *Cambridge Ancient History* (1924), had no doubts that this was the case, and that a dynasty ruling here during the Late Bronze or early Iron Age was behind the Greek traditions about the Tantalids.[44]

The only real question was: where was the capital of this kingdom? In other words, where was the city of Sipylus or Tantalis? Its exact location has always been confused by uncertainty about the ancient names for the two mountains of the region. The north-eastern mountain, Manisa Dagh, also known as Spil Dagh, was definitely known as Sipylus in classical times. What is not certain is whether the south-western mountain, Yamanlar, was also considered a part of Sipylus.

This element of doubt has given rise to two schools of thought on the whereabouts of Tantalus' city. Our main guide, the Greek geographer Pausanias, says that the inhabitants of Magnesia, a city which lies to the north of Sipylus, have among them 'the most ancient of all the statues of the Mother of the Gods' which was carved by Tantalus' son Broteas. Pausanias, who is thought to have been born in Magnesia, must be referring to Magnesian claims again when he says that evidence of the dynasty of Tantalus and Pelops is 'still left in our country today' – such as the lake of Tantalus, his magnificent tomb and the throne of Pelops on the mountain 'above the sanctuary of Mother Plastene'.[45] On the other hand, Aristides, a famous mystic, poet and orator who lived

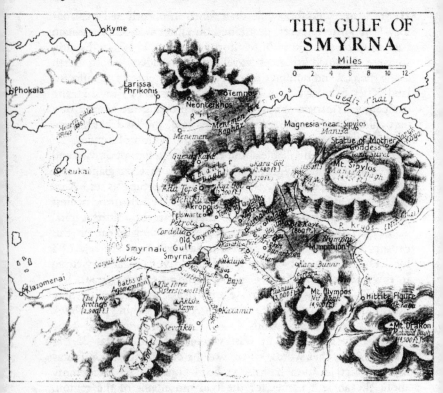

FIG. 19 Map showing the environs of Izmir (Smyrna). Modern names are shown in italics. Large areas of the Gulf of Izmir have silted up since classical times: the dotted line marks the present coastline (*from Cadoux 1948*).

in Smyrna in the second century AD, suggests much closer links with *his* city, which lies on the coast at the foot of Yamanlar Dagh. In speeches eulogising the history of Smyrna, Aristides said it had three phases. The 'first city' was that founded 'on the Sipylus' by Tantalus: 'the nymphs have received that city and now it is under the water, submerged in its lake.' The next was founded near the coast by the Athenian Theseus after he had defeated the Amazons, while the third was the present city of Smyrna.[46]

There is one other key piece of evidence. It is usually understood that Pliny stated that Lake Saloe which covers Tantalis is twelve Roman miles from Smyrna.[47] Even as the crow flies, this distance (about 11.35 modern miles) does not reach Manisa Dagh, let alone the land of the Magnesians to the north of it. On this point Aristides and the Smyrnaean school seem to have a distinct advantage.

Old Smyrna

The Smyrna of Roman times where Aristides lived was situated in precisely the same place as modern Izmir. From the citadel of Kadifekale, high on Mount Pagus behind the town, the columns of the classical market-place can be seen, peeping out between the morass of modern buildings. From the same vantage point, looking north across the Bay of Izmir, the view takes in the suburb (once village) of Bayrakli, which now sprawls across the foothills of the Yamanlar Mountain. Bayrakli is the site of the original Smyrna, settled by the Aeolians from northern Greece in about 1000 BC (on the traditional chronology).[48] The city went through both economic and political doldrums during the Persian period and was refounded at its present site on the inspiration of Alexander the Great, who, taking a nap on Mount Pagus, dreamt of restoring it to its former glory.

The Aeolian city, Old Smyrna, was the second in the series described by Aristides. So it was here that the French explorer Charles Texier arrived in 1834 to search the nearby hills for the remains of Aristides' 'first city', the seat of Tantalus and Pelops. On a hilltop behind Bayrakli, Texier discovered an enormous stone-built tomb, which he promptly identified as the 'tomb of Tantalus', mentioned by Pausanias. The drum-shaped base, composed of large polygonal blocks, was some ninety-seven feet in diameter, capped with a cone-shaped roof, which reached ninety feet above the ground. The overall style of this unique construction has been compared to the 'beehive tombs' of Mycenae. It was certainly grand enough to match Pausanias' description of the tomb of Tantalus as 'his by no means inglorious grave'.[49]

Having identified the 'tomb of Tantalus', Texier proceeded to demolish it in order to find how it was constructed. Mercifully he prepared a drawing of it before committing this amazing act of vandalism (see Fig. 20). The lowest part of the tomb and the rubble left by Texier were still visible in 1968 when Bean photographed it.[50] On our visit, after a difficult search to locate the site, we were dismayed to find that a house had been built over it. Some large stones were barely visible underneath the lowest courses of the modern masonry.[51] Still, imposing as the tomb once was, it is most unlikely that it had anything to do with Tantalus. In the opinion of modern researchers, it was built by a local magnate or governor during the Persian period.[52] If this is the grave to which Pausanias was referring, he was misinformed.

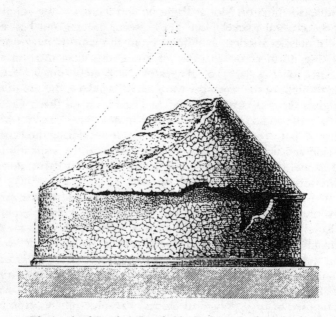

FIG. 20   The 'tomb of Tantalus' identified by Texier in the foothills of Yamanlar, near Izmir (*from Perrot & Chipiez 1890*).

The other Tantalid sites identified by the nineteenth-century explorers in the hills near Old Smyrna proved equally disappointing. Texier also spotted a small pond on the slopes behind Bayrakli and identified it as Lake Saloe, but it was so unconvincing that only he seems to have remarked on it.[53] The search was taken up by Weber, who announced confidently in 1898 that he had found Pausanias' 'sanctuary of Mother Plastene', a key landmark in Tantalid geography. On the hill of Ada Tepe, about three miles due north of Old Smyrna, Weber had discovered the remains of an enormous fortified enclosure, encompassing two crags of rock.

The southern crag was artificially levelled and furnished with steps, and an elaborate chamber open to the sky was cut into one corner – all of which suggested to Weber a sacred precinct. As for the 'throne of Pelops' which Pausanias said lay above the sanctuary, Weber argued that this must have been a local name for the one of the peaks lying nearer the summit of Yamanlar.[54] Ramsay examined these structures in 1880 and decided that their scope argued against their being simply a religious sanctuary; he felt that they were the remains of a defended acropolis. The problem was not solved until 1945, when Bean excavated the site with Rüstem Duyuran, Director of the Izmir Museum. Weber's chamber for the worship of the Mother goddess turned out to be a water-cistern, while the site as a whole proved to be a military installation, built for the defence of Smyrna during the Hellenistic period (3rd–1st centuries BC).[55]

One by one, the 'Tantalid' monuments identified by earlier explorers in the hills around Smyrna have been eliminated by subsequent research: they were either misidentified or far too late to have any genuine connection with the Tantalid dynasty, which, if real, must have reigned during the Bronze Age. Yet there are Bronze Age remains in the vicinity – not (as far as is known) in the surrounding hills but in Old Smyrna itself.

Old Smyrna, first extensively excavated between 1948 and 1951 by an Anglo-Turkish team, is an exciting site to visit. The visible excavated remains date largely to the 8th–6th centuries BC, the heyday of the city as the main Aeolian Greek colony on the coast. The Greeks believed it to be the birthplace of Homer.[56] There are no serried ranks of columns to view as there are at Sardis and other well-preserved classical sites. Instead one can enjoy restoring in the mind's eye Old Smyrna as a peninsula, surrounded on three sides by sea, or investigate parts of the enormous siege-ramp which runs up against the city wall, either laid by the Lydians at the end of the seventh century or by the Persians in the mid-sixth.[57]

Underneath the earliest remains of the Aeolian Greek colony, established about 1000 BC, deep soundings revealed Bronze Age levels containing Mycenaean pottery, though the finds are generally 'more akin to Anatolian than Aegean cultures'. The British director of excavations was the late John Cook, a ferocious walker who knew the monuments on the hills around Smyrna intimately. His assessment was that the site of Old Smyrna, was 'the centre of habitation in these parts from the beginning of the Bronze Age into Hellenic times.'[58] Cook also had great sensitivity for the value of the traditions, noting that the Byzantine encyclopedist Stephanus said that Tantalus had founded a town called Naulokhon at Smyrna, though there is no implication that this was his capital.[59] (It was gratifying to see Tantalus credited as the founder on the official placard of the excavation.) Cook carefully weighed up the possibility that Old Smyrna itself may have been the seat of the Tantalid dynasty, but concluded that 'tempting as it is to see in this modest peninsula site the capital of Tantalus and the rival of that of Ilus [of Troy], against whom Tantalus is reputed to have waged an unsuccessful war, the discoveries in the prehistoric levels . . . do not suggest a splendour in any way comparable to that of Troy.'[60]

Cook's assessment must be accepted. The excavations at Old Smyrna show that while it might have been the harbour of a Bronze Age kingdom it was not its political centre. Overall, the case for locating Tantalis in the immediate region of Smyrna and the lower foothills of Yamanlar is extremely weak, and the area has now been too well explored to produce any surprises. Furthermore Aristides, chief spokesman for the Smyrnaean school, clearly spoke of a mountain location, 'on the Sipylus'. So it was further into the mountains we went.

The Black Lake

If the standard interpretation of Pliny is accepted, then the site of Tantalis lay twelve miles from Smyrna. This distance takes us into the heart of Yamanlar Dagh, where there are two small lakes, Kara Göl and Kyz Göl. Kara Göl, the larger of the two, has actually been the favourite candidate for the lake of Tantalus since the late nineteenth century.[61]

The enchanting Kara Göl ('Black Lake') lies in a hollow near the top of Yamanlar Dagh, 2,680 feet above sea-level, surrounded by a beautiful pine forest. Fed by a small mountain stream, it is now stocked with freshwater shrimps as well as fish, and is a perfect, secluded picnic and fishing spot. The lake is about 31,000 square metres, according to the keepers of Kara Göl, who also told us that it was only five metres deep. Perhaps they misunderstood our question, as their estimate disagrees with everything else we have heard. Locals I spoke to at the mountaineering club of Manisa tell the story of a car that was pushed into the lake and disappeared without trace. Likewise Cecil Cadoux, the greatest expert on ancient Smyrna (he was born there), referred to it as 'deep mysterious Kara Göl'.[62]

Looking at the map, there seemed nothing untoward with the idea that there may have been an ancient settlement at the site of Kara Göl, though a very different opinion was expressed by twentieth-century archaeologists who had visited the site. Cadoux noted that 'the situation is not a very likely one for a real city'; Bean thought it 'improbable in the extreme'.[63]

Seeing, it is said, is believing. On the drive up to the lake, we engaged in a debate as to the likelihood of any major settlement existing at such an inaccessible altitude. When we arrived, we realised our speculations were pointless. Kara Göl is picturesquely beautiful but, without question, no place to build a town or even a village. It just doesn't feel right. Apart from the problems of hauling supplies up the difficult mountain roads, the area of the lake itself – a steep, roughly circular depression – is simply too restricted. There would be no room to grow anything but a handful of vegetables or tether more than the smallest of flocks. To make matters worse, Pliny talks about Tantalis being replaced by *three* successive cities on the same site, each of which succumbed to a similar fate. This would multiply by four the problem of siting a city at Kara Göl, turning improbability into sheer impossibility. Pliny's comments could simply be rejected, of course, but this would defeat the point of the exercise, which was to try to discover where he and our main source, Pausanias, believed the site to be. If we treated their views lightly we would lose our guides and might as well give up.

To make matters worse there was no trace whatsoever of any past habitation near the lake. As we walked around we searched keenly for sherds of pottery. Such surface finds are often the telltale sign of ancient occupation. (Even in unploughed areas, sherds can rise to the surface.) In the day we spent at the lake we found absolutely nothing. As we were about to leave, some locals turned up. They had heard we were archaeologists and, with the all-too common assumption that this means coin-collectors, they started to intimate about ancient things to be found near the lake. After some time it became clear what they were talking about. In the nearby hills they claimed that there were some graves of the Byzantine period. Were we interested? 'No thanks, not our period,' we said, and even if it had been, we were not interested in buying coins.*

As regards the Byzantine material, the story is feasible. In the fifteenth century, the cities nearby (Smyrna and Magnesia) were conquered by the Ottoman Turks, and many of the local inhabitants would have run for their lives; some would have escaped to the mountains to hide their savings, if not their mortal souls, in the remote hideaways offered by Yamanlar mountain. Such hoards or burials would be no surprise, and this possibility only confirms Kara Göl as the most unlikely place for a major settlement. It was a place of refuge at most, and unlikely to have been used as anything more since Stone Age times.[64]

Despite a century's search, there were no other features within a twelve-mile radius of Smyrna that might provide a realistic candidate for the site of the lost city. Shrugging off a feeling that we might be on a wild-goose chase, we went back to the drawing board – in this case, the ancient sources.

On further re-examination, Pliny's statement about the 'twelve miles' seemed to make no sense at all. In another place Pliny makes it clear that he located Tantalis 'in Magnesia', presumably not directly inside the city itself, but within its immediate district.[65] Yet Magnesia is much more than twelve Roman miles from Smyrna. So do the two passages simply contradict one another? We concluded that they did not – the 'twelve miles' claim is actually a red herring. Pliny's mention of Tantalis comes in a brief digression to his discussion of the Aegean coast of Asia Minor. Listing the important towns and features of Ionia, he proceeds northwards along the coast to the promontory of Mount Mimas. He continues in the same direction along the coast, and next mentions Clazomenae and two islands called the Chytrophoria which Alexander joined to the mainland. Then, as an aside, comes the important passage about Sipylus/Tantalis:

Places in the interior that exist no longer were Daphnus and Hermesta and Sipylus previously called Tantalis, the capital of Maeonia, situated where there is now the marsh called Sale; Archaeopolis which replaced Sipylus has also perished, and later

---

* In Turkey it is not only immoral, but a criminal offence carrying heavy penalties to take coins, or any other antiquities, from the country without special licence.

Colpe which replaced Archaeopolis and Libade which replaced Colpe.[66]

The next sentence begins: 'on returning thence to the coast at a distance of twelve miles we come to Smyrna, founded by an Amazon and restored by Alexander . . . '[67] The key question, of course, is from which spot the twelve miles were measured. Since the Sipylus passage is a digression (today we might have used brackets or a footnote), it is surely best to assume that the distance was measured from the last coastal place mentioned. This was the understanding of the translators of the Bohn edition of Pliny, who took Clazomenae as the starting point. Cadoux, in his definitive work on ancient Smyrna, disagreed, as Clazomenae is about twenty-four Roman miles from Smyrna.[68] Everyone since seems either to have followed him and the early explorers in looking for Lake Sale in the Yamanlar region – or to have simply given up. In any case, it would not be unreasonable to conclude that an extra 'x' (ten) was accidentally dropped from our text of Pliny during copying rather than that he misunderstood how far Clazomenae or Sipylus lay from Smyrna. Twenty-two Roman miles (about 20.8 of ours) are enough to bring us comfortably to either place.

If Pliny's contribution on this point is based simply on a misunderstanding, then the only evidence left for the Smyrnaean case is the impression given by Aristides, who was, after all, writing a poetical account of his city's history, and not a geographical or scientific handbook – as Pausanias and Pliny were. Abandoning the twelve-mile limit thought to be imposed by Pliny meant that the evidence of Pausanias could come fully into its own.

Ancient Magnesia

When we arrived in Magnesia (now Manisa) we were pleasantly surprised. There were numerous monuments and features associated with Tantalus, not by antiquarian speculation but by genuine ancient tradition. *Every* feature that Pausanias described – the sanctuary of Mother Plastene, the statue of the Mother Goddess, the throne of Pelops, the tomb of Tantalus, even Lake Saloe – could be matched on the ground or located. They were all clustered together, just as Pausanias describes them, in a small area just outside Magnesia.

As Bean realised long ago, the strongest card of the Magnesian school is the Mother of the Gods and the carving and sanctuary associated with her. Two pieces of solid archaeological evidence enabled us to locate them beyond any reasonable doubt.

The first piece is the Hittite carving of the Mother Goddess, or Cybele. Its air of mysterious antiquity and its position on the northern slope of nearby Sipylus confirm that this was the 'statue' described by Pausanias:

> The Magnesians to the north of Mount Sipylus have the most ancient of all statues of the Mother of the Gods on the rock of Koddinos; the Magnesians say it was made by Tantalus' son Broteas.[69]

It is to the credit of Magnesian tradition that it associated Tantalus, who must be placed in the Late Bronze Age, with a monument from that very period.

The second piece of key evidence comes from two Greek inscriptions of the Roman period, found on the plain beneath the Hittite goddess in 1887. The inscriptions record dedications to 'Mother Plastene'. One is on a marble statuette representing the Phrygian goddess Cybele seated on a throne, with a lion on each side of her. Unfortunately the exact location of these finds was never marked on a map, although we know it was only a short distance (about fifteen minutes' walk) away from the Cybele sculpture.[70] But they demonstrate the existence of a cult of the goddess, with the rare title 'Plastene', in the immediate vicinity. It is fair to assume that they came from the sanctuary of Mother Plastene, mentioned by Pausanias in connection with the other Tantalid landmarks:

> Some traces of the line of Pelops and of Tantalus are still left in our country today: the lake of Tantalus named after him and his by no means inglorious grave, and Pelops' throne on the mountaintop at Sipylus, over the sanctuary of Plastene the Mother; also a statue of Aphrodite at Temnus across the River Hermus, carved from myrtle wood.[71]

If the sanctuary of Plastene is located near the Hittite rock carving on the north side of Mount Sipylus, then it follows that the Tantalid monuments of 'our country' (with the exception of the statue at Temnus which Pausanias placed elsewhere) were all in the vicinity of Magnesia. Indeed, this has been the conclusion of all the careful scholars who have studied the matter, from Ramsay to Bean.

Despite this, there has been much confusion over the location of Pausanias' Tantalid monuments. No scholar suggested a better identification than Cybele for the relief carved by Broteas, but the matter was obfuscated for almost a century because of another landmark mentioned by Pausanias – the rock of Niobe.

The Weeping Rock

Niobe, a daughter of Tantalus, is renowned for the cruel fate accorded her by the gods. She bore fourteen children and lost them all in a single moment of pride. According to the Roman geographer Solinus, the city of Tantalis was given its second name in memory of one of her sons, who was called Sipylus.[72]

The story is most vividly told by the Roman poet Ovid, who places the scene at Thebes in Greece. Niobe had come there from Sipylus to marry the Theban king, the skilful lyre-player Amphion. Niobe's pride was her downfall. The Titaness Leto had born to Zeus Apollo and Artemis. Annoyed by the homage that mortals paid to Leto, Niobe boasted that she too had divine ancestry – in her veins flowed the blood of the Titan Atlas and, through her father Tantalus, that of Zeus himself. And whereas Leto had born only twins, Niobe had no less than seven sons and seven daughters. Leto told Apollo and Artemis of the insults she had received at the hands of Niobe, and they speedily dispatched all of her sons with arrows. So dismayed was Amphion that he killed himself with a sword. Niobe, however, was unrepentant, so Apollo and Artemis shot all of her daughters as well. So acute was Niobe's misery at the loss of her entire family that she was turned to stone. Ovid concluded the story thus:

> A violent whirlwind caught her up and carried her away to her own country, where she was set down on a mountain-top. There she wasted away and even now tears trickle from her marble face.[73]

Others report her metamorphosis as an act of mercy on the part of the gods. Apollodorus says that Niobe 'quitted Thebes and went to her father Tantalus at Sipylus and there on praying to Zeus she was transformed into a stone and tears flowed night and day from the stone.'[74]

The story is at least as old as Homer, who tells how Niobe now 'stands among the crags in the untrodden hills of Sipylus'.[75] Centuries later, the rock that had been Niobe was still visible. Pausanias wrote that:

> I myself have seen Niobe when I was climbing up the mountains to Sipylus. Niobe from very close up is a rock and a stream and nothing like a woman either grieving or otherwise; but if you go further off you seem to see a woman downcast and in tears.[76]

Clearly there was a rock formation on Mount Sipylus that resembled a weeping woman. The belief also seems to have been widespread that tears actually did flow from the rock, like the weeping statues of the Madonna still venerated today. A possible explanation given locally is that the 'tears' were formed by the melting of ice and snow that had settled on her head. Pausanias was clearly not impressed by this miraculous aspect of the story:

> And they say Niobe on Mt Sipylus weeps in the summer. And there are other stories I have heard told: that griffins have spots like leopards and tritons [mermen] speak in human voices . . . People who enjoy listening to mythical stories are inclined to add even more wonders of their own, and in this way they have done injuries to the truths, which they have mixed up with a lot of rubbish.[77]

What was this marvellous monument? For a hundred years explorers were deceived by the Hittite carving of the Mother Goddess (Tash Suret) into believing that they had seen Niobe. Some were disappointed. The English classical scholar Cecil Torr made these tart remarks after he had 'taken the trouble' to climb up to what he was told was 'Niobe' in April 1882:

> The figure has been worn down by weather to an almost shapeless mass, and it is not big enough to be impressive . . . After going to Niobe, I felt there must be something in what Philo of Byzantium says at the beginning of his book about the Seven Wonders of the World – instead of taking troublesome journeys people had much better stay at home and read his book.[78]

Torr would have been less sarcastic if he had known he had been looking at the wrong thing. What is missing from the Hittite goddess, of course, is the *trompe l'oeil* described by Pausanias. Besides, neither he nor the poet Quintus of Smyrna refers to Niobe as a carving. In fact Quintus said that 'when you come close it is seen to be just a high rock, a fragment broken off Sipylus'.[79] Yet, as late as 1938, Cadoux was still putting forward Tash Suret as Niobe, as 'all efforts to discover a natural Niobe rock other than Taş Suret had failed'.[80] Yet as Bean noted, almost immediately after the appearance of Cadoux's book, Helmut Bossert discovered the true Niobe, a marvellous freak of nature which is once again a local tourist attraction, just as it used to be in Roman times.

As Pausanias said, Niobe is found on the way up the top of Mount Sipylus. The ascent is too steep to the east of Manisa, so instead the road goes southwards following a route which eventually curves around the mountain to a point near the summit. At the beginning of this route sits Niobe, near the foot of the mountain and the edge of the modern Spil National Park. Walking straight up to it from the road, one sees, as Pausanias said, 'just a rocky cliff bearing no resemblance to a woman' (Plate 8). Take a step back to the western side, there you see her (Plates 9 and 10). By viewing her at different heights and bobbing up and down one can see her streaming hair, her hooked nose and nuances of her agonised expression: but, of course, if one comes too close the illusion is lost.

As Bean notes, 'that this is the figure of Niobe described by Pausanias and Quintus cannot be doubted'.[81] Being natural, it is not an archaeological feature in the normal sense of the word. Even so, its identification as the real Niobe provides two important historical clues. It has often been assumed that the stories of Tantalus and his family orginated on the other side of the Aegean and that they were transposed by Greek colonists to a Lydian setting, localising them around Mount Sipylus. A motive for such a shift is never given. In the case of Niobe it seems absurd to imagine that the Greeks developed the story of a woman so distraught that she turned to stone and that they *then* searched western Anatolia for a feature to fit the tale. It is far more economical that the simulacrum near Manisa inspired the story in the first place – whether the locals were Greeks or native Anatolians. The story of Niobe's transformation would have then spread to Greece with the rest of the Tantalus corpus.

The second fallout from the correct identification of Niobe is

FIG. 21   The 'throne of Pelops' on Mount Sipylus, carved at an unknown date
(*from Perrot & Chipiez, after a photograph by Humann*).

that it has finally removed all coi.fusion over the identification of
the Hittite carving of Tash Suret in Pausanias' writings. Tash Suret
was Pausanias' 'Mother of the Gods', carved by Broteas and the
centre of the nearby cult of Mother Plastene. She is the vantage
point for locating all the other remains of the Tantalid dynasty.

The Throne of Pelops

On top of Mount Sipylus, above the sanctuary of Mother Plastene,
wrote Pausanias, lay the 'throne of Pelops'. This feature was identified by archaeologists late in the last century. About half a mile east
of Cybele, on an almost inaccessible crag overlooking the plain,
there is a strange shape like a seat or a bisected cube cut into the
rock.

The way up to the 'throne of Pelops' takes in another conspicuous feature of the mythological landscape. Democles says Mount
Sipylus was 'shattered' in the reign of Tantalus and Pausanias talks
of a crack in the mountain from which waters flowed to drown the
lost city and form Lake Saloe. They could hardly be referring to
anything but the deep ravine or canyon which interrupts the cliff
face below the throne of Pelops.

Known in Turkish as Yarikkaya ('rifted rock'), the ravine is about 100 feet wide, its sides sheer walls of rock about 500 feet high (see Plates 15 and 16). Yarikkaya has a mysterious and slightly sinister quality: it is easy to see how it was associated with the legend of the earthquake that destroyed Tantalus' city. To the layman's eye it looks as if the mountain has simply been ripped in two by titanic forces, in Ramsay's words 'cleft as if by some terrible convulsion of nature, right down to the level of the Hermus valley'.[82] Whether it was really caused by an earthquake is another matter. James Frazer, in his classic commentary on Pausanias, said it 'was plain' that the ravine had been scooped out by a stream gradually wearing away the limestone rock.[83] Ramsay ventured a similar opinion, noting that he had consulted the geographer Sir Charles Wilson, but omitted to add whether Wilson examined the ravine personally.[84] On the other hand, while it is 'plain' that the sides of the ravine have been smoothed by the action of water, this does not show that the canyon was originally formed by water action. It would hardly be surprising to see earthquake scars in a region where earthquakes are so common and so violent. So far I have been unsuccessful in tracing any modern geological research on this part of Manisa Dagh, which seems to have been strangely forgotten by academics in recent years.

For the ascent up to the throne of Pelops near Yarikkaya, we have to follow Frazer as the perilous track used by him in 1898 has long since disappeared.[85] A few travellers had preceded him, including Ramsay and the German archaeologist Karl Humann. The accounts and detailed sketches of such early explorers reveal more than any photography could today (see Figs 21 and 22). Above Yarikkaya on its western side is a towering crag, which partly hangs over the ravine. There is no way up to it through the ravine. We crawled along for some way but any further progress upwards was impossible – the rocks are too smooth. The way up taken by Frazer and his predecessors was not from Yarikkaya, but from the front of the mountain:

> Even to reach the foot of this crag from the plain, stout limbs and a steady hand are needed; for the ancient mule path, partly hewn out of the rock, partly supported on walls on the edge of precipices, has mostly disappeared; and there is nothing for it but to cling as best you can to the bushes and the projections of the rock. In this way you at least reach the foot of the cliff, the sheer face of which bars all further advance. However,

on the western side of the crag there is a cleft or 'chimney' . . .
which leads up to the top, otherwise quite unapproachable . . .

We discovered later from the mountaineering club at Manisa
that there is a slightly safer, roundabout route to the top of the
crag, approaching it via a long haul from the eastern side of
the mountain.* Time was too short on our journey to organise
a trip with them, so for the moment we will have to continue
up with Frazer, who did it the hard way:

In antiquity there seems to have been a staircase in the 'chimney'. The first few steps of it may be seen under the bushes
with which the rocky fissure is overgrown. The upper surface
of the crag reached through this cleft is nowhere level; on the
contrary it slopes like the roof of a house and is indeed so steep
that to climb it is difficult. There are, however, twenty or thirty
foundations of houses cut in the rock and rising one above
another like steps of an immense staircase. Also there are seven
or eight bell-shaped cisterns.

The so-called houses and cisterns can be seen on Humann's
plan. At the topmost point of the crag lay the throne of Pelops,
which Frazer describes with some exhilaration:

On the very topmost pinnacle of the crag there is a square cut
into the rock, resembling the seat of a large armchair . . . It is
about five feet wide, three feet from front to back and three
feet high at the back. The back of the seat (as it may be called)
is simply the top of the precipice, which falls straight down
into the ravine, a sheer drop of 900 feet. Across the ravine soars
the arid rocky wall of Sipylus. On the other side the eye ranges
over the valley of Hermus, stretched like a map at one's feet.
There seems to be little doubt that this remarkable rock-cut
seat, perched on the pinnacle of the dizzy crag, is no other
than the 'throne of Pelops' mentioned by Pausanias.[86]

Frazer, along with Ramsay, Humann and others, was undoubtedly right, but, as he said, 'what the original intention of the
cutting may have been is a different question'. Ramsay suggested

* It should be stressed that it is inadvisable to attempt the climb without professional
help. Local hotheads occasionally make the climb, but while we were in Manisa
the mountaineering club had to rescue two youths who were completely stuck on
their way up to the crag.

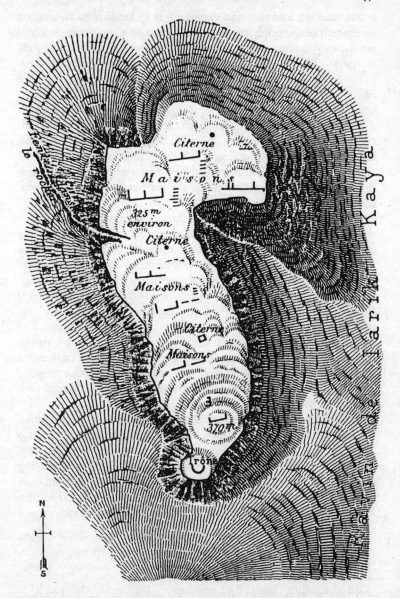

FIG. 22   Plan of the structures on the steep crag overlooking the ravine of
Yarikkaya, including cisterns and 'houses' cut from the rock. The 'throne
of Pelops' is at the southern tip (*from Perrot & Chipiez 1890*).

it was an altar, and the crag site as a whole lends itself to a cultic interpretation, though perhaps it doubled as a look-out post and emergency stronghold. Ramsay thought that the site was a small 'fortress' and the crag was certainly a naturally defensible position.[87] That it was used as a regular settlement seems the least likely explanation of the site. The so-called 'houses', of which only 'bases' cut into the rock exist, make unconvincing dwellings. The ascent by way of a mule-track, supports and even steps was certainly easier in antiquity, but that houses were placed on this exposed, acutely sloping crag still seems unlikely. A place for the rituals of a mountain-cult, probably connected with the worship of Cybele whose image hangs on the rock only half a mile away, seems more feasible.

The date of these archaeologically unique structures remains a matter of guesswork. Ramsay examined the pottery lying on the surface of the crag, including 'an abundance of broken tiles like those on all sites in the district', 'fragments of common red ware' and a vessel with black glaze 'of the ordinary Hellenic style'.[88] To judge from his comments elsewhere he was talking of the 5th–3rd centuries BC. Of course, this scatter does not show when the crag site was built, only when it was last frequented heavily. The structures may predate Greek settlement in the area in about the eighth century, but the suggestion that they are Mycenaean seems groundless.[89] The truth is that the only serious archaeological work on the site was done in the late nineteenth century, so a more accurate assessment is presently impossible.

All we know for certain is that the Magnesians of Pausanias' time (second century AD) knew about these curious rock cuttings and pictured the great Pelops, son of Tantalus, sitting in the seat-shaped niche at the top to survey his kingdom. This is interesting in itself. As Frazer notes, the 'throne' gives a commanding view over the plain, including Magnesia (Manisa) and the Hermus Valley beyond. Is this then where the kingdom of Tantalus and Pelops was believed to have been?

'His by no means inglorious grave'

With the other Tantalid monuments in context, the tomb of Tantalus is easy to identify. The road to the north of Sipylus (an old caravan route) hugs the base of the mountain quite closely and if one travels eastward for about half a mile beyond the

Yarikkaya ravine, one comes to an impressive stone tomb cut about forty feet up into the side of the mountain. It is not easy to spot. The tomb's façade is formed from the slope of the mountain itself, and the trees now obscure it almost completely. Bean described it in his popular account of the area in 1968, but the tomb seems to have been forgotten by locals and archaeologists alike and now provides a quiet home for scorpions. It was once known locally as the 'tomb of St Charalambos', after a medieval hermit took up residence there, but now it has no name at all. (Plates 11 to 13 are the first modern photographs of the tomb to be published.)

The construction of the tomb is unique. Even the steps are cut entirely from the living rock, showing the immense skill of the builders. The deep rectangular cutting around the tomb defines its shape and serves the added function of channelling off rainwater to protect the façade from erosion. Inside are two low chambers, one behind the other. There can be little doubt that this grand edifice was what Pausanias recognised as the 'by no means inglorious grave' of Tantalus. As Ramsay noted, 'there are practically only two tombs in Sipylus which so far surpass their

FIG. 23 The 'tomb of St Charalambos' near Manisa (Magnesia). This was the real tomb of Tantalus mentioned by Pausanias (*after Humann 1885*).

neighbours in size or beauty that popular tradition can have seen in them the tomb of the great legendary hero of the district.'[90] The other is that near Smyrna destroyed by Texier. Texier's tomb can be ruled out as it is too far from the other Tantalid remains, while the 'tomb of Charalambos' fits the bill perfectly. Its splendid construction suggests it was indeed the tomb of a local king.

Whether it was really associated with the Tantalids as a Bronze Age dynasty is another matter. Unfortunately the tomb was practically empty when Humann examined it in 1888 and guesses as to its date are all based on vague analogies with other tomb types.[91] It is certainly not Roman or Greek in style. Rock-cut tombs were a tradition in Anatolia, the finest and most famous examples coming from the kingdom of Lycia between the fifth and third centuries BC. But, apart from being rock-cut, there is really no point of comparison between the Lycian examples and the tomb of Tantalus. Nearer home, the Phrygians (just to the east of Lydia) also cut rock tombs. At the most splendid example, from Arslan Tash (probably 8th–7th century BC), the tomb entrance is flanked by two enormous rampant lions, one each side of a false column.[92] Again, there is no specific Phrygian parallel to the tomb of Tantalus. Ramsay, the great expert on Phrygian tombs, found it 'one of the most remarkable rock tombs I have seen'.[93]

Given their proximity, the Phrygian tombs and the tomb of Tantalus are probably related by the same tradition of rock cutting and tomb building. The first Phrygian examples seem to be from the ninth century at the earliest. Could the tomb of Tantalus be earlier, even a genuine relic of the dynasty that once ruled this mountain during the Bronze Age? For the moment the best thing is to accept Bean's assessment that 'it is undoubtedly very ancient'.[94] A Bronze Age date cannot be ruled out.

The Lake of Tantalus

We had now put every feature mentioned by Pausanias into place: Niobe; the oldest statue of the Mother of the Gods (Cybele); the sanctuary of Mother Plastene; the crack in the mountain (Yarikkaya); the throne of Pelops; and the tomb of Tantalus. Every feature, that is, except the lake or lakes he mentioned.

The list in which Pausanias groups most of these features begins with 'the Lake of Tantalus named after him'. He alludes to this lake elsewhere in a completely different context, discussing the rarity of white animals and birds: 'at Sipylus around Tantalus' lake I have seen some eagles they call swan eagles which are as white as swans.'[95] Was this lake 'at' or 'on' Sipylus? Unfortunately the Greek preposition (*en*) used here can mean either (as well as 'in'). The reference to eagles makes a mountain location like Kara Göl spring to mind, but on second thoughts it is hardly conclusive. Eagles may nest in mountain eyries, but this is not what Pausanias seems to have been talking about. He was surely referring to eagles flying around a lake, and they may well have left a nearby mountain crag to hunt for fish.

The second lake is Saloe, which Pausanias said covered the lost city. Pausanias' Lake Saloe is indisputably the same as Pliny's marsh of Sale, site of the city of Tantalis. As Tantalis was named after Tantalus, the most economical solution would seem to be that the Lake of Tantalus was one and the same as Saloe.

Whether or not it was identical with the Lake of Tantalus, Saloe does not seem to have been situated on a mountain, as Ramsay noted long ago: 'A scrutiny of Pausanias' words shows that his city was not in the heart of the mountains.'[96] In the passage where he talks about the city falling into a chasm, Pausanias refers to the mountain not as the site of the lost city – only as the source of the water which flowed from a crack in the mountain to drown it. Pliny's evidence corroborates this impression. As noted earlier, the idea that the site of Tantalis, succeeded by three further settlements on the same spot, actually lay *on* the mountain rather than next to it seems extremely unlikely. Pliny clearly refers to the city of Tantalis not as 'on Sipylus', but as 'in Magnesia', the district of the classical city on the plain.

The belief that Saloe/Sale, and therefore Tantalis, was located on top of the mountain has been the second major stumbling block, along with Pliny's twelve-mile limit, to previous interpretations. It seems we have the orator Aristides to thank for the misconception. Yet his lyrical descriptions of the lost city hardly weigh against the evidence of the matter-of-fact accounts of Pausanias and Pliny. As Ramsay pointed out, 'Aristides was not a native of the district, he was a great invalid who had certainly never gone to Sipylus and probably never been at Magnesia.'[97]

The Site of Tantalis

We can now assemble all the clues from the mythological land-scape described by Pausanias and Pliny, to see where they thought the lost city of Tantalis lay:

1 Under a lake or marsh called Saloe/Sale.
2 On the plain, near the northern side of Mount Sipylus.
3 Not too far from the tomb where Tantalus was believed to have been buried.
4 Near the ravine of Yarikkaya, apparently thought to be the source of the water that drowned the city.
5 Not too far from Cybele, believed to have been carved by Tantalus' son Broteas.
6 Probably overlooked by the throne of Pelops on the mountain top.

These criteria narrow the search down to a fairly restricted area, just east of ancient Magnesia. Yet today there is no lake, nor even a marsh in the vicinity. Fortunately when we travelled to Sipylus we had a copy of the map prepared by the great anti-quarians Georges Perrot and Charles Chipiez in 1890 (see Fig. 24). This, curiously enough, shows a small lake directly in front of Cybele, the Hittite Mother Goddess (mislabelled 'Niobe' on their map) – fitting perfectly all the requirements of Lake Saloe, except perhaps for its size. Now the area is simply farmland, but enquiries in Manisa showed that the lake existed not so long ago. A photograph we were shown depicts it as a local swimming spot, and older members of the mountaineering club remember taking a dip there before the lake was drained. It seems that Lake Saloe, the last resting place of Tantalus' legendary city, had been ungraciously pumped out to make room for more crops.

On rereading Frazer's and Ramsay's investigations, I was pleased to find that they had not only beaten me to the same conclusion about the lake – they could also give something of its history. In 1898 Frazer wrote: 'Below the image of Mother Plastene there is a small lake of clear water, fed by countless springs that gush from the rocky foot of the mountain. The water is dammed up and turns a mill. Some forty or fifty years ago, before it was dammed up, the lake covered a much larger area. It is probably the Saloe of Pausanias, the Sale of Pliny.'[98]

Sixteen years earlier Ramsay had reached the same conclusion, identifying Saloe as the 'tiny lake' beneath Cybele, 'which is said to have been much larger till it was drained about forty years ago'.[99] The size of the lake as it was in Frazer's and Ramsay's day can be judged from the map published by Perrot and Chipiez. Exactly how big it was in about 1840, before it was first drained, I am still investigating.

After a fairly long haul it was ironic to find that Pausanias' Lake Saloe had been 'on the map' all the time – but had been drained and simply forgotten. Yet there can be little doubt that it was here that Pausanias was told that, in days gone by, one could see the remains of a city beneath the waters, until mud had covered them.

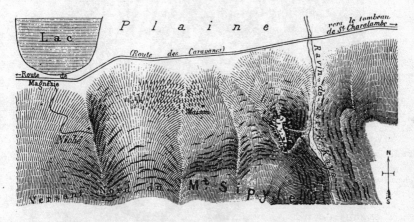

FIG. 24 Sketch-map by Perrot and Chipiez (1890) showing the small lake which once lay opposite the Hittite carving of Tash Suret ('Cybele') on the northern side of Mount Sipylus. (Here Tash Suret is mislabelled 'Niobe', following the error current until the real Niobe was discovered this century.) To the east of the lake are the ravine of Yarikkaya and the 'tomb of St Charalambos', known to Pausanias as the tomb of Tantalus.

Before turning to the wider historical evidence there is one thought to share, which came as we tramped through the field which lies opposite Cybele. We turned back and were struck by something which in retrospect seemed so completely obvious. The image of the Mother Goddess 'looks' directly across the field where the lake used to be. It was meant to be viewed from this spot.

The image of Cybele, carved in the Late Bronze Age is thirty feet high and is positioned three hundred feet up the face of the mountain. A marvel of ancient sculpture, its construction was not the work of a few passing shepherds. It would have needed the labour, organisation, indeed motivation, of a large and prosperous settled community. Where then did those people live? Many miles away? Or immediately below the image of the Mother, where she could smile on them every day?

FIG. 25   The Hittite carving of the Mother Goddess on the north face of Mount Sipylus (*from Perrot & Chipiez 1890a*).

CHAPTER 10

A Sunken City

Finding where a legendary city is said to have been is one thing. Discovering whether there was any reality behind the story, especially when the city is supposed to have disappeared into a chasm and been submerged by water more than three thousand years ago, is, of course, a very different matter.

One wonders why the nineteenth-century scholars Ramsay and Frazer, after successfully locating the legendary resting place of Tantalis, then gave up the chase. The problem was that they really had only the classical sources to go on, and after locating the site, both were quite happy to treat the matter purely in terms of folklore. Ramsay decided that the story of the sunken kingdom had been generated by confusion in the retelling of the story. The 'city', for him, was really the small acropolis on the mountain near the throne of Pelops; oral tradition had somehow relocated it beneath a nearby lake, while a cataclysmic earthquake, suggested by the ravine of Yarikkaya, was added as a mythical explanation of its demise. So Ramsay left it. Frazer took a similar line, and no later work of any seriousness was done to investigate the Tantalid remains near Magnesia.

Indeed, enthusiasm for the whole matter waned towards the middle of this century. When Cadoux wrote his history of Smyrna in 1938, he included a fairly thorough review of all the theories about the monuments scattered around the Yamanlar and Manisa mountains. However, he glossed over the conclusions of Ramsay and Frazer and monstrously recomplicated the problem by insisting that Pliny's Tantalis lay no more than twelve miles from Smyrna. He decided that the mysterious Kara Göl was an appropriate candidate for Lake Saloe, but because this was certainly never the site of a Bronze Age settlement, it only went to show that the story of the lost city was a fantasy.[1] The search for Tantalis, rather like that for Atlantis itself, was relegated to the sidelines of archaeological research.

Of course, the classical traditions were not enough to go on by themselves, though there are good grounds for supposing that Sipylus was once the seat of a Bronze Age kingdom. The rock-carvings at Kara Bel ('Sesostris') and Sipylus ('Cybele') show that this was an important region – both politically and religiously – during the Bronze Age and they were once accepted as evidence that Sipylus had been the seat of a Hittite client kingdom.

The problem was that, while the existence of such a kingdom was not denied, there was nothing to clinch the matter. At the time that Ramsay and Frazer wrote, barely anything solid was known of the Hittites, let alone the western lands of Arzawa. In 1879 the great Orientalist Professor Archibald Sayce examined the 'Sesostris' and 'Cybele' reliefs and recognised that they belonged to the same sculptural tradition as the carved rock sanctuary of Yazilikaya on the central Anatolian plateau. In a paper read to the Society of Biblical Archaeology in 1880 he was bold enough to draw the conclusion that they were all products of a 'lost Hittite Empire'. His hunch was corroborated in 1887, when letters from the Hittite Emperor Suppiluliuma were discovered at El-Amarna in Egypt, then completely confirmed in 1906 when the archives of the Hittite emperors at Boghazköy were excavated. The Hittite empire, stretching at its maximum extent from the Aegean to Damascus in Syria, now became a reality.[2]

Sipylus, with its rock carvings once so special to the nascent field of Hittitology, now became a backwater of study. Why spend time on this remote, peripheral area when the capital of the Hittites was producing thousands of tablets documenting political history, religion, trade and almost every other aspect of Hittite culture? While the existence of Arzawa, great rival of the Hittites, was known about since the discovery of the El-Amarna tablets, its location continued to be uncertain. Scholars were still free to argue that it lay in southern Anatolia, for example in the classical region of Cilicia close to northern Syria. So the Hittite sculptures of Sipylus, with their faint, uninformative inscriptions, remained politically, geographically and culturally anonymous. Efforts to link them with the legendary Tantalid dynasty must have seemed trivial when there was so much work on the Boghazköy Hittites to be undertaken.

The 'Mountain Land of Zippasla'

The last thirty years have seen momentous developments in Hittitology. Major areas of Hittite geography and chronology that were once murky have now been clarified, and one of the main areas to benefit has been the Arzawa lands of western Anatolia.

The texts of the Hittites have much to say about their traditional Arzawan enemies. At times, it seems, there were life-and-death struggles between the two, but which of them eventually won is hard to say. At the point when the Hittite empire collapsed, its records accordingly dry up, though Arzawan enmity certainly played a part.[3] Since 1970 it has been known that there was a far earlier crisis point in their relations which is actually better documented. Near the end of the fifteenth century BC a coalition of Arzawan states effectively smashed the power of the Hittites and appears to have taken control of all western and southern Anatolia. This extraordinary episode is known from a lengthy text from Boghazköy which catalogues the repeated treachery of an Arzawan vassal known as Madduwattas.[4] The text, known as the 'Indictment of Madduwattas', used to be dated to the reign of Hittite Emperor Tudhaliyas IV, in the late thirteenth century, but has now been reassigned to the reign of Tudhaliyas II (c. 1450–1430).[5] Once thought to chronicle the events which led to the final downfall of the Empire, it is now seen as documenting an earlier collapse, from which the Hittites eventually recovered.

According to the 'Indictment', Madduwattas was a western vassal of the Hittite emperor who had been displaced from his lands by a Mycenaean king or warlord referred to as 'Attarssiyas, Man of Ahhiya[wa]'. Madduwattas took refuge at the court of Emperor Tudhaliyas, who installed or reinstated him as vassal ruler of Zippasla.[6] Madduwattas was again attacked by Attarssiyas, this time with an army including a force of a hundred chariots, but Tudhaliyas sent a Hittite general to support him. Attarssiyas was defeated and Madduwattas' position at Zippasla consolidated.

The ambitious Madduwattas then took steps to shake off his dependence on the Hittites. Step by step he made neighbouring cities tributary to himself, rather than the emperor, and inveigled the emperor into ceding him control of important Arzawan territories. Eventually he made himself master of all the Arzawa lands, next moving towards the central Anatolian region of Pitassa, where he persuaded the local aldermen to accept him as overlord.

Finally, in coalition with his old antagonist Attarssiyas, we find Madduwattas raiding the island of Alashiya (Cyprus). Unfortunately, the text, already very fragmentary at this critical point, then breaks off completely.

Among the many puzzles posed by this text is the location of Zippasla, the kingdom used by Madduwattas as the springboard for his takeover of the Arzawa lands. In the past, no precise locations for Zippasla were offered, due to a number of obstacles. First, the references to Zippasla in the Indictment are the only Hittite source on its location.[7] Second, the text ranges over a very broad geographical area, following Madduwattas' career from its beginnings in the west to its culmination in the raid on Cyprus. Until recently, there was continuing uncertainty regarding the location of the larger units of Hittite geography, including Arzawa, Ahhiyawa and Alashiya. Locations suggested for Zippasla were thus very generalised, although it has usually been accepted that it lay to the west of the Hittite lands (*Hatti*).[8]

The broader questions of Hittite geography have now been finally settled, particularly since the discovery of new textual evidence in 1986. The Hittite terms for southern Anatolia have been clarified, with considerable knock-on effects for the west.[9] For example, there is now no room for the people called Lukka on the southern coast: it is clear they lived further to the west, most likely in classical Lycia (*Lukia*) on the south-western coast of Anatolia, a possibility long suspected from their name.[10] Nor is there any sense in still trying to locate Arzawa on the south coast. It must have lain in western Anatolia – as argued some thirty years ago[11] – and the obvious identification of the Arzawan capital of Apasas with classical Ephesus now becomes a certainty. Other developments have settled beyond reasonable doubt the identifications of Ahhiyawa with Mycenaean Greece and Alashiya with Cyprus. The irony is that after several decades of uncertainty, a whole string of attractive identifications with classical place-names, for many years held in doubt as being rather 'too good to be true', have now turned out to be right after all: Ahhiyawa was Achaea, Lukka was Lycia, Millawanda was Miletus, Apasas was Ephesus, Lazpas was Lesbos and so on.

This growing confidence in the location of the larger units of Hittite geography means that attention can be turned again to the location of smaller polities, such as the 'mountain land of Zippasla'. In fact enough clues can be drawn from the Indictment of Madduwattas to give a good idea of Zippasla's location.[12]

Zippasla must have been one of the states of Arzawa, or at least very close to it, and thus lay to the west of the Hittite heartland in central Turkey. A far western location is strongly supported by the progression of Madduwattas' conquests. Early on he seized Dalawa/Talawa, generally thought to be the Lycian city of Tlawa (Tlos), on the south-western coast.[13] Various districts of Arzawa followed, then the land of Pitassa in the heart of central Anatolia. The sphere of combat was clearly moving in an easterly direction from the region of the Aegean coast. While there is no suggestion that Zippasla actually lay on the sea (e.g., no reference to a port or it being raided by ships), it must have been near the Aegean seaboard, as the Mycenaean adventurer Attarssiyas of Ahhiyawa was able to attack it (perhaps twice).[14]

These factors already tend to narrow down the search considerably to the strip of western Anatolia parallel to the Aegean coast. The name of Madduwattas, prince of Zippasla, provides a further clue. It is of a distinctive form shared by many of the kings of Lydia in historical times, such as Sadyattes, Alyattes, etc.[15] Indeed, from his name and general geographical location, Madduwattas has been fairly described as a 'proto-Lydian'.[16] The final clue is in the term 'the mountain land of Zippasla' used by the Indictment.

There are no 'mountain-lands' in western Anatolia that fit these requirements as perfectly as Sipylus itself. It is a conspicuous mountain, about as far to the west as one could get from the centres of Hittite power, near the coast (but not on it) and is, of course, in what later came to be known as Lydia. Philologically the equation Zippasla=Sipylus is unexceptionable. 'Z' and 's' are frequently exchanged in both ancient and modern languages (Lesbos/Lazpas and Smyrna/Izmir for instance), while nothing could be easier than the transposition (metathesis) of the consonants 'sl' into 'l(o)s'. To cap everything Sipylus also has the outstanding credential of being the only mountain near the Aegean coast to possess Hittite rock sculptures. As the Hittites knew of Mount Sipylus they presumably had a name for it and it seems fair to say that this could have been Zippasla. To approach the question from a different direction, if Madduwattas was a 'Proto-Lydian' king as his name suggests, in classical terms he would have been the ruler of Maeonia, the ancient capital of which was Sipylus. The equation Zippasla=Sipylus at least stands on a par with Apasas=Ephesus, Lazpas=Lesbos and the other classical identifications currently accepted by Hittite scholars.

Archaeological Prospects

If Zippasla was Sipylus then a totally different light is thrown on the traditions about Tantalus' city. We are no longer looking for a fairy-tale city, but the centre of a historically attested and, for a short time, extremely powerful Bronze Age kingdom.

From purely historical and archaeological evidence it can be argued that the capital of Zippasla lay in exactly the same place as the legendary Tantalis. It was in these terms that I expressed my arguments to the local archaeological expert, Professor Recep Meriç, when I had the opportunity to meet him in Izmir. Meriç is a polymathic scholar with an impressive command of a wide range of fields. He began as a classical archaeologist, and is still excavating the massive Greco-Roman site of Philadelphia in Lydia, but his personal interests have now drawn him towards prehistory, including the archaeologically neglected subject of Arzawa. When I began by saying I was investigating traditions he was not too interested – archaeologists often tend to distrust traditional evidence. When I mentioned Zippasla he became seriously intrigued by my identification with Sipylus. He pulled a translation of the 'Indictment of Madduwattas' from his shelves and we went through it together as I explained my arguments for its location. He agreed the identification could work, at least philologically, and encouraged me to pursue it further.

I came away with the impression that Meriç already suspected the existence of an Arzawan centre somewhere in this region. After all, he himself had identified a number of fortified points running along the Gediz (Hermus) Valley which he felt were part of an Arzawan defence system against the Hittites. Logically, one of the Arzawan heartlands would have lain behind this defence system, near where the Gediz meets the coast. The Indictment of Madduwattas shows that the kingdom of Zippasla must have had at least one major urban centre within it. At the very least Madduwattas must have had a base (a palace or fortified settlement or both) from which to maintain his protracted intrigues and organise his military campaigns further south and east. Madduwattas kept up a lengthy correspondence with the Hittite emperor, so his centre must have also had scribes, possibly even an archive.

To treat it as a boyscout problem – take one Bronze Age city and situate it on or near Mount Sipylus where it is best situated for trade, communications, water-supplies, arable land and defence. The mountain itself is unlikely to have sustained any sizeable Late Bronze Age settlement – the terrain is simply too difficult, although one of the heights may have been used as an acropolis stronghold in times of emergency. (The Magnesians had a defended acropolis on the lower slopes behind their city.) The most logical area for a regional capital would be on one of the nearby plains, and the most attractive is certainly that which lies at the foot of the sharp northern slopes of Sipylus, towards the valley of the Gediz (classical Hermus) river. The plain is rich alluvial farmland, well watered by springs from the mountain (some of which now supply modern Manisa) as well as by the river. A settlement here would have command of the traditional caravan route from the interior to the central Aegean coast which runs along the southern edge of the plain at the foot of the mountain. In short, there is no site as good for the capital of Zippasla as the spot where Pliny and Pausanias located Tantalis/Sipylus.

These are the theoretical considerations. The hypothesis of a Late Bronze Age centre near the northern slopes of Sipylus seems virtually confirmed by the existence of the carving of the Mother Goddess on the mountain side, erected by a sizeable community most likely living very close to the monument itself.

A full answer can, of course, only come from excavation of the area. This would be a large undertaking, but it should be immediately rewarding. Field walking and surface collection of sherds would be the first task and this should be able to confirm the site of the Greek sanctuary of Mother Plastene which the inscriptions (and Pausanias) show was situated here. If Pliny was right in saying that Tantalis was followed by later cities on the same site, classical and archaic sherds may well be found from one of its later successors, and possibly material going back through most of the Iron Age. As for the city of Tantalis or the capital of Zippasla – call it what you will – this may be buried tens of feet below ground level. If I am right about the city's location, then deep coring should find Bronze Age (including perhaps Mycenaean) pottery. It will surely be worth the effort.

No major Arzawan city has yet been excavated and the prospect here is particularly exciting. The Boghazköy archives show that there were direct relations between the Mycenaeans and Hittites and that their spheres of influence overlapped on the coast of Anatolia. Yet, other than the Mycenaean pottery found on the Aegean coast and along the Gediz Valley, there is little archaeological reflection of any cultural interaction between Greek and Hittite cultures at this period. Only a few pieces of Mycenaean ware have been discovered in the Hittite heartland of central Anatolia, and only a dozen or so Hittite objects have been discovered in Greece. A site like Tantalis/Zippasla, in the 'no-man's land' between the two, holds the promise of providing the missing interface between Hittite and Mycenaean civilisations.

The Rise and Fall of Zippasla

The implications of the 'Indictment of Madduwattas', king of Zippasla, still need to be fully assessed by historians. Although written from a Hittite perspective, this remarkable text actually records the systematic dismantlement of their empire from the Aegean as far as Cyprus. Slice by slice, Madduwattas and his confederates (including Mycenaeans) swallowed up all the states of western and southern Anatolia and then even began to challenge Hittite authority in Cyprus.

The outcome of these events, which culminated about 1400 BC, is not well documented, except that it is fairly certain the Hittites went into political recession, while the Arzawan rebels came out on top. The immediate successors of Tudhaliyas II, against whom Madduwattas rebelled, are nonentities whose accounts are so skimpy that Hittite history only really begins again with the great conqueror Suppiluliumas, who took the throne around 1345 BC. In his time an account was written which looked back on the evil times which preceded. Enemies from every quarter attacked and encroached on the 'land of Hatti'. The worst was the incursion from the west: 'From beyond the lower land came the enemy from Arzawa, and he too sacked the Hatti lands and made Tuwanuwa and Uda his frontier.' Tuwanuwa is the classical city of Tyana, about 100 miles due south of the Hittite capital at Boghazköy. The Arzawan enemy – perhaps Madduwattas himself – had clearly bitten deep.

Oliver Gurney, Britain's senior Hittitologist, assessed the implications of this catalogue of disasters and, while noting that 'it seems scarcely credible that all these attacks could have occurred simultaneously', had to admit that they fitted with the known historical facts from the mid-fourteenth century.[17] In particular Tarkhundaradu, King of Arzawa in about 1350 BC, was so powerful that he was able to correspond directly with the Egyptian pharaoh on equal terms, as 'great king' to 'great king'. One of the El-Amarna letters records the consignment of gifts he sent to the pharaoh, which included gold, lead, ivory, a chariot, and furniture made of precious wood.

As the overall king of Arzawa, Tarkhundaradu was a political successor of the adventurer Madduwattas, who had initiated the brief golden age of Arzawan power. Suppiluliumas restored Hittite fortunes, and in about 1300 BC his son Mursilis marched on the Arzawan capital of Ephesus. Arzawa was reduced to its constituent parts and for the next century the Hittites maintained a whip hand over the west through a divide-and-rule policy.

In the meantime what happened to Zippasla? It is unfortunate that Hittite texts from the later fifteenth and earlier fourteenth centuries are so rare. Zippasla is actually known only from the miraculous survival of the Indictment of Madduwattas. It is very dangerous to produce arguments from silence when dealing with historical texts, but it has to be accepted that Zippasla, the centre of the Arzawan rise to power c. 1430 BC, was no longer in that position about 1300 BC, when Ephesus was the seat of the Arzawan king. It had not been destroyed by the Hittites, though of course it may have succumbed to an internal struggle within Arzawa. If we accept its identification with Sipylus, tradition could provide an answer: it disappeared in a natural disaster.

Swallowed by the Earth

Could the ancient city of Tantalis near Sipylus really have been 'swallowed by the earth' as Pliny stated? There is no doubt that earthquakes in this part of Lydia can be particularly severe. In fact Sipylus lies in one of the worst earthquake zones of the world. The Roman historian Tacitus gives a graphic account of the catastrophe which struck Lydia in AD 17:

> In the same year twelve famous cities in the province of Asia were overwhelmed by an earthquake. Its occurrence at night increased the surprise and destruction. Open ground – the usual refuge on such occasions – afforded no escape, because

the earth parted and swallowed the fugitives. There are stories of mountains subsiding, of flat ground rising high in the air, of conflagrations bursting out among the debris. Sardis suffered worst and attracted most sympathy. Tiberius promised it ten million sesterces and remitted all taxation by the Treasury or its imperially controlled branches for five years. Magnesia-by-Sipylus came next, in damage and compensation.[18]

Tacitus' statement that the ground opened and swallowed people is reminiscent of Pliny's account of the disaster which struck Tantalis. Sometimes, he wrote, 'the earth is eaten up by herself. She has devoured the highest mountain in Caria, Cibotus (together with the town of that name), Sipylus in Magnesia, and previously the very celebrated city in the same place that used to be called Tantalis.'[19] Can the ground literally open up and swallow people, buildings, and even cities, as these ancient accounts suggest?

In the sense that most people imagine it – of a crack in the ground opening up like jaws and then snapping shut on its victim – the answer must be that such occurrences are extremely unlikely. Cracks in the ground opened by earthquake tend to be quite shallow and the common fear that people are often swallowed up by bottomless chasms seems to be largely grounded in folklore. Very few reports of fatalities from earthquake fissures are accepted by seismologists. Most cases of people being 'eaten up' by the earth seem to arise when soft, unconsolidated ground is shaken so violently that objects, including people, are drawn into it like quicksand.[20]

Yet there are other mechanisms at play during violent earthquakes which could give the same impression of the ground 'swallowing' things up, or the 'earth eating herself'. There are 'grabens', the trenches that appear when weak areas of ground suddenly slump and collapse. During the New Madrid earthquake of 1811, probably the strongest in the recorded history of North America, such collapses produced holes in the ground twenty feet deep, some of which are still visible today. The most massive collapse resulted in the formation Reelfoot Lake (north-eastern Tennessee). A swampy tract of land sank many feet and filled with water, creating the lake which is nine miles long and two miles across.[21] We are reminded of the words of Strabo, who said that during the earthquake in the reign of Tantalus, 'lakes arose from swamps'.[22]

As we were to discover, these slumps of land can be particularly catastrophic in mountainous regions. We took the question of how a large piece of land near a mountain like Sipylus could sink beneath the water-table to Professor Ilhan Kayan, a geomorphologist at the Bornova University (in Izmir) who specialises in western Anatolia. Somewhat to our surprise he seemed to think that there was no theoretical problem involved. The mechanism is actually quite simple. The mountains of Turkey have been rising over the last few thousand years. The continental plate of Arabia is gradually rotating (in an anti-clockwise direction), and pushing up against the plate of Turkey. The result is that Turkey is slowly uplifting or, rather, buckling up. The process is usually a gradual one, but at times of earthquake, when some of the pressure which has been accumulated is released with awesome suddenness, things go with a skip-and-jump. Kayan explained that if a mountain-plate suddenly thrusts up, space is created around and underneath it. And in this case, when something goes up, something else must come down.

In the case of Sipylus, an area of land on a underlying plain could crumble and completely collapse. Buildings on it would of course be thrown down and destroyed. It may have also suffered from avalanche, an added hazard to settlements situated near mountains. In May 1970 the towns of Yungay and Ranrahirca in Peru, together with tens of thousands of inhabitants, were completely buried within four minutes by the debris shaken down from Mount Huascaran during an earthquake.[23]

Covering the ruins of Tantalis after such an earthquake would be the easiest thing imaginable. Mount Sipylus is full of water, and is noted for its springs; a slice of land which had collapsed alongside it would be drowned rapidly, and a marsh or lake formed.

It seems that Pausanias may not have been repeating just an old wives' tale when he talked about the ruins which could once be seen under Lake Saloe.

CHAPTER 11

The Travels of Solon

Plato believed that Solon brought the tale of Atlantis from Egypt, but we have seen so many reasons why this is unlikely. On the other hand, the Lydian tradition of the lost city of Tantalis has all the basic ingredients for Plato's story: a rich and powerful kingdom which fell out of favour with the gods and was destroyed by earthquake and flood. The resemblances are not coincidental, but due to a genetic relationship between the two stories. Tantalus, founder of Tantalis, is known to be a mythological variant of Atlas, first king of Atlantis. Other details come into focus when we investigate how Solon could have come across the Lydian story of the sunken kingdom.

Solon's Mediterranean travels not only took him to Egypt. According to Herodotus his other main destination was the court of the Lydian king Croesus at Sardis. Welcomed by Croesus as a famous 'wise man', Solon was given a guided tour of the palace and treasury. Croesus then asked to hear from Solon about the happiest man he knew. Solon responded with the story of an Athenian citizen who lived to see his grandchildren and died nobly in the service of his country. Next happiest, in Solon's opinion, were two pious Greek youths who died after dragging the cart of the priestess of Hera when there were no oxen available. Croesus was irritated that his own good fortune was rated below that of these ordinary folk, so Solon lectured him on the meaning of happiness: luck can change, and a man can only be deemed to have been truly happy if he dies happy. Many years later, when he had lost everything to the Persian conqueror Cyrus, Croesus was said to have remembered Solon's words.[1]

It was natural enough for a sage and politician such as Solon to touch on the theme of the fragile fortune of kings. From fragments of his poetry it is known that one of his favourite subjects was the transience of wealth: 'riches change their owner every day'.[2] 'Pride comes before a fall' is the theme of Solon's response to Croesus. It is also implicit in the moral edge to Plato's Atlantis story and is probably a genuine Solonic element.

The Empire of Tantalus

It would be hard to imagine that this spinning of yarns was a one-way traffic. According to Plutarch, Solon met the great fable writer Aesop at the Lydian court, where they discussed the best way to give advice to kings. The story of their meeting may be a fable in itself,[3] but it surely reflects the kind of exchange possible at the bustling Lydian capital.

It is easy to picture Solon being taken aside by a Lydian courtier – a historian, poet or perhaps priest – and told that his point about the fickleness of good fortune was well illustrated by the tragedy of a Lydian king even more rich and powerful than Croesus. All ears, Solon listens to the legend of Tantalus. It is worth trying to reconstruct what Solon was told:

Tantalus, son of the mountain-god Tmolus, or some say Zeus, was one of the earliest kings of Lydia. He built the first city – the parent of Smyrna, Sardis and all the other great cities of Lydia – at the holy mountain of Sipylus, sacred to Cybele, Mother of the Gods. In the Greek tongue its name was Tantalis – city of Tantalus. His wealth was unsurpassed and no king (excepting his august majesty Croesus) has ever been so blessed by the gods. Tantalus' kingdom was the mightiest in the world – he ruled the Lydians, the Phrygians and the Paphlagonians, indeed, all the peoples of Asia; Troy alone was his rival. In those days the Lydians were many and moved across the sea to colonise other lands as the Greeks were doing in Solon's time. Ascalus, brother of Tantalus, marched against the Syrians and reached the border of Egypt, where he founded the city of Ashkelon in Palestine. Another colony went to Tuscany in Italy, where they became the powerful Tyrrhenians (Etruscans). So great was the reputation of Lydia's kings that Pelops, son of Tantalus, was welcomed into Greece as a king.

Yet the gifts of the gods belong to the gods. Tantalus wanted more. He pried into their secrets and blabbed them to mortals. The gods took an awful revenge. In a single day and night they destroyed his power. The ground opened like the jaws of a giant and swallowed his city. The whole of Asia shook with earthquakes and the gods sent rains and great waves which flooded the land from here to Troy. Tantalis was covered by waters and still lies beneath a deep lake. Tantalis himself lies either at the bottom of the lake or crushed by the very mountain. The ancients believed that the sky rested on this mountain, and that the mountain rested on Tantalus – an eternal punishment for his crimes.

This narration is conjectural, but all the beliefs expressed in it are feasible for the kind of exchange that could have taken place between a Lydian scholar and Solon. The only detail not directly connected with Tantalus in the extant sources is the story of the Lydian colonists who settled in Italy and became the Etruscans, which actually relates to an even earlier king.[4] The exploits of Lydia's legendary age of expansion could easily have been drawn together. In AD 26 the Emperor Tiberius received deputations from all the cities of Asia in order to decide which community would benefit from housing his personal temple. The people of Sardis pleaded their case by stressing their glorious history, mentioning the colonisation of Italy and the story of Tantalus' son in the same breath:

> The Sardians claimed kinship with the Etruscans, quoting a decree of the latter. They explained that the original nation, owing to its size, had been divided between the sons of Atys – Tyrrhenus, who had been dispatched to create new homes, and Lydus, who had stayed in his fatherland – the two countries, in Italy and Asia, taking the names of their rulers; while the Lydians had extended their power by planting settlements in that part of Greece called the Peloponnese after Pelops.[5]

Whether there was any truth behind these claims does not matter. The Lydians sincerely believed them and may already have done so by the time of Solon's visit. At the court of the imperialist adventurer Croesus traditions which strengthened Lydia's territorial claims would have been encouraged. It was only a hundred years after Croesus that Xanthus recorded the Lydian claim to have founded Ashkelon in southern Palestine and Herodotus the Lydian colonisation of Italy. We are reminded of what Plato (*Critias* 114C) said about the Atlantean empire, which held sway 'over the Mediterranean peoples as far as Egypt and Tyrrhenia'.

What of the Athenians, whom Plato says were the only ones brave enough to march against the Atlanteans? Can the Athenian part in the story be explained in terms of the kind of information that Solon would have heard in Lydia?

There are legends about Athenian activity on the Aegean coast of Anatolia during the Heroic Age. By the early fifth century there was already a story that Theseus, king of Athens, had led an expedition to Asia Minor against the Amazons.[6] A later tradition claims that Theseus founded Smyrna after defeating the Amazons (Arzawans?) who lived at Ephesus.[7] Herodotus reported that Theseus' uncle Lycus migrated from Athens to Asia Minor and gave his name to the Lycians.[8] Such stories would have been popular among the Ionian Greeks of the coast, who were kinsmen of the Athenians. They were also subjects of King Croesus, and the legends of an early Athenian involvement in this region could well have been known at his court.

The legends may also reflect historical reality. It is a fact that the Greeks were active on the Aegean coast of Asia Minor throughout much of the Late Bronze Age. The story of the Trojan War concerns a Mycenaean attempt to control the northern part of the coast towards the end of the Bronze Age, c. 1200 BC. The Indictment of Madduwattas shows that the 'mountain land of Zippasla', argued here to be Sipylus in Lydia, was the focus of Mycenaean aggression about two centuries earlier. A memory of this struggle, preserved in Lydia and transmitted by means of Solon, might be echoed in Plato's account of the war between the 'Athenians' and 'Atlanteans'.

This point is speculative, but should be weighed against the generally accepted scenario: that Solon (or Plato) drew the raw material for the Atlantis story from Egypt. The idea that the Egyptians had either the desire or the means to record detailed descriptions of two foreign civilisations, together with the history of their mutual struggle, is manifestly absurd. If Solon learnt the story at the Lydian court, the picture changes completely. That Solon used traditions preserved by a people about *their own* ancestors is plausible. As it happens, the ancestors of the Lydians are known to have been involved in struggles with the early Greeks for control of the Aegean coast of Turkey. This, after all, is how the Greek colonies of Ionia and Aeolia, which had roots going back to the Bronze Age, began.

Tantalis and Atlantis

It would be useful at this point to take stock of the evidence that the legend of Tantalus and his city lay behind the story of Atlas' sunken kingdom. The essential parallels discussed here and in earlier chapters can be summarised as follows:

TANTALUS	ATLAS
King of Lydia and Phrygia	Son of the nymph 'Asia' (= Lydia)
Husband of Dione, the Pleiad	Father of Dione, the Pleiad
Ruler of Tantalis	Ruler of Atlantis
Tantalus' descendants famous lyre-players	Atlas a master lyre-player
Wealth proverbial	Wealth of Atlantis
Ancient Lydian empire reached borders of Egypt	Atlantean empire reached borders of Egypt
Ancient Lydians colonised Tyrrhenia	Atlantean empire reached as far as Tyrrhenia
Tantalus rebels against gods (sin of hubris)	Atlas rebels against gods (Atlantean hubris)
Sentenced to hold up sky	Sentenced to hold up sky
Crushed under Mt Sipylus	Transformed into Mt Atlas
Kingdom destroyed by earthquake and flood	Kingdom destroyed by earthquake and flood
Tantalis submerged under water	Atlantis submerged under water

It would not be difficult to produce numerous other parallels between Tantalis and Atlantis. One could point, for example, to the fact that red, black and white stone can be found on Mount Sipylus; that it has both hot and cold springs;[9] that ivory – in which Atlantis was rich – was sent to Egypt by the king of Arzawa in the fourteenth century BC; that the climate of this part of Turkey is so congenial and the soil so fertile that a vine at Smyrna was said to have produced two crops of grapes a year;[10] that the name of Poseidon's wife, Cleito, the mother of the Atlantean dynasty in Plato, was given by the poet Quintus of Smyrna as that of a Maeonian woman;[11] or that Poseidon, the national god of Atlantis, was also the patron of Pelops.

I would not set much store by these extra parallels, which could simply be due to coincidence. It is a common temptation of Atlantis theorists to try to show that the 'original' Atlantis (whether Crete or Troy) can satisfy every word that Plato wrote. The approach here is different – to trace the development, transmission and growth of the story. In terms of circumstantial detail there are large areas of 'Platonic overlay', such as the observations on the geology and archaeology of Attica, and the obsessively geometrical description of the idealised Atlantean capital, which reflects Plato's personal preoccupation with mathematics. He borrowed from Herodotus for the Egyptian part of the story, and from Homer's account of the Phaeacians for the Atlantean. There is no need to over-egg the pudding by trying to argue that every detail could have been based on the legendary city at Mount Sipylus. The differences between the Lydian story of Tantalis and Plato's account are equally important.

Older than Egypt

If the original Atlantis story concerned events in the second millennium, how did it come about that Plato placed it at such a remote period, even before the founding of Egyptian civilisation? The links with Athens actually posed something of a problem for Plato here, as they meant he had to adopt a mythical time-scale completely at variance with those of his contemporaries. The Athenian heroes Cecrops and Erichthonius, who lived around 1500 BC on the traditional dating, were whisked by Plato backwards in time to 9550 BC. Did Plato do this simply to give his story greater importance? Or was he, or Solon, genuinely confused about its dating?

Placing the complex figure of Tantalus on the traditional Greek time-scale would certainly have involved considerable headscratching. While most genealogies placed him a few generations before the Trojan War, there was a different tradition which presented him as a more primordial figure. Tantalus built the first city of Smyrna on Mount Sipylus and his son Broteas carved the first image of the Mother Goddess. His daughter Niobe often seems like a Greek Eve. She was said to be the first mortal woman with whom Zeus slept, and some legends describe her as the wife or daughter of Phoroneus,[12] the first man and the inventor of fire.[13]

As the mythologist Kerenyi noted, these 'firsts' show that in one view 'Tantalus came at the very beginning'.[14] Tantalus lived before the fall of man, when gods and mortals mingled freely, and it was his sins that severed the ties between them and brought the Deluge down on his people. Perhaps his most abysmal crime was setting the flesh of his own son (Pelops) before the gods at dinner. The same crime was thought to have provoked the great Flood of Deucalion. Disguised as a mortal, Zeus visited Lycaon, king of Arcadia, and was offered the cooked flesh of a male child. Zeus revealed himself, kicked the table over in disgust and, after striking down Lycaon and his sons with thunderbolts, decided to destroy mankind with the Flood.[15] Lycaon, incidentally, was reckoned to be a grandson of Niobe,[16] showing again how Greek myth swirled around groups of names and elements into different patterns like a kaleidoscope.

A remarkable story told by Ovid blends the traditional deluge story with the destruction of land which can only have been the kingdom of Tantalis. One of his characters relates how he was sent on a mission to Phrygia. There, near an oak and a linden tree growing side by side, is 'a stagnant pool: once it was habitable country, but now it has become stretch of water, haunted by small marsh birds.' Jupiter and Mercury had visited this land disguised as travellers and found the inhabitants so wicked that they decided to exterminate them, with the exception of an impoverished old couple who had given them hospitality. Instructed by the gods, the old couple climbed up the mountain, where they gazed in amazement as their country was drowned in marshy waters.[17] The marsh overlooked by a mountain can be none other than Pliny's Sale, clinched by the fact that Ovid specifically locates this catastrophe in the land 'where Pelops was once king'.

Let us assume that Solon discussed the mythological links of Tantalus' family with the Lydians in an effort to date them in terms of the traditional framework followed by the Greeks. If the connections with the 'first' men of Greece and the Flood arose, Solon may soon have come to the conclusion that the story was one of the earliest human memories. There is a strong clue that he did. It is curious that Tantalus' daughter Niobe and her husband Phoroneus are mentioned together with the Flood at the beginning of the Atlantis account in the *Timaeus* (22A). Solon is talking to the 'Egyptian priests': 'And wishing to lead them on to talk about early times, he embarked on an account of the earliest events known here [Greece], telling them about Phoroneus, the first man, and Niobe, and how Deucalion and Pyrrha survived the flood . . . ' We may even have here a genuine fossil from the original conversation between Solon and his Lydian hosts, perhaps preserved in a snippet of Solon's poetry or notes to which Plato had access.

If he associated Tantalus with Niobe, Phoroneus and the Deluge, Solon would have been led to place the Tantalis story at the very beginning of mortal history. His Lydian hosts would have encouraged him. The Egyptians were not the only race to look down on other peoples as 'young'.

Tantalus was said to have been the king of both the Lydians and their neighbours, the closely related Phrygians. Indeed, whether Sipylus lay in Lydia or Phrygia was a matter of some dispute, and Tantalus and his family were frequently represented as Phrygians by the Greek dramatists. Little is known about Lydian estimates of their antiquity, but there is some information on the Phrygian view. The 7th-5th centuries BC saw the rise of a widespread interest in national history throughout the Eastern Mediterranean. The Egyptians of the Saite Dynasty (665–525 BC) were particularly interested in the glories of the past and it may have been under them that the enormously long chronologies for Egyptian history told to the Greeks were developed. In the mid-sixth century Babylonian scholars were calculating impossibly high dates for the kings of ancient Mesopotamia.[18] The Phrygians, it appears, also joined in the game.

According to Herodotus, the Phrygians were the main rivals to the Egyptians for the title 'earliest race'. In Egypt Herodotus was told that the Saite Pharaoh Psammetichus, 'devised an ingenious means to decide the matter'. In the belief that there must have been one original language, Psammetichus commanded two babies, one Egyptian, one Phrygian, to be brought up in isolation – so that the first word spoken by either infant would determine what that language was. Their first utterance was supposedly the Phrygian word for bread, so Psammetichus conceded that the Phrygians were indeed older than the Egyptians.[19]

Whether the story is true or false does not matter. It was widely talked about, and Herodotus says that the Greeks had slightly different versions that all came to the same conclusion – the Phrygians were first. Indeed, the Greeks highly revered the antiquity of the Phrygians, believing that the Mother of the Gods

(Cybele or Rhea) came from their country. Her Phrygian attend-ants, the Curetes, were thought to have discovered a wide range of skills, from honey-making to the manufacture of swords and helmets, at a time so remote that house-building had not yet been invented.[20]

So if Solon was related the story of a primeval Lydian/Phrygian king, he could have been told in the same breath that it all happened before even the Egyptians were around. If he got the raw material for Atlantis from Lydia rather than Egypt, then an ugly problem in the transmission of the story can be resolved. The absurdity of the Egyptians giving a detailed history of a civilisation a thousand years older than their own is removed.

So it was probably Solon, following the cues of his Lydian hosts, who placed the sunken kingdom earlier than any other civilisation. The supposedly great antiquity of the story may have been one of the things which whetted his appetite and sparked the desire to turn it into an epic poem. It would have remained for Plato to add dates to the rough chronological fix of 'before Egyptian civilisation'. In the *Laws* Plato reckoned Egyptian civilis-ation was some 10,000 years old (see Chapter 7). In the *Timaeus* he used a slightly more conservative estimate for Egypt, 8,000 years before Solon, and placed the war between Atlantis and Athens a thousand years before that.

The Move to the West

It was probably also Solon who 'translated' Tantalus of the Lydian tale into his Greek equivalent, Atlas. If he understood that the story of the sunken kingdom belonged to the very beginning of history, he would have had a problem accepting that its primordial king was the familiar Tantalus of Greek legend, who reigned only a few generations before the Trojan War. This might have prompted him to think that the Lydians were really talking about the similar character Atlas, and that the story was close to the time when the Titans, rather than mortals, ruled the Earth.

Once Tantalus had been translated into Atlas, the mechanism was in place for a radical break with the story's original location. A simple confusion between Atlas' original domains (in Anatolia) and the western 'kingdom' where he was confined by the Olympi-ans would have allowed the whole story to shift in the same direction. Once moved to the Atlantic, Tantalis would have transmuted into Atlantis.

There was actually a large-scale drift of Greek mythical geography in a westerly direction, and Solon, or whoever was responsible for moving it there, would simply have been letting his story be carried along by the current. During the Archaic period (8th–6th centuries BC) the geographical horizons of the Greeks expanded immeasurably. Greek traders and settlers worked and lived in thriving communities throughout the coasts of the Eastern and Central Mediterranean, and the west was opening up to them as well. The first Greek colonies in Sicily had begun by about 700 BC, and around 600 BC Marseilles was founded by settlers from Phocaea, near Smyrna. The Phoenicians of Carthage in North Africa became the rivals to the Greek expansion westwards. The Carthaginians controlled the trade routes through southern Iberia and northern Africa to the Atlantic. This region, western Mediterranean and the African coast beyond Carthage, was the *terra incognita* for the Greeks, containing mysterious tribes and exotic flora and fauna, access to which was jealously guarded by the Carthaginian traders. As the real world of the Greeks expanded, so did their mythological one. The homelands of fabulous creatures are always best pushed to the furthest limits of the world, where imagination rather than knowledge is the only guide. 'Here be dragons' has been a caption to places on the extreme edges of maps from Babylonian times to the Renaissance. For the Greeks of the Archaic period the far west was the unknown.

Among the legends to be moved westwards during this period was the tale of Perseus and the Gorgons. The eminent mythologist Joseph Fontenrose wrote a penetrating study of Perseus which documented the story's original setting. From an early date Perseus' adventures seem to have been intimately associated with the Eastern Mediterranean – Palestine, Syria and the southern coast of Anatolia. Perseus was particularly remembered in Cilicia, where he was thought to have founded Tarsus and other cities on his way to find the Gorgons. Aeschylus, the earliest source giving a precise location for the Gorgons, places them near Kisthene, the name of a city on the coast of Lycia in south-western Anatolia. On his return Perseus stopped at Joppa in Palestine and rescued the princess Andromeda from a sea-monster.[21]

Later mythographers commonly located the Gorgons in Libya

(the Greek name for north-western Africa) and the rescue of Andromeda in Ethiopia. Euripides seems to be the first to have given a Libyan location (in his lost drama *Andromeda*), though Hesiod may hint at it in his vague description of the Gorgons 'dwelling beyond glorious Ocean in the frontier land towards Night'. Pindar, on the other hand, describes Perseus as travelling to the land of the Hyperboreans in the extreme north. 'It is evident', Fontenrose concluded, 'that the Gorgons could be placed on any edge of the world; but that the Greeks seem in general to have settled finally on west or south-west.'[22]

The west was also a suitable place to locate Giants and Titans, particularly defeated ones. Ogyges, a Titan king who helped Cronus in his war against Zeus, was said to have fled to Tartessus in Spain after the Olympian victory.[23] Cronus himself was thought to have been imprisoned by Zeus on an island in the western ocean.[24] The idea that redundant gods (Cronus, Ogyges, Atlas) were banished to the far west has a neat mythological and symbolical logic to it. For such Titans it was literally the 'evening' of their careers and they went towards the sunset (as things still 'go west' today when they have had their time). It provided a mythical rationale for the trend to push other related monsters and deities (such as the Gorgons and Hesperides) to the western limits of the world.

The shift of mythological locales to the west continued apace throughout the classical period. Anatolia was the original location of much of the shifted material and there is some evidence of a reciprocal effect: hellenised Anatolians, such as the Lydians, became so conversant with classical mythology that they began to claim back material which, rightly or wrongly, they believed had been moved from their country to the west!

Signs of the Lydian backlash come in a curious tale told by Pausanias about another famous western giant, the three-headed monster Geryon. Geryon owned a herd of marvellous cattle, which Heracles had to seize for his Tenth Labour. The whereabouts of Geryon's kingdom was, like that of other mythological lands, a matter of dispute. Locations in Greece, Italy and Sicily were argued, but most mythographers plumped for the far west – in Spain, at the city of Gades (Cadiz), where two pine trees that dripped blood were supposed to mark his grave, or in Tartessus, which was clearly a favourite resort of Greek giants.[25]

So when Pausanias visited his homeland, he was completely

amazed to hear that not only the bones of Geryon but also his throne, cut into a mountain top, were said to have been discovered near a small town in upper Lydia. The well-travelled Pausanias was not to be taken in so easily:

> When I opposed them and demonstrated that Geryon was in Cadiz, where they have no tomb, but a tree that takes different shapes, then the Lydian sacred officials revealed the true story: it was the body of Hyllus, the son of Earth, and the river was named after him; they said Heracles had called his son Hyllus after this river because of having lived once with Omphale [queen of Lydia].[26]

And, so it appears, Pausanias managed to nip in the bud another shift in mythical geography – one presumably attempted by the Lydian villagers to make their giant's bones more valuable as a tourist attraction. Were the Lydians aware that the stories associated with their old giants (such as Atlas and Tantalus) were being robbed by the west, and so felt justified in claiming something back?

Mythologial watchdogs such as Pausanias were rare. Without similar efforts on the part of others, the location of myths continued to slosh about between east and west in a highly undisciplined fashion. The world of mythology, of course, can cope with such things. Gods, giants and monsters are no respecters of national boundaries and can roam wherever they wish.

Some of the most flagrant examples of geographical distortion occur in the versions of the myths recorded by Diodorus of Sicily in the first century BC. His source was a mythographer known as Dionysius 'Leather-Arm', an Alexandrian scholar of the mid-second century BC. Little is known of him, except that he seems to have taken the trend to 'libyanise' Greek mythology to its logical extreme. Dionysius' versions of the myths read like fantastic science fiction tales, as he suffered from the ancient trend known as euhemerising, which believed that all the gods were really mighty kings of the Earth's remote past.

Dionysius really went to town with his account of the Amazons, the famous female warriors of Greek legend. All earlier writers had described the Amazons as an Asiatic race. The libyanising Dionysius, however, decided that the original Amazons had lived in North Africa. Diodorus introduced the new version as follows:

The majority of mankind believe that the only Amazons were those who are reported to have dwelt in the neighbourhood of the Thermodon river on the Pontus [Black Sea]; but the truth is otherwise, since the Amazons of Libya were much earlier in point of time and accomplished noble deeds. Now we are not unaware that to many who read this account the history of this people will appear to be a thing unheard of and entirely strange.[27]

Ancient readers would have been surprised with good reason. The mythical Amazons had long been associated with the Thermodon river in southern Russia as well as a number of Anatolian cities such as Ephesus. Yet Dionysius explained that the Amazons really started in Libya, where 'a longing overcame them to invade many parts of the inhabited globe.' First they attacked the 'Atlantians' on the western coast of Africa, who turn out to be a curious mixture of Plato's island race and the Atlantes said by Herodotus to live near Mount Atlas. After crushing the Libyan Gorgons, the Amazons went on to Egypt, where they signed a treaty with King Horus and marched victoriously through Arabia, Syria and Cilicia. They conquered all of Anatolia and planted colonies along the coast, which people mistakenly took to be their original settlements.

The most surprising element in Dionysius' bizarre account is the amount of genuine Anatolian detail that managed to survive the rough ride westwards. Dionysius concludes by saying that the power of the Libyan Amazons was crushed by two generals called 'Mopsus the Thracian' and 'Sipylus the Scythian'. The name Sipylus needs no introduction. Mopsus is an Achaean adventurer familiar from Greek legend and often thought to be a historical character mentioned in the Hittite text about Madduwattas of Zippasla![28] The mythological cocktail has been strongly shaken this time, leaving a few elements of traditional Lydian history peeping through the farrago of nonsense offered by Dionysius.

In his detailed account of 'Atlantian' customs, Dionysius even states that the 'Great Mother' of the gods (Cybele), usually reckoned to have been born in Phrygia, was actually born near the coast of Libya. What bitter irony that even Cybele, whose 'first image' on Mount Sipylus overlooks the original site of the sunken kingdom, was eventually transplanted to a non-existent Atlantic civilisation. The drift to the west was relentless.

From Solon to Plato

I have often been asked how the motif of Atlantis, if it really originated with the story of Tantalis in Lydia, could have been switched to the far west. The answer is, 'All too easily.' The popular trend to push mythological locations towards North Africa, Spain and the Atlantic was irresistible. In this case there was the added confusion between Atlas' eastern and western domains to trigger the process and set Atlantis adrift.

The step of relocating the story does not appear to have been taken by Plato. In the *Cratylus* he alludes to the destruction of Tantalus' kingdom and appears to have been quite unaware that the Atlantis tale was simply a version of the same story. The change may, of course, have happened during the story's transmission in the Critias family, but one suspects that it was Solon, as I have argued, who not only tampered with the chronology but translated Tantalus to Atlas and moved the story to the Atlantic.

The value, in storytelling terms, of moving something to the far west was obvious: Solon now had infinite freedom for his planned epic poem about the sunken kingdom. Once in the Atlantic, Atlantis could become as large and as grand as he liked. There was a whole ocean to fill. Solon, as his later biographer Plutarch tells us, eventually found the task too great:

> Solon also attempted to write a long poem dealing with the story of legend of the lost Atlantis, because the subject, according to what he had heard from the learned men of Sais in Egypt, had a special connexion with Athens. He finally abandoned it, however, not, as Plato suggests, for lack of time, but rather because of his age and his fear that the task would be too much for him.[29]

There is nothing incredible in the idea that the Critias family (to which Plato belonged) preserved the skeleton of Solon's planned epic and maybe even his notes on the names used in the story. Exactly where he found the story they seem to have forgotten, though they knew it was collected on his travels. One of the family, perhaps Plato himself, assumed this was Egypt, the other famous destination of Solon's Mediterranean wanderings.

When Plato came across the Atlantis story it must have seemed like a gift from the gods. The downfall of such a great kingdom at the dawn of time was perfect material for the catastrophist interpretation of the past he was already developing for philosophical reasons. The claim that it involved a people even older than the Egyptians led him to introduce a novel time-scale to the story, drawing in his own observations on Egyptian art and his reading of Herodotus. If Atlantis was older than Egypt, then it had to be placed some nine thousand years in the past. Linking it with Athens – correctly or otherwise – left him room to include his own well-considered points on the prehistory and geology of his homeland. After adding echoes of the Persian Empire and Homer's mythical Phaeacians to add epic colour to the Atlantean way of life, Plato used the story as a platform to air his theories on the importance (and fragility) of our environment, at the same time making some political allusions about contemporary Athens.

The result was a multi-layered masterpiece that has baffled everyone since it was written – primarily because the basic source for the story could not be found. What is ironic is that Plato, as much as Solon, seems to have found the story of Atlantis, now so vast in its scope and implications, too much to master. Plutarch concluded:

> Plato was particularly ambitious to create an elaborate masterpiece out of the subject of Atlantis, as if it were the site of some fine estate, which was still unbuilt on, but to which he had a special claim by virtue of his connexion with Solon, and he began the task by laying out great porches and enclosures and courtyards on a magnificent scale, such as no story or myth or poetic creation had ever received before. But he was late in beginning and the task proved too long for his lifetime, so that the more we enjoy what he actually wrote, the more we must regret what he left undone. Like the great shrine of Olympian Zeus among the temples of Athens, so among the many beautiful works which Plato's vision conceived the tale of the lost Atlantis is the only one to be left unfinished.

I am sure that, in his account of the story's development, Plutarch was absolutely right, except for the Egyptian connection. Solon got the story not from Egypt but from Lydia.

CHAPTER 12

The Unfinished Story

The *Critias* breaks off halfway through, with the story of Atlantis left hanging in mid-air, and there is no evidence to suggest that Plato attempted to continue it. In fact it appears that he simply flung his pen down in mid-sentence. Why? Plutarch says the task proved too long for Plato's lifetime, but it should not be imagined that old age or ill health made him leave the work unfinished. Classical scholars usually believe that, after abandoning the Atlantis story, Plato moved on to write the massive *Laws*. Though he clearly had plenty of energy left, he had obviously reached a creative impasse with the theme of the *Critias*.

The problem must have been the sheer immensity of the Atlantis theme. The additions of Solon and Plato – and possibly other members of the Critias family – had transformed the relatively simple tale of a sunken city into a story massive in its scope and implications. It seems that it was starting to raise far more difficulties for Plato than it solved.

In particular, the inflated mythological time-scale that gave the theme such grandeur created serious historical problems. How could Plato reconcile the idea that the founders of his city, the kings of Athens' Heroic Age, really lived 8,000 years earlier than was generally believed? Plato had identified remains of the Heroic Age around the Acropolis, and skilfully included them in a brilliantly intuitive sketch of Mycenaean society, but he was in deep water when he tried to remove all this material to such a remote period of time.

There is a noticeable vagueness to the way the traditional heroes of Athens are introduced in the narrative. It says that Cecrops, Erichthonius and 'most of the other heroes recorded before Theseus' ruled at the time of the war with Atlantis. The vagueness surely results from Plato's reluctance to admit that his chronology was tearing asunder the traditional history of Athens: a group of

Athenian heroes was whisked back some 8,000 years in time and
separated from Theseus, who had to remain in his traditional
position in the thirteenth century BC. Theseus was intimately
linked by tradition with the Trojan War – he was said to have
abducted Helen of Sparta to be his bride before she came to
maturity. Plato could not possibly break such links, and to have
tried to shift Theseus, and the Trojan War along with him, would
have been blasphemy. Indeed, he would have had to challenge
every hard-held belief of the Greeks about Homer's role as the
interpreter of a dim, but far from utterly remote past. There was
great continuity between the Mycenaean and Archaic Ages of
Greece.[1] At the very least, the Greeks recognised the tombs of the
Mycenaean period as the resting places of their heroes, and dozens
of them were turned into hero-shrines.

Plato was left with the awkward, and not explicitly stated, result
that the heroes of prehistoric Athens were to be split into two
groups: one at the time of Theseus and another 8,000 years earlier.
This would involve tearing to shreds the cherished traditions of
Greece, backed up by local cults and the genealogies by which
Greek kings measured their descent from the great heroes of the
past. The genealogies, running back through the Trojan War to
Heracles, Pelops, Perseus and the other great heroes, fitted neatly
into the picture that Argos, Mycenae, Thebes, and the other great
cities had been founded in the second millennium BC.

The citizens of Athens, proud as they were of their past, would
have had difficulty swallowing the idea that their own traditional
history should be divorced from that of the other Greeks. The
citizens of other Greek states must merely have looked askance:
Plato, the great critic of his home town, was trying to make
everyone believe that Athens was, after all, the most special and
the most ancient city on earth. Plato had gone too far and argued
himself into a corner.

The crux of the matter was that, having interposed some 8,000
years between Theseus and his traditional forebears Cecrops and
Erichthonius, Plato had to explain what had happened in the
intervening period. Should he suggest that Athens had simply lain
deserted? The idea would hardly have pleased his countrymen. If
the *Hermocrates*, planned as a sequel to the *Critias*, was to continue
history down to the present time, the reconstruction of 8,000
years of missing history would have been an insuperable task.
When he returned to the theme of catastrophic history in the

Laws, Plato simply glossed over the problem by leaving out the legendary history he had reconstructed in the *Timaeus* and *Critias* and starting with the Flood of Deucalion – in his model the last in a series of deluges. Plato seems to have accepted its traditional date, *c.* 1500 BC, as his narrative history then flows smoothly from the Flood through the foundation of Troy to the Trojan War (*c.* 1200 BC), the Dorian invasion and the origins of contemporary Sparta. In short, Plato never found a way out of the dilemma he created by dating Atlantis and Proto-Athens so early.

There was also a philosophical and ethical problem. It was a central tenet of Plato's theory of global catastrophes that when a conflagration or deluge struck the Earth, everything, good and bad together, was wiped out: that is why his idealised Proto-Athenians went down at the same time as Atlantis sank. People were only saved by special environmental conditions. The Nile safeguarded the Egyptians, and a few shepherds who happened to be on mountain-tops would always escape the floods. People would make their way back down to the plains when the world had stabilised, and civilisation would slowly start again.

Yet the story of the sunken kingdom had a moralising theme from its very inception. It was the crimes of Tantalus – ranging from hubris to infanticide – that destroyed his kingdom. With this theme of sin built into his very source material, it is not surprising that Plato succumbed to the temptation of adding a moral reason for the downfall of the Atlanteans, particularly since he was also subtly using them as a cautionary tale about contemporary Athens. In almost all his detailed description of Atlantis, Plato refrains from making any judgment about their lifestyle. In fact, everything is deemed praiseworthy. The attention he lavished on his description of Atlantean civilisation gave it the utopian splendour that has immortalised it. It is only shortly before the *Critias* breaks off that Plato begins to explain that the Atlanteans were in moral decline. Their divine blood was increasingly diluted by mortal stock and they began to suffer from human weaknesses such as greed. His Atlanteans were men of the Silver Age of Greek myth, the first to suffer from the law of inexorable decline. Hesiod said of the men of the Silver Age that 'Zeus the son of Cronus was angry and put them away, because they would not give honour to the blessed gods who live on Olympus.'[2] Similarly Plato, near the end of the *Critias*, explained that the degeneration of the Atlanteans angered the immortals: 'The god of gods, Zeus, who reigns by law, and whose eye can see such things, when he perceived the wretched state of this admirable stock, decided to punish them and reduce them to order by discipline.'

Zeus' scheme was outlined earlier in the *Critias* – he led them to attack the Athenians, and they were defeated. This humiliation was not the end of the Atlanteans' punishment: just as the war finished Atlantis sank. It would be absurd to see it as coincidence that this happened at the very time Zeus was intent on punishing the Atlanteans. It is clearly a second punishment. So Plato's theme has changed – he is about to imply that the catastrophe that destroyed Atlantis was brought about by the sins of its inhabitants, just as Tantalis was devastated because of its ruler's crimes. What has happened to the idea, so well developed in the *Statesman* and the *Timaeus*, that the upheavals which periodically rack the universe are simply the result of an imperfection in nature?

In describing the moral decline of the Atlanteans – as opposed to the steadfastly simple Athenians – Plato was running straight up against the classic dilemma that has always faced theologians – if God is good, why does he let innocent people die? If it was the corruption of the Atlanteans that brought about the end of the Silver Age, then why were the blameless Athenians destroyed in the same cataclysm? If it was an imperfection in creation that brought about the catastrophe, the degeneration and punishment of the Atlanteans is a dramatic irrelevance. Maybe Plato had in mind a solution to the dilemma. All the same, it seems no coincidence that his pen dropped at the very moment when Zeus called the gods together to decide the fate of the Atlanteans:

> He called all the gods into their most holy habitation, which being placed at the centre of the universe, beholds all created things. And when he had called them together, he spake as follows . . .

Zeus' speech was never written.

The Growth of a Legend

In 1981 the American classical scholar Daniel Dombrowski stated confidently that:

> Atlantis was only a powerful literary device invented by Plato, which was to act as a means of highlighting the fate of the

ideal state created in Plato's mind's eye. The only place in which Atlantis can be found, in addition to the writings of Plato, is in the minds of those with an imagination as vivid as that of Plato.[3]

Dombrowski's scepticism was premature. It now seems clear that Plato did have a source for the legend of Atlantis. He freely embellished it, but the core of the story was not his own creation. It came from Lydia, where the memory of the sunken kingdom of Tantalis was preserved until Roman times.

It had never occurred to me, during the many years in which I mulled over the problem of Atlantis, that Plato might open a window on the history of Bronze Age Lydia and the earliest Greek struggles to obtain a foothold on the coast of Asia Minor. Yet it is to this period that the traditions of the lost kingdom of Tantalus at Mount Sipylus refer. There is persuasive evidence that there was a Bronze Age kingdom in this area. Most surprisingly, it appears to be described in contemporary Hittite texts as 'the mountain land of Zippasla', a kingdom with Mycenaean connections which flourished briefly as the head of an anti-Hittite coalition in about 1400 BC, and then disappeared again from the records. The final proof that there was a major Bronze Age centre here will only come from excavation. We will then also learn whether it really succumbed to an earthquake as Pausanias, Pliny and others describe. There is no serious reason to doubt the legend: the circumstantial evidence from history, archaeology and geology adds up very strongly in its support. Troy and Mycenae were located by Schliemann using traditional evidence. At Mycenae Pausanias was an invaluable guide, used by Schliemann to locate individual tombs and other structures. Pausanias may turn up trumps again in helping to recover the lost kingdom of Sipylus. The site holds extraordinary promise – this one place could be the missing centre of the Arzawan state of Zippasla, the traditional home of Agamemnon's ancestors Tantalus and Pelops and, of course, the prototype of Plato's Atlantean royal city.

In the meantime Plato has already been vindicated. Since the time of his pupil Aristotle he has been accused of fabricating Atlantis – but now we can see that the story was 'true' in the sense that he did not invent it. Solon collected the story from the court of Croesus in Lydia and developed the theme as the subject of a planned epic poem. Had he finished it, Plato claimed (*Timaeus* 21C–D), Solon would have outshone in fame even Homer and Hesiod. Plato took up the challenge and began writing a prose epic on Atlantis. Although he bit off more than he could chew and left the *Critias* unfinished, Plato's work on Atlantis can hardly be called a failure. It gave the world one of the most enduring and visionary of all its literary themes.

Now that the raw material for Plato's Atlantis can be identified, it can be seen far more clearly why and how he used it in his philosophical interpretation of history. The charge that Plato created it from thin air to be a foil to his idealised prehistoric Athens can be dropped. Instead it seems that the basic outline of the story came to him ready made from the Critias family, who had preserved it from Solon's time. There is no longer any reason to see Plato as a gratuitous fantasiser. He took it for granted that the story was a genuine tradition from the distant past – it was, like every other myth he used – and he set about interpreting its meaning. Plato's goal, in so many matters, was to provide an interface between ancient myth and the new scientific world view, based on reason and logic, that was beginning to emerge among the Greeks. For him the Atlantis story was another myth holding invaluable clues about our past history and the nature of the world. So he fitted it into his philosophical framework and, by adding the requisite Platonic twist, used it to convey what he saw as fundamental truths.

Strangely enough, classical scholars and historians of science seem, until quite recently, to have been oblivious to the message that Plato was trying to convey through his story of Atlantis and Athens, and even reluctant to accept that it was anything but a frivolity. In fact they have glossed over, or deliberately ignored, a large part of Plato's philosophical thinking – encompassing astronomy, geology, archaeology, history and myth – and concentrated almost obsessively on the 'Socratic' and political sides of his work. On the other hand, traditional Atlantologists, from Donnelly to the modern occultists, have long understood Plato's message. Like it or not, scholars must accept that Plato's message was a catastrophist one. A major theme of his work – developed through four of his books – is that the universe is inherently unstable, and that the myths of deluges and conflagrations reflect the repeated interruption of our history by massive, sky-borne disasters. At the same time the world view of Aristotle, who developed the concept of a well-behaved, intrinsically benign, universe and rejected the myths of past catastrophes, is still so dominant that it is really only the so-called cranks who have paid any attention to Plato's explicit teachings.

For example, Plato's belief that the civilisation of the Greek Heroic Age was brought to an end by a natural upheaval is barely even recognised. It now has to be taken seriously, thanks to the pioneering work of Zangger at Tiryns which has shown that large parts of the city were devastated by earthquake and flood. Future archaeological work may well confirm that Tantalis, the prototype of Atlantis, was terminated by similar causes a century or two earlier. These, of course, are only two individual sites. Work is still continuing to correlate evidence on earthquakes, climate patterns and environmental and cultural change, in order to understand why at certain periods – particularly the ends of the Early, Middle and Late Bronze Ages – so many destructions seem to cluster together. Eventually underlying causes may be found. The mythological record so treasured by Plato suggests that extra-terrestrial causes, such as meteorite and cometary impact, were involved.

As I completed this book grim reminders of Plato's message about the fragility of our environment seemed to be everywhere. Two of the most technologically advanced regions of the world – Japan and western Europe – were upset by appalling natural disasters. In Japan, the earthquake that shook Osaka and Kyoto – and devastated Kobe – claimed at least 4,000 lives. Only about a week later western Europe was struck by heavy rains, and the floods were so severe that many towns in Holland had to be evacuated. Shocking as these events were, they occurred at a time in our history that is otherwise extremely stable – in terms of both climate change and geological activity – and were nothing compared to the scope of the upheavals that devastated past civilisations.

Ironically enough, it never seemed to occur to Plato that mankind itself could become an extra threat to the fragile environment. As if we were totally oblivious to the possibility of natural catastrophes – and as if these were not enough – we have now reached the point where the world is now also threatened by entirely man-made ecological disasters.

Were he around today, Plato might have had less trouble completing his epic. We, the new Atlanteans, would have provided the model and the answer to the philosophical dilemma which seemed to halt his writing. Our appalling greed and abysmal lack of respect for the environment make the hubris of the old Atlanteans seem trivial. To Plato the gods were guardians and embodiments of natural order, whose laws must be respected. Offend them beyond a certain point and the gods of nature will destroy us. Perhaps that is what Plato was struggling to express when he gave up on the project, except that he did not have as an illustration our shining example of how greed can directly cause environmental catastrophe. Our overweening pride can easily tip the fragile balance of nature against us. All the wealth, knowledge and advanced technology of Plato's Atlanteans did not save them – will ours save us? The Atlanteans paid the full price for their over-confidence. We would do better to check ours and listen to the warning of Plato, a wise man who tried to wake us from the dream that the world is always a safe place to live in.

The Atlantids

The descendants of Atlas' seven daughters, the Pleiades, were summarised by Hellanicus of Lesbos (5th century BC) in a genealogical work called *Atlantis*. All the Pleiades married gods, except for Merope. She was the wife of Sisyphus king of Corinth, a Tantalus-like figure who offended Zeus by trying to imitate him and was condemned to spend eternity in Hades rolling a massive rock up a hill. When Atlas' seven daughters were transformed into the constellation of the Pleiades, Merope was said to have hidden her face in shame for having married a mortal: only six of the seven stars in the group are clearly visible.

Of the other Pleiades, three had children by Zeus. Maia was the mother of the god Hermes. Taygete, who gave her name to a mountain in the southern Peloponnese, was the mother of Lacedaemon, ancestor of the Spartan kings. Electra's son Dardanus was the founder of Troy. (Some say that she rather than Merope, became the dimmest Pleiad, so grieved at the fall of Troy that she hid her face in her hands.) The sea-god Poseidon mated with two other Pleiades. Celaeno bore him Lycus, who was settled by his father in the 'Isles of the Blest'. Alcyone bore him a daughter, Aethusa, whose descendants settled in Boeotia (central Greece); her great-great-grandsons Amphion and Zethus built the walls of Thebes. By the war-god Ares, Sterope was the mother of Oenomaus king of Pisa or Lesbos, whose daughter Hippodameia became the wife of Pelops. (A variant makes Sterope the wife of Oenomaus.)[1]

With the exception of Maia, all the daughters of Atlas are connected in some way or another with Anatolia or with Tantalus and his descendants: Electra's descendants were the kings of Troy; the name of Celaeno's son Lycus connects him with Lycia in southwestern Anatolia; Merope was the wife of the Tantalus clone Sisyphus; and the families of Alycone, Sterope, Taygete were connected by marriage with the Tantalids.

Further links between the two groups come from names.

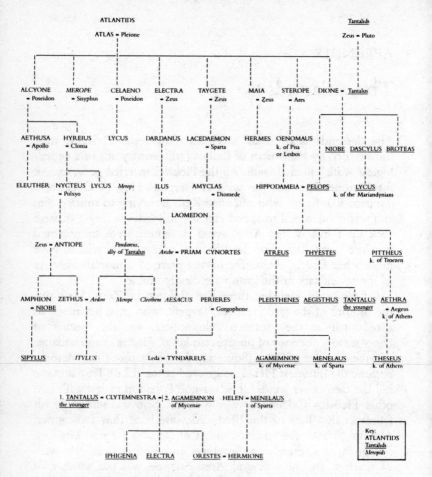

FIG. 26   The Descendants of Atlas and Tantalus

'Lycus' occurs among the Atlantids and the Tantalids. Names beginning with Merop- recur in the mythology surrounding both families. Pandareus, son of Merops and father of Merope, was Tantalus' main ally and his family married into two Atlantid lines. The name 'Merops' has a curious history. At the most general level it means 'endowed with speech' or 'articulate', and was sometimes used as a poetical epithet for the human race. The name seems to have been used in a more specific sense for some of the communities of the Aegean islands and the coast of Asia Minor. Meropie or Merope was another name for Siphnos in the Cyclades[2] and Meropis was a name for Cos (off the coast of southwestern Anatolia) whose first king was called Merops.[3] Another Merops (the father of Pandareus) was the king of Percote near the Hellespont and father-in-law of Priam of Troy. As Astour remarked, 'the common derivation from *meropos* "human, mortal" does not fit here at all; which island of the Archipelago was not one of human beings?'[4] Astour himself suggested that these Meropids were connected with the cult of a Semitic healing god called *merappê* (not actually attested as a deity in any Near Eastern texts). More likely the name reflects a connection with the Atlantids, as it appears that Merops was another name for Atlas himself.[5] The Meropids would then be another tribe claiming descent from the old Titan.

Notes and References

1 Hellanicus, *FGrHist* F19b. For information not in Hellanicus' fragments see Apollod. *Bibl.* XXX, x-xii and references in Frazer 1921, II, 2–4 (n. 1), 159 (n. 4).

2 See Astour 1965, 239.

3 Strabo XV, 686, Thuc. VIII, 41; Antoninus Liberalis: *Transformations* 15.

4 Astour 1965, 245, n. 7.

5 Taygete daughter of Atlas is referred to in Eur. *Helen* as 'Titanis, daughter of Merops' – see Fontenrose 1981, 131–133, 140–141.

APPENDIX 2

The Tale of Silenus

The idea that Solon found the raw material for the Atlantis story in Lydia, rather than Egypt, may not be so new. A curious tale generally neglected in Atlantological literature suggests that the real origin of the Atlantis story may have been known in antiquity. Aelian, a compiler of anecdotes in the second century AD, includes a tale drawn from the writings of Theopompus of Chios, a historian who was a later contemporary of Plato.[1] It concerns Silenus, leader of the brutish satyrs (part-horse or part-goat) and a familiar figure of Greek myth and comic theatre. Dissolute and drunken, Silenus was tutor to the young Dionysus, god of wine, and the adventure concerns a time when the god's debauched army was passing through Phrygia. Drunk, Silenus fell asleep in the rose gardens of King Midas and was left behind by Dionysus' band. Midas' gardeners brought him before their master, and Silenus entertained his host with a story. According to Theopompus:

> Silenus told Midas that Europe, Asia and Africa were islands surrounded by the ocean; that there was but one continent, which was beyond this world, and that in size it was infinite; that in it were bred, besides other very great creatures, men twice as big as those here, and they lived double our age; that many great cities are there, and peculiar manners of life.

Silenus' unknown continent is obviously a doublet of Atlantis – except that its marvellous inhabitants dwell on an outer continent, rather than a continent-sized island in the 'true ocean'. The tale continues:

> there are two cities far greater than the rest, nothing like each other; one named Machimus ('Warlike') and the other Eusebes ('Pious'); that the Pious people live in peace, abounding in wealth, and reap the fruits of the earth without ploughs or

oxen, having no need of tillage or sowing. The inhabitants of the city Machimus are very warlike, continually armed and fighting, and this one city predominates over many. The inhabitants are not fewer than 2,000,000. They die sometimes of sickness, but this happens very rarely, for most commonly they are killed in wars by stone or wood, since they are invulnerable to steel . . .

There can be little doubt that this is a parody of the two idealised societies in Plato's account – the worthy Athenian farmers and the aggressive Atlanteans. The people of Machimus, like the Atlanteans, make an expedition to the known world, but with a rather different result:

He [Silenus] said that they once planned a voyage to our isles and sailed the ocean, being 10,000,000 in number, till they came to the Hyperboreans [of northern Europe]; but understanding that they were the happiest men amongst us, they despised us as persons who lead a mean and inglorious life, and therefore thought it not worth their while to go further.

Silenus continued with further descriptions of what can be found on the unknown continent, noting that 'there are men living among them called Meropes, who inhabit many great cities'. The land is thus known as 'Meropis'. While *meropes* can mean simply 'mankind', in this context it is more likely that Meropes is an oblique reference to the name Atlantis. Merops seems to have been an alternative name for Atlas (see Appendix 1).

Midas was delighted with Silenus' tale and entertained him for five days and nights before returning him safely to Dionysus. It was then, according to other writers, that Dionysus granted Midas the unfortunate 'Golden Touch', which he could only rid himself of by swimming in the River Pactolus (see Ch. 9).

What are we to make of this curious tale of the drunken Silenus, with his news of an unknown Atlantic continent? English poet and mythologist Robert Graves provided an intriguing analysis:

Why the story of the Atlantic Continent should have been attributed to the drunken Silenus may be divined from three incidents reported by Plutarch . . . The first is that Solon travelled extensively in Asia Minor and Egypt; the second, that he believed the story of Atlantis and turned it into an epic poem; the third, that he quarrelled with Thespis the dramatist who, in his plays about Dionysus, put ludicrous speeches, apparently full of topical allusions, into the mouths of satyrs . . . Aelian, who quotes Theopompus as his authority, seems to have had access at second or third hand to a comedy by Thespis, or his pupil Pratinas, ridiculing Solon for the Utopian lies told in the epic poem, and presenting him as Silenus, wandering footloose about Egypt and Asia Minor. Silenus and Solon are not dissimilar names and as Silenus was tutor to Dionysus, so Solon was tutor to Peisistratus who – perhaps on his advice – founded the Dionysian rites at Athens.[2]

Graves' interpretations of Greek myths are often rather wayward and his speculation that Theopompus used a lost work by Thespis seems unnecessary. In other respects his analysis is spot-on, and it is generally accepted that Theopompus' Meropis is a take-off of Atlantis.[3] Silenus would be the perfect figure to use in a parody of Solon, who in old age 'became even fonder of leisure and entertainment, and for that matter of wine and song too'.[4]

There is a further parallel in the story which has been overlooked. If Silenus stands for Solon, then Midas, who entertained him at his court, can only stand for Croesus. The similarities between Midas and Croesus hardly need spelling out, except, perhaps to note how they were both intimately associated with the Pactolus: King Midas created the gold in the river, and Croesus was the last Lydian monarch to enjoy its benefits. Though Solon (Silenus) is cast as the inventor, rather than the recipient, of the Atlantis (Meropis) story, the fact that Theopompus used the court of Croesus (Midas) as the scene of its transmission suggests he was aware of the story's true origin – Lydia rather than Egypt.

Notes and References

1 *FGrHist* 115 F 75; Aelian: *Varia Historia* III, xviii.
2 Graves 1960, I, 284–5.
3 Gill 1980, vii; Vidal-Naquet 1986, 264–5; Ferguson 1975, 122–3; Romm 1992, 67, n. 51.
4 Plut. *Life of Solon* 29.

The Bull Cult of Atlantis

Supporters of the Minoan-Atlantis school have always made great play with the fact that there were religious cults involving bulls on both Crete and Atlantis. Bulls figured conspicuously in Minoan culture and the image created by the famous frescoes showing the ritual sport of bull-leaping is compelling. The bulls were more than likely sacrificed after the 'games' finished. Yet the ritual described by Plato (*Critias* 119D–E) involved no bull-leaping. The Atlantean ritual was conducted by the ten kings of the island, who hunted the bulls which roamed at large in the grounds of Poseidon's temple. When a bull was caught it was sacrificed, by having its throat slit, on, or against, the top (*kata koruphên*) of the sacred pillar of Poseidon, so that its blood trickled down over the sacred laws engraved on it. Nothing like this is depicted in Minoan art or reported in Cretan tradition.

The problem was appreciated as long ago as 1927, by the Cambridge scholar Jane Harrison, who pioneered an anthropological approach to the study of ancient Greek religion. In her detailed analysis of the bull cults of the classical world she made the following remark about Frost's hypothesis that Atlantis was an echo of Minoan civilisation (see Chapter 3):

> It has been happily suggested that the lost island of Atlantis reflects the manners and customs, the civilisation generally, of Crete, which after its great Minoan supremacy sank, for the rest of Greece, into a long oblivion. It is also very unlikely that Plato would *invent* ritual details which in his day would have but little significance. But we have definite evidence that the ritual described is actual, not imaginary, though the evidence comes not from Crete but from another region of the 'Mycenaean' world.

The evidence which struck Harrison came from coins minted in Roman times at Troy. These depict a bull cult and one coin, as Harrison noted, shows very clearly how the bull was sacrificed.

FIG. 27   Coin from Troy (Ilium), Roman
period, showing (right) a sacrificial bull suspended
from a pillar.

On the left is shown the goddess Athena with her spear, 'but to
the right is an older sanctity, a pillar *on to which is hung a bull*. He
will be sacrificed, not on the pillar's top, which would be
extremely awkward, but with his head and his throat to be cut
against the top, alongside of it, down over it (*kata koruphên*).'[1]

The resemblance between the bull cults of Troy and Atlantis is
undeniable. The striking thing is that it presents a precise parallel,
of a quite different order to the vague resemblances offered by
the Minoan-Atlantis school. The awful possibility that the Trojans
of Hellenistic times invented such a cult after reading the *Critias*
can be discounted. Ancient cults were notoriously conservative
and it would take more than a short passage in Plato to inspire and
institute a new one.

How, then, can the parallel be explained? Zangger, had he
known the Roman coin evidence, would certainly have taken it
in support of his theory that Troy was the prototype of Atlantis.[2]
As shown (Chapter 8), his argument suffers from many weaknesses, not the least being the idea that details about the culture
of Bronze Age Troy were preserved in Egypt and relayed to the
Greeks several hundred years later – a highly unlikely and circu-
itous route since the Greeks were surely better informed about
Trojan traditions than the Egyptians ever were. An alternative
explanation is that Plato simply borrowed the details from contemporary Trojan practice. Yet it seems unlikely that Plato would
have plucked a detail from a relatively obscure Trojan cult as an
embellishment for his description of Atlantis; it is hard to imagine
a motive for such a decision. (On Zangger's model Plato was
supposedly unaware that his Atlantis was really Troy.) The third
possibility is that the detail of the bull cult was already embedded
in Plato's ultimate source – the story of a sunken kingdom told
to Solon in Lydia – and that this preserved a genuine recollection

of a distinctive Anatolian custom. The custom of sacrificing bulls need not have been exclusively Trojan. There is evidence that Troy and Sipylus (where Tantalus' kingdom lay) had similar religious cults, particularly with respect to the worship of the Phrygian Mother Goddess Cybele (in Greek, Rhea). The geographer Strabo complained that the dramatist Aeschylus located king Tantalus at Mount Ida near Troy, apparently muddling it with Mount Sipylus.[3] Elsewhere, as Harrison noted, Strabo provides an explanation for the confusion, due to the identity of cults in the two places:

> The Berekyntes and the Phrygians in general, and the Trojans living at *Ida* worship Rhea with mystical rites . . . and after the various places of her cult, they call her Idaean, Dindymene, *Sipylene*, Pessinutis, Cybele . . . The Greeks call her attendants Curetes.[4]

If, as Strabo states, the Trojans worshipped the Mother Goddess under the name 'Sipylene', then we can only assume that there was cultic borrowing from the worship of Cybele on Mount Sipylus. Bull sacrifice was a major feature of the Phrygian goddess Cybele, and the curious custom of sacrificing bulls hung from a sacred pillar may even have been borrowed by the Trojans from the cult of the Sipylene Mother Goddess. Thus the 'Atlantean' custom reported by Plato may be another genuine relic of the civilisation of ancient Sipylus.

Notes and References

1 Harrison 1927, 164.
2 Zangger (1992, 166–7) tried to match the description in the *Critias* with archaeological evidence from Bronze Age Troy (VI). He noted that four pillars set against the outside of the fortifications were assumed by the excavator Blegen to be cultic installations, while a nearby house containing a thick stratum of burnt debris, including many animal bones, was thought to belong to a cult of burnt offerings. Zangger argued that these two features belonged together and that they reflected a ritual of sacrificing bulls on pillars like that described by Plato. The evidence is hardly convincing.
3 Strabo XII, 580, citing Aeschylus Fr. 156.
4 Strabo X, 469, translation and emphasis Harrison (1927, 246).

Notes and References

Abbreviations

AJA	*American Journal of Archaeology*
ANET	J. B. Pritchard (ed.), *Ancient Near Eastern Texts Relating to the Old Testament*, Princeton University Press (3rd edn with supplement), 1969.
Apollod.	Apollodorus mythographus:
Bibl.	*Library*
Epit.	*Epitome*
Arist.	Aristotle
CAH	*Cambridge Ancient History*
Diod.	Diodorus Siculus: *Library of History*
Diog. Laert.	Diogenes Laertius: *Lives of the Eminent Philosophers*
Eur.	Euripides
FGrHist	F. Jacoby (ed.), *Die Fragmente der Griechischen Historiker*
Hes.	Hesiod:
Th.	*Theogony*
Op.	*Opera et Dies (Works and Days)*
Hdt.	Herodotus: *The Histories*
Hom.	Homer:
Il.	*Iliad*
Od.	*Odyssey*
JEA	*Journal of Egyptian Archaeology*
JHS	*Journal of Hellenic Studies*
JNES	*Journal of Near Eastern Studies*
Ov.	Ovid: *Metamorphoses*
OJA	*Oxford Journal of Archaeology*
Paus.	Pausanias: *Guide to Greece*
Plut.	Plutarch

Notes

1 THE LOST CONTINENT

1 Abridged from Verne, Everyman trans. (1908), 196–7.
2 Bramwell 1937, 13.
3 For the genre of science fiction writing which grew around Atlantis during the late 19th and early 20th centuries see de Camp 1970, 155–75.
4 Bonewitz 1983, 95, 158.
5 For an example of this sort of paranoid reaction see the aptly named Rufus Fears quoted in Chapter 3.
6 For those who like definitions: I follow the dictionary in using 'story' as a description of events, real or imaginary, written or told to entertain. This includes the categories 'myth' and 'legend', for definitions of which I have tried to follow the guidelines of Sir James Frazer (1921, I, xxvii-xxviii). 'Myths' he defined as 'mistaken explanations of phenomena, whether of human life or of external nature . . .', from the origin of the world and natural phenomena to the beginnings of society and the mystery of death. I would only disagree with the word 'mistaken', a value judgment based on the assumed superiority of 20th-century scientific knowledge, understandable in Frazer's day. By 'legend' Frazer understood 'traditions, whether oral or written, which relate the fortunes of real people in the past, or which describe events . . . said to have occurred at real places . . .'
7 Greek *oreichalkos* (Latin *orichalcum*) means 'mountain copper' and was regularly used for copper ore and the brass made from it. By saying that it 'survives today only in name' (*Critias* 114E), Plato indicates that *oreichalkos* was once used to indicate another, more precious metal.
8 Gill 1980, 64. Plato is not precise about the height of the temple; he says (*Critias* 116D) it was a stade (about 600 ft) in length, three plethra (about 300 ft wide), and 'proportionate in height to look at'.
9 E.g. Diod. I, lxix, 3–5.
10 Hdt. II, 43 & 50.
11 Arist. cited in Strabo II, iii, 6.
12 Plut. *Life of Solon* 29.
13 The Parian Marble, a chronicle of Greek history from Cecrops, mythical first king of Athens, down to the archonship of Diognetus in 264–3 BC, dates Deucalion's Flood to 1529 BC. For a translation and discussion of the prehistoric entries see Forsdyke 1957, 50–61.
14 For a study of Greek mythical genealogies see Parada 1993.
15 The meeting between Socrates, Timaeus, Critias and Hermocrates may never have happened as such – if it did it would have taken place about 420 BC – see Taylor 1928, 17.
16 The reality of Solon's travels to Egypt and Lydia has been doubted on chronological grounds, but Miller (1969) has demonstrated that only late sources contradict the consistency in accounts of Solon's career and the tradition that he went to Egypt in the reign of Amasis (570–526 BC) and Lydia in the reign of Croesus (561–547 BC). The conventional chronology for the Greek 6th century, which would push all the events

of Solon's career back about twenty years in time, and break these synchronisms, is, as Miller realised, inflated – cf. James *et al.* 1991, 328–330. The problem is an old one. Plutarch (*Life of Solon* 27) noted that chronological arguments had often been used to 'prove' that Solon never met Croesus, but refused to believe that their much attested meeting, which bore the stamp of Solon's 'greatness of mind', should be rejected on chronological grounds. He was right.

17 For Solon as a poet see Anhalt 1993; for classical sources on Solon generally, including his fragments, see Martina 1968.

18 Cf. Luce 1969, 35.

19 Matthiae 1980.

20 For an introduction to the Indus Valley civilization and its script, see Renfrew 1987, 183–91; for some of its technological highlights see James & Thorpe 1994, 356–7, 361–2, 442–3, 454–5.

21 E.g. Berlitz 1984, 23–6.

22 Mellaart 1979, 22–33.

23 Hawkes 1974, 139.

24 For Jericho and early agriculture see James & Thorpe 1994, 200–1, 354, 381.

25 Parker 1990.

26 See James & Thorpe 1994, 300–1.

2 THE ORIGIN OF CIVILISATION?

1 So described in the excellent sketch of Donnelly by Michell 1984, 201–11. For other accounts of Donnelly's life see de Camp 1970, 37–43 and E. F. Bleiler's introduction to the 1976 Dover facsimile edition of Donnelly 1882.

2 de Camp 1970, 28–30, 250.

3 Donnelly 1882, 23.

4 Donnelly 1882, 1–2.

5 Cited in Donnelly 1882, 326.

6 Donnelly 1882, 172.

7 Donnelly 1882, 171.

8 E.g. Berlitz 1984, 20–21.

9 Vaillant 1965, 85–6, 94–5, 106–8.

10 Brundage 1972, 22, 195, 298.

11 Donnelly 1882, 46.

12 Cited in Donnelly 1883, 53.

13 Donnelly 1882, 44.

14 Donnelly 1882, 49.

15 Michell 1984, 205.

16 Trans. (Han Kloosterman) from de Launay 1905, 256.

17 Trans. (Han Kloosterman) from de Launay 1926, 72.

18 For an account of Wegener's contribution see Smith 1981.

19 Hess 1962.

20 Bucher 1950, 40.

21 Smith 1981.

22 Smith 1977.

23 Wood 1980.

24 For some recent objectors see Chester 1993, 25, 47–8.

25 For an extreme case see the essay 'Velikovsky in Collision' in Gould 1978, where continental drift is misused in an attempt to debunk a theory of cometary catastrophism, and my review (James 1982).

26 Clube & Napier 1982; 1990; Huggett 1988.

27 An old chestnut, still frequently referred to (e.g. Berlitz 1984, 158) is the piece of vitreous lava (tachylite) discovered in the seas near the Azores during the laying of a telegraph cable in 1898. French geologist Termier declared that the structure of the tachylite showed it solidified in the open air. For explanations of this apparent anomaly see Galanopoulos & Bacon 1969, 59–61 and Vitaliano 1973, 223–4.

28 Galanopoulos & Bacon 1969, 60–1.

29 Warlow 1982, 129.

30 Warlow (1982) did not follow this path to explain the submergence of Atlantis as he does not accept the conventional Ice Age model. His own model for the glaciations involves a shift in the polar position, which would involve little net exchange between the quantities of water stored in the oceans and polar caps.

31 Emiliani et al. 1975, 1086.

32 Wright 1978, 173.

33 Fairbanks 1989; van Andel 1990.

34 Barbetti & Flude 1979.

35 Spedicato 1985.

36 van Andel 1989, 736.

37 For convenient summaries of information on Old and New World Pyramids see Mendelssohn 1974.

38 Spence 1924; for an assessment of Spence see de Camp 1970, 91–8.

39 The world's major deluge myths are collected in Gaster 1969, 82–131.

40 Brotherston 1989, 282.

41 Ginzberg 1909, 162.

42 Mundkur 1976.

43 Gordon 1970; James & Thorpe 1994, 504–6.

44 Wahlgren 1986.

45 For other possible Greek references to the Americas see Gordon 1971.

46 Harden 1971, 170. For Phoenician knowledge of the Atlantic islands (notably the Madeiras) see Keyser 1993, 164, n. 101 for further references on the alleged Azores hoard.

47 Kehoe 1971.

48 See Cross 1979 for the notorious Paraiba Stone from Brazil.

49 See discussion in Mundkur 1976, which argues that the similarities are due to a common cultural heritage before the migration of the Palaeo-Indians across the Bering Straits.

50 Klein 1989, 389–92.

51 James & Thorpe 1994.

52 Emery 1961, 38.

53 Cf. Rowling 1989.

54 Donnelly 1882, 139.

55 For an account of the hyper-diffusionists see Daniel 1964, 88–107.

56 For an exemplary account of the growth of the 'new archaeology' see Malina & Vašíček 1990; reviewed in James 1992a.

57 Renfrew 1973, 132, 160; Renfrew 1987, 147–52.

58 See Redford 1992, 17.

59 Daniel (1971, 91–2) gives a wonderfully evasive compromise: 'I would suggest that the origins of Egyptian civilisation are to be explained in terms of stimulus diffusion from Sumeria [sic] to an essentially African society in the Nile Valley – a society which was already well on its way to civilisation, and might well have got there independently without benefit of Sumer.'

60 Redford 1992, 23–4.

61 From the pottery connections between Buto and Amuq in Syria, Redford (1992, 22–3 & Fig. 1) has suggested that the newcomers to Gerzean Egypt came by ship from the Levantine coast.

62 See for example the excellent work on the origin of cuneiform in Schmandt-Besserat 1992.

63 For accounts of these reported finds see Ebon 1977, 102–18; Hitching 1978, 141–3 & Zink 1978.

64 McKusick and Shinn 1980.

65 McKusick 1982, 116.

66 Cayce, readings 440:5 and 958:3 – from Cayce (ed.) 1969.

67 For example by Valentine himself, as interviewed in Berlitz 1984, 97.

68 They are published, conveniently, in Berlitz 1984, Pls. 5–7.

69 See the interview with Egerton Sykes, former British diplomat and grand old man of British Atlantology, in Berlitz 1984, 87–8.

3 THE DESTRUCTION OF THERA

1 Letter to his father John Evans, Nov. 1900, quoted in Cottrell 1955, 125, still the best popular account of the discovery of Knossos.

2 Frost 1913, which wrongly dates his article in *The Times* to January 19th, 1909.

3 Jowett 1892, III, 431.

4 Hdt. II,30, II,177; Plut. *Life of Solon* 26.

5 Hdt. II,178.

6 Bietak 1992.

7 The idea that all these figures are people from Keftiu and that Keftiu = Crete is wrong, but is one of those assumptions that, once made, refuses to go away quietly. In fact, the *only* instances in which a person from Keftiu is clearly identifiable show people wearing typically Syrian costume. A typical Egyptological reaction to this has been to assume that the Egyptian artists did not know how to draw Keftiu people properly (i.e. as Minoans)! A more logical approach (to the admittedly limited evidence) leaves two choices: that Keftiu was not Crete but somewhere nearer the Levant such as Cyprus (Strange 1980); or that the ruling class of Crete had a Levantine element (Bernal 1991, 413–15).

On the other hand people of undeniably Minoan appearance occur in the tomb paintings. The problem, complicated by the uncertainty of the location of the 'Isles in the Midst of the Sea' (from which some of the people shown may have come), is still not resolved.

8 Frost 1913, 205.

9 Regarding the origin of the Vapheio cup, see Hooker 1976, 62–3.

10 Frost 1913, 204.

11 See Hutchinson 1962, 300–5. There have always been problems with the idea of an Achaean invasion around 1400 BC – see Hooker 1976, 59–80; Dickinson 1994, 304.

12 Plut. *Life of Theseus* 19.

13 Marinatos 1969, 5.

14 See Marinatos' own account of the development of his theory in Marinatos 1969, 5–6 (reprinted from Marinatos 1950).

15 Marinatos 1939, 439.

16 Marinatos 1969, 33–4.

17 Details from Vitaliano 1973, 184–7 & Marinatos 1969, 34–5.

18 The calculation based on caldera size is simplistic. As Vitaliano (1973, 187–8) noted, what is important is not the total amount of energy released, 'but *how that energy was partitioned*.' I.e. if it was all released in a few rapid explosions it would have far more devastating consequences than a slow sequence of smaller explosions; likewise the size of the tsunami created is governed by how much of the cone collapsed at any one time. For the most recent estimates of the force and effects of the Thera explosion see Hardy & Renfrew (eds.) 1990, Vol. 2: *Geology.*

19 Marinatos 1939, 432.

20 Marinatos 1969, 41–2.

21 Augustine: *City of God* XVIII, 10–11.

22 For Deucalion's Flood and the Exodus see Galanopoulos & Bacon 1969, 192–9. The link between Thera and the Exodus has subsequently been developed by many authors, e.g. Bernal 1991, 291–3.

23 See Mavor 1969 for his account of these events.

24 Marinatos 1969, 7.

25 The authenticity of the *Minos* as a Platonic work has been disputed on rather weak grounds – for a defence see Morrow 1960, 35–9.

26 Gill 1980, xi.

27 Galanopoulos & Bacon 1969, 170.

28 Galanopoulos & Bacon 1969, 134.

29 Luce 1969, 181.

30 Plut. *Life of Solon* 25–26.

31 Mavor 1969, 33–4.

32 The more common belief was that Egyptian civilisation preceded Greek, see e.g. the tradition that Athens was founded by colonists from Sais (Diod. I, xxviii, 4). A different claim was that the Egyptian cities of Heliopolis and Sais were founded by Greek colonists from Rhodes and Athens respectively. The Greeks forgot these events, as well as their primacy in astrology – which the Egyptians claimed to have invented – due to a flood which destroyed all their written records (Diod. V,

lvii, 2–5). The story looks like a late creation, produced by nationalists as a counterweight to the persistent traditions about the Greek debt to 'barbarian' civilisations. It was also clearly influenced by Plato's writings – see Cameron 1983, 86–8.

33 Hdt. II,142.

34 See James *et al.* 1991, esp. 291–3.

35 See Miller 1965, 113.

36 See for example the Abydos kinglist, discussed in James *et al.* 1991, 224.

37 Galanopoulos & Bacon 1969, 125; Vitaliano 1973, 240–1.

38 Vitaliano 1973, 240.

39 Vitaliano 1973, 241; see also Luce 1969, 182–3.

40 Vitaliano 1973, 242–3; see also Galanopoulos & Bacon 1969, 146–51 and Luce 1969, 182.

41 Vitaliano 1978, 159.

42 In Doumas (ed.) 1978–80, II, 396.

43 See papers by S. Hood, D. Page, W. Schiering and J. V. Luce in Doumas (ed.) 1978–80, I.

44 For criticisms of the proxy dating of Thera by ice-cores and tree-rings see Warren 1984, Muhly 1991; James *et al.* 1991, xix-xx. In defence of proxy dating see most recently Manning 1992. My present view is that neither side in the debate over the 'high' and 'low' datings for the Thera eruption is right – or completely wrong. The 'low' school, currently led by Warren, is correct in rejecting the ice-core and tree-ring proxy dates as an irrelevance, while the radiocarbon dates used to support the high date are frankly a mess. (They are almost certainly affected by old carbon from the volcano.) The 'high' school, on the other hand, seems to have the edge in demonstrating through archaeological synchronisms that the eruption took place earlier than the 18th Dynasty. If, as we have argued (James *et al.* 1991, 1991a, 1992), the accepted chronology for Egypt should be considerably reduced, the upshot may be that the 'low' date-range for Thera (1525–1400 BC) is correct, but, ironically, that the 'high' chronologists are right in saying that the eruption took place a century or so before the 18th Dynasty.

45 For an overlap of the end of Late Minoan IB with the reign of Thutmose III in Egypt – see Hankey 1987, 44–6.

46 Davis (1990) suggests that a document from the early 18th Dynasty describes the long-range effects of the Thera eruption.

47 Vitaliano & Vitaliano 1974.

48 Vitaliano 1978, 158.

49 Luce 1978, 67.

50 E.g. Bernal 1991, 295–8. The latest book on the Minoan-Atlantis theory is Pellegrino 1991, a work which contributes nothing of value to the case.

51 Fears 1978, 133–4.

52 For authors and dates of these theories see de Camp 1970, 314–18.

53 Hdt. IV, 42.

54 For some Celtic sources see Bromwich 1961, 397–400. Evidence for

modern, medieval and earlier erosion of the coasts of the British Isles is discussed in Pennick 1987 – a useful book despite the frustrating lack of proper references. We know that stories of sunken kingdoms were told in Europe as early as the Iron Age from Timagenes (quoted in Ammianus Marcellinus XV, ix, 2), who in the 1st century BC cited the Druids of Gaul as saying that while some Gallic peoples were indigenous, 'others also poured in from the remote islands and the regions across the Rhine, driven from their homes by continual wars and the inundation of the stormy sea.'

55 I explored this idea in a talk ('Plato's Atlantis and Prehistoric Europe') given to the Ancient History Society at University College (London University) in 1981.

4 PLATO'S WORLD

1 R. Kraut: 'Introduction to the Study of Plato', in Kraut (ed.) 1992, 1.

2 For recent bibliographies see Brisson 1997; Brisson & Ioannidi 1983; Kraut (ed.) 1992, 439–529.

3 Thuc. I, 23, 118. See Hornblower 1991, 88–93 for an analysis of Thucydides' description of the causes leading to the war.

4 See Diod. XII, i, 3–4. For a curious mismatch between the historical and archaeological records, with a possible resolution involving a shift in the dating of Athenian pottery, see James et al. 1991, 96–8, 359.

5 For the importance of Persian bullion in the economic flowering of 5th-century Athens, see Vickers 1985, 24–5.

6 Thuc. VI, 76; Taylor 1928, 14.

7 Vidal-Naquet 1986, 268; see also Gill 1980, xviii.

8 Gill 1977, 298.

9 de Camp & Ley 1952, 30–1; cf. Cameron 1983, 89. The theory that the name Atlantis was copied from Atalante fails to explain the evidence (see Chapter 8) that the story was intimately connected with the cycle of legends surrounding Atlas and related figures. There is no reason to doubt that the name Atlantis was derived from Atlas, as Plato suggests.

10 Plut. Life of Pericles 13.

11 See Luce 1978, 76–8 on the confusion of the two Critiases.

12 Plato: Epistle VII, 324B–325D; trans. K. Stott. For its authenticity see Bury 1929, 391–2 & 463 and Penner 1992, 130.

13 See Plato: Gorgias, esp. 509.

14 Cicero: Talks at Tusculum V, xxxii, 91.

15 Diog. Laert. I, 37; Plut. Benefit from Enemies 90E.

16 For the Ionian scientists see Sarton 1952, I, 160–98, 238–59; Vernant 1983, 343–4.

17 Burnet 1908, 29.

18 Xenophon: Memorabilia I, 13.

19 Xenophon: Memorabilia I, 16.

20 See Bury 1927, 382–5.

21 In the Laws Plato argues that homosexuality should be legislated against.

22 Penner 1992, 130.

23 Other biographers such as Xenophon provide different perspectives on Socrates which balance Plato's picture. For the classical writings on Socrates, including a selection from Plato, see Ferguson 1970.

24 Penner 1992, 121–69.

25 This was too subtle for Aristotle. In *The Politics* (V, 12) he spends some time pointing out the obvious, e.g. that 'surely there are also changes in the reverse direction, as from democracy to oligarchy even more than to one man rule'. He then finds fault with the idea that a tyranny will turn into a timarchy, having set up as a straw man a theory of repeating and continuous political cycles which is not to be found in *The Republic*.

26 Friedländer 1958, 201.

27 Sarton 1952, 413.

28 On Hermes see Brown 1969 & Vernant 1983, 128–30.

29 See Friedländer 1958, 41.

30 *Meno* 81C–D, trans. K. Stott.

31 Morrow 1960, 591.

32 Saunders 1970, 27–8.

33 Morrow 1960, 591.

34 *Laws* 714, trans. K. Stott.

35 Explicitly stated in Ov. I 113–15; cf. Plato: *Statesman* 272B.

36 I have used the rather archaic 'Brazen' Age here rather than the more common 'Bronze' Age to avoid confusion with archaeological terminology.

37 It is generally thought that Hesiod interpolated the Age of Heroes into an already existing sequence of Gold-Silver-Brazen-Iron – see Vernant 1983, 4, 26, n. 10. Vernant provides an interesting structural analysis of Hesiod's narrative. On the origins of Hesiod's Age system see also Fontenrose 1974 & Griffiths 1991, 237–51.

38 *Laws* 713, trans. K. Stott.

39 The same conclusion has been reached by Reiche 1981, 170–171.

40 Hes. *Op.* 134; see Vernant 1983, 11.

41 *Critias* 120D-121B, trans. K. Stott

42 Despite its title, Settgast 1990 (*Plato Prehistorian*) contains no cogent argument for seeing Plato as a prehistorian. It takes the chronological setting of the *Critias* and *Timaeus* literally and compares it to the archaeological record of prehistoric Europe in an utterly naive fashion. It is surprising enough that Plato's writings contain genuine echoes of the Mycenaean world – ignored by Settgast. To expect him to have accurate knowledge of Mesolithic Europe and Egypt is simply beyond belief – and unnecessary.

5 A PLATONIC AFFAIR

1 See Diog. Laert. VIII, 85.

2 Heath 1913, 94–7; Sarton 1952 I, 288–90; Koestler 1968, 43–5.

3 Friedländer 1958, 249. It is usually assumed that Timaeus, main speaker

in the dialogue, was a fictional character, as there is no independent evidence for the existence of a Greek astronomer of this name. This is, however, only an argument from silence.

4 *Timaeus* 30B, trans. Bury 1929.

5 Sarton 1952 I, 421.

6 Sarton 1952 I, 451.

7 Sarton 1952 I, 435.

8 Sarton 1952 I, 451, citing Arist. *On the Heavens* II 293b & Theophrastus in Plut. *Platonic Questions* VIII.

9 As well as Sarton, see e.g. Cornford 1937, 134 and Koestler 1968, 59; even Temple (1976, 236), in his stirring defence of Platonic tradition, describes Plato as 'a feeble astronomer'.

10 Bury (1929, 85, n. 6) justifies his supposition by making another about relative motions in Plato's cosmos: 'Her [Earth's] potential motion (we may assume) is equal and opposite to that of the Universe, of which she is the centre, and by thus neutralising it she remains at rest.'

11 Jowett 1892, III, 459 & n. 1; Lee 1971, 55.

12 See Heath 1913, 174-89.

13 Cornford 1937, 120-34.

14 See discussion in Guthrie 1939, 220-3, note *a*.

15 Vlastos 1975, 37-51.

16 *Phaedo* 108E; *Laws* 677; *Timaeus* 40B; *Republic* XI, 616-617 & *Cratylus* 409A: '. . . his [Anaxagoras'] recent discovery, that the moon receives her light from the sun'; *Epinomis* 983A.

17 Plut. *Nikias* 23, trans. K. Stott.

18 Sarton 1952 I, 423.

19 Sarton 1952 I, 423, 222.

20 Diog. Laert. V, 2.

21 Cited in Farrington 1953, 117.

22 Koestler 1968, 55.

23 Aristotle is usually praised for his biological classification, though it led him to the absurd result that animals evolved (by degeneration) from mankind, and plants from animals. The real advances in this field were made by Theophrastus, a student of both Plato and Aristotle, who completely overturned Aristotle's work (see Farrington 1953, 159-69). Theophrastus was one of the greatest scientists of ancient times, yet our educational system still allows his brilliance to be overshadowed by the reputation of Aristotle.

24 Heath 1913, 171; cf. Farrington 1953, 218.

25 Gribbin 1980. For an impassioned attack on the contemporary prostitution of cosmology see Bennett 1994.

26 Lee 1955, 33.

27 *Republic* 529, trans. K. Stott.

28 *Statesman* 269E; 270B-C; cf. *Epinomis* 982C.

29 *On the Heavens* I, iii, 270b.

30 *Meteorologica* I, xiv, 352a.

31 *Meteorologica* I, viii, 345a-346b.

32 *Meteorologica* I, xiv, 352a-b.

33 de Camp 1970, 18.
34 Julian: *Against the Galileans* 49A.
35 Augustine: *City of God* VIII, 11.
36 Augustine: *City of God* VIII, 12.
37 Athanassiadi 1993, 24; Sarton 1952 I, 399–400.
38 Koestler 1968, 111.
39 de Camp 1970, 19.
40 Koestler 1968, 62.
41 Arist. *Meteorologica* I, vi; cf. Seneca: *Naturales Quaestiones* VII.
42 King-Hele 1975, 1–5.
43 Koestler 1968, 61.
44 See Koestler 1968, 200–2.
45 Field 1982.
46 Drake 1957, 188.
47 For the Cambridge Platonists see Stewart 1905, 475–519 (p. 489 for the Earth's motion).
48 Levinson 1953, 12–13, 441, 498–504.
49 De Camp 1970, 87–9; Pauwels & Bergier 1963, 139, 153–79.
50 Rauschning 1939.
51 Levinson 1953, 22.
52 Sarton 1952 I, 420, 421.
53 One shining exception is Friedländer (1958, 247 ff), who, for example, considers Plato a precursor of modern molecular theory. Another is Vlastos (1975) which provides a refreshingly unbiased approach to Plato's contribution to astronomy.
54 Farrington 1953, 120.
55 E.g. Farrington 1953, 101.
56 Athanassiadi 1994, 1.
57 Temple 1976, 228. The first edition of the *Oxford Classical Dictionary* (1949) did not even consider Proclus worthy of an entry, though this was corrected in the second edition of 1970.
58 *Timaeus* 92C, trans. Lee 1971.
59 Kraut (ed.) 1992. The bibliographical guide includes entries on the *Meno, Phaedo, Symposium, The Republic, Phaedrus, Parmenides, Theaetetus, Timaeus, Sophist, Statesman, Philebus, Laws* and *Letters*. Atlantis does not appear in the index and is only mentioned in passing (p. 15) in a discussion of the relative order of the *Timaeus* and *Critias*.
60 See e.g. Brisson 1977; Brisson & Ioannidi 1983.
61 Vidal-Naquet 1986, 277.
62 Dombrowski 1981, 117 (his emphasis).

6 ATHENS OF THE HEROES

1 Vidal-Naquet 1986, 264 (essay originally published 1964).
2 On the earliest efforts to write Athenian history see Jacoby 1949. Gantz 1993, 233–49 provides a useful summary of the sources and material for the mythological history of early Athens.
3 It features prominently, for example, in Eur. *Ion*.

4 Hom. *Il.* II, 547; Eur. *Ion* 1163; Aristophanes: *Wasps* 438; Apollod. *Bibl.*
   III, xiv, 1 & 5; Paus I, ii, 6.

5 Apollod. *Bibl.* III, xiv, 6; the myth seems to have been described in a
   lost play of Euripides – see Gantz 1993, 235–6.

6 Isocrates: *Panathenaicus* 124–5.

7 Eumolpus was a King of Thrace who laid claim to the Athenian throne.
   Invited by the people of Eleusis, the last independent city in Attica, to
   defend them against Athens, he invaded with a massive force but was
   defeated by King Erechtheus. (Apollod. *Bibl.* III xv, 4–5.) The war of
   Erechtheus and Eumolpus is mentioned in Thuc. II, 15 and was the
   subject of a tragedy by Euripides, now lost (Gantz 1993, 242–244). The
   invasion of the Amazons was thought to have been repelled by Theseus.
   The growth of the Amazon legend was surely influenced by the Persian
   invasion of Attica in 490 BC, yet it existed before. According to Plut.
   Life of Theseus 28, the author of the 6th-century epic known as the
   Theseis also wrote an epic on the Amazon invasion called *Rising of
   the Amazons*. The detailed references to the invasion in Aeschylus
   (*Eumenides* 680ff) show that the tradition was well developed by 458
   BC. On early sources see Gantz 1993, 284–285.

8 Thuc. I, 2, cf. Hdt. I, 56.

9 E.g. Eur. *Hippolytus* 421ff; Sophocles: *Oedipus Coloneus* 913; for further
   references and discussion see Davie 1982, 28 & 33.

10 See Davie 1982, 26–9; Jacoby 1949, 126.

11 Isocrates: *Helen* 36; on the dilemma posed by the figure of Theseus the
   'democratic king' see Davie 1982, 28.

12 Isocrates: *Panathenaicus* 128.

13 Crantor, cited by Proclus: *On the Timaeus* 76.

14 For the Boutads (priests of Athena and Poseidon) see Apollod. *Bibl.* III,
   xv, 1; for other sources see Frazer 1921, II, 101, n. 2; for the Kerykes
   or 'Heralds' (priests of the Mysteries of Demeter at Eleusis), Paus. I,
   xxxviii, 3.

15 Plut. *Life of Theseus* 25.

16 *Parian Marble*, 11, 4–7 (see Frazer 1921, II, 88, n. 2); Apollodorus (*Bibl.*
   III, xiv, 5–6) agrees, and notes that Cranaus was succeeded as king of
   Athens by Amphictyon, son of Deucalion.

17 Lecture by Papadimitriou cited in Cottrell 1963, 183. P. was wrong in
   inferring that Brauron was completely abandoned. While very little
   LHIIB and no LHIIIC pottery was discovered during excavations, there
   are surface finds of LHIIIA-B sherds and one house has been identified
   as an LHIIIB structure (Simpson 1981, 49). Though P's claim is exaggerated, the idea of the unification of Attica during the Late Bronze Age
   is implicit in the archaeological literature, e.g. even in Simpson (1981,
   41), which notes that 'synoecism under Attica may not have been
   complete even in the LHIIIB period'.

18 Saccon 1974, 113.

19 On the conventional chronology, literacy disappeared in the early 12th
   century and only resurfaced with the introduction of the alphabet c.
   800 BC. For the problem of Greek literacy in the Dark Age see James

et al. 1991 (81–5, 319), where we argued that the end of the palaces should be redated to c. 950 BC. This would shorten the period of illiteracy considerably – indeed it is possible that the use of Linear B and the alphabet slightly overlapped at some Greek centres.

20 Hooker 1976, 183.

21 Hooker 1976, 188.

22 Broneer 1956, 11–12. Simpson (1981, 43) claims that 'it is probable that Mycenaean settlement to the south of the Acropolis was as extensive as that to the north of it', but his 'considerable, though sporadic, evidence' for occupation there during Mycenaean and Submycenaean times consists only of burials.

23 Thuc. II, 15.

24 Broneer 1949, 53; 1956, 12–13.

25 See Mellaart 1971, 406–10, for the disasters at the end of EBA II in Anatolia. (For simplicity I have referred here to the catastrophe at the end of the Early Bronze Age, though the terminology for Anatolia, the Aegean and the Levant allows the period to continue after the major disasters c. 2300/2200 BC – e.g. the cultural phase in Anatolia between 2300 and 2000 BC is described as EBA III.) Striking evidence of the catastrophic nature of the events at the end of the EBA has come from the excavation of several sites abandoned in northern Mesopotamia at this time – analysis of their soil shows a sudden change in climate (from a settled regime to one of desiccation punctuated by severe rainstorms), coincident with the fall of considerable amounts of tephra (probably from volcanoes in eastern Turkey). It seems clear that these upheavals played a major part in the fall of the Akkadian Empire, c. 2200 BC (Weiss *et al.* 1993).

26 Schaeffer 1948.

27 Breasted 1927, III: §580.

28 Carpenter 1966, vii.

29 See Neumann and Parpola 1987 and James *et al.* 1991, 288–9, 313.

30 For references see conveniently Drews 1993, 35–6, 43.

31 Schaeffer 1968, 607–8 – see James *et al.* 1991, 314, 394 & Drews 1993, 33–4, 42, 78.

32 James *et al.* 1991, 71–2, 311–14.

33 Drews 1992; 1993.

34 Kilian 1980.

35 Zangger 1992, 81–5.

36 Zangger 1992, 7.

37 Zangger 1992, 5.

38 Platt 1889, 136.

39 Kukal 1984, 22.

40 Zangger 1992, 126. Apart from the exceptions noted I have only found Platt cited (within mainstream literature) by Stewart (1904, 465).

41 Vidal-Naquet 1986, 263–84.

42 Dombrowski 1981, 123 (his emphasis).

43 Dombrowki 1981, 122.

44 *Laws* 676–682; trans. K. Stott.

45 Levinson 1953, 507; cf. 626.

46 Another exception is Gill (1980, 56) who refers to Plato's 'theory of periodic natural catastrophes'. Otherwise, appreciation of this aspect of Plato's work tends to be restricted to Velikovskian, catastrophist literature, see e.g. Mage 1981.

47 Stecchini (1984a, 1984b, 1984c).

48 MacLaurin 1775, 409–10.

49 Stecchini 1978, 100–6.

50 See Gould 1984. For the 19th-century struggle between catastrophism and uniformitarianism see Gillispie 1951 and Huggett 1990.

51 Velikovsky 1950.

52 For the 'Velikovsky Affair' see de Grazia (ed.) 1978 and Bauer 1984.

53 Stecchini 1978, 117–8.

54 Nininger 1959, 265–78.

55 Moore 1972, 55; Moore 1983, 52.

56 'We thought that Shoemaker-Levy was broken up into very small particles that would simply cascade down onto Jupiter's outer gas without making very much of a disturbance. That hasn't happened. They've hit and they're chunks several miles across and that, frankly, we did not suspect.' P. Moore, interview, ITN News, 21 July 1994.

57 Clube & Napier 1982 & 1990; see also dendrochronologist Baillie (1994), who allows the possibility that an asteroid strike may have been responsible for a dust-veil event in the 6th century AD, and geographer Huggett (1988, 1990) who provides sympathetic reviews of the effects which various catastrophist models would have on the Earth. For the record, the major pioneer in synthesising the evidence for a global catastrophe c. 2300 BC from archaeological, geological, climatological and other evidence is American radar engineer Moe Mandelkehr (1981).

7 THE EGYPTIAN CONNECTION

1 Luce 1969, 12.

2 Muck 1978, 16–17.

3 Taylor 1820, I, 64.

4 Cameron 1983, 82. Cameron argues that 'the ultimate source of confusion' was ·T. H. Martin's *Études sur le Timée de Platon* (Paris, 1841), the first comprehensive survey of ancient, medieval and modern writing on Atlantis, but allows (p. 82, n. 9) that 'Taylor had already made his misinterpretation public in the brief introduction to his translation of the *Timaeus* itself (London, 1804).'

5 Plut. *Life of Solon*, 2; for a summary of classical sources on Plato's Egyptian trip see Davis 1979, 122, n. 3.

6 Luce 1978, 60.

7 Saunders 1970, 505, n. 18; Griffiths 1991, 16.

8 Luce 1978, 66.

9 Luce (1978, 60) notes that Solon's fragment of verse about the Nile is the 'best testimony' for Solon's visit, the tradition of which 'runs back to Plato', forgetting that Herodotus reported Solon's Egyptian trip

nearly a hundred years before Plato!

10 One such passage is that in the *Timaeus* (20E), where Critias introduces the Atlantis story, speaking of 'the great and admirable exploits performed by our city long ago, which have been forgotten through the lapse of time and the destruction of human life'. Vidal-Naquet (1989, 267) has pointed out that these words seem to paraphrase those of Herodotus' introduction, where he expresses his intention of 'preserving from decay the remembrance of what men have done, and of preventing the great and wonderful deeds of the Greeks and barbarians from losing their due meed of glory . . .' Vidal-Naquet implies from this and other similarities that Plato's Atlantis story is a Herodotean pastiche with political and philosophical overtones – this is taking the similarities too far. Substantial parallels occur really only in the Egyptian portion.

11 Hdt. II, 83–4; see Griffiths 1991, 5.

12 Hdt. II, 142, trans. K. Stott.

13 For a translation of Sinuhe see J. A. Wilson, *ANET*, 18–22.

14 See Spanuth 1979, 217.

15 See Finley 1962, 116–118.

16 Luce 1969, 171–2 [Crete]; De Camp & Ley 1952, 78 [Tartessus]; Spanuth 1979, 213–44 [Heligoland]; Zangger 1992, 181–96 [Troy]; on other locations see de Camp 1970, 201–3.

17 *Odyssey* VI, 23, 205, 280; VII, 320.

18 Cited by Strabo: *Geography* I, 24.

19 See de Camp 1970, 197–203; Vidal-Naquet 1986, 266.

20 *Odyssey* VII, 84ff, trans. Lawrence 1932.

21 *Odyssey* VIII, 563ff.; XIII, 146–64, 181–7.

22 *Odyssey* VI, 270–2.

23 Vidal-Naquet 1986, 266–7.

24 For a selection see Gaster 1969, I, 157–8.

25 *Atrahasis Epic* A, II, ll. 1–8; trans. E. A. Speiser, *ANET*, 104.

26 Seneca: *Naturales Quaestiones* III, xxix, 1, trans. Burstein 1978, 15.

27 Drews (1976, 51–4) and Burstein (1978, 31–2) provide effective rebuttals of the pseudo-Berossus theory.

28 Olmstead 1948, 200–1.

29 Drews 1975, 52.

30 For a recent translation and commentary, see Kramer & Maier 1989, 12–13, 22–30.

31 Trans. Gordon 1971, 63.

32 Gordon 1971, 63–4; Griffiths 1991, 9–11.

33 Vycichi 1986. See Herodotus II, 156 for the tale of the floating island of Chemmis in the Delta.

34 Herzog 1968.

8 IN SEARCH OF ATLAS

1 For a survey of Atlas in Greek, Etruscan and Roman art see de Griño *et al.* 1986.

2 On Poseidon as father of giants and monsters see Fontenrose 1959, 31, 282, 330–2.

3 For Prometheus, Epimetheus and Pandora see Gantz 1993, 152–66.

4 Hes. *Th*. 514–16.

5 Hyginus: *Fabulae* 150.

6 Genealogical information from Hes. *Th*. 133–6, 359, 508–11 & *Catalogues of Women and Eoiae* Fr. 1; Apollod. *Bibl*. I, ii, 3. A variant tradition made Atlas a son of Uranus (Diod. III, lx, 1 & III, lvii, 2) or Earth and Air (Hyginus *Fabulae* Praef. 3).

7 Apollod. *Bibl*. II, v, 11, probably following Pherecydes.

8 Hes. *Th*. 518, 744–7.

9 Pindar's reference (*Pythian* IV, 289–290) comes at the end of a poem (462 BC) concerned with the legendary history of Libya – this suggests a Libyan location for Atlas as well. Hdt. IV, 184.

10 *Odyssey* I, 51–4, trans. Lawrence 1932.

11 See Gantz 1993, 46, 306–307.

12 Pomponius Mela: *Description of the World* III, x.

13 Hdt. IV, 184.

14 For references see Bernal 1991, 298–299, where the unconvincing suggestion is made that Atlas derives from Egyptian *itru,* 'river'.

15 As argued by Griffiths 1991, 22.

16 Diod. V, lxvi, 4.

17 Pindar: *Pythian* IV, 289–290.

18 Paus. IX, xx, 3.

19 Apollod. *Bibl*. III, x, 1.

20 Dionysius of Halicarnassus I, 61 & II, 70–1; Apollod. *Bibl*. III, xii, 1–2.

21 *FGrHist* F19b – see Gantz 1993, 216. Hellanicus' other genealogical works were the *Phoronis* (on the daughters of the Argive king Phoroneus) and the *Asopis* (daughters of the river-god Asopus).

22 Gantz 1993, 132–5; Keyser 1993, 149–52.

23 Diod. V, lxxix, 1.

24 Pliny: *Natural History* IV, 58.

25 Diod. V, xxci, 7 – xxcii, 4.

26 Diod, V, lv, 4–lvi, 2 & V, lvii, 2–3.

27 Scholiast on Eur. *Orestes* 990; see Frazer 1921, II, 159.

28 The 'Table of Nations' in *Genesis* 10 gives Japheth as the father of Gomer (the Cimmerians of southern Russia), Magog (?), Madai (the Medes of Iran), Javan (the Greeks), Tubal (= Tibal, a kingdom of southern Anatolia) and Meshech (= Mushki, another name for the Phrygians of Anatolia). Javan was father of Elishah (probably from Alashiya, a name for Cyprus), Tarshish (= Tarsus in Cilicia?), Kittim (another name for Cypriots), and Dodanim (variant Rodanim = people of Rhodes). From its composition the list seems to have been compiled in the 6th century BC, clearly from information provided by Jews acquainted with Anatolia, and reflects the veneration in which Atlas' family was held by the East Greeks. The translation of Iapetus into Japheth presumably came about when Jewish scholars investigated the genealogical traditions of the East Greeks. Since Iapetus was the furthest

that these Greeks could go in terms of human ancestors (Iapetus' parents Uranus and Gaea would not have made sense in Jewish theology), it would have been logical for the Jews to conclude that Iapetus was the son of Noah.

29 Stephanus, *s.v.* Adana & Anchiale.

30 Apollod. *Bibl.* I, ii. 3. Hes. *Th.* 507–9 calls Atlas' mother Clymene. Hdt. IV, 45 makes Asia the wife of Prometheus.

31 Fontenrose 1959, 211.

32 For translation and bibliography of 'Kingship in Heaven' see *ANET*, 120–1.

33 On these similarities see Walcot 1966 & Kirk 1974, 117. Kumarbis is identified with El in a Hurrian text from Ras Shamra, and El with Cronus in hellenistic Phoenician texts, assuring the equation Kumarbis = Cronus. See Fontenrose (1959, 213).

34 Kirk 1974, 254–75.

35 Trans. A. Goetze, *ANET*, 125.

36 In hellenistic and Roman times Atlas was frequently depicted carrying a globe on his shoulders, sometimes decorated with zodiac signs indicating that the whole universe was intended – see de Griño *et al.* 1986, 9, 15–16.

37 For the earliest literary and artistic sources for this myth (mid-6th century), see Gantz 1993, 410–13.

38 For Anatolian mountain gods see Haas 1982.

39 For introductions to Yazilikaya see Gurney 1954, 141–4 and Alexander 1986.

40 van Loon 1985, 22, Pl. XXVIIb.

41 Frankfort 1969, 129–30; van Loon 1985, Pl. XVII c.

42 Loud 1939, Pl. 11.; Frankfort 1969, 130–1.

43 Alexander 1986, 151, n. 9.

44 van Loon 1985, 35 & Pl. XLVd.

45 'Ritual for the Erection of a New Palace', *ANET*, 357–8.

46 van Loon 1985, 21.

47 Atlas became a sky-supporting mountain; Prometheus was chained to the Caucasus; the giant Typhon, or in another version Enceladus, was crushed by Zeus under Mount Etna; Zeus also put a mountain on top of the dragon Ophion. Sources in Fontenrose 1959, 231, 241–2.

48 For an illustration see Singh 1993, 29.

49 Egyptian Shu provides a similar concept to Atlas, but hardly enough to suggest that he was the prototype. Luce (1969, 56; 1978, 68) argued a different Egyptian antecedent for the role of Atlas in Plato's story, claiming that 'Keftiu', ostensibly the Egyptian name for Crete, is derived from an Egyptian root ('keft-') meaning 'pillar', and that the Egyptians conceived Crete as one of the four pillars of the world. If Solon (or Plato) had understood this meaning he might have translated Keftiu as 'island of Atlas'. Unfortunately, as Griffiths (1991, 22) notes, there is serious doubt about the existence of 'keft-' as an Egyptian word for pillar.

50 Kantor 1957, 148–9; Beyer 1982, 72–5; Alexander 1986, 151, n. 9.

51 A slot near LHIIIB/IIIC transition is still generally favoured for the context of the Trojan War. See Easton 1985; Hiller 1991.

52 Zangger 1992, 103.

53 *Iliad* XXII, 148–56.

54 Servius on Virgil's *Aeneid* XI, 262.

55 Zangger 1992, 221.

56 Kayan 1991.

57 Pers. comm. I. Kayan, May 1994.

58 James 1992.

59 For discussion see Easton 1985 & Hiller 1991. It has long been suggested, by those who favour Troy VI as the Homeric candidate, that the story of the Wooden Horse might echo the city's destruction by earthquake. (The horse was the sacred animal of Poseidon, god of earthquakes.) See e.g. Broneer 1956, 17.

60 Dionysius of Halicarnassus I, 61 & II, 70–1.

61 Strabo I, iii, 17.

62 Diod. IV, lxxiv, 4 states that Tantalus was driven from his (original?) kingdom in Paphlagonia by Ilus, king of Troy. We must envisage him moving from there to Sipylus, where Paus. II, xx, 4 says he was buried; enmity with Troy continued, as Paus. notes that Pelops had to flee Sipylus 'when Ilus of Phrygia brought an army against him'.

63 *Odyssey* XI, 582–93, trans. Lawrence 1932.

64 Apostolius Paroemiographus XVI, 16.

65 Antoninus Liberalis: *Metamorphoses* 36.

66 Pindar: *Olympian* I, 60.

67 Eur. *Orestes* 10.

68 Diod. IV, lxxiv, 2.

69 Pindar: *Olympian* I, 24–82; Apollod. *Epit.* II, 3.

70 Athenaeus: *Deipnosophistai* 281 B.

71 Hyginus: *Fabulae* 9, 83, cf. Ov. VI, 174. The Vatican Mythographer (I, 1. 3, 204) said that another daughter of Atlas, the Pleiad Sterope was Tantalus' wife. Others named her Euryanassa, daughter of the River Pactolus – see Gantz 1993, 536.

72 Apollod. *Bibl.* I, i, 3; Hes. *Th.* 353 makes Dione a daughter of Tethys.

73 Kerenyi 1959, 58.

74 Ov. VI, 174–6.

75 Nymphis (*FGrHist* 432 F4).

76 Sergent 1987, 74–6 suggests that literary mythology may have deliberately obscured the identity of the two families, as marriage within the *genos* was proscribed – a hard argument to prove. Why should the poets and others have worried that 'incest' was committed by such remote dynasties? While I accept Sergent's basic point that the Atlantids and Tantalids were identical, I do not agree with his assumption that they were originally a Boeotian group.

77 Apollod. *Epit.* II, 1.

78 *Olympian* I, 57–58; cf. *Isthmian* VIII, 21.

79 Archilochus Fr. 55 – see Paus. X, xxi, 2.

80 Scholiast on Homer's *Odyssey* XI, 582.

81 Eur. *Orestes* 5–7 & 983–5.

82 West 1987, 252.

83 *Phaethon*, Eur. Fr. 783N

84 Scholiast on Pindar's *Olympian* I, 97; his opinion is also accepted by the Scholiast on Eur. *Orestes* 981.

85 E.g. Kerenyi 1959, 60–61.

86 Cook 1940, 418.

87 Scholiast on Eur. *Orestes* 982.

88 Cited in Cook 1940, 417; for the identity of Atlas and Tantalus see also Sakellariou 1958, 227.

89 Sergent 1987, 74. *Tlaô*, to 'bear', 'suffer', 'endure' (with the participle *tlas*), certainly provides a reasonable origin for *Atlas*. Plato (*Cratylus* 28) derived *Tantalus* from *talantatos* ('most wretched') which comes from *tlaô* via *talas*, 'suffering, wretched'. One could, however, argue that *Tantalus* comes from *tantaloô*, 'to swing'; the passive participle *tantalotheis* means 'swung', 'hurled', or 'dashed down', which would suit the fate of Tantalus.

90 Virgil: *Aeneid* I, 740–1.

91 Paus. IX, v, 4.

92 Diog. Laert. II, 8.

93 Diod. III, lx, 2.

94 This view is contrary to the often-expressed (and unfounded) assumption that the stories of Tantalus and Pelops were developed in Greece and transplanted to Lydia after the Ionian migration, c. 1100 BC. The assumption is hellenocentric, and would presuppose that Atlas and Tantalus had 'separated' already in Greece before the Ionians brought the latter to Lydia. It is simpler to assume that Tantalus and Pelops were Anatolian characters who were subsumed into Greek myth.

95 See discussion in Cook 1940, 417.

96 Antoninus Liberalis: *Metamorphoses* 36.

97 Stephanus, *s. v.* Tantalos & Polion.

98 I have speculated on the idea that the interface between the two aspects of Tantalus (man and mountain) may lie in the derivation of his name from Hittite Tudhaliyas (suggested by Poisson 1925). This was a common Hittite royal name (borne, for example, by the Emperor who was the overlord of Madduwattas of Zippasla), taken by kings from that of the mountain-god Tudhaliyas. Thus Tantalus might have originated as a local ruler called Tudhaliyas, confused in the telling of history with the mountain-god. However, I am advised by David Hawkins (pers. comm.) that a derivation of the name Tantalus from Tudhaliyas seems unlikely on philological grounds.

99 Paus. VII, xxiv, 6–7, trans. Frazer 1898. Ironically, Giovannini (1985) argues that the whole Atlantis motif was derived from the disaster of 373/2 BC mentioned by Pausanias, when the Achaean city of Helice disappeared into the sea, and overlooks the promising lead which Pausanias gives about Tantalis.

100 Pliny V, 31; cf. II, 13.

9 IN THE KINGDOM OF TANTALUS

1 Bean 1966, 58–9.
2 Mitten & Yügrüm 1974, 26; Hanfmann (ed.) 1983, 19.
3 Ov. XI, 137–41; for other classical sources on the Pactolus, Pedley 1972, 70–2.
4 Olmstead 1948, 187. In the 1st century AD Strabo (XIII, iv, 5) reported that the gold of the Pactolus 'had failed'.
5 For Sardis in the Bronze and Iron Ages see Mellink 1987 and Ramage 1987.
6 Olmstead 1948, 187–9.
7 Hdt. I, 93.
8 Ratté 1994; his doubts about the identity of the 'Tomb of Gyges' might be extended to that of Alyattes – the evidence is equally uncertain.
9 Hanfmann 1972, 155.
10 For Herodotus' Lydian chronology see Miller 1965 and Drews 1969.
11 Hdt. I, 7. On Maeonia as an earlier name for Lydia, see also Pliny V, 110; Strabo XIII, iv, 5; Dionysius of Halicarnassus I, xxvii, 1.
12 For sources see Pedley 1972, 6–7 , 12.
13 J. Spier in Hanfmann (ed.) 1983, 25.
14 The earliest Mycenaean material from these sites is LHIIIA 1–2 – see, conveniently, Mellink 1983, 139 & Spier in Hanfmann (ed.) 1983, 24.
15 See J. Spier in Hanfmann (ed.) 1983, 25.
16 Güterbock 1983 & 1986; Mellink 1983; Bryce 1989 & 1989a.
17 Hom. Il. X, 431; XVIII, 288–92; XX, 382–92; II, 864–6.
18 Mitten & Yügrüm 1974; Hanfmann (ed.) 1983, 20
19 French 1969, esp. Fig. 6, p. 71.
20 Pers. comm. R. Meriç, May 1994.
21 Garstang & Gurney 1959, 88.
22 Strabo XIX, v, 28; XII, viii, 18; Athenaeus (Deipnosophistai XIV, 625e-f) says Pelops came from the city of Sipylus.
23 Pliny V, 31; Solinus XL, 14.
24 Strabo XII, viii, 18.
25 Tacitus: Annals II, 47; see Kokkinos 1992, 47–49.
26 Arist. Meteorologica II, viii.
27 Pherecydes, FGrHist F38; Aeschylus, Fr. 154a R.
28 Aeschylus: Agamemnon 1468–69.
29 Orestes, son of Agamemnon, led a colony to Aeolia – Pindar, Nemean XI, 34–5; Orestes' son Tisamenus lost the throne of Mycenae to the Heraclid invaders and moved to Achaea where he fell in battle (Paus. II, xviii, 6–7; VII, i, 3); Tisamenus' oldest son Cometes migrated to Asia (Paus. VII, vi, 2).
30 Quoted by Plato: Republic II, 381.
31 FGrHist 765 F10 – for translation see Pedley 1972, 13; the same story appears in Nicolas of Damascus, FGrHist 90 F18.
32 For early sources on the chariot race see Gantz 1993, 540–5.
33 For a convenient account see Kerenyi 1959, 302–7.
34 E.g. Athenaeus (Deipnosophistai XIV, 625e-f) claimed that the 'Lydian

mode' of Greek music was brought to Greece by Pelops from Sipylus. Pausanias (VI, xxii, 1) said that the cult of Artemis Kordax at Elis (near Pisa) was named after the *kordax*, the local dance of the people of Sipylus – perhaps he had noticed a real similarity in the cultic dance of the two places.

35 *ANET* 319, 395.

36 Güterbock 1983, 136; Smit 1990–1991, 99.

37 J. Spier in Hanfmann (ed.) 1983, 95. The name of Myrtilus, the treach- erous charioteer of Oenomaus, is also Anatolian; it was used by the Lydian King Myrsilus or Candaules in the early 7th century, and by the Hittite Emperor Mursilis in the 14th.

38 Sergent 1987, 78.

39 Leaf 1915, 70.

40 Ramsay 1880, 63.

41 The short inscription apparently gives a name, the second part of which reads -*mu(wa)*. A second worn inscription has been discovered in a niche to the right of the figure – it may give the name *Zuwala*, and his title – Güterbock & Alexander 1983.

42 For an explanation of how Herodotus' apparently confused description of their location should be read, see Cook 1956.

43 Hdt. II, 106.

44 Hogarth 1924, 501–4.

45 Paus. V, xiii, 7.

46 Aristides: *Orat.* XVII, 2–3; XVIII, 8; XXI, 3.

47 Pliny: *Natural History* V, xxxi, 117.

48 Boardman 1964, 49–50.

49 For an account of the tomb and early views see Cadoux 1938, 42.

50 Bean 1966, Pl. 5.

51 Though we were naturally unsatisfied that we had been shown the right spot, when we checked with archaeologists at the Ege University, Izmir, we were reassured that the tomb had indeed been built over.

52 Bean 1966, 50, 61.

53 See Cadoux 1938, 38.

54 For description and bibliography of Weber's discoveries see Cadoux 1938, 40.

55 Bean 1966, 61, 65–6.

56 It is clear from his brief notes on the subject that Cook (1958/1959, 12 & n. 15) was tempted to see Smyrna itself as the prototype of Homer's Scheria. As Scheria (see Ch. 7) is thought to be one of the sources for Plato's Atlantis, Cook's speculation suggests a potentially interesting line of investigation.

57 Vickers 1985, 19.

58 Cook 1958/1959, 9.

59 Stephanus, *s.v.* Smyrna.

60 Cook 1958/1959, 9–10.

61 Cadoux 1938, 38 & n. 2.

62 Cadoux 1938, 5.

63 Cadoux 1938, 38; Bean 1966, 59.

64 Kyz Göl, the tiny lake close to Kara Göl, has been less enthusiastically suggested as a candidate for Lake Saloe. Maps and the evidence of local people made clear its similarity to Kara Göl. Located 2,200 ft up, on the other side of the mountain ridge, it is so small that a Turkish airforce officer we met in Izmir had never seen it, though he had flown over the mountain dozens of times on training exercises. Ramsay (1882, 65) remarked: 'The Kyz Göl, Maiden's Lake, looks to a great extent artificial, is exceedingly small and in no respect impressive: probably no Greek legends are associated with it.'

65 Describing 'towns that have been eaten up by the earth', Pliny (*Natural History* II, xcii, 205) included 'Sipylus in Magnesia, and previously the very celebrated city in the same place that used to be called Tantalis.'

66 Pliny: *Natural History* V, xxxi, 117.

67 *Regredientibus inde abest XII p[assum] ab Amazone condita, restituta ab Alexandro, in ora Smyrna.*

68 Cadoux 1938, 38, n. 3.

69 Paus. III, xxii, 3.

70 For text and translations see Frazer 1898, III, 554; for their discovery see Perrot & Chipiez 1890, 62–3; and comments in Bean 1966, 62.

71 Paus, V, xiii, 7.

72 Solinus 40, 14.

73 Ov. VI, 147–312.

74 Apollod. *Bibl.* III, v, 6.

75 Hom. *Il.* XXIV, 602–17. For other early sources on Niobe see Gantz 1993, 536–40.

76 Paus. V, xxi, 5.

77 Paus. VIII, ii, 7.

78 Torr 1923, 29.

79 Quintus Smyrnaeus: *Posthomerica* I, 293–306.

80 Cadoux 1938, 26, n. 1.

81 Bean 1966, 55.

82 Ramsay 1882, 36.

83 Frazer 1898, 552.

84 Ramsay 1882, 36, n. 1.

85 Frazer 1898, 552. To judge from the description given by Bean (1966, 63), which is a paraphrase of Frazer, he did not make the ascent himself.

86 Frazer 1898, III, 553.

87 Ramsay 1882, 36.

88 Ramsay 1898, 37

89 For theories on the dating see Cadoux 1938, 38, n. 2.

90 Ramsay 1882, 67.

91 For references see Cadoux 1938, 39, n. 3.

92 See James *et al.* 1991, 93 for an illustration and Ramsay's comparison with the Lion Gate at Mycenae.

93 Ramsay 1882, 37. Nothing like it appears in the catalogue of Phrygian rock-cut monuments published by Haspels in 1971.

94 Bean 1966, 62.

95 Paus. VIII, xvii, 3.

96 Ramsay 1882, 65.

97 Ramsay 1882, 65.

98 Frazer 1898, III, 554.

99 Ramsay 1882, 65.

10 A SUNKEN CITY

1 Cadoux 1938, 38.

2 For the rediscovery of the Hittites see Gurney 1954, 1–7; James *et al.* 1991, 113–118.

3 Singer 1983.

4 Text and (German) translation in Goetze 1928.

5 For the redating and some historical implications see Houwink ten Cate 1970; for the repercussions on later Arzawan history see Singer 1983.

6 Houwink ten Cate (1970, 63) assumes that Zippasla was was Madduwattas' original kingdom.

7 Houwink ten Cate (1970, 63) has pointed to wording in the text which shows that Zippasla was distinct from the 'Mountain Land of Hariyati', mentioned as being 'near to Hatti'. Hariyati was originally offered to Madduwattas by Tudhaliyas so that he would be more easy to control, but he demanded Zippasla instead. As Houwink ten Cate notes this suggests that Zippasla 'was much further to the west' than Hariyati.

8 Gurney (1954, 54) grouped Zippasla 'among the most westerly provinces of the Hittite empire'; Goetze (1975, 264) placed it in northwestern Anatolia.

9 See Gurney 1992. The discovery of the 'Bronze Tablet' has enabled the borders of the kingdom of Tarhuntassa to be defined – it lay to the southwest of the Hittite heartland and seems to have been roughly equivalent to classical Pamphylia and western Cilicia.

10 Bryce 1992. Gurney 1992 prefers to link Lukka with Lycaonia.

11 Garstang & Gurney 1959.

12 I have considerably simplified the arguments for identifying Zippasla with Sipylus – I hope to give them a fuller treatment elsewhere. Bernal (1991, 454) has also argued that Zippasla was Sipylus, but the only evidence he adduces is a somewhat garbled rendition of the career of Pelops.

13 Güterbock 1983, 134.

14 See Mellink (1983, 139), who notes that Madduwattas was 'evidently a coastal potentate with his own ships'.

15 Goetze 1928, 40; Barnett 1975, 363.

16 Vermeule 1983, 141.

17 Gurney 1954, 27–28.

18 Tacitus: *Annals* II, 45.

19 Pliny: *Natural History* II, 93.

20 Vitaliano 1973, 95–100.

21 Vitaliano 1973, 87–8, 99.

22 Strabo: *Geography* I, iii, 17.

23 Bryant 1991, 251–2.

1 Hdt. I, 29-33, 86.

2 Solon Fr. 15, quoted by Plut. *Life of Solon* 2-3.

3 Plut. *Life of Solon* 71. According to Herodotus (II, 134), Aesop was a slave on the island of Samos, and lived in the reign of the Egyptian king Amasis, a contemporary of Croesus. While there were undoubtedly relations between Lydia and Samos (just off the coast of Asia Minor), the appearance of Aesop at Croesus' court looks like a plausible detail added to the tradition of Solon's visit.

4 Dionysius of Halicarnassus (I, xxvii, 1-2) says that Atys was the grandson of Manes, the very first king of Maeonia. The story of the Lydian migration to Italy is first mentioned in Hdt. I, 94. See Drews 1992 for a recent discussion of this tradition which concludes, on slender grounds, that Herodotus fabricated it.

5 Tacitus: *Annals* IV, 55.

6 Pherecydes and Hellanicus, cited in Plut. *Life of Theseus* 26.

7 Tacitus: *Annals* IV, 56. See Cadoux 1938, 47-8 and Sakellariou 1958, 224-34 for other sources and discussion. The claim of an Athenian foundation must have been developed after Smyrna was conquered by the Ionians, the coastal Greeks who were kinsmen of the Athenians, who seized it from its Aeolian founders around 700 BC (Cadoux 1938, 66-7). Though Tacitus is our earliest source for the Theseus foundation it may have already been current in Solon's day.

8 Hdt. I, 173.

9 Ramsay 1882, 37.

10 Cadoux 1938, 21.

11 Quintus Smyrnaeus: *Posthomerica* XI, 67-9.

12 By Zeus Niobe was said to be the mother of Argos and Pelasgus, who gave their names to the city of Argos and the Pelasgians, the earliest inhabitants of the Peloponnese – Apollod. *Bibl.* II, i, 1-2. Pausanias (II, xvi, 1) refers to 'Argos, son of Phoroneus' daughter', clearly refraining from giving her the name Niobe, whom he claimed for his Lydian homeland. The connection of Niobe with Phoroneus dates back to the 6th-century Argive writer Acusilaus (*FrGrHist* 2 F23) – see Gantz 1993, 198-9. In Boeotia Niobe was thought to be the wife of Amphion, who built the first walls of Thebes, or of Alalkomeneus, the first man, who sprang spontaneously from the soil (see Kerenyi 1974, 57).

13 Paus. II, xv, 4; II, xixx, 5.

14 Kerenyi 1974, 57.

15 Kirk (1974, 239-40) argues that the Tantalus myth preceded, and gave rise to, the Lycaon version.

16 Lycaon was the son of Niobe's son Pelasgus (Apollod. *Bibl.* II, viii, 1).

17 Ov. VIII, 611-724; see Hollis 1970, 106-12 & Fontenrose 1945.

18 See James *et al.* 1991, 293.

19 Hdt. II, 2-3; see James *et al.* 1991, 291.

20 Diod. V, lxv. Strabo (X, iii, 19) cites the early epic *Phoronis* as saying that the Curetes were Phrygians. In the same place he cites a fragment

of Hesiod (Fr. 123) which made the Curetes grandsons of Phoroneus. See Gantz 1993, 147, 199. Hippolytus (*Refutation of all Heresies* V, vi, 3) reports the varying claims as to who were the 'first men': among them he lists the 'Idaean Curetes' and 'the Phrygian Corybantes'. Egyptians are never mentioned in such contexts.

21 Fontenrose 1959, 276-81.

22 Fontenrose 1959, 288, giving references.

23 For sources on Ogyges see Fontenrose 1959, 236. Ogyges was thought to have been the first king of Thebes or Eleusis, during whose reign a great flood occurred. His association with primeval kingship, a deluge and the Titans suggests a link with Atlas, confirmed by the name 'Ogygia' given by Homer to the island where Atlas' daughter Calypso dwelt. For hints of Ogyges' Lydian connections see Fontenrose 1959, 237, n. 27.

24 Plut. *The Face on the Moon* 941.

25 Fontenrose 1959, 335-7.

26 Paus. I, xxxv, 7.

27 Diod. III, li, 1.

28 A person named Mukshush is mentioned in a highly fragmentary context near the end of the extant Indictment of Madduwattas. A bilingual inscription of the rulers of 1st-millennium Adana in Cilicia calls them descendants of one Muksas, in Phoenician *Mpš*. It is often argued that this individual is the same as that in the Indictment, and that they should be identified with the Mopsus of Greek traditions who founded cities in Cilicia. See Barnett (1975, 363-5), who sees Mopsus as 'an undeniable historical personality'.

29 Plut. *Life of Solon* 31-2.

12 THE UNFINISHED STORY

1 See James *et al.* 1991.

2 Hes. *Op.* 137-9.

3 Dombrowski 1981.

Postscript: Near completion of this work I discovered that two writers – outside the mainstream of classical scholarship – had already noticed the link between Atlantis and Tantalis. Ev Cochrane ('Kadmos: The Primeval King', *Kronos* XI: 3, 1986, 3-14) suggested the Tantalis story as a parallel to that of Atlantis, but drew no further conclusions. Credit for first spotting the parallel goes to the mystical Russian novelist Dmitri Merejkowski (1865-1941). In *Atlantis/Europe: The Secret of the West* (New York, 1931, p. 446), Merejkowski alluded to 'the Tantalus myth, which is perhaps the most abysmally ancient of all myths, time-worn almost out of recognition – like an old coin worn smooth at the bottom of the ocean: TANTAL. ATLANT.' Though he recognised the underlying identity of Atlas and Tantalus, Merejkowski left the matter there, apparently unaware of the significance of his discovery.

Bibliography

Alexander, R. L., 1986. *The Sculpture and Sculptors of Yazilikaya* (Newark: University of Delaware Press).

Anhalt, E. K., 1993. *Solon the Singer: Politics and Poetics* (Lanham, Maryland: Rowman & Littlefield).

Astour, M. C., 1965. *Hellenosemitica* (Leiden: E. J. Brill).

Athanassiadi, P., 1993. 'Persecution and Response in Late Paganism: the Evidence of Damascius', *JHS* 113, 1–29.

Barbetti, M. & Flude, K., 1979. 'Geomagnetic Variation During the Late Pleistocene Period and Changes in the Radiocarbon Time Scale', *Nature* 279, 202–5.

Baillie, M. G. L., 1994. 'Dendrochronology Raises Questions about the Nature of the AD 536 Dust-veil Event', *The Holocene* 4:2, 212–17.

—— 1995. 'Patrick, Comets and Christianity', *Bulletin of the Navan Research Group* 13, 69–78.

Barnett, R. D., 1975. 'The Sea Peoples', *CAH* II:2 (3rd edn), 359–78.

Bauer, H. H., 1984. *Beyond Velikovsky* (University of Illinois Press).

Bean, G., 1966. *Aegean Turkey: An Archaeological Guide* (London: Benn).

Bennett, C., 1994. 'Science as Showbusiness', *Fortean Times* 75 (June-July), 51–3.

Berlitz, C., 1984. *Atlantis: The Lost Continent Revealed* (London: Macmillan).

Bernal, M., 1991. *Black Athena, II*, (London: Free Association Books).

Beyer, D., 1982. 'Le sceau-cylindre de Shahurunuwa, roi de Karkémish', in *La Syrie au Bronze Récent*, Extraits de la XVIIe Recontre Assyriologique Internationale, Paris 1980 (Paris: Editions Recherche sur les Civilisations), 67–78.

Bietak, M., 1992. 'Minoan Wall-paintings Unearthed at Ancient Avaris', *Egyptian Archaeology. Bulletin of the Egypt Exploration Society* 2, 26–8.

Boardman, J., 1964. *The Greeks Overseas* (Harmondsworth: Penguin).

Bonewitz, R., 1983. *Cosmic Crystals* (Wellingborough, Northamptonshire: Turnstone Press).

Bramwell, J., 1937. *Lost Atlantis* (London).

Breasted, J. H., 1927. *Ancient Records of Egypt* (University of Chicago Press, 3rd edn).

Brisson, L., 1977. 'Platon 1958–1975', *Lustrum* 20, 5–304.

Brisson, L., & Ioannidi, H., 1983. 'Platon 1975–1980', *Lustrum* 25, 31–320.

324 BIBLIOGRAPHY

Bromwich, R., 1961. *Trioedd Ynys Prydein: The Welsh Triads* (Cardiff: University of Wales Press).

Broneer, O., 1949. 'Plato's Description of Early Athens, and the Origin of Metageitnia', *Hesperia* Suppl. 8, 47–59.

—— 1956. 'Athens in the Bronze Age', *Antiquity* 30, 9–18.

Brotherstone, G., 1989. 'Zodiac Signs, Number Sets, and Astronomical Cycles', in A. F. Aveni (ed.), *World Archaeoastronomy* (Cambridge University Press), 276–288.

Brown, N. O., 1969. *Hermes the Thief* (New York: Vintage Books).

Brundage, B. C., 1972. *A Rain of Darts* (University of Texas Press).

Bryant, E. A., 1991. *Natural Disasters* (Cambridge University Press).

Bryce, T. R., 1989. 'Ahhiyawans and Mycenaeans – an Anatolian Viewpoint', *OJA* 8:3 (1989), 297–310.

—— 1989a. 'The Nature of Mycenaean Involvement in Western Anatolia', *Historia* 38:1 (1989), 1–21.

—— 1992. 'Lukka Revisited', *JNES* 51:2, 121–30.

Bucher, W. H., 1950. 'The Crust of the Earth', *Scientific American* 182, 32–41.

Burnet, J., 1908. *Early Greek Philosophy* (London: Black).

Burstein, S. M., 1978. *The* Babyloniaca *of Berossus*, Sources from the Ancient Near East 1:5 (Malibu: Undena Publications).

Bury, J. B., 1927. 'The Age of Illumination', *CAH* V (1st edn), 376–97.

Bury, R. G. (trans), 1929. *Plato. Timaeus, Critias, Cleitophon, Menexenus, Epistles* (Harvard University Press: Loeb Classical Library).

Cadoux, C. J., 1938. *Ancient Smyrna* (Oxford: Basil Blackwell).

Cameron, A., 1983. 'Crantor and Poseidonius on Atlantis', *Classical Quarterly* 3:1, 81–91.

Carpenter, R., 1966. *Discontinuity in Greek Civilization* (Cambridge University Press).

Cayce, H. L. (ed.), 1969. *Edgar Cayce on Atlantis* (London).

Chapman, J. J., 1931. *Lucian, Plato and Greek Morals* (Boston: Houghton Miffin).

Chester, D., 1993. *Volcanoes and Society* (London: Edward Arnold).

Clube, V. & Napier, W., 1982. *The Cosmic Serpent* (London: Faber & Faber).

—— 1990. *The Cosmic Winter* (Oxford: Basil Blackwell).

Cook, A. B., 1940. *Zeus: A Study in Ancient Religion* III:1 (Cambridge University Press).

Cook, J. M., 1956. 'The Reliefs of "Sesostris" in Ionia', *Türk Arkeoloji Dergisi* VI:2, 3–9.

—— 1958/1959. 'Old Smyrna 1948–1951', *Annual of the British School of Athens*, 1–34.

Cornford, F. MacDonald, 1937. *Plato's Cosmology.* (London: Kegan Paul, Trench, Trubner & Co.).

Cottrell, L., 1955. *Bull of Minos* (London: Pan Books).

—— 1963. *The Lion Gate* (London: Pan Books).

Cross, F. M., 1979. 'Phoenicians in Brazil?', *Biblical Archaeology Review* V:1 (Jan/Feb), 36–43.

Crossman, R. H. S., 1939. *Plato Today* (Oxford University Press).

Daniel, G., 1964. *The Idea of Prehistory* (Harmondsworth: Penguin).

—— 1971. *The First Civilizations* (Harmondsworth: Penguin).

Davie, J. N., 1982. 'Theseus the King in Fifth-century Athens', *Greece and Rome* 29, 25–34.

Davies, J. K. 1971. *Athenian Propertied Families 600–300B.C.* (Oxford: Clarendon Press).

Davis, E., 1990. 'A Storm in Egypt during the Reign of Ahmose', in Hardy & Renfrew (eds) 1990, 232–5.

Davis, W. M., 1979. 'Plato on Egyptian Art', *JEA* 65, 121–7.

de Camp, L. S., 1970. *Lost Continents* (New York: Dover, rev. edn).

de Camp, L. S. & Ley, W., 1952. *Lands Beyond* (New York).

de Grazia, A. (ed.), 1978. *The Velikovsky Affair* (London: Sphere).

de Griño, B., Olmos, R., Arce, J. & Balmaseda, L. J., 1986. 'Atlas', in *Lexicon Iconographicum Mythologiae Classicae* III:1 (Zürich & München: Artemis), 3–16.

de Launay, L., 1905. *La Science Géologique* (Paris).

—— 1921. *Où en est la Geologie* (Paris).

de Sélincourt, A. (trans.), 1954. *Herodotus. The Histories* (Harmondsworth: Penguin).

Dickinson, O., 1994. *The Aegean Bronze Age* (Cambridge University Press).

Dombrowski, D. A., 1981. 'Atlantis and Plato's Philosophy', *Apeiron* 15, 117–28.

Donnelly, I., 1882. *Atlantis: The Antediluvian World* (New York: Harper).

—— 1883. *Ragnarok: The Age of Fire and Gravel* (New York: Harper).

Doumas, C. (ed.), 1978/1980. *Thera and the Aegean I: Papers Presented at the Second International Scientific Congress, Santorini, Greece, August 1978* (London: The Thera Foundation), 2 vols.

Drake, S. (trans. & ed.), 1957. *Discoveries and Opinions of Galileo* (New York: Doubleday & Co).

Drews, R., 1969. 'The Fall of Astyages and Herodotus' Chronology of the Eastern Kingdoms', *Historia* 18, 1–11.

—— 1975. 'The Babylonian Chronicles and Berossus', *Iraq* 37, 39–55.

—— 1992. 'Herodotus 1.94 and the Drought ca. 1200 BC, and the Origin of the Etruscans', *Historia* 41, 14–39.

—— 1993. *The End of the Bronze Age* (Princeton University Press).

Easton, D., 1985. 'Has the Trojan War been Found?', *Antiquity* 59, 188–96.

Ebon, M., 1977. *Atlantis: The New Evidence* (New York: New American Library).

Emery, W. B., 1961. *Archaic Egypt* (Harmondsworth: Penguin).

Emiliani, C. *et al.* 1975. 'Paleoclimatological Analysis of Late Quaternary Cores from the Northeastern Gulf of Mexico', *Science* 189 (26th Sept.), 1083–88.

Fairbanks, R. G., 1989. 'A 17,000–year-old Glacioeustatic Sea Level Record', *Nature* 342, 637–42.

Farrington, B., 1953. *Greek Science* (Harmondsworth: Penguin).

Fears, J. R., 1978. 'Atlantis and the Minoan Thalassocracy: A Study in Modern Mythopoeism', in Ramage (ed.) 1978, 103–34.

Ferguson, J., 1970. *Socrates: A Source Book* (London: Macmillan/Open University).

—— 1975. *Utopias of the Classical World* (London: Thames & Hudson).

Field, J. V., 1982. 'Kepler's Cosmological Theories: Their Agreement with Observation', *Journal of the Royal Astronomical Society* 23, 556–68.

Fite, W., 1934. *The Platonic Legend* (New York: Scribner).

Fontenrose, J., 1945. 'Philemon, Lot, and Lycaon', *University of California Publications in Classical Philology* 13:4, 93–119.

—— 1959. *Python* (University of California Press).

—— 1974. 'Work, Justice, and Hesiod's Five Ages', *Classical Philology* 69:1, 1–16.

—— 1981. *Orion* (University of California Press).

Forsdyke, J., 1957. *Greece before Homer* (New York: W. W. Norton & Co.).

Frazer, J. G. (ed. & trans.), 1898. *Pausanias's Description of Greece* (London: Macmillan).

—— (trans.) 1921. *Apollodorus. The Library* (Harvard University Press: Loeb Classical Library).

Friedländer, P., 1958. *Plato: An Introduction* (London: Routledge).

Frost, K. T., 1913. 'The *Critias* and Minoan Crete', *JHS* 33, 189–206.

Galanopoulos, A. G. & Bacon, E., 1969. *Atlantis: The Truth Behind the Legend* (London: Nelson).

Gantz, T., 1993. *Early Greek Myth* (Johns Hopkins University Press).

Garstang, J. & Gurney, O. R., 1959. *The Geography of the Hittite Empire* (British Institute of Archaeology at Ankara: Occasional Pub No. 5).

Gaster, T. H., 1969. *Myth, Legend and Custom in the Old Testament* (New York: Harper & Row).

Gill, C., 1977. 'The Genre of the Atlantis Story', *Classical Philology* 72, 287–304.

—— 1980. *Plato: The Atlantis Story. Timaeus 17–27, Critias with Introduction, Notes and Vocabulary* (Bristol University: Bristol Classical Press).

Gillispie, C. C., 1951. *Genesis and Geology* (Harvard University Press).

Ginzberg, L., 1909. *The Legends of the Jews* (Philadelphia), Vol. I.

Giovannini, A., 1985. 'Peut-on démythifier l'Atlantide?', *Museum Helveticum* 42, 151–6.

Goetze, A., 1928. *Madduwattaš* (Leipzig: Mitteilungen der Vorderasiatisch-Aegyptischen Gesellschaft).

—— 1975. 'The Hittites and Syria', *CAH* II:2 (3rd edn), 252–73.

Gordon, C. H., 1970. 'The Accidental Invention of the Phonemic Alphabet', *JNES* 29, 193–7.

—— 1971. *Before Columbus* (London: Turnstone Press).

Gould, S. J., 1978. *Ever Since Darwin* (London: André Deutsch).

—— 1984. 'Towards the Vindication of Punctuated Equilibria', in W. A. Berggren & J. A. Van Couvering (eds): *Catastrophes and Earth History: The New Uniformitarianism* (Princeton University Press), 9–34.

Graves, R., 1960. *The Greek Myths* (Harmondsworth: Penguin, rev. edn).

Gribbin, J., 1980. *The Strangest Star* (London: Athlone/Fontana).

Griffiths, J. Gwyn, 1991. *Atlantis and Egypt: with other selected essays* (Cardiff: University of Wales Press).

Guralnick, E. (ed.), 1987. *Sardis: Twenty-Seven Years of Discovery* (Chicago: Archaeological Institute of America).

Gurney, O. R., 1954. *The Hittites* (Harmondsworth: Penguin, 2nd edn).

—— 1992. 'Hittite Geography: Thirty Years On', in H. Otten *et al.* (eds), *Hittite and Other Anatolian and Near Eastern Studies in Honour of Sedat Alp* (Ankara: Türk Tarih Kurumu Basimevi), 213–21.

Güterbock, H. G., 1983. 'The Hittites and the Aegean World: Part 1. The Ahhiyawa Problem Reconsidered', *AJA* 87 (1983), 133–8.

—— 1986. 'Troy in Hittite Texts? Wilusa, Ahhiyawa and Hittite History' in Mellink (ed.) 1986, 33–44.

Güterbock, H. G. & Alexander, R. L., 1983. 'The Second Inscription on Mount Sipylus', *Anatolian Studies* 33, 29–32.

Guthrie, W. K. C. (trans.), 1939. *Aristotle. On the Heavens* (Harvard University Press: Loeb Classical Library).

—— (trans.), 1956. *Plato. Protagoras and Meno* (Harmondsworth: Penguin).

Haas, V., 1982. *Hethitische Berggötter und Hurritische Steindämonen* (Mainz am Rhein: Philipp von Zabern).

Hamilton, W. (trans.), 1973. *Plato. Phaedrus & Letters VII and VIII* (Harmondsworth: Penguin).

Hanfmann, G. M. A., 1972. *Letters From Sardis* (Harvard University Press).

—— (ed.), 1983. *Sardis from Prehistoric Times: Results of the Archaeological Exploration of Sardis 1958–1975* (Harvard University Press).

Hankey, V., 1987. 'The Chronology of the Aegean Late Bronze Age', in P. Åström (ed.), *High, Middle or Low?* (Gothenberg: P. Åströms Förlag), 39–59.

Harden, D., 1971. *The Phoenicians* (Harmondsworth: Penguin).

Hardy, D. A. & Renfrew, A. C. (eds), 1990. *Proceedings of the Third International Congress, Santorini, Greece, September 1989* (London: The Thera Foundation), 3 vols.

Harrison, J. E., 1927. *Themis* (Cambridge University Press).

Haspels, C. V. E., 1971. *The Highlands of Phrygia: Sites and Monuments* (Princeton University Press).

Hawkes, J., 1974. *Atlas of Ancient Archaeology* (New York: McGraw Hill).

Heath, T., 1913. *Aristarchus of Samos* (Oxford: Clarendon Press).

Herzog, R., 1968. *Punt* (Glückstadt: Augustin).

Hess, H. H., 1962. 'History of Ocean Basins', in A. E. J. Engle *et al.* (eds), *Petrologic Studies* (Colorado: Geological Society of America), 599–620.

Hiller, S., 1991. 'Two Trojan Wars? On the Destructions of Troy VIh and VIIa', *Studia Troica* 1, 145–54.

Hitching, F., 1978. *The World Atlas of Mysteries* (London: Collins/Pan).

Hogarth, 1924. 'Lydia and Ionia', *CAH* (1st edn) III, 501–26.

Hollis, A. S., 1970. *Ovid Metamorphoses Book VIII* (Oxford: Clarendon Press).

Hooker, J. T., 1976. *Mycenaean Greece* (London: Routledge).

Hornblower, S., 1991. *The Greek World 479–323 BC* (London & New York: Routledge, rev. edn).

Houwink ten Cate, P. H. J., 1970. *The Records of the Early Hittite Empire*

(Istanbul: Nederlands Historisch-Archaeologisch Instituut in het Nabije Oosten).

Huggett, R., 1988. 'Terrestrial Catastrophism: Causes and Effects', *Progress in Physical Geography* 12, 509–32.

—— 1990. *Catastrophism: Systems of Earth History* (London: E. Arnold).

Hutchinson, R. W., 1962. *Prehistoric Crete* (Harmondsworth: Penguin).

Jacoby, F., 1949. *Atthis* (Oxford University Press).

James, P., 1982. 'Ever Since Darwin: A Review [of Gould 1978]', *Kronos* VII:4, 26–32.

—— 1992. 'Digging for Theories' [review of Malina and Vašíček 1990], *New Scientist* 1 February, 53.

—— 1992a, 'Atlantis Lost From Our Sight Again' [review of Zangger 1992], *New Scientist* 29 August, 45.

James, P. & Thorpe, N. [I. J.], 1994. *Ancient Inventions* (New York: Ballantine 1994/London: Michael O'Mara 1995).

James, P., Thorpe, I. J., Kokkinos, N., Morkot, R., Frankish, J., 1991. *Centuries of Darkness* (London: Jonathan Cape 1991/ New Jersey: Rutgers University Press 1993).

—— 1991a. 'Centuries of Darkness: Context, Methodology and Implications', *Cambridge Archaeology Journal* 1:2, 228–235.

—— 1992. 'Centuries of Darkness: A Reply to Critics', *Cambridge Archaeology Journal* 2:1, 127–30.

Jowett, B., 1892. *The Dialogues of Plato* (Oxford: Clarendon Press).

Kantor, H. J., 1957. 'A "Syro-Hittite" treasure in the Oriental Institute Museum', *JNES* 16, 145–62.

Kayan, I., 1991. 'Holocene Geomorphic Evolution of the Besik Plain and Changing Environment of Ancient Man', *Studia Troica* 1, 79–92.

Kehoe, A. B., 1971. 'Small Boats Upon the North Atlantic', in C. Riley *et al.* (eds): *Man Across the Sea* (University of Texas Press), 275–92.

Kerenyi, K., 1959. *Heroes of the Greeks* (London: Thames & Hudson).

Keyser, P. T., 1993. 'From Myth to Map: The Blessed Isles in the First Century B.C.', *The Ancient World* 24:2, 149–67.

Kilian, K., 1980. 'Zum Ende der mykenischen Epoche in der Argolis', *Jahrbuch des Römisch-Germanischen Zentral-Museums Mainz* 27, 166–95.

King-Hele, D. G., 1975. 'Truth and Heresy over Earth and Sky', *The Observatory* 95, No. 1004, 1–12.

Kirk, G. S., 1974. *The Nature of Greek Myths* (Harmondsworth: Penguin).

Klein, R. G., 1989. *The Human Career* (University of Chicago Press).

Koestler, A., 1968. *The Sleepwalkers* (Harmondsworth: Penguin).

Kokkinos, N., 1992. *Antonia Augusta* (London: Routledge).

Kramer, S. N. & Maier, J., 1989. *Myths of Enki, the Crafty God* (Oxford University Press).

Kraut, R. (ed.), 1992. *The Cambridge Companion to Plato* (Cambridge University Press).

Kukal, Z., 1984. *Atlantis in the Light of Modern Research* (Earth Sciences Reviews, Special Issue 21).

Lawrence, T. E. (trans.), 1932. *Homer. The Odyssey* (New York)

Leaf, W., 1915. *Homer and History* (London: Macmillan).

Lee, H. D. P. (trans.), 1955. *Plato. The Republic* (Harmondsworth: Penguin).

—— (trans.) 1971. *Plato. Timaeus and Critias* (Harmondsworth: Penguin).

Levinson, R. B., 1953. *In Defense of Plato* (Harvard University Press).

Luce, J. V., 1969. *The End of Atlantis* (London: Thames & Hudson).

—— 1978. 'The Sources and Literary Form of Plato's Atlantis Narrative', in Ramage (ed.) 1978, 49–78.

McClain, E. G., 1976. *The Myth of Invariance* (York Beach: Maine: Nicolas Hays Inc.)

MacLaurin, C., 1775. *An Account of Sir Isaac Newton's Philosophical Discoveries* (3rd edn, London).

McKusick, M., 1982. 'Psychic Archaeology: Theory, Method and Mythology', *Journal of Field Archaeology* 9, 99–118.

McKusick, M. & Shinn, E. A., 1980. 'Bahamian Atlantis Reconsidered', *Nature* 287, 11–12.

Mage, S., 1981. 'Plato and the Catastrophist Tradition', *Kronos* VI:2, 33–46.

Malina, J. & Vašíček, Z., 1990. *Archaeology Yesterday and Today* (Cambridge University Press).

Mandelkehr, M., 1981. 'An Integrated Model for an Earthwide Event at 2300 BC. Part 1: The Archaeological Evidence', *Society for Interdisciplinary Studies Review* V:3, 77–95.

Manning, S. W. 1992. 'Thera, Sulphur and Climatic Anomalies', *OJA* 11:3, 245–53.

Marinatos, Sp., 1939. 'The Volcanic Destruction of Minoan Crete', *Antiquity* 13, 425–39.

—— 1950. 'On the Atlantis Legend', *Cretica Chronica* 1950, 195–213.

—— 1969. *Some Words about the Legend of Atlantis* (Athens: Archaiologicon Deltion 12).

Martina, A., 1968. *Solon: Testimonianze sulla vita e l'opera* (Roma: Edizioni dell'Ateneo).

Matthiae, P., 1980. *Ebla: An Empire Rediscovered* (London: Hodder & Stoughton).

Mavor, J. W., 1969. *Voyage to Atlantis* (London: Souvenir Press).

Mellaart, J., 1971. 'Anatolia, c. 4000–2300 B.C.', *CAH* I:2, 363–416.

—— 1979. 'Early Urban Communities in the Near East, c. 9000–3400 B.C.', in P. R. S. Moorey (ed.), *The Origins of Civilization* (Oxford: Clarendon Press), 22–33.

Mellink, M. J., 1983. 'The Hittites and the Aegean World: Part 2. Archaeological Comments on Ahhiyawa-Achaians in Western Anatolia', *AJA* 87 (1983), 138–41.

—— (ed.) 1986. *Troy and the Trojan War* (Bryn Mawr College).

—— 1987. 'Lydia and Sardis in Anatolian Context', in Guralnick (ed.) 1987, 16–25.

Mendelssohn, K., 1974. *The Riddle of the Pyramids* (New York: Holt, Rinehart and Winston).

Michell, J., 1984. *Eccentric Lives and Peculiar Notions* (London: Thames & Hudson).

Miller, M., 1965. 'Herodotus as Chronographer', *Klio* 46, 109–28.

—— 1969. 'The Accepted Date for Solon: Precise but Wrong?', *Arethusa* 2:1, 62–86.

Moore, P., 1972. *Can You Speak Venusian?* (London: Michael Joseph).

—— 1983. *Countdown!* (London: Michael Joseph).

Morrow, G. R., 1960. *Plato's Cretan City* (Princeton University Press).

Muck, O., 1979. *The Secret of Atlantis* (London: Fontana).

Mundkur, B., 1976. 'The Cult of the Serpent in the Americas: Its Asian Background', *Current Anthropology* 17:3, 429–55.

Muhly, J. D., 1991. 'Egypt, the Aegean and Late Bronze Age Chronology in the Eastern Mediterranean: A Review Article' *Journal of Mediterranean Archaeology* 4:2. 235–47.

Neumann, J. & Parpola, S., 1987. 'Climate Change and the Eleventh-Tenth Century Eclipse of Assyria and Babylonia', *JNES* 46, 161–82.

Nininger, H. H., 1959. *Out of the Sky* (University of Denver Press).

Olmstead, A. T., 1948. *History of the Persian Empire* (University of Chicago Press).

Parada, C., 1993. *Genealogical Guide to Greek Mythology* (Studies in Mediterranean Archaeology CVII – Jonsered: Paul Åströms Förlag).

Parker, A. J., 1990. 'Classical Antiquity: the Maritime Dimension', *Antiquity* 64, 335–46.

Pauwels, L. & Bergier, J., 1963. *The Dawn of Magic* (Anthony Gibbs & Phillips Ltd).

Pedley, J. G., 1972. *Ancient Literary Sources on Sardis* (Harvard University Press).

Pellegrino, C., 1991. *Unearthing Atlantis* (New York: Vintage).

Penner, T., 1992. 'Socrates and the Early Dialogues', in Kraut (ed.) 1992, 121–69.

Pennick, N., 1987. *Lost Lands and Sunken Cities* (London: Fortean Tomes).

Perrot, G. & Chipiez, C., 1890. *Histoire de l'Art dans L'Antiquité* V (Paris: Librarie Hachette 1890).

—— 1890a. *History of Art in Sardinia, Judaea, Syria and Asia Minor* II (London: Chapman & Hall).

Platt, A., 1889. 'Plato and Geology, *The Journal of Philology* 18, 134–9.

Poisson, G., 1925. 'Tantale, Roi des Hittites', *Revue Archéologique* 22, 75–94.

Popper, K. R., 1945. *The Open Society and its Enemies* (London: Routledge).

Ramage, A., 1987. 'Lydian Sardis', in Guralnick (ed.) 1987, 6–15.

Ramage, E. S. (ed.), 1978. *Atlantis: Fact or Fiction?* (Bloomington: Indiana University Press).

Ramsay, W. M., 1880. 'Newly Discovered Sites Near Smyrna', *JHS* 1, 63–74.

—— 1882. 'Studies in Asia Minor', *JHS* 3, 31–68.

Ratté, C., 1994. 'Not the Tomb of Gyges', *JHS* 114, 157–161.

Rauschning, H., 1939. *Hitler Speaks* (London).

Redford, D. B., 1992. *Egypt, Canaan, and Israel in Ancient Times* (Princeton University Press).

Reiche, H. A. T., 1981. 'The Language of Archaic Astronomy: A Clue to the Atlantis Myth?' in K. Brecher & M. Feirtag (eds), *Astronomy of the Ancients* (Cambridge, Mass./London: MIT Press).

Renfrew, A. C., 1973. *Before Civilization* (London: Jonathan Cape).

—— 1987. *Archaeology and Language* (London: Jonathan Cape).

Romm, J. S., 1992. *The Edges of the Earth in Ancient Thought* (Princeton University Press).

Rowling, J. T., 1989. 'The Rise and Decline of Surgery in Dynastic Egypt,' *Antiquity* 63 (1989), 312–19.

Saccon, A., 1974. *Corpus delle Iscrizioni Vascolari in Lineare B* (Rome: Edizioni Dell'Ateneo).

Sakellariou, M. P., 1958. *La Migration grecque en Ionie* (Athens: Centre d' Études d'Asie Mineure).

Sarton, G., 1952. *A History of Science I: Ancient science through the golden age of Greece* (Harvard University Press).

Saunders, T. J. (trans.), 1970. *Plato: The Laws* (Harmondsworth: Penguin).

Schaeffer, C., 1948. *Stratigraphie comparée et chronologie de l'Asie occidentale (IIIe et IIe millénaires)* (Oxford University Press).

—— 1968. *Ugaritica: Mission de Ras Shamra* V (Paris).

Schmandt-Besserat, D., 1992. *Before Writing* I, (University of Texas Press).

Scott-Kilvert, I. (trans.), 1960. *The Rise and Fall of Athens. Nine Greek Lives by Plutarch* (Harmondsworth: Penguin).

Sergent, B., 1987. *Homosexuality in Greek Myth* (London: Athlone Press).

Settegast, M., 1990. *Plato Prehistorian* (New York: Lindisfarne Press).

Simpson, R. Hope, 1981. *Mycenaean Greece* (New Jersey: Noyes Press).

Singer, I., 1983. 'Western Anatolia in the Thirteenth Century B.C. According to the Hittite Sources', *Anatolian Studies* 33, 205–17.

Singh, M., 1993. *The Sun in Myth and Art* (London: Thames & Hudson).

Smit, D. W., 1990/91. 'KUB XIV 3 and Hittite History', *Talanta* 22/23, 79–111.

Smith, P., 1977. 'Evidence for Earth Expansion', *Nature* 268, 200.

—— 1981. 'Wegener's Legacy', *Society for Interdisciplinary Studies Review* V:I, 30–2 (reprinted from *Open Earth*).

Spanuth, J., 1979. *Atlantis of the North* (London: Sidgwick & Jackson).

Spedicato, E., 1985. 'Apollo Objects and Atlantis', *Quaderni del Dipartimento di Matematica, Statistica e Informatica e Applicazioni* 3 (Istituto Universitario de Bergamo).

Spence, L., 1924. *The Problem of Atlantis* (New York: Brentano's).

Stecchini, L. C., 1978. 'The Inconstant Heavens', in de Grazia (ed.) 1978, 80–119.

—— 1984a. 'The Newton Affair', *Kronos* IX:2, 34–8.

—— 1984b. 'Newton's World View', *Kronos* IX:3, 52–9.

—— 1984c. 'Newton and Historical Science', *Kronos* X:1, 62–8.

Stewart, J. A., 1905. *The Myths of Plato* (London: Macmillan).

Strange, J., 1980. *Caphtor Keftiu: A New Investigation* (Leiden: E. J. Brill).

Taylor, A. E., 1928. *A Commentary on Plato's Timaeus* (Oxford: Clarendon Press).

Taylor, T., 1820. *The Commentaries of Proclus on the Timaeus of Plato* (London).

Temple, R. K. G., 1976. *The Sirius Mystery* (London: Sidgwick & Jackson).

Torr, C., 1923. *Small Talk At Wreyland* (Cambridge University Press).

Vaillant, G. C., 1965. *Aztecs of Mexico* (Harmondsworth: Penguin).

van Andel. T. H., 1989. 'Late Quarternary Sea-level Changes and Archaeology', *Antiquity* 63, 733–45.

—— 1990. 'Addendum to "Late Quaternary Sea-level Changes and Archaeology" ', *Antiquity* 64, 151–2.

van Loon, M. N., 1985. *Anatolia in the Second Millennium B.C.*, Iconography of Religions XV:12 (Leiden: E. J. Brill).

Velikovsky, I., 1950. *Worlds in Collision* (London: Victor Gollancz).

Vermeule, E. T., 1983. 'Response to Güterbock', *AJA* 87 141–3.

Vernant, J.-P., 1983. *Myth and Thought Among the Greeks* (London: Routledge).

Verne, J. (trans. H. Frith), 1908. *Twenty Thousand Leagues Under the Sea* (Everyman Library).

Vickers, M., 1985. 'Early Greek Coinage, a Reassessment', *Numismatic Chronicle* 145, 1–44.

Vidal-Naquet, P., 1986. *The Black Hunter* (Baltimore & London: Johns Hopkins University Press).

Vitaliano, C. & Vitaliano, D., 1974. 'Volcanic Tephra on Crete', *American Journal of Archaeology* 78, 19–24.

Vitaliano, D., 1973. *Legends of the Earth: Their Geologic Origins* (Indiana University Press).

—— 1978. 'Atlantis from the Geologic Point of View', in Ramage (ed.) 1978, 137–60.

Vlastos, G., 1975. *Plato's Universe* (University of Washington Press).

Vycichi, W., 1986. 'L'île de Chemmis "qui flotte au gré des vents" ', *Discussions in Egyptology* 4, 73–6.

Wahlgren, E., 1986. *Vikings and America* (London: Thames & Hudson).

Walcot, P., 1966. *Hesiod and the Near East* (Cardiff University Press).

Warlow, P., 1982. *The Reversing Earth* (London: Dent).

Warren, P., 1984. 'Absolute Dating of the Bronze Age Eruption of Thera (Santorini)', *Nature* 308, 492–493.

Weiss, H., Courty, M.-A., *et al.* 1993. 'The Genesis and Collapse of the Third Millennium North Mesopotamian Civilization', *Science* 261, 995–1004.

West, M. L. (ed. & trans.), 1987. *Euripides. Orestes* (Warminster: Aris & Phillips).

Wood, R. M., 1980. 'Geology Versus Dogma: the Russian Rift', *New Scientist* (12 June), 234–8.

Wright, H. E., 1978. 'Glacial Fluctuations, Sea-level Changes and Catastrophic Floods' in Ramage (ed.) 1978, 161–74.

Zangger, E., 1992. *The Flood from Heaven* (London: Sidgwick & Jackson).

—— 1993. 'Plato's Atlantis Account – A Distorted Recollection of the Trojan War', *OJA* 12:1, 77–87.

Zink, D., 1978. *The Stones of Atlantis* (New York: Prentice-Hall).

Index